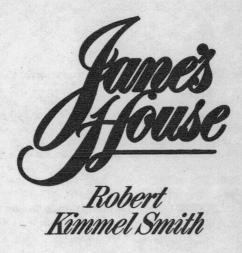

Jane's House

Robert Kimmel Smith

PUBLISHED BY POCKET BOOKS NEW YORK

Grateful acknowledgment is made for permission to reprint the following:

On page 234, lines from the song "The Road to Morocco" by Johnny Burke and Jimmy Van Heusen
Copyright 1942 by Paramount Music Corporation
Copyright © renewed 1969 by Paramount Music Corporation

POCKET BOOKS, a division of Simon & Schuster, Inc.
1230 Avenue of the Americas, New York, N.Y. 10020

For Claire,
for Heidi,
for Roger

PART
ONE

1

_____

HE WAS JUST two blocks from home when he remembered that he had forgotten to take anything out of the freezer for dinner. "Damn," he said aloud, looking at the clock on the dashboard. Six-twenty. He could still make the supermarket before it closed. He pulled up to the red traffic light on Beverly Road, angry at himself.

It's such a simple thing. All you have to do is remember in the morning to take something out to defrost. Providing you remembered to shop for meat sometime, and wrapped it carefully in aluminum foil, and then put on a clearly legible label so that when you went fishing in the frost-clouded freezer at eight o'clock in the morning you could actually tell what was in there.

He gazed up the street as he waited for the traffic light to change, looking at his house, third one in from the corner, three stories of frame and brick Victorian with a wraparound porch big enough to hold a dance on. Between the tall Norway maple tree on the front lawn and the big forsythia hedge at the curb, a yellow tennis ball flew to the porch steps and then rebounded to the curb. That had to

3

be Bobby, playing one of his endless games of throw and catch, pitching to a home plate that existed only in his ten-year-old mind, striking out George Brett or some other American League terror. Paul honked the horn just as the light broke green. He pulled forward into the intersection and honked again, but Bobby did not look his way.

He found a parking space across the street from the supermarket, almost directly in front of the pizza joint. Through the dirty window he could see Guido taking a pie out of the oven on his long wooden scoop, putting it down on the counter into a box. Paul watched him take the little wheel cutter and segment the pizza into eight steaming slices. He was tempted to forget about dinner and just bring home a pizza. *Again?* That was the problem. They'd shared a pizza only three or four nights ago, and he'd brought home Chinese food last night, and Kentucky Fried chicken sometime in the last week.

Continuity.

Yes, Dr. Wirtz, he thought, continuity. The kids needed it, he needed it. Perpetuate the patterns of the past as much as you can. Regular meals at the regular time, table talk over dinner, share the kids' thoughts, let them tell you about their days, see that they go to bed and get up at their regular time. Continuity, that's the ticket. Easy to say, Doctor, hard to do.

He pushed the shopping cart past the dairy case, trying to remember the state of the refrigerator at home. Milk? Certainly, Bobby and Hilary were both good milk drinkers. And this being a Wednesday, and the main grocery shopping being done on Saturday, another carton of orange juice was a good bet too. He walked through the cake, bread and cookie section and headed for the meat case.

"Mr. Klein?"

Paul turned. An elderly woman in a short fur jacket smiled at him. She looked vaguely familiar, a neighborhood face, but who?

"Sylvia Fox, from Marlborough Road."

"Of course," Paul said. Who was Sylvia Fox?

"I knew your wife from the P.T.A. I just wanted to tell you how sorry I am."

"Thank you."

"She was a lovely woman, a lovely woman."

"Thank you."

"So bright and sweet. My grandchild, Jason Brandt? From Rugby Road? He had her in the third grade and he used to talk about her all the time. She was a very good teacher. Not like some of these young ones they have now. You know, coming to school in pants, and even blue jeans. I ask you, is that a thing for a teacher to do? Is that an example to set?"

Oh, God, Paul thought, not now, please. He didn't want to hear about what a fine teacher Jane was, how well she always dressed, what a force for peace and understanding she was in a school that had half its kids bussed in from a black neighborhood across Ocean Avenue. It was all true, and more besides, but he just did not want to hear it now from Mrs. Sylvia Fox of Marlborough Road.

"And so young," Mrs. Fox went on, shaking her gray head, "a real tragedy to lose a young woman like that."

"Mrs. Fox," he said.

"I'll bet she wasn't even forty years old, was she?"

Paul shook his head.

Mrs. Fox's quick intake of breath hissed through her teeth. "A real tragedy."

God in heaven, what a stupid woman. A flare of rage welled in him. He wanted to push this old hag into the meat case and hold her there until her ass froze solid. Who the hell was she to talk about Jane? What did she know about her? Why did people think that walking up and saying "sorry" was the thing to do? Sorry, sorry, what the hell good was *sorry*? Didn't they know that he just wanted to be left alone, that he didn't need reminding, that all the sorrys and sympathy in the world didn't mean shit? "I'm in kind of a hurry," Paul said, his voice barely in control.

"Of course," said Mrs. Fox. "My sympathy."

He pushed the cart down the aisle, his hands white-knuckled on the bar. He wanted suddenly to scream, to push the cart full-force down the aisle so it crashed against the shelves, toppling boxes and cans to the floor. He would run through the cereal section in front of him, tearing and smashing the boxes of corn flakes and Cocoa Puffs, making huge piles of Captain Crunch and Count Chocula, a mountain of Rice Chex and Sugar Smacks. Grieving widower goes berserk in local supermarket. Mrs. Sylvia Fox found buried under cold cereal mountain. "I just said sorry and he went crazy, I don't know why."

Slow down, kimosabe, he told himself. He took a deep breath, then another. With a shaking hand he found his cigarettes, fished one out of the pack, and managed to light it.

Dinner.

He stared into the meat case. Broil a piece of meat, open a can of peas, instant mashed potatoes. Chicken? He looked at the gleaming plastic-wrapped packages. Legs and thighs, breasts, drumsticks, fryers, and broilers. How long does it take to cook a chicken? Are parts faster than a whole chicken? Had to be. But how long? He moved on down the case. Liver? Forget it. Only Jane could make them eat liver, and then she had to hide it under a mound of sweet onions. Maybe lamb chops. They were probably Hilary's favorite meat. Those little baby chops she used to eat as a small child. What did she call them? P-bones. Right. And the first time Jane cooked shoulder chops Hilary couldn't believe they were lamb. "They have . . . *unusual* bones, Mommy." That's what Hilary still called them, unusual-bone lamb chops. Sure she did, and there was a package of them at home in the freezer, stupid, and if you'd remembered to take them out this morning you wouldn't be standing here staring into the meat case.

Paul walked past the veal, the roast beef, all the red and bloody cuts of beef you had to pot and simmer for hours and hours. Hamburger? Hamburger was fast and easy, which is why they had it so often. He hesitated. Why was it so hard to make up his mind? He felt the time passing. Hamburger or not? To be or not to be. He walked on down the meat case.

Flank steak. Of course. It had been so long he'd almost forgotten how much they all loved flank steak made Jane's way. She put soy sauce, lemon juice, and lots of chopped scallions on top and broiled it. The old favorite. The recipe was in the Julia Child cookbook on the shelf near the radio. He could almost see the page open before his eyes, the way Jane left it open when she cooked, a thumb print of grease, the page splattered with soy-sauce spots. Yes, he could do that. It probably wasn't even difficult.

He put a flank steak into the shopping cart and moved on. Fruit-and-vegetable section. Scallions, a couple of lemons, and a honeydew melon, the one both Bobby and Hilary liked. He squeezed and prodded, trying to decide which was ripe. How the hell could you be sure? You can't, buster, you just pays your money and takes your chances. He took a two-dollar melon and moved on.

There was a short line at the check-out. He looked at his watch. Dusk outside now, the yellow streetlamps on. He felt a lot better. An old-fashioned flank-steak dinner, success guaranteed. He'd get Hilary and Bobby to help in the kitchen. They'd open up and talk over dinner. The latest gossip from Hilary's high school, Bobby and his long subway rides to and from school. Perhaps they would even laugh tonight, like they used to do. Continuity. Hell, yes, Dr. Wirtz.

Bobby was still throwing the tennis ball against the steps when he pulled into the driveway. In the almost dark, the streetlight shining yellow against the trees, Bobby tugged his Yankee cap low over his eyes. The boy's lips were moving as he announced himself pitching in the big leagues. Paul gathered his supermarket bundles from the seat, took up his briefcase, watched Bobby's left arm flash forward and throw the ball. Two southpaws in the family, both kids, and he and Jane were right-handed all the way. Somewhere in Jane's family a left-hander lurked, coming out in this generation.

"Hi there." The little left-hander was opening the car door, taking Paul's briefcase. "You're late."

"A little. I did some shopping at the supermarket." He reached out and squeezed Bobby's pitching arm. "How'd the game go?"

"Four-all tie, bottom of the ninth, Yanks and Pittsburgh in the last game of the World Series."

Paul got out of the car, locked the door. He and Bobby began walking across the lawn toward the front steps. "Was Ron Guidry pitching?" he asked, smiling. Bobby identified strongly with the Yankee left-handed ace. Bobby *was* Guidry, in fact, most of his make-believe playing time.

"Of course. Struck out Dave Parker four times."

"Terrific. What'd you do, smoke him inside?"

"Twice. Curve balls low and away the other times. He can't hit that pitch."

The porch lights were not lit and the inside hall light was dark. The only light came from Hilary's windows upstairs.

"Homework done?"

The boy nodded.

"Kind of late for you to be outside playing. It's after seven."

Bobby shrugged. "Peter's here," he said.

"Again?"

"I feel funny when he's here. Hilary gets . . . weird, you know?"

"Weird how?"

"She's showing off for Peter. Calling me 'little brother.' And she's so lovey-dovey with Peter it makes me feel . . . funny."

"Left out, kind of a fifth wheel?"

"Yeah."

Paul opened the front door with his key, then the inner foyer door. He snapped on the foyer light and the porch lights.

Peter Block, the boyfriend, with his skin-tight jeans, flannel shirt, scraggly hair, and that ridiculous growth that would someday be a moustache. Paul had nothing against the boy, except for the facial hair that needed shaving, but he was seeing too much of Hilary. And vice versa. Peter wouldn't be hanging out here so often if Jane were alive. Keeping tabs on Hilary's love life was Jane's department. Scratch that, now it was his department, along with all the other departments that mattered.

He heard music coming from Hilary's stereo upstairs, rock with a heavy beat. "Take these into the kitchen for me, chum," he said, handing the supermarket packages to Bobby.

"What's for dinner?"

"A surprise."

"Uh-oh."

"What do you mean, 'uh-oh'?"

"Hamburgers again?"

"No, wise guy," Paul said in his mock-hurt voice. "Flank steak, rice, and peas." He looked into Bobby's eyes, trying for a smile from the boy and not getting it. Bobby turned and headed for the kitchen.

Paul hung his topcoat in the foyer closet and started upstairs, the music getting louder as he neared Hilary's room. The door was closed. He stood for a moment, listening. Why weren't they talking in there? What was going on? He knocked loudly. He heard a groan, a moment passed, and then Hilary's cheery "enter."

They were sitting on Hilary's bed, side by side. Hilary's usually sallow cheeks were bright pink, her face flushed. "That's my dad," Hilary said, as if he and Peter had not seen each other countless times over the past year. The boy was almost a boarder in the house.

"Hello, Mr. Klein," said Peter. His face was flushed as well, and he looked embarrassed.

They've been necking for hours, Paul decided, then pushed the thought away. "Greetings from the outside world," he said. "What's that music?"

"Elvis Costello," Hilary said.

"My favorite," he said with a wry grin.

"He hates Elvis Costello," Hilary said to Peter.

"I didn't like the original Elvis either," he said. "Now if he was *Abbott* and Costello, you'd have something. Homework all done?"

"Most of it. I have some French left."

"Right," he said. "Dinner as soon as I can make it." He left the door to her room open and went down the hall to his bedroom. He hung his suit jacket in the closet and was taking off his tie when Hilary appeared behind him.

"Are you mad at me?" she asked.

"No." Ah, conscience, conscience. Her face was so serious.

"You don't look too pleased."

I come home to find you on your bed with Peter, he thought, the door closed, the house dark downstairs, your brother playing outside after seven, and your homework not done. But he did not say any of it.

"Can Peter stay for dinner?"

"No."

"Why not?"

"He has a home, you know."

"Why can't he stay?"

"Look, sugar, he's in the next room. Can we not discuss it right now?"

"He's my boyfriend," she said, her voice rising.

He put a finger to his lips, afraid the boy would hear. "Not to-

9

night, okay. We'll talk about it later." He watched her face go hard; sulky sixteen, he thought. Where did the girl's flighty temperament come from? He wasn't so edgy, nor had Jane been. It was a mystery, like her left-handedness, and she'd been that way long before Jane died.

"Christ!" Hilary snapped and stomped out of the room.

Downstairs, he rolled up his cuffs and washed his hands in the kitchen sink, drying them on a sheet of paper toweling. Bobby was sitting at the kitchen table, in the alcove near the picture window, reading his baseball magazine. The packages from the supermarket were on the chopping block. He heard the front door slam shut, then Hilary's footsteps start up the stairs to her room. He went to the dining room and called out to her. "Sugar! Could you give me a hand down here?"

She'd sulk all night now, he knew, but it couldn't be helped. A line had to be drawn somewhere with Peter; she couldn't spend all her time with him.

He poured himself a small bourbon and took a sip, remembering the simple pleasure of sitting at the table before dinner, having a drink and talking with Jane as she finished preparing the meal, telling her about his day, hearing about hers, joking with the kids as they waited. His simple plan of flank steak and a happy meal seemed very far away. Bobby was off in his own world; Hilary stood behind him, arms folded, staring out the window into the dark garden.

The whiskey bit his throat, but it felt good. He took another sip, looking at his children, the loudest sound in the kitchen the humming of the refrigerator. They were coming apart, the three of them, each in his own way, as they tried to find some method of coping with the hurt that wouldn't go away. Happy families are all alike, with lines of love and tenderness, duty and obedience that hold them together. With Jane gone they had lost their very center. Bobby had become silent and brooding. Hilary had found her anodyne, Peter Block. In a way, it was much simpler for himself. He had his answer right in front of him, the children. He had to be strong now, be mother and father rolled in one to keep them all together and functioning. That was his job, his responsibility, and by God, he wouldn't permit them to fall apart. But how do you mend a broken family?

"Okay, crew," he said, as gaily as he could, "let's get with it. Flank steak, rice, and peas time." He turned the broiler on to pre-heat and began opening the packages on the counter. The children did not respond. "Hil, you make the rice, okay? Three-quarters of a cup should do." The girl turned to look at him. "C'mon, sugar, you know how to make rice. Use the measuring cup, wash it in the big strainer in the sink under cold water, put it into the small pot with the copper top. And then you . . ."

"I *know* how to make rice," Hilary said. She went to the cabinet under the island stove and took out the small pot.

"Right. Bob-o! Flank steak with scallions and stuff."

The boy looked up from his magazine. "Will it be like Mom's?"

"I sure as hell hope so. Get me the recipe, will you? It's in the little Julia Child on the cookbook shelf." Paul took the steak out of its wrap and put it on the chopping block. With a knife he trimmed some fat and scored the steak in a crosshatching, then flipped it to do the same on the other side.

"How much water do I put in for the rice?" Hilary asked.

"Good question."

"We used to use two cups of water for one cup of rice."

"Like twice as much water as rice, huh? So use twice three-quarters of a cup. Which is . . . what?"

"Cup and a half," Bobby said. He brought the cookbook to Paul.

"Thanks. At least we have one mathematician here." Paul found the recipe in the cookbook and began preparing the marinade. "It's going to be a great dinner," he said, "a great dinner."

"Wait a minute," Hilary said. "I remember how Mom made this. You have to marinate the steak for about two hours."

"What?"

"Yeah," Bobby said, "that's right. I remember once she had to go someplace after school and she left me a note to turn it after one hour. It takes a long time."

"It's going to be great anyway. Fabulous! And I'm going to save half to make a Chinese dish tomorrow."

"If you remember," Hilary said.

"I'll remember," he said, grinning at the girl. " 'I have just be-gun to cook,' said John Paul Klein."

11

"Huh?"

"A joke. Never mind." He took another sip of his drink as Bobby went back to his magazine. "Bob, how about you set the table, okay? And I think those place mats have had it. Just throw them in the washing machine and put out some new ones. In the cabinet behind the stove. Good."

Hilary watched the rice water come to a boil. She covered the pot, lowered the flame, and set the timer for fifteen minutes. "So how long will you marinate the steak?" she asked.

"As long as the rice takes. Fifteen minutes. Then I'll cook the steak."

"And then the rice will get cold."

"Not if we keep it covered. You'll see. Will you open a can of peas and put them in a pot, babe?"

Bobby was at the silverware drawer. "What do we need?"

"Steak knives, teaspoons."

"And forks?"

"Unless you want to eat rice with your fingers."

"That's not funny, Dad."

"I'm trying, I'm trying," Paul said. "Oops, forgot the melon." He took down three small plates from the cabinet near the sink, found a sharp knife, and cut three melon slices, tipping the seeds into the garbage pail. He put the three plates of melon on the table, before the three places Bobby had set. The boy sat and read his magazine again. Paul put the melon plate on top of the magazine. "Supper time, not reading time," he said, meeting Bobby's eyes. "A little human commoon-ication here—isn't that what the Two Thousand Year Old Man says?" Paul went into his Mel Brooks voice, trying to get Bobby to respond. The boy loved the Two Thousand Year Old Man album; he played it over and over and even made cassettes of it on his tape recorder. "What did we eat in the old days? Only the natural things . . ." Paul waited for Bobby to supply the punch line, and when he didn't, went on. "Clouds, rocks, stars!"

Nothing. The boy took his spoon and began to eat the melon.

"You had to be there," Paul said. "Okay," he said to Hilary, "how's our rice doing?" He put a small flame under the peas.

"Five more minutes on the timer."

Paul took the steak over to the counter near the broiler. "Hurry up and marinate," he said to it. "Listen, marination can be fun, right, Bob?"

"What?"

"That's your joke, remember? When we were talking about chewing your food and I called it mastication. And you said, 'Mastication can be fun?' A long time ago."

"Yeah?"

"Marination can be fun. Same joke."

"It's not funny."

"I'm trying. Another five minutes and I start tap dancing."

"You're really weird tonight, you know that?"

"That's me. Old weird Paul."

"You can say that again," said Hilary.

"I will. Old weird Paul. Listen. Why does an elephant have a trunk?" Maybe he *was* crazy. The children were looking at him as if he were, as if cracking a smile was some kind of crime. "Because he doesn't have a glove compartment, that's why. No good? I got a million of 'em. Panhandler walks up to me on the street and says, 'I haven't had a bite in three days.' So I bit him. Nothing, right? You want more?"

"No," Hilary said.

"Guy finds another guy in the jungle, see? Big spear right through this guy's chest. And the guy who finds him says, 'My God, man, a spear through your chest—that must hurt plenty.' And the other guy says, 'Only when I laugh!' " At least they were staring at him. He had their interest. "These are the jokes, folks."

"Cut it out, Dad," Bobby said.

"What's the matter, is laughing so bad? God knows we've been crying for three months. Has that helped?"

The timer rang in the silence. "Perfect timing," Paul said. He turned off the heat under the rice and slammed the steak into the broiler. He was angry and he didn't know why. "The world goes on," he said. "We may not like it, but the goddamn world goes on. Words of wisdom and you heard it here first. The goddamn world goes on."

He felt weak suddenly, the anger fading. He stared into the electric broiler, knowing the children were silently staring at him. He felt old, tired, used up. He wanted Jane here, needed her here, to hold him in her arms, one small hand rubbing at the back of his

13

neck, one small warm hand that could make everything right. DON'T CRY! Too late, he knew, as the tears stung his eyes, rolled down his cheeks. He kept his face turned away, staring into the broiler, watching the scallion edges turn brown, the fat searing and hissing in the orange-red light, sobbing as behind him the children, too, began to cry.

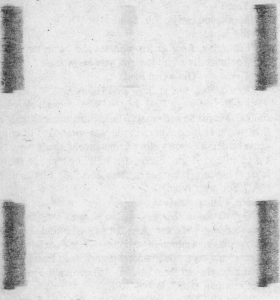

2

THIS WAS WHAT he was doing at five minutes to midnight: squatting down in front of the stupid washing machine in the kitchen, watching T-shirts, shorts, and socks go by, feeling the floor shake as the machine rumbled through the lock-and-spin cycle, rattling the dishes in the cabinets and making the dryer on top jump and squeak on its bolts. Oh, yes, we're having a midnight laundry party tonight and you are all invited. Bring along your white wash, ladies, please, coffee and Danish will be served. Paul toasted his reflected image in the washing-machine door, taking a sip of the brandy and laughing at himself. When all else fails, smile.

Why was he there? Because when he puts Bobby to bed, the boy casually says there are no more socks left in his drawer. Wrong, of course. Checking, Paul finds one pair of rolled-up white tube-socks. Unrolling, putting one sock on his hand, two fingers stare back at him from where the toes ought to be. No toes. Checking further in the underwear drawer, the boy has only one T-shirt and one pair of undershorts; still further, he and Hilary are low on underwear as well. "I'll do a fast wash," he tells the boy, in bed now in blue flannel pajamas, teeth brushed, face and hands washed, the little wet edges of his long hair spiky and cute; Paul has to stop himself from curling them on his fingers. No good, Bobby is too grown-up in his own mind for cuddling and petting. Severe rations for a father: one kiss in the morning when he leaves for school, one when Daddy gets home, one when he tucks him into bed and straitjackets him tight under the quilt. Even after ten years, Paul's heart still jumps when the boy submits to a hug.

No toes.

Seated on the edge of the bed, he tells Bobby about no toes. "When I was a boy, Grandpa Herman came home from work one evening with a package of a dozen pairs of socks rolled up with string. You remember where I lived when I was a boy?"

"We rode past there once and you showed me. It was a yucky neighborhood."

"Well, it wasn't when I was a boy. It was nice then."

"Not as nice as here, though."

"No, but we were poor. Anyway, your grandpa comes in and says, 'Look at this for a bargain! I bought it from a pushcart by the subway. One dollar for a dozen pairs of socks!' He's so proud of himself, you see. My pop loved a bargain. So he takes a knife and cuts the string and spreads the socks on the table, and when he gets them unrolled, guess what?"

"What?"

"No toes. None of those socks had any toes at all. Just a neatly bound edge where the toes ought to start. And the terrific part was that the man who sold Pop the socks from a pushcart near the subway station had been so smart. He'd tied all his packages of socks so cleverly that you couldn't open them without cutting the string. And until you did that, there was no way to see that the toes were missing."

"So the guy was a crook."

"Of course."

"What happened?"

"Well, I laughed but my mother didn't. She knew my pop better than I did. He got very red in the face, rolled the socks back up again the way they were to begin with, and retied them with the string. 'Hold dinner,' he says, 'I'm going to return these socks.'

Now remember, it was eight long blocks back up that steep hill to the subway, and eight blocks back again. That's what a dollar was worth in those days, when you were poor.''

"Did he have a fight with the pushcart man?"

"That's what my mother kept saying while we were waiting for Pop. 'He'll get into a fist fight, they'll call the police, he'll end up in jail, all for a dollar.' So, about half an hour later Pop comes in, doesn't say a word, just washes his hands in the sink and sits down at the table. 'What happened?' my mother says. Pop kind of shakes his head, he's smiling. 'What a *goniff*,' he says, not mean, but kind of admiring the nerve of the guy, 'what a *goniff*.' ''

"What's a *goniff?*"

"A thief."

"Did they fight?"

"Wait. 'The guy is standing on a box by his pushcart,' Pop says. 'He's yelling at the top of his lungs—"Socks a dollar a dozen! Come and get 'em! a dozen for a dollar!"—and he sees me coming, the socks in my hand, a mad look on my face. The guy doesn't turn a hair, just goes on yelling, peddling his socks to the people crowded around the pushcart. But all the time, with his eyes on me.

" 'I get to the pushcart but before I can say a word, the guy takes the socks from my hand and slips me my dollar back. I look at him. He gives me a wink. Then he leans down, his finger to his lips, shushing me, you know, not to say anything. He draws me close and he whispers in my ear: "Mister, even in America, you don't get a dozen for a dollar." ' ''

Now Paul waited. "That's the story?" Bobby asked.

"Yup."

"Grandpa didn't call the police?"

"Nope."

"He didn't warn the other customers?"

"No."

"Why not?"

Paul planted a kiss on the boy's brow. "That's just what I asked *my* father. 'The man was right,' he said. 'I let my greed for a bargain overcome my good sense. To learn that for a dollar, that was cheap, and I even got my dollar back.' ''

Bobby's small lips pursed. "But what about the other people?"

"What about them?"

17

"They got cheated . . . and Grandpa didn't do anything."

" 'A man's got to make a living,' that's what he said. And for a guy to have so much *chutzpah*, to have nerve enough to sell socks without toes, that tickled my pop."

"He was wrong."

"Maybe." Paul shrugged. "I understand why he didn't, though, perhaps because I'm my father's son and I knew him. Like I hope someday, Bob-o, you'll understand me. Oops, I almost forgot the rest of the story. From that day, whenever Pop saw an advertisement that promised too much, or we heard a politician making promises, one of us always said: 'A dozen for a dollar,' and it gave us a good laugh."

"A dozen for a dollar."

"The moral of the story. And good night."

Bobby kissed him on the cheek, a Colgate-with-MFP-fluoride kiss, wet, cold, minty, and the high spot of his day.

He'd forgotten to add the fabric softener, of course. He almost always forgot. Why, he asked the world at large, why did Westinghouse design a washing machine that didn't stop itself and remind you when it was time to add the fabric softener? You had to catch the stupid machine right on the button after the second wash and before the long soak, which was very hard to do unless you were actually standing there watching. So simple. Put an "add-fabric-softener-now" buzzer on the machine, a clanging bell perhaps, skyrockets, something. Without the fabric softener all their underwear was going to come out stiff and boardy. "My T-shirts itch me," Bobby would complain, and what was there to say: "I'm not as smart as your mother was"?

When the machine wheezed to a stop and clicked, Paul unloaded the clothes and dumped them into the twin dryer above. He set the timer on the dryer, pushed the button, and listened to it whoosh to life.

He took another sip of the brandy and sat down. Before him, in a pile on the polished teak table that seated four comfortably, six if they were good friends, were the month's bills, his checkbook and bank statement, a yellow pad for figures, and a felt-tip pen.

Paying the bills had been Jane's job, decided in the early years of their marriage when he had taken on the task and failed miserably. He had lost track of their balance and caused half-a-dozen checks to bounce, making such a mess that it took careful, organized Jane three months to set it right. That's how long it had taken for the check he had written in Cleveland, one of five checks not recorded on his stubs, to come back. One shirt, purchased at Halle's—blue, button-down collar, eleven dollars and thirty cents—worn to impress a restaurant owner whose account he had not gotten anyway.

He remembered it all now. That had been in their first apartment, the two-room basement with the water bugs that scared her; Jane in her blue terry bathrobe, sitting at the little desk in the corner of their bedroom, holding out the canceled check that brought their account back in balance and made her so happy. "From now on, especially out of town, you charge everything on your credit card, promise? Because American Express keeps better records than you do." Of course, cross my heart and hope to die. And then, after he'd grabbed that serious imp face with the pixie haircut and kissed it, he picked up all ninety-eight pounds of her, carried her over to the bed, and that was the end of high finance for that night.

He lit a cigarette and looked out the picture window into the floodlit garden, listening to the dryer turn over, hearing the rumble of a subway train passing through the cut two blocks away. A cold October wind stirred the few remaining brown leaves of Boston ivy that clung to the garage. He looked at the little vegetable plot Jane had planted across the driveway back in April. It was a jungle now, uncared-for all summer, tomato vines overgrowing brown zucchini leaves, eggplant and pepper shrubs twisted together. "My ratatouille garden," Jane always called it, and she kept it as neat as herself . . . those long sunny Sundays when she would stand for hours at the stove, browning eggplant and zucchini, the whole house fragrant with the aroma of sautéing onions and garlic.

Oh, Jane. She was everywhere in this house, in this kitchen. Everything was her touch, her taste, her life. Her plants in the small clay pots on the windowsill, the two woks nestled on the shelf alongside the stove, the straw baskets she'd hung on the wooden wall above, the pegboard wall near the oven, covered with implements and gadgets she loved to use, the old schoolhouse light fixtures she'd found at an auction and dragged home all by herself, spending more on the taxi fare than the fixtures had cost. On the long counter were her matching glass jars that held spaghetti, rice, beans, coffee, sugar, and those shiny aluminum weights she used when making pies and quiche. He could see Jane now, performing her "bottle trick" for the kids, popping the black tart pan down on the wide top of an upturned jar to free the quiche from its rim, then holding it up high, saying, "Thank you, thank you," as Bobby and Hilary applauded the performance.

Lighten up, kimosabe. Pay the bills. Work, do not think. He wrote checks; the gas bill for heating the house, the electric bill, and the big one for the mortgage. Pay to the order of Citibank the amount of four hundred sixty-four dollars and fifty-six cents or they will take this house away and put you out on the street.

Out on the street . . .

> Bobby and Hilary standing out on the street . . .
> Bobby and Hilary standing crying out on the street
> . . . Bobby and Hilary standing crying out on the
> street with their mother dead inside the house . . .

Sunlight on that Saturday morning in July, filtering through the blinds in the bedroom, awakening him as he sleeps beside her in the big bed, glancing at the clock to see it was after ten. Jane on her back, still asleep, one hand pressing against his side as he turns to look at the little sleepyhead; not like her to be in bed this late, not on a Saturday, when she does the supermarket shopping and goes to the butcher and later they're going to run downtown to buy new jeans for Bobby, how that boy is growing, why only last night she went through his closet with him, Bobby trying on shirts too short in the sleeve and his jeans above his sneaker tops with white socks showing and . . . he wonders then why she does not move. . . . "Hey, sleepyhead, it's after ten." A kiss on her brow, cold brow kiss on her cold brow . . . funny twist to her little mouth I've kissed ten thousand times. One eye slightly open but no brown pupil showing and no breathing? "Jane? Honey!" And shake her a little and she doesn't move, so stiff her body in the big bed and why is she not breathing, not waking up? So stiff and cold and shoving her hard and shaking her and she does not move. . . . Kiss of life but her lips won't open, can't force those lips open, her jaw set and can't force those lips open to breathe for her my Jane my Jane . . .

and shrieking now, leaping out of the big bed and running where? The telephone and nine-one-one police emergency come quick my wife is not breathing, and the lady cop on the other end saying calm down and where do you live and hanging up. Jane uncovered on the big bed, her shortie blue nightgown above her dark pubic hair showing and one leg twisted, and behind him in the doorway Hilary and Bobby, and they must not see this SHE'S DEAD. And his tears and his sobbing and their childeyes and white faces and chasing them out of the room and down the hall and "Go outside, go outside, something's wrong with your mother," and he can't say *dead* although he knows. Calling Dave Berg down the street, his friend, her friend, the doctor pediatrician who is there in three minutes in jeans and pajama top and no socks, and Dave pulling him away from Jane's body on the big bed and covering her, oh so finally covering her with the brown quilt over her head the brown quilt over her little body on the big bed.

And the two cops and the city ambulance and the paramedics upstairs with him.

And the stretcher with the green blanket they put her under and why won't they let him say good-bye to her? Why do they hold him away as they take her downstairs and out on the lawn as they come through the big front door on the porch and down the steps and there are the children, his children, his Hilary, first-born, and his Bobby he loves so much, and their childeyes are staring at the form of their mother under the green blanket and their eyes, he will never forget their eyes their eyes their eyes on that sunny Saturday morning in July. . . .

The clothes dryer buzzes, an ugly sound, strident and harsh. Paul gets up and goes swiftly to the machine. He opens the door to silence the noise, feels the hot underwear, all dry now. Piece by piece he takes the dry laundry out. On the clean maple chopping block he matches socks, rolls them into balls, folds flat Bobby's T-shirts and small briefs, his own underwear, folds five pairs of Hilary's once colorful and now faded bikini panties, one button-down white blouse of hers, one white shirt of Bobby's. He puts them into the yellow plastic laundry basket to take upstairs.

A quarter to one in the morning. Paul tosses off what remains in the brandy snifter, rinses it, and puts the snifter in the dishwasher.

He double locks the big front door, sets the chain bolt on the inner door of the foyer. Crossing the foyer to turn off the downstairs lights, he sees himself in the mirror, his eyes red-rimmed, his face pale, hair ends shaggy, in need of a haircut. No object all sublime, he says to himself. He takes the laundry basket and starts upstairs. The Austins, next door, have left the floodlight on in their driveway and a pale rosy light comes through the twin stained-glass windows on the landing.

Paul pauses, looking at the gilt-framed photographs on the wall. Jane's parents, Sam and Sylvia, standing next to their brand-new 1934 Chrysler Airflow sedan, Bobby in his bath at two years of age, Hilary in pigtails grinning through her missing teeth, a smiling Jane as a baby, holding a doll almost as big as she is. Their wedding picture, September 1962; his hair was curly then, Jane's teased up high to hold the white veil and crown, her lace gown flowing in a graceful line to the floor, a picturebook bride with the warm smile that always lit her face. He can remember every detail of their wedding and how he felt on that warm Saturday evening. The wonder of it, that this small smart happy little girl he could almost pick up and put in his pocket had chosen to spend the rest of her life with him. He thought himself the luckiest man on the face of the earth.

Upstairs, he separates the laundry on his bed and takes Bobby's underwear and socks to the boy's room, putting them on top of the dresser. The thin quilt is pulled up around Bobby's chin. Paul goes to the bed and looks down, runs his hand lightly over the boy's dark curly hair. Leaning down, he kisses Bobby's brow, then tiptoes from the room.

Hilary's panties in his hand, he opens her bedroom door a crack and reaches in to put them on her dresser.

"Daddy?" Her voice is thick with sleep.

"Yes. Sorry I got you up." Keeping his voice a whisper.

"I wasn't sleeping. What time is it?"

"Late. Go back to sleep."

"Could we talk? I'm not sleepy." With a graceful gesture, she sweeps a long strand of hair from her face. "Please?"

Paul walks a few steps into her room. In the dim light from the hallway he sees Remus, her old and only teddy bear, propped up on the pillow beside her head. Good old Remus, sixteen years old like

22

Hilary, who has survived being lost twice, having an ear torn off, losing a shoe-button eye, and countless spins through the washing machine. Smiling in the dark, Paul sits on the chair by her desk. "I have to be up at six-thirty," he says.

"You really don't. I can get Bobby off to school."

"Nope, my job."

"I *could* do it, you know."

"I know, babe. But it gives us a chance to talk. Bobby's still worried about the new school, I think."

"I know. He's such a baby."

"He's ten years old, puss. It's a long trip by subway for a kid, for anyone, an hour with two changes."

"He's been doing it for two months."

"He's a worrier. He's not like you."

"I know," she says, sighing. In the dark, she seeks her father's eyes. "He misses Mom."

"Yes."

"I miss her, too. A lot."

"I know, sugar. We all do."

"It's a shitty deal," she says, her voice harsh.

"Yes it is."

After a silence, Hilary says, "Daddy?"

"Yes."

"I want to talk to you about Peter."

"It's very late, babe."

"You don't like Peter."

"I never said that."

"You act like it."

"Did I ever say I don't like Peter? Be fair. He's a nice kid, he's always polite to me, he seems to be fairly smart. It's just . . . sometimes I think you're seeing too much of each other."

"Daddy . . . I think I'm in love with Peter."

"Oh?" he says, surprised and not surprised. All the signs were there, he could have seen this coming. Jane would have, certainly.

"And Peter loves me."

"Uh huh." Even in the near-dark, he can see the anxiety on her oval face. She has his nose, but the questioning eyes are Jane's.

"Is that all you're going to say?"

23

"Oh, babe," he sighs, "what can I say? You're sixteen years old. Peter is . . . what?"

"Two months younger than me."

"The same age. You're together practically all the time, you go to the same school, you listen to the same music, you even wear the same ratty jeans. So the two of you are . . . *simpatico*, okay?"

"It's not puppy love, Daddy, if that's what you're going to say. I'm old enough to know my feelings. I love Peter. He's like another part of me. When we're together sometimes . . . Daddy, we even *breathe* in unison."

In spite of himself, Paul laughs. "I'm sorry. I know it's not funny to you."

"You can't talk me out of it," she interrupts.

"Of course not. Look, honey, you're very young, and right now I think you're very vulnerable, too. Hell, the three of us are. I could cry sixteen times a day for no reason at all. And Peter is nice, like you say, and maybe, I think, you're grabbing on to him more because of Mom. Do you think that's possible?"

"Even if Mom were here, I'd still love Peter."

The intensity of her voice sounds a warning. "Okay, I'll give you that. And you are a pretty mature sixteen. But is it really love?"

He tells Hilary about himself at sixteen, slightly overweight, thinking his nose was too long, deathly afraid of making a fool of himself before girls and yet seeking their company. It wasn't until he was in college that he had his first real girl friend, and he thought that was love, too, at the time. Until they broke up, and he found another girl friend after a while, and then still another.

"It wasn't till I met your mother that I knew I was really in love. I know this is ancient history, and you've heard it before."

"No, that's okay. She was nineteen."

"Almost twenty. And I was twenty-four, out of the army, and not really looking to get married. But after about three months, I knew it. Oh, boy, did I know it. And your mother was the same way. We'd go places, to restaurants, and just sit and stare at each other across the table, looking into each other's eyes, just gaga . . . like two idiots, two crazy people. We didn't care about anything else, back then, just being together. I'd spend an evening with her, we'd neck in the car for hours, then I'd go home and we'd talk *on the telephone* for another hour. Is that crazy?''

"Like Peter and me."

Paul sits on the edge of Hilary's bed. He takes her hand and holds it. "Here's the point, babe. By the time Mom met me she'd had two or three boyfriends already. And one near-engagement. When we fell in love, she knew it was the real thing. Peter is your first love, honey, and that's very special. But someday—I'm not going to say it will happen, just that it might—someday you might break up and I'd hate to see you get hurt."

"Don't worry."

"I'm not worried, just saying it might happen."

"We won't break up, Daddy."

"We'll see." He squeezes her small hand in his. "In the meantime, I'm glad someone around here is happy."

Hilary sits up and hugs her father, then kisses his cheek. "I'm so relieved," she says, grinning at him.

"Relieved?"

"I was afraid to tell you. I thought you were going to be so angry with me."

"For what?"

"For falling in love with Peter."

Standing before the mirror in his bathroom, he is still thinking about Hilary's last words to him. "I thought you were going to be so angry with me." Is that what Hilary thinks of you, truly? Is he some sort of ogre in her eyes, the big bad Father Bear? The truth is, he is not pleased with her relationship with Peter. Because . . . say it, he really doesn't know how to handle it. Jane would know, of course. Jane was the one the kids brought their problems to. It was her job, after-school mommy, weekend mommy, and general wise-woman of the Western world thrown in. He'd been busy building a business, working his tail off, investing time away from home like bonds that would pay dividends at some later date.

Father knows best. The hell he does.

Paul stares at the pink Librium spansules in the prescription bottle. They are not supposed to keep him from sleeping, but somehow they do. And they don't lift his goddamn spirits, either.

He settles for a Klein Special: two extra-strength Tylenol washed down by a healthy slug of Jack Daniels.

25

He gets under the quilt on the big bed and sets the clock-radio alarm for six-twenty, telling himself not to worry about how late it is. Jesus, another wonderful day to be faced on less than four hours' sleep. Groaning, he pulls Jane's pillow to his chest and turns over on his side. *"Me strong like Fodder."* The punch line to a joke Herman, his father, used to tell—a joke he can't remember, but the punch line had become a family saying when he was a boy. He thinks of Herman, a skull face in the hospital bed, dying of cancer at age sixty-three. Not strong like Fodder at all. And then Jane's father had gone the following year, and his mother two years later. Only Sylvia was left, Jane's mother, living in the little condo apartment in Fort Lauderdale and crying her eyes out on the phone once a week when she calls.

Sleep, he tells himself, all engines dead stop.

You never got a chance to say good-bye, that was what haunted him. Never got a chance to hold that small form against himself, to look in those sweet brown eyes and say how much he loved her, had always loved her, and loved her still.

A pillow wasn't Jane. Cradling it close, he remembers the feel of her lying next to him as they fell asleep, two spoons nestled up tight, his arm under her neck, left arm lying loose in the soft curve of her hip, the smell of her hair tucked up under his chin. In the Widdicomb bed Jane had picked out, on the sheets and pillowcases she had bought, in the bedroom painted blue at her choice, Paul Klein falls asleep.

3

_____

". . . TEMPERATURE FORTY-EIGHT DEGREES, going up to fifty-five," said the news-radio voice. Paul groaned, stirred, rolled over, and looked at the clock. Six-twenty.

He found his slippers and sleepwalked into the bathroom. He held his head under the faucet and let the cold water run full-force. Water on the hair awakened him, opened his eyes, let his brain operate. When Jane was alive she would wake him with a kiss at about eight o'clock. By that time she had seen the kids off to school, breakfasted, showered, and was heading off to her own school to teach. Leaving him a warm bathroom, a warm shower stall, a warm beginning to each day.

Paul put on his terrycloth robe against the morning chill and went into Bobby's room. The boy was lying on his back, quilt up to his chin, his snub of a nose pointing at the ceiling. My one and only son, my perfect little boy. In the dim light he gazed at Bobby's thick black eyebrows, the delicate tracery of his long eyelashes. "Why didn't Hilary get those eyelashes?" Jane would ask when Bobby was a baby. "He's so beautiful!"

27

He leaned down and kissed Bobby's brow. "Good morning, chum, rise and shine."

The boy's eyes fluttered open, settled upon Paul. He stretched and yawned. "Morning."

"Did you sleep okay?"

"I guess so. Is it cold out?"

"About the same as yesterday. No sun, though. Are you ready for the light?"

Bobby nodded. Paul got up, walked to the wall switch, turned on the bright overhead light. Bobby pulled himself out from under the quilt and sat up, shielding his eyes from the glare.

Paul opened the bottom drawer of the dresser and took out a pair of clean blue jeans, checking to see that the knees were not worn through.

"What day is today?" Bobby said.

"Thursday."

"Oh, God! Science lab the first two periods."

"Not your favorite, huh?"

Bobby struggled into his T-shirt, getting angry as he flailed about trying to put his arm through the right opening. Paul had tried to teach him to roll the T-shirt first, then stick his head through the center hole, his arms through the others. But Bobby did it his own way, his arms straight up in the air as he slipped into the shirt, letting it work its way down while he fought to find the right openings.

"Mr. Bressant is such an idiot! He gives us all this stupid homework and he never checks it." With a sudden thrust, Bobby's hand and arm came ripping through the white cotton shirt. "Shit! I tore it." The boy wrestled the shirt off and threw it on the bed.

"Don't get upset, you've got other T-shirts."

The boy glared at him. Paul turned away, found another, and tossed it to Bobby. "What would you like for breakfast?"

Bobby stood mute, the T-shirt in his hand; he shrugged. He began to cry.

Paul took him in a hug, holding Bobby's head to his chest. "It's okay," he said, "it's only a T-shirt, it doesn't matter." The boy sobbed once, then pulled away from his father, wiping his eyes with balled fists, angry at his tears.

Paul felt tears brim at the back of his eyes. *Don't!* "Scrambled eggs? French toast? Hot cereal?"

Bobby rolled his shoulders in a shrug.

Say something, come on, talk to me, Paul pleaded silently. "I'll see you downstairs," Paul said, his voice husky.

"Yeah."

In the front hallway Paul snapped off the porch light, undid the locks and chain, stepped out onto the porch to bring in the newspaper. A car came down the street, slowing for the red light at the corner. Across the way, a light came on in the Dawsons' bedroom. Paul looked at the bank of orange and white impatiens that had grown knee-high in front of the Dawsons' shrubbery, fronting their house with a splash of bright color that set off the dark brown shingles. In a few weeks the flowers would be gone as the cold set in, but still they flourished, even in the October chill.

In the kitchen, he opened *The New York Times,* found the sports section, and put it on the table before Bobby's chair. He poured a glass of orange juice and put it with a vitamin pill on the place mat. From the refrigerator he took a package of bologna to make Bobby's lunch sandwich. He pulled open the bread drawer and his heart sank. There was a package of white bread that appeared to be mostly plastic wrap and no bread. Only an end slice inside, with a corner torn off. How the hell did this happen? Yesterday morning there had been about half a loaf left, enough not to worry about. Had Hilary had a sandwich after school? Gemma, the cleaning lady? How could he make Bobby a sandwich with no bread?

Bobby came into the kitchen and went silently to the table.

"We have a slight emergency here," Paul said. "Somebody seems to have made off with the bread."

Bobby gulped his vitamin pill down with a swallow of juice. "No French toast then?"

"No toast, period."

"I'll have cold cereal."

"Which kind?"

The boy shrugged and busied himself with the newspaper, which meant he didn't care. Paul opened the cupboard door and looked at the cereal packages. "I could make you hot cereal. Oatmeal? Wheatena?"

Silence.

Paul poured Cheerios into a bowl, added milk, took a spoon from the drawer, a napkin from the plastic dispenser, and set them down alongside the newspaper in front of Bobby. He poured a glass of milk and started to bring that, too, when he checked himself. He had forgotten the ice cube. Bobby had a passion for freezing cold milk, couldn't drink it without an ice cube. Paul pulled a cube from the container, plopped it into the glass, then glanced at the clock. Ten of seven. "It's getting a little late, Bob."

The boy put the cereal bowl on top of the newspaper and began to eat. Paul poured himself a half-glass of juice and sipped it while he looked out the window into the back garden. Bobby would have to buy lunch at school, as much as he disliked—make that hated; no, make that *refused*—to do it. They'd had two previous arguments about purchasing school lunches. Bobby insisted that a) he had a thirty-five-minute lunch period and it took thirty minutes to go through the lunch line, and b) it nauseated him just to pass in front of the steam tables because they stank so much, they used the wrong kind of bologna, yucky peanut butter, they put celery in the tuna sandwiches and he hated celery, and the milk wasn't just warm, it was hot and undrinkable.

Paul felt suddenly tired. He was running on empty, with two flats and no spare.

"Look," he said, more harshly than he intended, "you'll just have to buy your lunch in school today. I don't want any arguments."

Bobby looked at him, surprised. "What?"

"No bread, remember? So you'll have to buy lunch. You'll survive it."

Bobby took a long slug of his milk, emptied the glass, and got up. "I'm not buying lunch," he said. He began to cross the kitchen on his way upstairs. Paul stopped him, taking hold of his arm.

"You're buying lunch today, okay? Get used to it."

The boy looked at him, his face sullen.

"I'm sorry about the bread. I forgot, or something."

"Just give me my milk and an apple," the boy said. "I'll mooch a sandwich from someone."

"What do you mean, 'mooch'?"

"You think I always eat what you give me? Sometimes I give it away to one of the guys. Or we trade."

Paul stared.

"Just give me a bunch of cookies and I'll trade with Sambo. Do we have Oreos? Sambo'll trade anything for Oreos."

"No. I'm not sending you to school with no lunch. When you go upstairs, take some money from on top of my dresser and you'll buy lunch."

Bobby shook his head. "No, I won't. By the time I get through the line, lunch will be over, Sambo and the guys'll be gone, and I'll have no one to sit with." He looked past Paul's shoulder at the clock on the oven wall. "Ten after seven. I'm late!" He pulled his arm out of Paul's grasp and dashed from the kitchen to his room.

"Take money!" Paul shouted after him. He felt weak, defeated. He couldn't push Bobby right now, not with all they were living through, but sometimes he had to. Oh, hell! He had forgotten to prepare the boy's thermos of milk. Hastily, he opened the cabinet above the sink and looked for the thermos. He'd filled the thermos to the top before he remembered the ice cubes. When he opened the freezer to take out an ice cube, his eye fell on a package that stood in front of a row of plastic containers of Jane's frozen Chinese soup stock. White bread, in its plastic wrap, almost covered with frost. Jane's emergency package of frozen bread, used for toasting some mornings when they ran out of bread. How old was the bread? Had to be at least five months. Could you still eat it? Paul opened the package and slipped out two rock-hard slices. They smelled funny, but frozen bread always smelled funny.

He piled bologna on a slice, topped it with the other slice, took a knife from the drawer and stopped himself. You couldn't cut this sandwich. He hoped the bread would thaw before lunch. Hastily, he tossed an apple and three Oreos into the bag. When Bobby reappeared in the kitchen, lugging a knapsack filled with books, his lunch was ready.

"I found bread," Paul said. The boy showed no surprise. He was busy filling his pockets from the small pile on the corner of the counter near the door. Every day, when he came home from school, Bobby unloaded his pockets right there in that spot. Paul watched him put two subway tokens in his pocket, his train-pass case, his school ID, his house keys on a little chain with a hockey-skate charm attached, and the dollar and dime he always carried; the dime for a phone call in case there was some emergency, the dollar to be surrendered to some hoodlum who might try to mug the boy.

"Do you have everything?"

Bobby nodded. He stuffed the lunch bag in among his books and secured the knapsack.

Paul followed him through the house to the front door. When Bobby put on his jacket and cap, Paul helped him heft the knapsack onto his back. It weighed twenty pounds at least. Why did they make little kids lug so many books back and forth to school each day?

"Gemma will be home after school, and maybe Hilary," Paul said.

The boy tilted his head up to be kissed. Paul pecked him on the cheek and gave his arm a squeeze. "See you tonight, chum."

Paul followed him onto the porch and stood watching as the boy went down the steps and turned toward the corner. Near the driveway, Bobby turned and looked back, waving once. Paul waved back. The boy looked so fragile to his eyes, so small, weighted down with a knapsack that made him walk hunched forward, wearing a baseball jacket and a Yankee cap, blue jeans and sneakers worn almost through in the toes. Bobby crossed at the light, then began to run at the sound of a subway train pulling into the station. He disappeared from sight behind the house at the far corner.

Paul heard a toilet flush and Hilary's footsteps as she padded about in her room upstairs. He boiled water in the brown kettle and made himself a cup of instant coffee. He was sipping his coffee and smoking his first cigarette of the day when Hilary came into the kitchen. "Good morning," she said in her cheery way.

"There's water in the kettle," Paul said.

Hilary nodded. She poured herself a glass of orange juice and took a vitamin pill. "You ought to stop smoking," she said.

"I know."

"It's a disgusting habit."

"Baby, please. Not today, okay? I *need* this cigarette."

Hilary put a tea bag into her special mug, the yellow one with the chip on the bottom—the one she wouldn't let anyone else use—and poured the boiling water into it.

"I had a thing with Bobby about lunch. There was no bread for his sandwich."

"Oops," Hilary said.

"You finished the bread?"

"After school yesterday, Peter and me. We pigged out on peanut butter and honey. Sorry."

"You should have told me last night. I could have run out and bought a loaf of bread."

"I said I was sorry." Hilary took a cup of yogurt from the refrigerator. As she came to the table, Paul took a good look at her. She was wearing a pair of her rattier jeans, with two patched knees and one torn belt loop, and above them she had on a tight-fitting blouse. The twin brown aureoles of her apple breasts showed much too clearly through the thin material. Hilary was able to read the expression in her father's face because she stopped and said: "What?"

Hilary's unconventional mode of dress was a contentious subject, one the girl and Jane had wrangled about for years. Hilary despised what she called "fashion," hooted scornfully at the "disco" crowd in her school who wore designer jeans and clunky shoes. But this was a matter that Jane had always handled, trying very hard not to nag Hilary about it, objecting only when the girl went too far. Paul grimaced. Say what you think, big daddy. "You need a bra under that shirt."

Hilary put her tea and yogurt on the table. "I don't own a bra." The girl sat down at her place before the window.

"It doesn't look right."

Hilary opened her yogurt and took a spoonful. She looked coolly at Paul. "What doesn't?"

That's right, he thought, make me say it. "Your breasts."

"Thank God I've got 'em."

Paul remembered a conversation he'd overheard, perhaps a year ago; Hilary on the telephone with a friend, wailing, "When am I going to grow tits!" They were small, like her mother's had been, but they were now large enough to show. Too much. "Honey, you can't wear that shirt without a bra."

"It's a body suit."

"Whatever. It's too sheer. Everything shows."

"I'm not ashamed."

"That's not the point."

"I like the way it feels. And I think it looks good."

"It's too . . . provocative, Hil."

"I think you're being silly."

He reached for his pack of cigarettes.

"And now you're so nervous you have to smoke another cigarette. Could you not, please?"

"All right. But I can't let you wear that outfit to school."

"Why not? Am I going to get raped or something?"

"Honey, I can see everything through it. And so can every boy in school."

"So what?"

"So plenty. Do you really want to get stared at, or have some wise-ass making cracks?"

"You think I care about that?"

"I know, I know. But why give them the chance? Sugar, I know what I'm saying. Wear a sweater over that shirt, okay?"

"Body suit," she said. "And I'll be too warm in a sweater over it." She pulled the newspaper from her brother's place mat and lowered her eyes to it, her signal that the conversation was over.

Paul stared at his lovely daughter, who used to be so happy-go-lucky, so giggly and bubbly only a few months ago. The light from the window made her long brown hair shine. He remembered the small pink baby he used to diaper, and the few wonderful times he had been privileged to give her a bath, and the time when she had suddenly put on weight and filled her jumpsuits to overflowing. And that fat little bundle had grown into a slim, tall, beautifully built young woman who was now angry with him.

It was time to be stern. Why did it make him hate himself?

"You're not leaving this house dressed like that," he said, a note of finality in his voice. Hilary did not look up. "Did you hear me?"

She nodded.

"Right," he said. "You'll change then."

"Uh huh."

"Right." He got up from the table and took his coffee cup to the sink. In the back garden, a male robin was pecking at something hidden in the grass. He had to go upstairs, shower, shave, get into his clothes, and go to the office. He had to work a whole day somehow and then come home to prepare dinner for the three of them.

34

At this moment, it seemed impossible. "Do you have enough money in your pocket?"

"Yes."

"Will you be coming straight home from school?"

"Yes."

The New York Times must be fantastic this morning, he thought; she can't take her eyes off it. Miss Frost, Jane used to call her when Hilary had one of these moods, Miss Hilary Frost.

He was about to leave the kitchen when he remembered dinner. He opened the freezer and looked in, pushing the foil-wrapped packages around so he could read the labels. "Lamb chops tonight?" he asked Hilary.

She didn't answer.

"Unusual-bone lamb chops," he said, smiling.

Nothing.

"I'll broil them with some soy sauce on top. Okay with you?"

"Sure."

He put the wrapped package on the counter by the sink. He wanted to give Hilary a hug or a kiss before he left the room, but he was afraid. If when he kissed her she sat still and cold, he would shrivel. It hurt him, always, that withholding of love, it felt like a kick in the gut. "When Bobby comes home, will you see he has some milk and cookies?"

"Sure."

He stared at the girl, who stared at the newspaper. "Honey, look at me. Please." Her face came up sullen, but she looked at him. "I'm sorry about your body suit. Really I am. But now I've got to be a mother and a father and I'm probably lousy at both jobs. We've got to stick together, Hil. You and me and Bobby, like glue now, you understand?"

"And what do I do when you give me shit, say nothing?"

"Just try to understand. And don't say words like *shit* to me. You never used language like that in front of Mom, did you?"

"You're not Mom."

"That's right. But I'm your father and I'm asking you to behave. Scratch that, I'm *telling* you to behave. We're still a family around here. We've got to feel for each other."

Hilary stared at him. "Even if you're wrong?"

That little girl is tougher than I'll ever be, he thought. And

35

maybe thank God for that. ''Yes, even when I'm wrong. Because we love each other, and we can forgive each other, and when I'm wrong it's because I'm doing what I think is right to look after you.'' He heard himself saying this and it sounded both pompous and weak. He was blowing it, and she wasn't helping him one little bit. Miss Hilary Frost. ''Kapeesh, kiddo?''

She nodded.

''Right.'' One kiss, one hug would say more than a thousand words, but she would not let him. Not yet a woman, but she had all the weapons in place. ''I've got to get showered and dressed and get out of here. See you tonight.''

Hilary lowered her eyes and looked at the newspaper again. He turned and walked away. Only eight o'clock in the morning of a day that promised to be about a thousand hours long.

4

"SO THE POPE comes back to Rome after his visit to America," said Michael Bradie, as the two partners sat having lunch at their customary table in Sweets Restaurant. "And his favorite cardinal asks him, 'Your Holiness, how did you enjoy your stay in the United States?' 'Terrible,' the pope says, 'very upsetting.'

" 'And why is that, your Holiness?'

" 'Two reasons,' says the pope. 'First of all, the so-called ethnic jokes. It was very upsetting to hear them, setting race upon race, religion against religion. Especially, I might add, the great number of Polish jokes. Very demeaning.' "

Jesse, the waiter who had served Paul and Michael Bradie for the past ten years, set their drinks down. Michael paused to take a sip of his vodka gimlet, then continued. " 'And the second reason, your Holiness?'

" 'The M&Ms,' says the pope, 'those tiny chocolate candies.'

" 'The M&Ms?'

" 'Yes,' says the pope. 'Very hard to peel.' "

Paul laughed, but not any harder than Michael Bradie, who enjoyed his own jokes very much. "Black Irish" was the way Michael had described himself twenty years ago, when he and Paul were both army second lieutenants stationed in Rüdesheim, West Germany. Michael's black hair was thick then, even with a crew cut. The hair was gone now, except for a dark fringe that framed his head and accentuated his jug-handled ears. Those ears were the subject of many jokes, told mostly and with great glee by Michael himself, but it was by his bushy eyebrows, which rose and fell when he told a story, and by his expressive brown eyes that Michael was now defined. "An Irish leprechaun," he called himself, those eyes twinkling and sparkling, winking to make a point. And that was how Paul thought of his partner of fifteen years: a short, well-built leprechaun who knew him better than any other man, and who had brought them both a great deal of luck and success in their business.

Michael took another sip of his drink. "Still not sleeping?"

"Is it that obvious?"

"You could go to the blood bank and have your eyes drained. I guess the Librium isn't helping."

"Not much."

"And the kids? How are they?"

"Do we have the whole afternoon?" Paul lit a cigarette and toyed with his lighter. "We're all the same, shell shocked, trying to cope. Bobby's the one I worry about. Hilary's finding her own way. But the little guy . . ."

"It's a tough age," Michael said, "even without losing your mother. And he's at the new school, of course. There's a lot on his plate, Paul."

"I wonder if I did the right thing, sending him to school so far away."

"One of the best schools in the city, if not *the* best."

"But I wonder if Bob wouldn't be better off close to home. He'd have more neighborhood friends, no long trip to school on the subway, and the work would be easier."

"Don't second-guess yourself. I remember how happy you and Jane were when the kid passed the examination and decided to go there. Hell, Bobby belongs there. And as for work, I think it's the best for all of you right now. Occupy your minds, leave you less time for brooding."

Paul took a sip of his Jack Daniels. "Is that a hint?"

Michael smiled. "Not really. We've been *schlepping* this long, we can still wait a while."

"Mike, I just can't spend a week in Chicago and a week in Minneapolis right now."

"Did I say anything?" Michael's busy eyebrows raised and lowered, but the expression in his eyes was warm.

"You don't have to. I know we're hurting out there. I'll take care of it, Mike, but not now. After New Year's, I promise."

"Minneapolis in January? You'll disappear into a snowbank and never be heard from again. Hell of a way to lose a partner."

"February or March. I can't put Carter off longer than that."

"Your department entirely, and besides, Carter can get stuffed as far as I'm concerned, he's never satisfied. How you get along with him, I'll never know."

"Personal charm," Paul said, smiling, "and picking up the tab while he stuffs his face at Charlie's Café. Speaking of that," he added, looking at his partner and setting up the private joke they shared, "shall we order lunch?"

"Lunch? We haven't finished drinking yet."

Paul Klein's friendship with Michael Bradie had been formed by the army and cemented during a thirty-day leave they had taken together in Europe. The itinerary had been arranged by Michael, a tour through the wine country of Germany, France, and northern Italy. They traveled first by train to Épernay, in the French champagne district. Paul was surprised when a limousine met them at the small country train station, and amazed when they were given a personal tour of the caves by the son of the local bottler who was most respectful of "Monsieur Bradie." They dined that evening at the home of the bottler, apparently a big man in that part of France, who inquired after the health of Michael's family.

"He's been doing business with my old man for forty years," Michael explained later that evening when they were having a brandy in the crystal-chandeliered bar of the guest house in Épernay. "I kept it a surprise because I wanted to see the look on your face," he grinned.

"Was I dumbfounded?"

"Better than that."

"Who is your old man, anyway?"

39

"Thomas Bradie of Thomas Bradie and Sons, Incorporated. Next to firms like Schieffelin and Julius Wile, he probably imports more wine into the United States than anyone."

The rest of their leave was equally impressive to Paul. Michael Bradie was greeted like a long-lost member of the family throughout France and Italy. He had made many buying trips as a young boy, along with his father and brothers, and he knew not only the shippers they visited but many of the members of their families as well. The red carpet was rolled out for the two lieutenants everywhere they went. They were taken shooting in Bordeaux, stayed at villas and châteaux, and in Lake Como a large and stately yacht was put at their disposal. But everywhere they went, Michael took time out to visit other local shippers, men with whom his father did not choose to do business. "They're the future, pal," he told Paul, "mine and maybe yours. Because with four brothers and me the youngest, there's one too many sons in Thomas Bradie and Sons." Not yet twenty-two years old, Michael Bradie had a plan for a business of his own, a business Paul could share someplace down the road, if he was interested. It was in most respects the business the two men now owned and ran, with Michael controlling sixty percent of it and Paul the rest.

Michael had explained that day as they took the sun on Lake Como, cruising slowly toward Bellagio. "The big boys, men like my old man, import the big wines, the famous names. They spend millions advertising and promoting them. But there's plenty of other wines to import, Paul, no-name wines, sure, but good wines of good value. There's a market there if you know what you're doing, and if you have the contacts and the push. We'd never get really rich, like my old man, say, but we'd make a damn good living."

"I don't have any money, Mike."

"There are banks for that. We get along, that's the main thing. You have a degree in marketing from NYU, no? And a damn sharp *Yiddische kopf.* Did I say that right?"

"Like my grandmother."

"So there, a Catholic and a Jew, Bradie and Klein. I'll handle Europe and the buying, you handle stateside distributors and selling, and we'll both share the worrying."

It had taken three years to launch the firm of Bradie and Klein,

Inc., three years in which Paul had worked for a distributor in Cleveland, a small import house in New Jersey, and Michael's father, Thomas Bradie. He schooled himself in every phase of the wine business, married Jane, fathered a daughter, secured an enormous bank loan, and did more than his share of the worrying. But from the moment they opened the doors of their warehouse and offices in Long Island City, they had done well. Not getting rich, but making a damn good living. They still maintained the warehouse, along with a larger one near the waterfront in lower Manhattan where their small but comfortable offices were located. Michael had found the Manhattan space, on a shabby street near the Brooklyn Bridge, and Paul still twitted him about it because when the wind was right the smell of the Fulton Fish Market pervaded their offices. Wonderful aroma, Michael always said, a constant reminder to sell more white wine.

Michael finished the last of his striped bass and put his fork on the plate. He was telling Paul about his wife Kathleen's latest campaign. "She's finally going back to school, she says, to get her nurse's degree. As if taking care of four daughters at home wasn't enough nursing for her. And the girls, of course, little Gloria Steinems every one, are encouraging her. Can you imagine? My own personal harem, turning on me that way. Women's lip, I call it, because I can't make the simplest remark without someone or other calling me a chauvinist, or worse."

"But you are, Michael," Paul said, knowing Michael's mock-chauvinist hyperbole was a pose; underneath he was a teddy bear who doted on Kathleen and the girls.

"Damn right, barefoot and pregnant is the ticket. Supper on the table, pipe and slippers handed over, and no back talk, thank you very much."

"That doesn't sound like the Kathleen I know."

"Not since she had her hysterectomy, my boy. That was the act of liberation and no mistake. Deny the possibility of pregnancy and a woman changes completely. A scrub nurse she wants to be, in the operating room and all. Kathleen, mind you, who can faint dead away at the sight of blood."

"More power to her."

"Oh, you would say that," Michael said, smiling impishly, "my liberated friend who had his balls cut off."

"Just a vasectomy, pal, the balls are still there."

"How could you let a man, even a surgeon, approach your balls with a knife in his hand, that's beyond me."

It had been six years since his vasectomy, but Michael never stopped kidding Paul about it. "I could show you my scars if you like."

"Now, now," Michael said. He reached into his suit coat and took out a cigar. "Speaking of which, and presuming they're still in place, have you given any thought to exercising your manly function?" Michael carefully unwrapped the Upmann Special.

"Not really."

"It might do you good, you know."

"That's not where my mind is, Mike."

"Never mind your mind. I'm talking about getting laid, to put it crudely."

"Don't you always?"

"Blunt yes, crude no. You know what they say, when you fall off a horse you have to get right back up again."

"I fell off the earth, Michael. It's more like that."

"Still that."

"Lost in space, the three of us."

"Time to come down, don't you think?"

"But how?"

"A vacation. Take the kids out of school and go off somewhere. You could have the beach house in Amagansett again. Just say the word."

"Thanks, but I don't think that'll help. I told you about the time we spent there in August. Three of us in that beautiful house, perfect weather. And each of us in his own world, sitting on the beach like pieces of driftwood, staring at the sea, afraid to enjoy ourselves because that would have been untrue to Jane. It was awful, Mike. We wandered around like three suntanned ghosts in bathing suits."

"From what you say, it hasn't been much better at home. Have you thought about moving out? Selling the house, say, and moving into an apartment in Manhattan?" Michael lit his cigar carefully with a match.

"Thought about it, yes. But doing it . . ." Paul paused while Jesse poured coffee into their cups. He looked at Michael through a haze of blue cigar smoke. "Our lives are bound up in that house, it connects us in a special way. Maybe sometime we could move away, but not now. Continuity, especially for the kids, that's the thing they need."

"That's Dr. Wirtz talking. Has he helped?"

"Who knows?" Paul shrugged. "Maybe we'd have been basket cases by now without him. He helped Hilary and me, I guess. Bobby doesn't like him."

"Why not?"

"I don't know. He just won't open up to him, though. And that scares me."

Michael sighed, exhaling a cloud of smoke.

"He loves you, Mike."

"My jokes. Bobby's always been my best audience. Jesus, the three of you are pathetic."

"And I'm getting sick and tired of being pathetic. It's getting old, Mike, just going on and on."

They were walking back to the office through the winding streets of the financial district. They walked as old friends do, almost touching, adjusting to each other's gait and staying in step. "Why," Michael was asking, "why don't you get rid of that housekeeper of yours? What's her name?"

"Gemma."

"Why don't you fire her, Paul, and get someone who'll live in and take care of things for you? That Gemma sounds like a loser."

"She is."

"So?"

"I can't, Mike. Gemma's worked for us for six or seven years. Bobby loves her. And she knows all of Hilary's little secrets. She's almost like a member of the family."

"Why does she let you run out of underwear? That's ridiculous."

Paul grinned, thinking of how many midnight washes he'd had to do over the past few months. It wasn't funny. So what made him smile, he wondered. *"Housekeeper* is the wrong word for Gemma. She worked Monday and Thursday and did the heavy cleaning for Jane. She's a middle-aged lady with two married kids. Her husband's a welder, works someplace in Jersey, and Gemma works to help out at home. Jane always knew how to handle her."

"And obviously you don't."

"She doesn't take direction well," Paul said, thinking it was the understatement of the week. "I'm glad she was able to give us an extra day. I don't know what we'd do without her."

Michael grunted. "She keeps screwing up and you love her. I don't get it. Paul, you're a guy who built a great sales force. If you had a salesman like Gemma working for us, you'd fire his ass in a minute."

"Probably. But I'd never have hired anyone like Gemma in the first place."

The cold wind coming off the East River made Paul hunch his neck down into the collar of his coat. Both men were chilled. They walked through the wood-paneled reception room and into the back corridor that divided their space into a long row of small cubicles with a large corner office at either end. "Hang in there," Michael said.

Lillian Lerner, Paul's secretary, who had been with him since the early Long Island City days, sat at her desk outside his office. "The usual nonsense," she said in reply to his questioning glance. Paul hung his coat in the small closet. "Oh," she went on, "Arlen Carter called in an order from Minneapolis. Routine, nothing big."

He sat at the desk in his office and picked up the order called in by Arlen Carter and written on the order pad in Lillian's small, neat hand. It was the usual, with perhaps a bit more of the sparkling wines and champagnes Carter would be selling as they moved toward Christmas and New Year's. There were none of the newer items on the order, the brands Carter had promised to take on. But then, the firm of Bradie and Klein had not delivered on its promise to carry out certain promotions in Carter's market, either.

Paul wished they could operate like some of the big boys in the business for once. Make a couple of television commercials, run the hell out of them, and then sit back while sales shot up to the moon. Going on the road to promote their products took so much time and energy, items he did not have in abundance right now.

Paul looked out the window of his office. A pale sun glinted on the dirty, cobblestone street, and if he craned his neck, he could see a small slice of the river. He'd missed important trips to Minneapolis and Chicago this year. More than that, he'd been away from the office for a solid six weeks, and almost useless when he'd returned. But just standing here, thinking about what remained to be done in Minneapolis and Chicago, he was feeling better. Put the mind to work and you close off the pain. Pain can only occupy one place at a time in your body. To cure a headache, stub your toe. To stop brooding about Jane and the kids, get down to business. He could begin planning his Chicago and Minneapolis promotions now. When would he go? February? Probably too soon. March, then. What kind of shape would Bobby and Hilary be in by then? Could he leave them for a week, two weeks?

He went to his desk and turned the Rolodex to Minneapolis, looking up the number of the public relations firm he'd used out there on his last trip. It was still early, but he could start making arrangements.

Paul was about to dial the Minneapolis telephone number when the intercom buzzed. "Bobby's school is on the line," Lillian said.

Paul punched the lighted button on his telephone, glancing across the desk at the photograph that stood in a silver frame next to the in-tray. It was his favorite photograph of the family, taken on a winter trip to Puerto Rico two years ago. Jane stood in the foreground on Loquillo Beach, sunglasses pushed back atop her head, with a laughing Hilary and Bobby nestled close under each of her arms. Hilary was fourteen then, braces still on her teeth, just about as tall as Jane; Bobby hadn't begun shooting up yet, skinny as a stick; you could see every rib.

"Mr. Klein?"

"Yes."

"Robert Klein's father?"

"Yes."

"I'm Patricia McNeil, Robert's grade adviser. I believe we spoke briefly when school began in September."

"Oh, yes, and I sent you a note about . . . Bobby's mother."

"That's correct. Robert has been involved in an incident, a scuffle with a classmate, and he's sitting outside my office right now."

"Bobby had a fight?"

"Not much of a fight, really. Some pushing and shoving. One or two punches perhaps. He's been crying the whole time since then, though, and I hesitate to send him home from school this way.''

"I'll be right there."

In midafternoon, traffic flowed easily on the northbound drive. His peaceful, gentle Bobby in a fight, that was hard to believe. Violence was so far from the boy's nature. Even as a little child Bobby had turned away from television shows involving shooting or fighting. He'd never wanted a cap pistol like most of the other kids, and when Hilary watched *Batman* (with great glee, as Paul remembered, shouting out every *Pow! Bam!* and *Sock!*) Bobby would leave the room. They couldn't get him to see a horror picture; he had balked at seeing *The Sting* because he'd heard there were a few scenes with shooting in them. Only Jane's coaxing had convinced him to go.

Jane. It always came back to Jane.

Marry a teacher and you get a wife who works yet still has time to be there for the children after school. And during school hours, too, he reminded himself, and for whole weeks when he was away. Hilary's broken arm. He'd missed the girl's fall on the patio out in the back garden, the sight of the bump under the skin of her forearm where the bone was pressing out, the dash to the hospital emergency room and the long wait.

Jane had handled it, as she always did.

He'd only known about it that evening when he'd come back to the hotel to find a pink message slip: "Mrs. Klein called." And Jane's calm voice on the telephone, saying first, "Everything's fine now, but," before telling him the rest.

And Bobby's meningitis, which had turned out to be only a mild case of the mumps. He'd been in Boston that time, at the Ritz-Carlton, and Jane could laugh about it by the time she told him. But how had she had the courage to help hold Bobby on the table while they performed a spinal tap? He would have been a blob by then, a small puddle of melted father on the floor of the emergency room. And how had Jane handled all those hours of waiting for a final diagnosis while young interns mumbled, "Meningitis"? An inflammation of the brain. Meningitis—you can die from meningitis— and Jane knew it. She was so strong, always, the calm one who knew what to do.

Paul found a parking space near the school, a minor East Side miracle, and walked a half-block to Park Avenue. Kids were streaming out of the school building into the gray afternoon, happy to be let out of confinement, laughing and shouting in their own small circles of warmth.

He mounted the stairway to the second floor and found the grade adviser's office. Bobby was sitting downcast on a chair in the outer office, crying quietly, not looking Paul's way. Paul stood for an instant in the hallway. There was a thin crust of dried blood under Bobby's nose, a dark smudge on one cheek where tears had flowed and been rubbed by the back of the boy's hand. A waif. A lost child waiting to be claimed.

"Hi." Bobby looked up at him. The boy began to sob as Paul held his head against his coat. There was a gray-haired heavy-bosomed woman at a desk in a cubicle Paul had not seen from the hall.

"Mr. Klein?"

"Yes."

"He just can't stop crying, the poor lamb. I told him it wasn't that tragic, but—"

Miss McNeil appeared at the doorway to the inner office. "You made good time," she said. "Will you come in, please."

"In a moment." Paul squatted down next to the boy. He took out his handkerchief and dabbed at Bobby's eyes. "Take it easy, chum, it's going to be all right." He put the handkerchief under Bobby's nose and wiped the dried blood. "Bob-o, please try to stop crying," he said, which seemed to make the boy sob louder. "Look—take the handkerchief and go to the boy's room and wet it, and see if you can get that blood off your lip, okay?"

Bobby nodded.

"Because it really looks yucky. Okay?" He helped the boy to his feet and kissed him quickly on the top of his head. Still sobbing, unable to speak, Bobby set off.

Paul sat in the visitor's chair next to Miss McNeil's desk. She told him about the fight. "The other boy was Sam Bockman, which is surprising because Sam is one of Robert's real friends in school."

"Sam Bockman? Yes, of course, the famous Sambo. Bobby's spoken about him at home."

"I have both of them in my math class, Mr. Klein, and they've always seemed to get along quite well. I don't know what the fight was about. Sam said it was over a chance remark, and Robert just couldn't speak at all, as you've seen. Sam was very surprised that Robert started swinging at him, like a tiger, he said, and he claimed he only defended himself. I don't think the fight is that important, although I'll have the Bockman boy's parents here tomorrow, but it is an indication of Robert's unhappiness. How is he at home?"

"Quiet. I don't think I've heard him laugh in months."

"Is he getting help from someone?"

Inwardly, Paul smiled at the code word. "A psychiatrist, yes. We've all been seeing him. Individually, and occasionally as a family group."

"Good."

"That remains to be seen, Miss McNeil."

"Mrs."

"Sorry." For the first time, Paul noticed the gold band. She was not yet thirty, this Mrs. McNeil, and she was quite attractive. Blond hair, a pale blue pants suit, a handsome silk scarf tied at her throat. *Happily* married, he'd be willing to bet. "So far, I haven't seen it help all that much."

"If Robert wasn't seeing someone, I was going to suggest it. As his grade adviser, I was given the note you sent and I've been keeping an eye on him. Losing a parent is about the greatest shock a child Robert's age can sustain. Different children react in different ways. Some act up, behave very badly, as if they're always daring us to discipline them. Others, like Robert, become withdrawn, put up a shell as a defense mechanism, have very few friends." Her smile was warm. "I can't help having more sympathy for the quiet ones, like Robert. He's so bright. I get the feeling he was a very happy child before . . . " She hesitated to say it so baldly.

"Before my wife's death, you mean. Yes, he was." We all were, Mrs. McNeil, happily married teacher like Jane. "He's always been a good student, too. He liked school right from the first. He was reading by the time he was four."

"A good student, yes, his work reflects it. Which is probably remarkable, given the circumstances. And conscientious, too. No missing homework, reports turned in on time . . . " She looked silently at the folder on her desk.

"And now this," Paul said.

"Yes. And is this just an isolated incident, or the beginning of a new pattern of behavior? That's the question I think we must worry about."

"I've been worried about him," Paul said. "He's been bottled up, afraid to let loose. I hope this isn't the way he's going to choose to release his anger."

"We'll see, Mr. Klein. In the meantime, I'll continue to keep a close eye on him. And you help him at home. I don't know what else we can do." She rose and came around from behind her desk, extending a cool hand. "I'm sorry about . . . your situation," she said as she shook Paul's hand. She walked the few steps with Paul to her office door. Bobby waited outside, by the door to the hallway, his face smudged where he had washed it, part of the tail of his flannel shirt sticking out of his jeans. Paul shot him a secret wink of reassurance. Killer Klein, Paul thought, his gentle boy who had slugged someone. It was so unbelievable, a lamb turning tiger. But more unbelievable things had happened to them all, to himself and Hilary too. It was not believable to have someone die like that. It was as if the sun had not come up one morning.

5

THEY WALKED DOWN the hill from Park Avenue toward Lexington in the gray afternoon; a tall man wearing a navy raincoat, a boy in jeans, New York Mets jacket, and a Yankee cap. The man carried the boy's heavy knapsack easily in his hand, but the boy beside him walked with his head down, as if the weight still rested upon his shoulders.

They got into the front seat of the Buick, buckled up for safety. Paul put the keys in the ignition. He looked over at Bobby, at the profile that reminded him always of Jane, at the tuft of curly hair that came out from under the back of his cap. "Feeling any better?"

Bobby shrugged.

"Can we talk about it?"

The boy said nothing.

Paul started the engine, pulled out of the parking space, and drove to the corner. The traffic light was red; they waited. "Does your nose hurt?"

Bobby shook his head.

When the light changed, Paul turned down Lexington Avenue, coming to a halt at the light on the next corner. He wondered who felt worse at that moment, the boy in his guilt and remorse, or himself, looking at Bobby's suffering face. Say something, he told himself, get through it and find out what happened and why. "What about the other kid, Bockman? Is that his name?"

"Yes."

"Is he the one you call Sambo?"

Bobby nodded.

"The one who loves Oreos?"

"Uh huh."

"I thought he was a friend of yours."

Bobby shrugged.

Stupid question. The light changed to green and Paul started the car forward, falling into the slow traffic pattern that moved downtown. "Did you hurt him?"

Bobby looked away as they went slowly through the intersection at Eighty-sixth Street.

The silence cut into Paul. He reached out with his right hand and took hold of his son's arm. "Bob-o, we've got to talk about this."

Bobby kept his face turned away. "I know what you think of me," he said quietly.

Paul wasn't sure he had heard the boy's words correctly. "What I think of you? Is that what you said?"

Bobby nodded.

"And *what* do I think of you?" Paul asked.

Even with his face turned away, Paul could see the thin smile at the corner of Bobby's mouth. It was chilling.

"What are you saying?" A bus swung out from the curb, blocking the street. "You think I hate you, or something? Because of what happened today?"

"I don't want to talk about it," the boy said.

Drivers behind them began to toot their horns. The bus swung farther out into the street, trying to move around a double-parked delivery van. "Bob-o, I love you," Paul said. "You're my son. My wonderful, smart, good boy of a son. Nothing can change that, not getting in trouble in school, or anything. Don't you understand that?"

Tears brimmed in Bobby's eyes. He shook his arm loose from Paul's hand and angrily rubbed his eyes.

"Talk to me, babe," Paul pleaded. "Please talk to me. I don't really care what happened. I know you, I know how good you are, and I'm not angry with you, please believe me." His words sounded hollow and stiff to his own ears. Words. How would his own father have handled this? Herman would be shouting at him for sure, taking him by the shoulders and shaking him roughly. He'd lived in fear of his father's temper when he was a boy. Herman blew up, the cords in his neck standing out as his face turned red, and he hit. One reason why he had never laid an angry hand upon Bobby. *"I know what you think of me."* It cut to the bone.

A quiet sob escaped the boy's lips. Paul fought against the seat belt, lifted up, and reached through his coat and under his suit jacket to find the handkerchief in his back pocket. The handkerchief, he realized as his fingers found an empty pocket, that was wet and bloody and in Bobby's jeans somewhere.

The traffic started moving again, slowly winding past the double-parked van.

"It was stupid," Bobby said.

"Right," Paul said.

"And . . . and my fault."

"Okay."

"We were . . . it was after math. In the hall. We were going to social studies. And I started it . . ."

"I don't think that matters now, who started it."

"I did." Bobby stared out the window in front of him. Bloomingdale's loomed three blocks away and traffic was slowing down again.

Paul waited for the boy to continue. There was a long silence. "Listen," he said after a while, "I got into plenty of trouble in school when I was a kid. Grandma had to come to school." Bobby turned to look at him. "Oh, yes, I wasn't an angel all the time. I remember once, it must have been in fourth or fifth grade. I was supposed to write something, a report I suppose, and I just didn't. And the teacher called on me to read it, of course. Mrs. Demlinger—hey, I even remember her name—an old biddy who was very, very strict. And I remember I took my loose-leaf notebook up to the front of the room, opened it to a blank page, and began to ad lib. You know, pretending to be reading this report." Paul smiled as the moment came back to him. Glib, even then, and full of confidence, enjoying the thrill of putting one over on the old teacher. " 'The Elephant' was my report. 'The elephant is the largest mammal among the jungle creatures,' I said. 'The elephant resides in darkest Africa and the jungles of Asia.' And I went on like that, you know, full of blah blah and faking it. Until in the middle of all this, Mrs. Demlinger suddenly came up behind me, looked over my shoulder, and saw that I was reading from a blank page. Oh, man. Then I'd had it. She blew her top. Not because I was a bad student, or I hadn't bothered to do this report. But because I was faking it, that's what got me in trouble." Paul grinned at Bobby, trying to coax a smile onto that pale, tear-streaked face.

"We were doing a rank-out," Bobby said.

"What's that?"

"Dumb, really dumb."

"Of course."

"You call each other names. And Sambo . . ." Bobby swallowed hard. "We say bad things, you know."

"The F-curse, you mean?" Oh, God, you sound stupid. He's not a baby anymore. "You were saying 'fuck'?"

"Yeah."

"And probably more than that, right?"

Bobby nodded.

"Only words, chum. Just words. And then what happened?"

Bobby's mouth opened briefly, but he said nothing.

"Your classic one-word-leads-to-another situation, right? And sooner or later, somebody starts swinging."

Nothing.

"Was that it?" Paul asked lightly.

"Yes."

"Aha! Now we're getting somewhere. So from cursing each other out, playing this game—"

"I said it was stupid."

"Understood. And then somebody started fighting."

"Me. I hit him."

"Slugger Klein." Lightly, lightly.

"It's not funny."

"It's not tragic, either. Just a fight between two friends. Bobby, it happens a lot. Probably more than you think."

"Sambo said something."

"Obviously." He waited to hear more, but Bobby had put on his silent face again. "Sticks and stones," he said, smiling. "Yes, words can hurt, too. Hurt a lot."

Bobby nodded.

They rolled to a stop at the traffic light in front of Bloomingdale's. Thick crowds of pedestrians passed in front of the car.

"It got me mad . . . what he said."

"Sure." Paul was surprised when Bobby took his hand. The boy held it to his cheek.

"I couldn't—" Bobby began, then went silent. Paul saw the boy's lips tremble. "Shit," Bobby said.

"Take it easy."

"Stupid."

"It's okay."

"I miss her so much," Bobby said in a voice that pierced Paul's heart. "Oh, God."

Paul released his seat belt and pulled Bobby to him. One foot on the brake holding the big car, with people outside walking by and looking in at them, he held Bobby against his chest and petted the boy's cheek. "I know, I know," he said, the boy's head tight against his raincoat, throbbing as he sobbed, a small bird beating its wings, "It's okay, baby, it's all right." The light changed and he heard car horns tooting behind them. Traffic on both sides of their car began to move forward. Wait, he thought, I can't move now, as the driver behind him leaned on his horn. Please wait. "It's okay, baby," he said, "it's okay." Knowing it wasn't okay, couldn't be okay, not for Bobby, nor for Hilary, nor for himself. "It's all right," he said, holding his wounded son to his wounded heart, the horns tooting behind them, the people walking by staring as he sat, dry-eyed, in his car in the middle of the street in front of Bloomingdale's on this cold, gray afternoon.

The tires thumped in rhythm as the car sped along the newly resurfaced roadway. *Cheerup, cheerup, cheer up*, it sounded in Paul's ears. Yes, yes, cheer up, indeed yes. He was slightly amazed at himself. Trauma in front of Bloomingdale's, widower

holds crying son in his arms to a symphony of auto horns and yet—
are you listening, Dr. Wirtz?—no tears. Not one tear did the old
man. shed. Dry-eyed through it all. *Mann weint nicht, verstehen
Sie?*

Amazing.

In fact, he felt good. Worried about Bobby, sure, but feeling
good. He thought of the man who jumped from the top of the Em-
pire State Building and as he passed the tenth floor said, "So far,
so good." Was it going to hit him later? Was this a reprieve from
the governor or only a temporary stay of execution? Don't ask, enjoy it.

Maybe, just maybe he had come out of the crying time. Drought
declared, turn off the waterworks. Could be. He was sick and tired
of feeling sorry for himself. Pathetic, Michael Bradie had said.
Yes, and pissed off at feeling that way. Who the hell wants to be
pathetic? Enough.

Bobby was still in his own world, but what more could he do?
He'd reassured the boy, told him the scuffle at school could be forgotten, held him, soothed him, hugged and kissed him. Hard fact:
Jane was not ever coming back. No more Jane would there be in
their house, forever and ever. Hilary knew that, she'd learned it before he did. Tougher by half, Hilary was, a direct inheritance from
her mother. And Jane had been tougher than he was. Better able to
face a situation and coldly handle it. He was the emotional one.
And Bobby the disturbed one. Oh, yes, don't dodge it, the boy has
a special grief, his own brand of guilt.

Guilty over what?

"I know what you think of me." What was that all about? The
kid was wearing his guilt like a fielder's mitt, catching everything
that came his way. Why?

He turned the corner of his street and drove slowly down the
block. What a lovely street it was, even with the bare October
trees. Big houses, built at the end of the Victorian Age, when gra-
cious living had meaning. High ceilings, oak paneling, stained-
glass windows. A wide street with broad lawns and stately old
trees. A quiet street where kids could roller skate and ride bicycles
in safety. And still could. But Bobby hadn't. Not once since Jane
died. Something wrong with that. Pleasure was not forbidden
after your mother died.

He pulled the Buick over the sidewalk cut and up the driveway. "Home, chum," he said. "Nice and early, too."

The boy sat like a lump.

Paul reached out and touched his chin. "Chin up, stiff upper."

Bobby got out of the car, then opened the rear door to fetch his knapsack.

"Coraggio, as the Italians say. *Coraggio!"* Paul got out and looked at Bobby over the roof of the car. Silent Sam. "Do you have much homework?"

"Some."

"Well, how about we get out the old basketball and toss in some hoops? A little five-three-one, maybe? How's about it?"

"It's cold out."

"Wear a sweatshirt. Hey, come on, it'll be fun." Paul looked into the party-pooper face. The boy shook his head and began walking down the driveway toward the front of the house, making Paul hurry to catch up with him. "We could get out the football," he said. "Toss it around, catch a few passes."

"The football's flat."

"We have a pin, and a pump. I'll blow it up in no time."

"Nah."

"Some fun you are. Once in a dog's age I get athletic and you aren't. Come on, forget about what happened in school, let's exercise these old bones."

Talk to the wall.

Paul opened the front door with his key. Immediately they heard the blasting stereo upstairs. "I hear your sister's home from school." He grinned at Bobby. He followed the boy to the front closet and hung his coat on a hanger. "Jesus, what the hell is that noise?"

Bobby shrugged. "Punk."

"You're not kidding, punk. And loud enough to hear in Jersey. How can she stand it up there?" The percussive bass beat of the music made his teeth vibrate. Hilary would be stone deaf by age twenty, no question. "Get yourself some milk and cookies, babe," he said, and headed upstairs.

The mistake was opening Hilary's door without knocking first.

The music was so loud they couldn't have heard him coming. Hilary was on her back on the bed, her blue sweater up about her shoulders, her breasts two round eyes that stared back at him. Peter was lying beside her, kissing her, one long arm stretched down her stomach; her jeans were open in front, his hand was down inside. Paul stared, blood draining from his face, so shocked for the moment he could not move.

In a rage, Paul shoved the door so it crashed against the door stop. *"Out!"* he shouted. *"Get out!"*

Peter looked up, eyes wide with sudden terror, and bounded from the bed. Paul wanted to run at him, arms flailing, start smashing that stupid face with the scraggly moustache which had just been rubbing against his daughter's breast. Instead he ran across the room to the stereo and snapped it off; the raucous noise died in a groan. Hilary had rolled off the bed. Crouching low on the lee side, she was zipping up her jeans, pulling down her sweater. *"Scram!"* Paul shouted at Peter, who had gone white. The boy stood rooted near the bed, tall and gangly, slightly stooped, expecting the world to fall on him. Paul took one sudden, threatening step toward Peter and the boy jumped away, turning in midair; long legs in motion, he scooted out the door, into the hallway, and down the stairs two at a time.

The front door slammed shut downstairs.

Paul sat on a lump in the chair near Hilary's desk. Peter's jacket, goose-down, blue, slightly crushed by one dazed father. "Pete's jacket," he said dumbly, his brain beginning to work again. It was cold outside. He rushed to the window and pulled it open. Peter was halfway to the corner. "Hey, Pete!" he shouted, "hey!" Peter stopped and looked back. "You forgot your jacket!" Father stared at would-be lover, lover stared back. "Your jacket," Paul shouted again. Peter stood looking, the tail of his flannel shirt half out of his jeans. The kid thinks it's a trap, Paul saw, a plot to get him back here so I can rip his moustache out by the roots. Caught *in flagrante delicto,* his hand in the cookie jar, the kid was scared silly. Not funny, kiddo, not when it's your own daughter.

A Mexican standoff. The boy who won't come in from the cold and the father at the window. Paul ducked back inside, grabbed Peter's bulky jacket. "Your jacket!" He held it outside the window so Peter could see it. Come fetch; that's a good dog.

The kid started walking back to the house, warily watching Paul. Probably thinks I'm going to jump down from here and land

57

on his neck. Now Peter stood on the lawn. Paul tossed the jacket to him. No good, too bulky, it caught in the wind and slid away on the overhang of the porch. Out of reach from the window and too far up for Peter to get from the ground or the porch.

Groaning and thoroughly disgusted, Paul put one anxious leg outside the window onto the sloping, shingled porch roof. What the hell am I doing, he thought, me with my acrophobia? One more leg and he was outside, squatting down and in fear of his life. The stupid jacket was twenty feet away, rippling in the wind. Desperate widower breaks leg falling from porch roof while rescuing jacket of daughter's seducer. They'd have to shorten that one for the *Daily News* headline. Meanwhile, it was freezing out here and— oh, shit!—his suit jacket caught on a protruding nail and he distinctly heard it tear. Good-bye, Brooks Brothers flannel.

Working his way very carefully, ass down and holding on for dear life, Paul sidled along the overhang. Why am I doing this, he wondered, when I ought to be kicking the kid's teeth in? Starting tomorrow, no more Mr. Nice Guy. *Shit!* He almost shouted as he slid a couple of feet toward the edge of the roof. Easy, take it easy. The jacket was almost within reach. Until a gust of wind blew it farther away down the roof. Gritting his teeth, Paul sidled on, his hands filthy from the detritus on the shingles. At last he reached the jacket, hooked it with one foot, and gathered it into his hands.

Peter was standing below in the shrubbery, bruising the rhododendrons. And Bobby was just a few feet away, looking up at him in total amazement. "What are you doing up there, Dad?"

Paul laughed, he couldn't help himself. "Catch," he called out to Peter as he threw the jacket down.

"Thank you, Mr. Klein," Peter said. He slipped his long arms into the jacket.

"Back in the house," Paul told Bobby. "It's cold out here." Cold? It was freezing. He watched Bobby disappear up the front steps.

Peter zipped the front of his jacket. He backed out of the shrubbery and Paul winced as he heard a rhododendron branch snap. "Mr. Klein? Look . . . I'm sorry."

Paul nodded at the boy. "Yeah, me too." Sorry I ever opened Hilary's door, that's for sure. "Pete, do me a favor. Go home. And I don't want you in the house when I'm not here, *comprende?* Apparently you guys need a chaperone. Or a watchdog. Or a straitjacket and chains.''

"It won't happen again," Peter said.

Oh, that was funny. It would happen again the very next time they were alone together. Or more. Don't think about that, a small voice said. "Go home, Pete." And take a cold shower, followed by a cold hip bath.

As Peter turned and headed down the block, Phyllis Berg came walking along the sidewalk, carrying a bundle from the supermarket. Tall Phyllis with the horn-rimmed glasses that gave her the look of a storkish owl. She and Dave were the Kleins' closest friends on the block. Their kids, a boy and a girl, were just slightly younger than his. "Paul, is that you?"

A nearsighted owl. "Hello, Phyllis."

"Are you all right?"

"Hotsy-totsy, kid. Just fine." Always-concerned Phyllis. She'd mother anything within six paces.

"What are you doing up there?"

I freaked out, Phyllis, haven't you heard? I may pitch a tent out here. Widowed father of two camps out on porch roof, neighbors concerned. "Just checking out the gutters. Lots of leaves stuck down in there."

"In a suit and tie?"

"Just an impulse. I'll be going in now, Phyllis." Scram, Phyllis. You don't want to see a man in fear of his life sliding on his ass along a porch roof.

"How is Sunday?" Phyllis asked. Walking up to Phyllis was Howard Austin, his next-door neighbor, coming home from his law office carrying a briefcase and a newspaper. Paul had never realized how short a day Howard worked.

"Hey, Paul," Howard called, stopping to watch what he was up to on the roof.

"Hi there, Howard." Down at the corner Myron Levy, neighborhood gardening authority, was heading home. Jesus, he could run a conversational salon out here; Fidel Castro could give a speech.

"Can you come for dinner on Sunday?" Phyllis asked.

"Sure, fine." Why didn't everyone go away? Hadn't they ever seen a man on a porch roof before?

"About seven o'clock. Or after the football game. Whichever comes first. Dave doesn't like to eat until the game's over."

"You're on. And thanks." Now go away already. But still she stood there, along with Howard and now Myron Levy. Paul heard Phyllis say something about a stopped-up gutter. He returned Myron's wave.

No good. They were all going to stand there until he was back inside. He began working his way back toward the open window, bumping along on his behind, knowing how foolish he looked. *Coraggio!* Turning over onto his hands and bent knees, his ass in the air, Paul scuttled like a crab toward the open window. Afraid to stand up or turn his feet toward the window, he crawled through the opening headfirst and tumbled to the floor. Staying low, out of sight of what must be a *minyan* by now, he snapped at Hilary: "Close the damn window and lower the shade."

The shade lowered, he stood up and looked at himself. His hands were black with dirt, the front of his suit coat was flecked with tiny red spots from the shingles, the knees of his pants were gray. Nobody ever said show business was easy, he thought. Next time he'd charge admission.

Hilary stood looking at him, her pale face serious.

"I'd better wash up," Paul said. "Come along and we'll talk." Hilary followed him down the hall and into his bathroom. He slipped out of his suit coat and handed it to her, then looked at himself in the mirror over the sink. There was a black smudge on his temple. But his yellow and blue silk tie, one of his favorites, was undamaged. He never liked to wash up with his tie on, however. It either dipped into the sink and got wet, or was splashed from his hand-washing. And he couldn't touch it until he'd cleaned his filthy hands. "Favor," he said, "would you slip my tie off?"

"Sure." Hilary came close, his suit coat over her arm; reaching up with both hands, she began to undo the knot of his tie.

Eyeball to eyeball, he looked into the face of his lovely daughter as she concentrated on his tie. Brown eyes, like Jane's, heavy eyebrows as yet unplucked, his nose but somehow lighter and more graceful, and Jane's sweet lips. Paul felt a surge of love for her, a heavy feeling of tenderness. If he felt anger before over catching her with Peter, it was gone now. Why on earth did he feel so good? Why, after months of misery and pain, was it draining away? Pooh,

pooh, spit over your shoulder or the evil eye will return. Don't question, just take it as she comes. This sweet girl before him, Jane's core and his trimmings, was a gift. She and Bobby were what was left now. They were his sanity and he theirs, and he had to grab on to them for dear life.

His tie was off. He grabbed Hilary, dirty hands and all, and enfolded her in a hug. "I love you, sweetness," he said.

"You're not mad at me?"

"Sure I am, but I'll get over it." He smelled the fragrance of the long hair she washed every day, then sniffed aloud so she could hear. "Lemon? Orange?"

"Balsam and citrus. Organic shampoo."

"Fantastic." He kissed her cheek lightly and released her from his grasp. "Is this a girl or a fruit stand?" he said to make her laugh.

Hilary smiled, which was almost enough. "I'm sorry."

"Yeah," he nodded, "me too. We'll talk about it later, after dinner. And several drinks. God, I suddenly have an appetite. It must be all that fresh air. I may take a stroll on the porch roof every night before dinner."

"Daddy," she giggled.

"Hey, why not? Fresh air, exercise, and you meet such interesting people." He started to laugh, then she did, then they were hugging again.

Laughter, he thought, it's better than Librium. Are you listening, Dr. Wirtz?

6

"ONE OF YOUR more fabulous dinners," he was saying later as they sat at the table in the kitchen. "My compliments to the chef."

"Pretty good," Hilary said.

"Pretty good? Is that all?"

"Okay, good."

"You throw compliments around like glue. And you, sir," he said to Bobby, "your honest opinion, please."

"Edible."

"Oh! Oh!" Paul held his hand to his heart, as though wounded. "Here I cook a meal that would make Julia Child insane with jealousy, and it rates only an *edible?* C'mon, give me a break."

"Fair," Bobby said, a trace of a smile beginning to show.

"Fair? Ungrateful wretch of a child, what do you know about fancy cooking? Fair, indeed."

"The lamb chops were overcooked," Bobby said.

"Slightly, yes," Paul said. "Probably broiled them a minute or so too much. But what about that fantastic crust? My gourmet secret right there, you know. The famous Kowloon Superior soy sauce."

"The potatoes were good," Hilary said.

"A little thin," Paul said. "The famous French's instant mashed potatoes. I'm beginning to wonder why they never come out right. I followed the instructions on the package, but they don't taste like they did when Mom made them."

"I think she put more milk in them," Hilary said, "and more butter, too."

"You may be right," Paul said. "The peas were good."

"The famous LeSueur canned baby peas," said Hilary, "left over from last night."

"They were green, weren't they?" Paul said, thinking of Jane's dictum of always having something green on the plate. Which in her idiom meant a fresh green vegetable, freshly prepared. He remembered broccoli, stir-fried in the wok, fragrant and garlicky, crisp green string beans, leaf spinach. Jane was a great cook. A great mother. A great teacher. A great woman.

He realized he was thinking of her now without pain. He could see her in his mind's eye at the stove, hands flying as food tossed and turned in the wok, wearing the blue apron the kids had given her one Mother's Day that said on the front: "My Mom Is the Greatest!" Nearby would be her rocks glass of scotch and water, one ice cube, which she would sip from time to time as he sat watching from this very seat at the table. Jane talking as she worked. About school, her day, the kids in her class, the nonsense and make-work of the board of education.

Jane remembered, without that catch in the throat, the pain, the brimming of tears.

Manic.

"She wasn't always a great cook, you know," he said. "Of course, once I gave her all my trade secrets, she improved." He sat back, smiling at the kids, seeing the look forming on Bobby's face. "Not funny, Dad," he said to the boy.

Bobby nodded. "Right."

"Only joking, chum. Listen, a joke is not a bad thing. Even a bad joke. Like the ones I usually tell. Which reminds me." He repeated the pope joke Michael had told him at lunch. Hilary laughed out loud, and Bobby giggled. How sweet it was to see a smile on the boy's face. "A story about how your mother learned to cook," he announced. "We were just married, living in a walk-down basement apartment."

"The one on Troy Avenue," Hilary said.

"Right. You remember, we drove past there once, Bob-o? I was working for this wine distributor in New Jersey, and your Mother had begun teaching. I liked a breaded and fried veal chop then, in fact I still do, and Mom liked lamb chops. And that's what she'd made for dinner that night. She'd gone to the butcher after school and bought lamb chops for herself and veal chops for me. The veal chops she breaded and fried, and the lamb chops she broiled, and when we sat down to dinner and she served me those beautiful breaded veal chops, guess what?"

"She mixed up the chops," Bobby said, matter-of-factly.

"You heard this story?"

"About a million times," Bobby said.

"Mom told us," Hilary said.

Where had he been? On the road, probably. He smiled to himself, remembering the highly distinctive taste of a breaded and fried lamb chop. "Oh, well," he said, and another memory came to him. "The first time Mom used the deep fryer was a disaster. We were living in Cleveland then."

"Is this about the French fried potatoes?" Bobby said.

"Yes." Another piece of ancient history shot to hell. He was surprised that Jane had told this story on herself.

"And you came home to find her crying," Hilary said, "with oil on the floor? Because she couldn't turn off the drain thing and the jar she was holding underneath overflowed?"

"That's the story," he said, grinning at them. "Oil City all over the floor and your mother crying like a baby."

"I'll bet she never made that mistake again," Bobby said.

"Nope, never did. She never used the fryer again, either."

Bobby's lip curled down. "It's a stupid story," he said. "She wasn't like that."

"Like what?"

"Dumb."

"I didn't say she was. Inexperienced, maybe. She learned fast, though, probably quicker than most."

"She was very smart," Bobby said.

"Very," Paul said. "Wait a minute, did you ever hear about the goldfish?"

The kids looked blank. Fresh territory at last, excellent. "You were just born, Hil, maybe you were three or four months old. Spending all your time in the crib. And I thought it would be a good idea for you to have something to look at."

"I had a mobile over my crib," Hilary said. "It played a tune."

"You don't remember that?"

"No. But I remember it over Bobby's crib. Mom said it was the same one I had."

"It was."

"It had birds on it," Bobby said, "pink, blue, and yellow birds. And the tune was 'Oh, Susannah.' It's up in the attic in a box."

"It is?"

Bobby nodded. "We were up there putting away some of my old toys a few years ago and she showed it to me."

"Wait a minute. She saved your old toys?"

"Didn't you know that?" Bobby said.

"No."

"Sure. Every once in a while, when my yellow cabinet got kind of overflowing, we'd sit down and sort them out. Together. And she would put the broken ones, and the ones I didn't play with anymore, she'd put them in one of the supermarket cartons and we'd take them up to the attic. And she wrote my age on the carton in Magic Marker."

Jane the pack rat. The compulsive saver of string and rubber bands, of garbage bags collected under the sink, of pictures neatly pasted in photo albums, mementos filed away in cigar boxes; even the congratulatory notes and telegrams on the birth of each child were somewhere saved. But why hadn't she thrown away the old and broken toys, or given them to some charity to be fixed for needy kids? Because of Bobby. Probably because this kid sitting here was so insecure as a baby, so prone to temper tantrums and fits of tears when he didn't get his way. So Jane had sat and sorted out the junk in his toy cabinet with the boy, and then she had saved them in a box, properly labeled, of course, and stored them upstairs in the attic. Bobby's history, told in boxes of old and broken toys, filed away for posterity. Another kind of security blanket for

Bobby, his past preserved by a woman who knew him much better than he did.

"What about the goldfish?" Hilary said.

Why hadn't Jane ever told him about the toys in the attic? Was it their secret, hers and Bobby's? How many more secrets were there between them? "Where was I?"

"I needed something to look at in my crib," said Hilary.

"Right. So one day I stopped at a pet shop and picked up a little bowl and a couple of goldfish. One was black and the other was gold, and I set them up on the shelves above your crib."

"When we lived on Beverly Road."

"Yes." Hilary was proud of having lived in the two-bedroom apartment on Beverly Road; Bobby had never set foot in the place. Beverly Road was Hilary's alone. "It was just like me, you know, to buy those goldfish. Impulsive, not planning ahead. Because I didn't buy a pump to purify the water in the bowl, or plants to put oxygen in the water, or even that stuff they sell to kill the chlorine and fluoride in tap water. So those fish had to die sooner or later. But I wasn't thinking of that. Just that you would have something real to look at in your crib, Hil.

"Anyway, about a week later, you must have been crying in the night, or something, and I got out to see what was what. We took turns then, when you were a baby, and I guess your mother pushed me out of bed. So I did whatever I had to do, probably changed your diaper, and then I noticed that one of the fish was belly up in the bowl. Dead. The gold one. So I fished out the dead fish, flushed it down the toilet, and got back to bed.

"The next morning when I got up, your mother was really excited. 'Wait till you see this,' she said. I thought nothing of it, shaved, showered, you know. But before I had breakfast she pulled me into your room and pointed at the fishbowl. 'One of the goldfish is missing,' she said. And she was amazed, of course. 'What happened to the other fish?'

"God help me, I couldn't resist it. 'Didn't I tell you?' I said. 'That black guy in there, he's a killer goldfish. The man in the pet shop said he's very rare.' And I made up a crazy name for the fish, *carpus cannibalis*. 'During the night,' I said, 'the black fish must have eaten up the other guy. Probably we should have fed them more.' "

Hilary began to giggle.

"There's more," Paul said, laughing. "I didn't think any more of it, just went off to work. But that night, as luck would have it, my parents came over for coffee. They were always coming over to see you when you were just born. And lo and behold, your mother drags them into your room and shows them the black goldfish and starts telling them all this malarkey about a killer fish, and *carpus cannibalis,* and I just fell on the floor, I was laughing so hard." Paul began to laugh again, remembering.

Hilary laughed with him, but Bobby looked puzzled. "Why did you do that?" he asked.

Paul shrugged. "For fun."

"Why did Mom believe you?" the boy asked.

"Why?" Paul repeated. "Because she always believed me. She always thought I knew everything. Which, of course, I do," he added, winking at the boy.

"So you made her look like a fool," Bobby said.

The champion of her memory, Paul thought. No one will say a bad word about Jane when Bobby's around. "It was a joke, Bob-o, that's all. Two people who love each other can kid and make jokes, even tease each other."

"She never teased you," Bobby said.

"Sure she did."

"I never heard her."

"How about my checkbook? Wasn't she always saying how I loused up our account? And I'd forget appointments sometimes, or I'd be late for dinner, and when I gained a little weight, she'd be calling me 'Fat Stuff' and things like that."

"You did it more to her than she did it to you."

"Maybe," Paul said, taken aback by the rising tone in Bobby's voice.

"Everything's a joke to you," Bobby said, "everything."

"Not everything."

"Almost everything."

Paul sighed. "Look, Bob-o—the world is a funny place. Things happen, people do weird things to each other. If you can't laugh about it you'll go nuts."

"Some things aren't funny," the boy said.

"You sure aren't," Hilary said to Bobby.

"Neither are you," the boy shot back.

"You're such an idiot sometimes," Hilary said.

"And you're a bum!"

"Hold it!" Paul said, his hands outthrust. "Calm down, both of you. No fighting."

"He's so stupid," Hilary said.

"Hilary!" Paul said sharply, "cut it out."

Bobby pushed his chair back from the table and stood up. "I've got homework," he said. He came around the table, on his way out of the kitchen.

Paul stopped Bobby by putting a hand on the boy's arm. "Don't be upset," he said.

"I'm not."

"Come on, sit down. I'll get you some ice cream."

"I'll have it later."

"We were having such a nice time," Paul said.

Bobby shrugged, his face sullen. He withdrew his arm from Paul's. "I'm going to do my homework." Turning, the boy left the room.

Another fun evening at home, Paul thought mockingly. "Thanks for all your help," he said to Hilary.

"Sor-ree," the girl sang in her familiar tune.

"And don't say sor-ree that way," he snapped.

They stared at each other for a long moment. Paul was not sure of what had just transpired. The evening, which had held such promise, seemed to collapse about him. He took a cigarette from his pack, lit it, and took a heavy drag. A cup of coffee was what he wanted right now. He realized that he had not made any coffee tonight, had not even thought about it.

Hilary stood and silently began to clear the table, taking dinner plates and stacking them near the sink. Now she began rinsing the dishes and putting them into the dishwasher.

The walls are up again, he thought, the private walls that shape our private worlds. He felt suddenly lonely, sitting there, watching the girl. There were things undone, words unsaid.

Hilary rinsed silverware and dropped it into the dishwasher basket. "I'll do the pots," he said.

She turned off the water in the sink, dried her hands on a sheet of paper toweling.

"We have to talk about Peter," Paul said. The girl nodded, her face cold and set. "I don't want him here in the house during the week. Not after school when Gemma's gone and I'm not home."

Hilary's face betrayed nothing.

"You see Pete plenty in school. And there are weekends. I don't mind his being here on Saturdays or Sundays, when I'm around. And you can go out with him, like you've been doing." Her cold silence cut like a knife. He found himself wanting her to speak up, react, defend herself. "Is that unfair of me?"

The girl shrugged.

"Say something."

"Why?" Hilary said. "It wouldn't make any difference."

"You think I'm being unfair?"

"You're the father."

"So?"

"What can I say?"

"Whatever you want. I'm not an ogre."

"Not after today. After . . . what happened."

"I've forgiven you for that," he said.

"Thanks," she said, her voice edged with irony. "I've got a French test. I've got to study." She turned away.

Paul watched her go, unable to find the words that would prevent her leaving. He stubbed his cigarette out in the ashtray. Another wonderful evening with the Klein family, he thought, entertainment for everyone. See Bobby close up like a clam. See the beautiful Miss Hilary Frost freeze her father's heart at ten paces. Hear a lifetime of intimate family stories totally misunderstood by your son.

See Father left alone to clean the pots.

He brought the broiler tray to the sink, removed the rack, peeled back the aluminum foil to find it had a leak. A pool of oil ran down the tray as it tilted in his hand. Sighing, Paul filled a pot with detergent and hot water. Using the sudsy water from that pot, he cleaned and rinsed another pot, and then the broiler tray. The rack on which the lamb chops had rested was greasy and crusted with bits of burnt meat and fat. He used a steel wool pad on it, but cautiously. He remembered his mother telling him that a bit of steel wool under the skin could cause blood poisoning and death. Which did not make it one of your better products. Hold it. Was that true? He'd accepted it at face value for thirty years. Would his mother lie to him? No, but how often was she right?

He scrubbed the inside of the pot the potatoes had cooked in. One of the ingredients in instant mashed potatoes must surely be glue, he thought. He scrubbed and rinsed three, four times, and still there was a filmy residue of potato left inside the pot.

Enough.

He shut off the running water and gazed through the kitchen window into the black garden. Stars were shining in the western sky and the pine tree at the back of the garden shivered in the brisk wind.

He had to talk to someone about the kids, preferably a woman.

Was there a mothering sense, a special skill fathers did not have? Or was that propaganda, fostered by the great sorority of Mothers United for Propagation of Faith in Mom? Incorporated. Maybe. Jane had had that mothering sense, in spades. But Jane had parenting sense, emotional sense, financial sense, and every other kind of sense that mattered.

A woman to talk with.

Kathleen Bradie. He could call her. She certainly knew how to handle girls. And Michael.

No, not Kathleen. Paul was close with her, loved her in fact, but they had never communicated on that personal a level. Which also left out his secretary—rational, sensible Lillian Lerner.

Phyllis Berg, right down the street. She was the one to talk to. He'd been relying on Phyllis ever since Jane died. Jane and Phyllis had been friends for years. Phyllis, in fact, was the one who had called Jane when this house became available; she had brought them to this street.

He'd put a lot on Phyllis's shoulders since July. No, Phyllis had taken it on herself in her own goodness. She'd given them dinner countless times, kept bringing baked goods over, had taken Bobby and Hilary shopping for clothing along with her own two kids, and more.

Paul turned off the lights in the kitchen and walked to the front hallway, took his sheepskin jacket from the closet and put it on. Upstairs, he could hear the beat from Hilary's stereo. "Hey, kids!" he called up the stairwell, knowing they would not hear. He climbed to the point on the stairs where he could see Bobby and Hilary's closed doors. "Hey, kids!" He waited. Bobby's door opened a crack, then Hilary's. Two faces stared at him. "I'm going out for a little while," he said. "Down the block to the Bergs'." Bobby nodded, Hilary said okay, then both doors closed. *Bang. Bang.* Two pistol shots in the heart.

Stay out, stay out, O father dear,

Leave me my sorrow and my fear . . . .

Easy, kimosabe. But even the masked rider of the plains had his faithful Indian companion.

The night was crisp and clear, beautiful, even with the wind that shook the heavy bare trees. Across the street the face of the Dawsons' house was dark. A scent of sweet woodsmoke came to him. Someone had a log fire burning in the fireplace. The Weisses, he thought, as he passed their house. Or the Martins, next door. The street was quiet and empty. For once there was not even the sound of traffic moving on Beverly Road. The pitched and gabled roof of the Turner house shone in the light of the streetlamp, the round tower that sprang from its lower story reaching above the roof and into the dark. Myron Levy's Ford was parked in his driveway, a sticker across the rear window read, "Wellesley College," his daughter, Joan, a freshman this year.

Paul turned up the Bergs' short walk. Under the overhang of their porch roof, the living room windows were lit. He climbed the stairs to the porch. Through the open curtain of the window nearest him he could see inside. He heard laughter, it sounded like Dave's cackle. He walked across the porch toward the window and looked in. Dave sat in the club chair, his feet on the ottoman, shoes off, looking at the television set beneath the window. Phyllis was on the couch, needlepoint in her hand, nestled against blond Amy, who at fourteen was becoming a copy of her mother, even to her

71

nearsightedness and horn-rimmed glasses. In front of the couch, sitting on the floor, his back against Phyllis's knees, was Billy, twelve years old in a few weeks and already half a head taller than Amy. The Bergs were watching television together, some show Paul could dimly hear. Now they were all laughing, Dave cackled again, Phyllis lowered her needlepoint into her lap. With one hand, Phyllis softly ruffled Billy's dark hair. Dave's head turned toward the couch to look briefly at his family, his lean hawk face relaxed and smiling, and Paul could see Dave's lips move. The three faces on the couch turned to Dave, listening, and then they laughed together.

Paul took a quiet step back from the window, suddenly feeling himself an intruder. A wave of loneliness and sorrow came over him. Through the window he had stolen a moment of intimacy that did not belong to him, a small instant like ten thousand others in the heart of a family that bound them together for all time.

Like his own, only last year. Never more like his own, to be together and share.

Nevermore.

He took another step back and turned away from the Bergs' window. *Nevermore* sang in his head. No! That thought led to despair and sorrow and surely they had had enough. Someday he and Hilary and Bobby would laugh again, joke again, be easy in each other's company, be free to kid and tease and reveal themselves without putting up walls. Or closing doors. Or donning masks of grief that kept them apart.

His Hilary. His Bobby. Himself. A new family of three souls, bound by blood and spirit and lives that intertwined under one roof.

Quietly, he stepped down the stairs. A lone dead leaf skittered across the walk, blown by the wind. He began walking slowly back to his own house.

There were no golden answers from the mouths of oracles for what they faced. Not from loving, kind Phyllis Berg, earth mother and open heart to the world. Not from Kathleen or Lillian. Or especially from Dr. Henry Wirtz, who seemed only to sit and listen, writing endlessly on his steno pad.

He stood on the street in front of his own house, the chill wind whipping at his ears. A spill of light came onto the porch roof from Hilary's window. He gazed up at the attic floor, at the dormer window shining black, the chimney rising high from the corner of the house. Jane's house no more, it belonged now to himself and the kids. Her ghost remained, her spirit, in every brick and tile and inch of painted wood and polished glass. But ghosts are of the past. They do not counsel or advise, they do not point the way.

Slowly, Paul walked up the stairs and across the broad wooden porch, back to the children who waited inside.

7

SOME NIGHT HE would get into bed and fall quickly asleep. Tonight wasn't it.

He put on the bedside lamp and sat up, found his cigarettes and lit one, smiling as he remembered another one of Jane's rules: No smoking in the dark in bed. Smoking had been her only bad habit, and at that, she smoked only about ten cigarettes a day. At breakfast, lunch, in the teachers' lounge during a break, walking home after school, while preparing dinner, and the few she smoked with him at the dinner table, especially with the second cup of coffee after the kids had left them.

And after sex.

How many times had they made love? He could figure it out if he really thought about it. Almost eighteen and a half years of marriage, about three times a week. . . . His old nemesis, math, reared its cold and logical head and he gave it up.

The blue silky nightgown that unzipped all the way down the front. The smell of her skin against his face, the taste of her shoulder, her warm sweet neck. Her small, perfect breasts with the uptilted pink nipples, under his hand, on his lips.

Cut it out.

Paul got out of bed, put on his slippers and robe. He raised the shade and looked down into the floodlit driveway. The small rounded yew shivered in the wind. Jane was still here, he thought, in this room, on that bed. He heard her quiet moan of pleasure as if they were making love at this moment. Her voice in his ear, "Paulie, oh Paulie . . ."

Not now, kiddo, not now.

Slowly, he walked to her closet, opened the door, the light inside coming on automatically. A big, walk-in closet, what delight it gave her after the tiny one she'd had in their last apartment. The shoe racks Paul had put up lined the closet door. Twelve pairs of shoes, neat, toes up, tiny like she'd been. The pair of navy suede pumps with red leather trim he'd always loved. On the floor lined up neatly, her tennis sneakers, the old pair of Keds she'd used for gardening, her open-toed gold house slippers. Teeny tiny baby shoes, so small they touched his heart.

He walked into the closet. Pocketbooks on the floor-to-ceiling shelves to his left, a plastic tray of gloves. Round hatboxes from Saks and Lord & Taylor's up above. On the short low rod her blouses and sweaters hung. Her dresses, suits, and pants were on the higher, longer rod. He moved the clothes, feeling, touching. Her yellow silk dress, one of his favorites, worn only once or twice a summer when they went someplace special. He took it off the rod and held it to his face. Only a trace of her, a lingering scent of perfume. He put the yellow dress back on the rod, moved the clothes along. At the end of the rod, her orange terry bathrobe, her long blue velvet house robe. He took the velvet robe and held it against himself, swaying for a moment in the closet, his eyes shut, remembering the feel of Jane in the robe as he'd held her.

"Love you, Janie," he whispered, holding the soft velvet to his cheek. The sound of his own voice disturbed him. Suddenly he felt foolish and put the robe back in its place.

He went to Jane's triple dresser of pale fruitwood. Opening the top drawer, he fingered her collection of scarves, handkerchiefs, neckerchiefs. They were so much a part of her style. Always, the small touch of color, a kerchief about her throat, a handkerchief on her handbag, the long silk scarf tied about her small waist as a belt.

He opened the drawer below. Her bras and panties. He picked up a pair of bright blue bikini panties, so impossibly small. They smelled of lilac and lavender, and looking deeper in the drawer he found small sachets at the bottom. A flesh-colored bra, soft and shapeless without her. He held it to his nostrils, closed his eyes. Opening them, he caught sight of himself in the mirror above the dresser.

A man with a bra on his nose, he thought comically. Sex-crazed widower goes berserk, found wandering streets in wife's underclothes.

Stop. Replace bra. Close drawer. Watch TV until you get sleepy.

He found an old movie, James Stewart in a battered cowboy hat, carrying a long rifle. Paul sat down in the club chair to watch. A short time later, he heard a quiet knock on the closed bedroom door.

Hilary's face appeared, peeking around the now partly opened door. "I thought I heard the TV go on. I couldn't sleep either."

"Come on in, butch." The girl was wearing the bottom half of a pair of yellow longjohns. Above this, Paul was surprised to see an old brown flannel shirt he thought he'd thrown away last spring. "I know that shirt," he said.

"You can't have it back."

"I don't want it back. In fact, I thought it was long gone."

Hilary smiled at him. "I found Gemma throwing it in the trash. I sewed up the holes myself."

"There's a paint smear near the collar."

"I love it." She sat down on the floor near Jane's dresser, folding her legs under her like a yogi. "What are you watching?"

"Anything. I think it's *Bend of the River*. Jimmy Stewart against the world."

They watched the film in silence. Paul was happy to have company and put away all thoughts of how early Hilary had to rise in the morning to go to school.

"We have to talk," Hilary said when the commercial break came on. A woman was singing about a detergent.

76

"About today?"

"Partly."

"I thought we'd settled that."

"Nope."

"All right." The telephone company was telling how cheap it was to call someone in California. Paul wished he knew someone in California, someone who might call him. He pulled his eyes from the TV screen and looked at Hilary.

"I don't know how to begin," she said, her face directed at the television set and not at him. Her mouth opened and closed, but no words came out.

"Is it about you and Pete?"

She nodded her head. There was a long silence in which a group of people at a county fair sang about Pepsi-Cola.

"Speak up," Paul said. "I won't bite."

Hilary cleared her throat. "I . . . uh, went to Planned Parenthood last week."

A stone shifted in Paul's chest. *"What?"*

"I want to get a diaphragm."

Hot blood rushed to Paul's head and pounded in his ears. "Wait a minute," he said, a little louder than he intended. He got up and switched off the television. Standing, he looked down at his daughter, feeling a rush of disbelief and anger. No, no! he thought, I don't want to hear this, knowing at the same time he must. He opened the sliding doors to the closet, one door slamming against the frame. Reaching in, he took his bathrobe from the hook on which it hung and put it on. He pulled the belt tight, staring at the girl.

"Did you hear me?" she said.

"I heard you." The message was loud and clear, girl, he thought. You and Pete, you want to start making love. His Hilary and the skinny kid with the funny moustache. She was a kid, a baby. "Forget it!"

"I knew you'd be mad."

"You bet I'm mad. Jesus!" He patted his pockets to find his cigarettes, then went to the night table where he'd left them. It was just one damn upsetting thing after another. Never a full day of peace and calm. Peace was buried at Mount Hebron with Jane. The world turns upside down and when you're used to that, it turns inside out. "You've sure got a lousy sense of timing, baby."

"I'm old enough," she said.

"I didn't mean that. And I don't agree."

"We're in love. And I really don't need your permission."

"The hell you don't. I'm your father. You're sixteen years old, for God's sake!"

"I didn't mean that. I meant that I don't need your permission to get a diaphragm. I just want to talk about it with you. Before. And I'll be seventeen in the spring."

"You're a baby!" he half-shouted.

"Don't get excited," Hilary said.

"I am excited!" he yelled. "Jesus, I'm fit to bust."

"I didn't come in here to make you angry."

"No? Well, you're doing a pretty good job of it."

"And I could have gone behind your back."

"The hell you could."

"Daddy, calm down. I could have asked for the pill, or been fitted already, and you wouldn't know anything about it. But I wanted to talk to you first."

"Thanks a lot," he snapped. How could the girl be so calm?

"You have no right to control my sex life."

"What is that, a quote from *Ms.* magazine? I'm your father, and I have every right a father ever had."

"You're not listening to me," the girl said. She shook her head.

"I'm listening all right, and I'm not liking what I'm hearing." His voice was hard and loud. "Hilary, your mother was a virgin when we got married. She was almost twenty years old."

"That's not today."

"What the hell is going on in this house?" He'd lost control of himself, he knew, but he was beyond that now. A fierce rage bubbled inside, a cold fury that spilled from his mouth as he shouted. "We're coming apart! Just goddamn falling into little pieces! There's no order, no sympathy . . . no bread and no underwear! You don't cooperate, you fight me! I get called to school because your brother had a fight, he's walking around like a brooding monk, you're on your bed with Peter, the world

has gone to hell in a handbasket and you want a *diaphragm?*
Good God!''

"Sor-ree.''

"And don't say that, you know it infuriates me!''

Bobby suddenly appeared in the doorway, tears in his eyes.
"I'm sorry,'' he said, "I know you're fighting about me.''

"What?'' Paul was startled.

"It's . . . it's my fault,'' the boy said. He turned, as if to run
away, but Paul was too quick. Crossing the room he grabbed hold
of Bobby's arm. "What's your fault?'' he asked. "What?''

Bobby tried to speak and couldn't. He spread his hands in a wide
gesture.

A hoarse cry of pain came from Paul. *"It's nobody's fault!"* he
shouted. "That's the hell of it. Nobody killed your mother, she just
died. Do you understand me? She had that little thing in her brain
and when the time came it broke. An aneurism they call it, a bubble
in her brain, and when it broke she couldn't live anymore. And
nothing you did, or Hilary did, or I did made it happen, nothing!''
He put his arms around the boy and held him tight. "Stop crying,''
he commanded, hating the words that came from him. "Just stop
it.'' Looking over at Hilary, he saw tears brimming in her eyes.
"No!'' he shouted to her. "Cut it out!'' Half-pulling Bobby, he
brought him to where Hilary sat and forced him to sit down on the
floor beside her. "Quit that blubbering,'' he said. A knot had un-
tied inside him and he felt strong.

"Mourning is over,'' he said cruelly. "Crying time is finished.
You want to bawl your heads off, go ahead, but leave me out of it,
understand? Your mother is dead. Dead! Get used to it. She's not
coming back. We put her in the ground, remember? And we
walked away and came back. That's it. The end. *Finito.*

"So what are you guys now, orphans? Hell no. You've got me,
your father, and by God I've got you and I'm not giving you up.
Hear that? Never! Wherever you go and whatever you do in your
whole life, I'm always going to be your father. Through thick or
thin, no matter what, you are *mine.* And I'm going to bust my gut
to do everything I can to take care of you. Get that! Me,'' he said,
thrusting a cocked thumb to his chest, "I'm the guy who's going to
take care of you.''

Both children had stopped crying. Struck by the ferocity of Paul's voice and the hard look on his face, they listened.

"Your mother knew you better than I do. That's what I'm finding out. But if she raised you, you've got to be the best damn kids in the whole world. And nobody loves you more than I do.

"But starting now, we've got to stop feeling sorry for ourselves. We've got to put an end to our grief, thinking only about ourselves, hiding away from each other behind closed doors. We're a family, flesh and blood! And I'm your father. You might not like what I say or what I do, but you'll listen to me. We're stuck with each other, kids, we're all the family we have, just the three of us."

Slowly, the hard look on Paul's face softened. The children looked cowed by what he had said, frightened perhaps. Or was it something else? He went down on his knees, put his arms around them, and hugged them tight. He felt Bobby's arms reciprocate, and then Hilary's, the three of them huddling tight and holding on to one another.

"That was a helluva speech," Paul said lightly. "If I'd known it was coming, I would have worn my formal pajamas." He held his hand to Hilary's face. "I'm sorry I yelled at you, baby. I wasn't being fair."

"That's okay, Daddy," she said.

"We'll have to talk about it, soon, I promise. In the meantime, please, baby, promise me you'll wait."

"I will." She kissed Paul's hand.

"My throat is dry as a bone," Paul said. "Too much yelling." He got up and found his cigarettes, lit one, and sat on the edge of the bed. Bobby stood up and came over to him. "I'll be better," the boy said.

"Of course you will."

"I'm sorry."

"There's nothing to be sorry about."

Bobby leaned down and kissed Paul on the cheek. "Good night, then."

"Wait a second," Paul said, not wanting the moment to end. "I want a cup of cocoa. How about we all go downstairs and have some?"

Bobby was surprised. "It's after midnight," he said.

"I know."

"There's school tomorrow."

"So what? Come on, chum. And you too, Hil. Let's have some cocoa and talk. Maybe we can even get this family organized."

8

HE HEARD BOBBY'S sneakered tread on the stairs. The boy came into the kitchen silently, his hair an uncombed tangle. "Good morning, chum. Did you sleep well?"

Bobby grunted, went to his place at the table, and opened the newspaper to the sports section.

"I slept very well, thank you," Paul said aloud to himself. "How did you sleep, Dad? Pretty good, thank you," he answered himself, "but not long enough."

Bobby turned to look at him, fish-eyed, Paul thought.

"Good morning." The sunny voice behind him was Hilary. She put her arms around him from behind and hugged him. Her breath smelled of mint. "Good morning, sugar," he said.

Hilary sat at her place at the table. Bobby kept his eyes on the newspaper, saying nothing.

"What's with him?" Hilary asked.

"Ignore him," Paul said, "maybe he'll disappear."

Hilary reached over and slipped the news section of the newspaper from Bobby's grasp. He didn't look up. She looked at the front page. "I need an article on Red China," she said.

"Red China," Paul said. "I'll tell you one thing, it doesn't go with an orange tablecloth." He began making French toast for the kids.

One of the things decided in the long family conference last night was that Hilary would get up earlier so they could breakfast together each day. Paul hoped Hilary would be a good influence in the morning.

She looked so adorable in his old flannel shirt, head down, reading the paper, the sun bringing out copper highlights in her hair. A feeling of love washed over him. They were good kids, both of them, even the grouchy boy who didn't laugh a helluva lot.

Paul made himself a cup of instant coffee, put his own French toast into the pan. He went to the freezer, opened it and looked in. Another day, another dinner. It was really endless, wasn't it? How did women do it? To shop and cook and put dinner on the table every night. Kathleen Bradie fed six. Even after Michael had inherited so much money when his old man died, Kathleen was the cook. Amazing. Yeah, but what do you eat tonight?

Endless.

He shut the freezer, went back to his toast, and turned the slices over. It was a form of love, really, cooking for your family. You set it down before them, a love offering, and they took it into their bodies to satisfy their hunger. Here, you were saying, I made this to keep you alive, a little token of love from my own two hands. Was that a crazy thought?

Demented widower philosophizes over breakfast, intellectual journals please copy. Sometimes, kiddo, you are ridiculous.

Sometimes it feels good to be ridiculous.

"Chillun," he announced in his hillbilly accent, "listen up good. Ah am dee-cidin' whut we-all is gonna eat fo dinnah." They looked at Paul, which made him feel even better. "You listenin' to yo Daddeh, honey chile?" he asked Hilary.

"Yes, Daddeh," she grinned.

"You bettah pay attention, boy, ah aims to ask questions later, you heah?" Was that a trace of a smile at the corners of Bobby's mouth? Good golly, Miss Molly!

"Well, now," he went on, "whut ah'm gonna do is get me one

o' them woks, what-you-call-it, see? An' then ah'm gonna melt me down a mess a bear grease.''

"Whut's bear grease, Daddeh?" Hilary said. Her hillbilly was pretty good.

"Grease from a bear, girl, that's whut it is. What are you, stupid or somethin'? Ah'm gonna get that bear grease real hot, see, and then ah'm agonna cook us up some supper. Whooeee!''

Hilary was giggling and Paul couldn't help grinning. "Whut you gonna cook, Daddeh?" Bobby asked.

"Frahd bicycle," Paul said.

"In the bear grease," Bobby said, liking it.

"In the bear grease. Gonna fry up them handlebars real fahn, give them to Hilary heah. Then ah'm gonna take da spokes offa them wheels and cook 'em up jus lahk spaghetti. That's fo you, son.''

"In the bear grease, Daddeh?" the boy asked.

"In the bear grease, son. Then ah'm gonna take that there bicycle seat and frah it up real fahn. That's the best part, you know. That there seat-meat. And that's for me.''

"Sounds good, Daddeh!" Hilary said.

"Real fahn," Bobby said.

"Well, ah should say so," Paul said. "An iffen there's any oh that seat-meat left over, why ah'll jus maybe make us one oh them there Chinee dishes wid it.''

"In the wok," said Hilary.

"In the bear grease," Bobby said, laughing.

"In the bear grease," Paul said.

It became a hillbilly breakfast, very silly, with the children chattering like refugees from the Ozarks. The first silly time they'd had in much too long.

In the front hallway, he helped Bobby heft his knapsack as the boy left the house. "Have a good day," Paul said.

Bobby stood on tiptoe to kiss Paul's cheek.

"How are you going to handle Sambo?"

"I don't know."

"No more fighting, got that? And if he wants to be friends again, you do the same."

"He won't."

"Don't be too sure."

Bobby opened the front door and stepped out onto the porch. Paul stood in the open doorway, feeling the cold through his thin pajamas and robe. "See you tonight, baby."

"In the bear grease," the boy said. He went down the steps and took off running toward the corner.

By nine o'clock he was showered and dressed and ready to go to the office. He waited for Gemma to arrive, sitting in his chair at the kitchen table, listening for the sound of the front door opening, sipping yet another cup of terrible instant coffee. The day was sunny, though cold. Paul looked out the picture window at the basketball hoop with its half-torn net, the tangled jungle of dead plants in the vegetable garden. The garden would wait until spring. And then what? He could clean it up, plant a small crop of vegetables. Tomatoes, Bobby's favorite, and lettuce for salads. But who would tend the garden? He would, of course, but he would get the kids involved too. He would show them what to do. *Show,* hell, first he'd have to learn what to do himself.

Nine-thirty. Where the hell was Gemma?

He called his office and spoke to Lillian. No, nothing was wrong, in fact, some things were better than they'd been.

Gemma Anne Davis, when are you going to show up?

By ten o'clock, Paul was thoroughly annoyed. The woman deserved to be fired; she was taking advantage of him. Gemma had always been Jane's responsibility, and he knew how well the two women got on. In all the years she'd worked for the Kleins, Paul had seen her only on those rare occasions when he was home ill or returning from a business trip. He barely knew the woman.

Waiting, growing more impatient, he found a yellow pad and began to make notes. At ten past ten he heard the front door open. The hall closet creaked open, clothes were hung on a hanger. Footsteps came across the dining room. "Mr. Klein? What are you doing here?"

"Hello, Gemma."

She was carrying a small paper bag. A large black woman in a cotton housedress and sweater, Gemma had a gold tooth in front that sparkled when she spoke. "I know I'm late," she said. Gemma ran water in the sink, filled the kettle, and put it up to boil. She opened the paper bag, took out a crusty roll and put it on a plate. Opening the refrigerator she brought butter and jelly to the table.

"I wanted to talk to you, Gemma," Paul said.

Gemma nodded. She took silverware and brought it to the table. "My second daughter," she said, "she's havin' a baby any day now. I stopped by there this mornin' to do some shoppin' for her, and to see if she was all right. I'm sorry." Gemma didn't look more than thirty-five.

"I can't believe you're a grandmother, Gemma. You're so young."

"Don't feel so young, Mr. Klein, that's for sure. Fact is, I thought about not comin' in today. I'm feelin' pretty low. My woman's time of the month." She sugared her tea and brought it to the table.

"How long have you been working for us, Gemma?"

"Let's see now." She took a sip of her tea. "Going on for eight years now. Missus Klein started me with one day for a while, then two. She always wanted another day, but I have these other ladies I do for, you know." She reached into the pocket of her housedress and withdrew a dainty handkerchief. "Stupid me," Gemma said in a voice that broke with emotion, "why didn't I give her what she wanted. Now I do it when she's dead and gone. It hurts me." She blew her nose loudly into the handkerchief.

Paul looked away, feeling the woman's sorrow himself.

"She was a wonderful lady," Gemma said. "So sweet and kind. It just don't make no sense, does it?"

"No. No sense at all."

"In the prime of life, two beautiful children, a lovely home like this." She dabbed at her eyes, looking down at the table. "Sometimes when I'm workin' in the afternoons, I'll think of somethin' I want to tell her, and I'll say to myself she'll *be here*. Comes three-thirty she'll walk in with that smile for me like she always had, and we'll just sit down here in the kitchen and have a nice talk." Gemma took a loud sip of her tea. "I miss her, Mr. Klein."

"I know, Gemma."

"I feel so sorry for you all. There's a lot of sorrow in that little boy, Mr. Klein. He was always so happy, with that little grin, always funnin' me, callin' me 'Fat Gemma' like only he could do. You gotta pay most attention to that boy now, Mr. Klein, because his little heart is broke in pieces. All the sorrow still in there and he can't get it out."

"Gemma, I need your help. Every time something goes wrong it's like a reminder, about Jane, telling us she's gone. Bobby ran out of socks this week and I had to do a wash. I don't want that to happen anymore."

"He needs socks," Gemma said. "And underwear, too. And I don't think those flannel shirts from last year fit him too well no more."

"Those are the kinds of things I wish you'd tell me," Paul said, making notes on the yellow pad. "I'm sure you told Jane about things you noticed we needed."

"I did. And she saw to things, too." Gemma thought for a moment. "We need fabric softener."

"Right," Paul said. "And I'm going to buy jeans and clothing for the kids this weekend. Bobby's jeans are too short in the cuff."

"He don't need new jeans, Mr. Klein. There's plenty of cuff left inside to be let down on 'em."

"You can do that?"

"Oh, Mr. Klein," Gemma said, smiling. "Your missus, she always gave me things like that to do. You know that skirt Hilary made out of an old pair of jeans? Who do you think did the hem for her, and helped her with the sewing?

"Put buttons back on shirts, mend torn seams, I do all that. Course Missus Klein always set those things aside for me. You could do that, too."

"I'll start paying attention to it," Paul said.

"Bobby and Hilary, they were just babies when I come here." Gemma bit into the roll, chewing thoughtfully.

"That girl of yours, she's grown up so fast. Smart as a whip, that one, and more than her share of sass. But underneath, she's as sweet as sugar. Never forgets my birthday. Even this year. And Bobby . . . well, me and him just get along. Always have."

Paul doodled a square on the yellow pad as Gemma spoke, then put a roof and chimney on it.

"I remember he was sick one time, must have been seven or eight then, and I made him something new for lunch. A scrambled egg sandwich. Oh, how he loved that! From then on he just wanted that every day." She smiled, thinking about the little boy years ago, who sat at this very table in his pajamas and robe. "That reminds me. How come you don't buy those Raviolios no more? Bobby loves them."

"Really? He's never said anything." He made a note on the pad.

"That, and a glass of milk—with an ice cube—that's a good lunch for him."

"Gemma," Paul said, "I'm going to ask you to do something for me. Something important. It would ease my mind to know that you were here every day, to see to the kids. Do you think you could do that for me? And for them?"

Gemma took a sip of her tea. "Now Mr. Klein . . . I told you back in summer I could only give you one more day, a Friday. And that's what I've done."

"I know that, and I appreciate it, Gemma. But if you came five days a week, things would be a whole lot better."

"What about them other ladies? What should I say to them?"

"Tell them you've got important work to do. And I don't mean washing floors or vacuuming carpet. You've got a family that needs looking after, a house to run. Two kids who need a woman to talk to sometimes, a woman who loves them. That's what you should tell them, Gemma. And tell them you're going to make more money, too, I mean it." He mentioned a figure to her, not nearly as much as he paid Lillian Lerner, but more than twice what he paid Gemma now.

Gemma was silent for a time, thinking, her large fingers playing with a paper napkin.

"I wouldn't care if you came in later in the day, Gemma, just as long as you were here when the kids come home. That's what's important to me, that time you could spend with them."

"Mostly with Bobby," Gemma said. "Hilary's got that Peter boy to talk to."

"I know."

"She told me she's in love with him. Very polite boy. And eat—why I don't think they feed him at home."

"You could keep an eye on them for me, Gemma. And I know you wouldn't work as hard, just looking after one house. And I would do my best to help you. What do you say?"

Gemma stared out the window, obviously concentrating. "I

could ask my cousin Gigi to do for Missus Miller," she said, almost to herself. "And Thelma, from my church, she needs steady work. Course she don't do ironing, but that don't seem so important these days." A sudden smile brightened her face. "All right. I'll try for every day. Till five o'clock, how's that? And I'll come in about ten."

"You could come in at eleven, I don't care."

"Eleven's too late. This is a big house."

"You decide," Paul said. "You're the boss now."

"Well, I'll try. You got to help me, though. My remembering ain't too good."

"I will," Paul said. "I'll leave notes for you, or call you from the office."

"Even so," Gemma said, "I'll mess up. Just don't get mad at me when I'm forgetful."

"I won't, Gemma, that's a promise."

9

"WHERE IS THE reef?" Jane said. "I don't see it."

"Right *there.*" His finger pointed offshore. A white line of foam in the turquoise bay.

"It looks awfully far, babe."

"Piece of cake." He took her hand and helped her down the rocky slope from the headland. The beach was powdery white sand, the water warm on their bare feet. Overhead, white clouds drifted in a high blue sky.

She sat down at the water's edge, wet her swim fins, and began to pull them on. "The famous Coki Point. Doesn't look like much."

"The best reef from here to Buck Island." He sat down on the warm sand, watching her struggle with the tight fins, a beautiful girl in a blue bikini. The mother of two young children? It didn't seem possible. She was a kid.

"What?" She smiled, reading his thoughts.

"You. Just you."

Jane grinned, squeezed his thigh with a small hand. She wet her snorkel mask and cleared it, spit into the face plate and put it on. She stood up in her swim fins and backed awkwardly into the sea, waiting for him.

"We'll just dog paddle out," he said when he joined her, "nice and easy. Save energy. You ready?"

"You realize we can't see the reef from here."

"Straight out; we can't miss it. Let's stay together."

"Maybe we ought to wait. Nobody knows we're out here."

"Come on, chicken, get started."

She grinned under the face mask. "If something happens to us, my mother will be very annoyed."

Laughing, Paul paddled off, waiting for her to catch up and swim beside him. Halfway to the reef, he felt the current pulling against his legs, trying to sweep them down the channel toward the open end of the bay. "Let's float awhile," he said to her, turning over on his back.

He pulled his mask atop his forehead. Looking back, he picked out the tree that was their marker on the headland. They were slightly off-course, not a lot, but the current would take them farther in the wrong direction.

"We'll have to swim left," he said, "at an angle," but when he turned back to say this she was gone.

"Jane?" The sunlight danced on the water, reflecting in his eyes. "Hey! Jane?" Where was she? Why had she swum off? *"Jane!"* Too much sun, he couldn't see. *"Jane! Wait up!"*

He sat up in bed, panic in his throat. Sunlight came strong through the venetian blinds. In the mirror above her dresser he saw himself, his hair crazy, slack mouth open. He felt cold and sweaty under his flannel pajamas.

A dream. A stupid dream.

Almost the way it had been, but not quite. He remembered the fright, but not panic. Jane had answered in the next instant; she wasn't far away, a few yards. In the water, she was better than he was. Had he been frightened for himself?

He remembered the rest of that day, the hours they'd spent exploring the reef, the coral formations, the incredible numbers of dazzling skipjacks, zebras, and angelfish swimming right up to their masks. The champagne he'd had waiting for them when they got back. The warm shower they took together, soaping her little rounded body, the big bed that faced the sea. Drinking the wine, naked under their robes, close together, knowing that when they finished they would make love.

Shit.

He found a cigarette, lit it, swung his legs off the bed. Horny widower goes berserk, attacks bag lady on street. Don't think about it, maybe it will go away.

What had he once told Jane? Yes, men are different, they can get the hots five times a day. Why are you laughing? Okay, three times a day. Would you believe twice? They have this twig between their legs that has a life of its own. And when the sap rises in the tree . . .

She'd never let him forget it. How's your twig, baby? Is your twig awake or sleeping? Uh-oh, the twig also rises.

He let the shower run hot while he shaved. Once in and soaped, he brought it down to lukewarm and then as cold as he could take it. Toweling off, he thought about the day. A shopping list for the supermarket, some kind of menu plan for the week, off to Macy's later with the kids. Tonight, a movie—any movie—dinner somewhere.

He folded his big bath towel and hung it over the bar behind the door. Not his bath towel anyway. It was a pink towel, one of Jane's. His bath towels were blue. Practical Gemma, she was still putting out towels for him without thinking which were which. Did it matter anymore that the pink ones were Jane's? They were just towels, weren't they? And where Gemma used to hang two face towels and two bath towels, a pink and a blue of each kind, there were now only two instead of four.

His and His.

Suddenly, jokes didn't seem funny. Naked in the bathroom, he was not alone. Jane was still here, surrounding him in a thousand memories. At any moment she could open that closed door and walk in, raising her eyebrows at him, saying, "A naked man in my bathroom, what's going on here? Some clothing I hope."

On the tile shelf, next to the potted philodendron, her lotions and perfumes. L'Interdit, the spray she put on before coming to bed. Audrey Hepburn's perfume. That was Jane, her style, her model. A small girl, under a hundred pounds always, with a beautiful slim neck like Audrey Hepburn; a *gamine*, a waif, a wife.

Under the corner sink cabinet stood the wastebasket. Paul took it to the tile shelf and tossed in the half-bottle of spray cologne. Next to it, a small bottle of L'Interdit perfume. Throw it out. Large bottle of Jean Naté. Into the wastebasket.

There was no reason for him to keep looking at her things every time he came in here. No goddamn reason.

He slid open Jane's side of the medicine cabinet. Out! Clean it out! Into the wastebasket went Etherea toning lotion, body lotion, small tan bottles of makeup, oils, creams, Cutex nail-polish remover, bottles of nail polish, emery boards, cotton balls, body powder, nose drops and prescription bottles, deodorants, a Lady Shick razor, a small box of Tampax, a pair of tweezers, bath oil beads, a hairbrush, two combs. In the corner of the bottom shelf, a rubber band was wound around ten packets of partly used book matches. Pack rat. *Out.*

He went to the built-in closet in the corner. Modess, more Tampax, sanitary belt, suntan lotion, an old hair dryer that hadn't worked for years, more emery boards, a whole collection of small wrapped soaps from hotels they'd visited.

He opened the drawer in the cabinet by the sink. Rubber bands, another hairbrush, loose books of matches, her nail clippers, a half-used bottle of Revlon nail polish, six lipsticks, eyebrow pencil.

Out. All of it. *Out!*

He came back into their bedroom, a fury building in him. Two of her framed needlepoints hung on the walls. Above his dresser, a sailboat scene in purples and blues. A zodiac in orange and brown over the television in the corner. They could stay.

He dressed in jeans and a flannel shirt, his stomach growling. Clean it all out, get rid of it. He didn't need reminders of what he had lost. He wanted breakfast, real coffee instead of rotten instant for once. Why was he so angry?

Downstairs in the living room, Bobby sat on the black leather loveseat, still in his pajamas and striped robe. The TV set was making a racket; animated cats chased a gray mouse. Paul took a deep breath. He ruffled the boy's hair, bent down to kiss his brow. "What are you watching?"

"Stupid cartoons."

Paul grunted. "Get dressed," he said, hard command in his tone.

Bobby's face turned to regard him. "Now?"

Easy, don't take it out on the kid. "Soon, okay? We've got a lot of work to do today."

In the kitchen, Hilary was at the table, reading the newspaper. She was wearing a rose sweater that gave color to her pale face. Looking up, she smiled at him. "Hey, Daddeh," she drawled.

He sat down in his chair, lit a cigarette. Hilary put the newspaper back together and passed it across the table. "What would you like for breakfast?" she asked.

"Would you make it?"

"Yes, indeed," she said cheerfully. "That's why I asked." She got to her feet and came around the table to kiss him on the cheek. "Is anything wrong? You look sad."

"Same old stuff."

"Poor Daddy." She touched his cheek. "Anything I can do?"

"Just be nice. Stay with me. I'm feeling lonely again."

"I'll be right here. Scrambled eggs, sunnies?"

"Toast is all. And some real coffee. Strong."

"Aye, aye, sir." Grinning, she saluted.

He munched the toast slowly, not really tasting it, but the coffee he savored. Hilary sat in Jane's chair, next to his, watching him.

"Peter called this morning. He wants me to go to a concert with him tonight. I told him I'd have to ask you."

"Where's the concert?"

"In the Village. We'd probably have pizza somewhere before."

"Good concert?"

"A group I like. The Lounge Lizards."

"Punk?"

She giggled. "New Wave. Dissonance. You'd hate it."

"What time would you be home?"

"Not late."

He nodded. "Make sure Peter brings you home, though. Right to the door."

"Sure. Thanks, Daddy."

He finished the coffee and put the cup in the sink. From the pantry closet he took a large plastic trash bag. "Come on upstairs," he said. "You can help me."

Bobby was fully dressed, lying on his bed, playing with an electronic game that beeped and buzzed. "Favor, Bob-o," he said. "Would you go up to the attic, please, and bring down all of our suitcases?"

Bobby put the game down on the bed. "Are we going somewhere?"

"No. Just bring them into my room, okay?"

Hilary followed him into the bathroom. She watched as he emptied the wastebasket into the trash bag. "What's up?" she asked.

"Cleaning out." He walked past her with the trash bag and went to Jane's dresser. Two slender vases were on top of the long piece of furniture; in one of them stood a red silk rose. He took the rose and dumped it into the trash bag. "That's been bothering me for months," he said. Also on the dresser, on four small feet, stood a large brass clamshell that opened. Inside were coiled strands of imitation pearls, ropes of bead necklaces. He picked these things up to dump them in the bag when Hilary stopped him. "Wait! Don't throw that away."

"Why not? You don't wear this stuff."

"I might. Someday."

"Here." He handed her the brass clamshell. "Put it away in your room. Out of sight. I just don't want to *see* it again, understand?"

Looking somewhat frightened, Hilary dashed down the hall to her room. An instant later, Bobby came in with a large suitcase in each hand. "Just put them down, Bob-o. And open them."

The boy did as he was told, saying nothing. He sat down on the bed, looking at Paul.

"We'll need the other suitcases, too. Bring them down."

"What are you doing?"

"Cleaning out things." He looked at the boy. "Get the suitcases."

Bobby left, Hilary came back in. He opened the top left-hand drawer of the dresser. Pantyhose, tights in many colors, down below a box from Lord & Taylor. Inside the box were sealed packets of nylon hose. He emptied the drawer into the trash bag.

"Are you okay?" Hilary asked.

"No."

"You're acting spooky."

"This stuff is driving me crazy," he said. The drawer below held a hundred envelopes. Canceled checks dating back five years, deposit slips; in some of the envelopes were receipts for items purchased years and years ago. He filled the trash bag with them. Next drawer down: shorts, summer tops, three bikinis. Out.

Top middle drawer. Behind him, Bobby came back. "What's he doing?"

"He's throwing out Mom's things."

"All of them?"

"Ask him."

Jewelry in the drawer, costume junk but some good things, too. The jade pin he'd given her, gold ropes he'd bought one Christmas when feeling flush, gold pins and bracelets. "Do you want any of this?" he asked Hilary.

"Yes."

"What?"

"I don't know. Some of it . . . maybe all of it. How do I know what I'll want when I'm twenty?"

He pulled out the entire drawer and marched it down the hall, putting it on Hilary's bed. "Take what you want, but hide it. I want that drawer to be empty when I put it back."

She followed him back to his bedroom. Next drawer. Sweaters. He pulled a suitcase over and opened it, began filling it.

"This is crazy, Dad," Hilary said. "Those are good sweaters."

"Who's going to wear them? You're three inches taller than she was and still growing." He kept unloading sweaters and putting them in the suitcase.

"That's a cashmere, that navy one."

He remembered how Jane felt in his arms when she wore it, how soft and cuddly. Stop.

Out.

Bottom drawer. Memorabilia. Picture albums, boxes of old letters, a stack of telegrams and old birthday cards. These he would save. If not for himself, for the kids. He slammed the drawer closed with his foot.

Top drawer, right, kerchiefs, scarves, and handkerchiefs. He began putting them into the suitcase, filling it. He zipped it closed.

"Dad." Hilary, her voice quiet.

"Yes." He opened the next drawer down. Panties and bras.

"Please don't throw everything away," the girl said. "There are some things . . . I want some things to wear sometimes. Her things."

"No!" He opened another suitcase, started throwing in the panties and bras.

"Please, Dad," Hilary said.

"I said no." Bottom drawer. Oh, hell, nightgowns.

"Why not? Don't you think I'd like some of her things to wear? She had good clothes."

Under his fingers, thin nylon, sheer cottons and silks, the pink slinky nightgown that unbuttoned all the way down the front. Into the suitcase, fast, don't think about it.

"Her skirts I could wear," Hilary said. "They just have to be lengthened."

He slammed the final drawer shut, took a deep breath. "No, Hil. I couldn't stand that. To see you wearing anything of hers, God, I think that would kill me. Even with these drawers closed, I'm haunted. All her things, still here, like I'm waiting for her to come back and wear them again."

He turned away from the children and looked at himself in the mirror. His heart was hardened now, somewhere beyond tears, the hurt like a lead weight cold inside. Easy boy, take it easy.

"I hate this," Bobby said. "It's like . . . like you're trying to throw Mom away."

"She is away, Bob." Go gently, gently, he told himself. "These are only the things she'll never use again. Things that have been hurting me. That's why I'm taking them away. Can you understand that?"

"No. It just seems . . . like it's *mean*. The way you're doing this."

"I should have done it long ago. But I don't think I was strong enough."

The closet waited, that whole huge closet.

He swung the door open, stripped the shoes from the racks, took the sneakers and slippers from the floor. He began taking things from hangers, dresses, suits, skirts with Lord & Taylor labels, Saks, Bloomingdale's. All good clothing, all her style, her colors.

At last, Hilary began to help, folding jeans and shoving T-shirts into the last of the suitcases. The closet poles were empty, rows of hangers swung and tinkled.

Behind him, shelves of pocketbooks and handbags. So many. He sent Bobby downstairs for more trash bags and filled two of them.

He cleaned the hatboxes off the upper shelves and stacked them on the floor in the hallway. The yellow straw cloche was in one of them, his favorite, the one she'd bought in Florence. Sitting in a café that overlooked the Arno, in bright sunshine, drinking Cinzano with Michael and Kathleen Bradie. Jane had worn that hat then, stirring his heart, her face all golden, the four of them resting, footsore from the Uffizi. *Out.*

Somehow he managed to drag everything downstairs and out to the car. He loaded the trunk, part of the back seat. The trash bags he set out at the curb. Hilary helped, Bobby only reluctantly. They put on their warm outer jackets, hats and gloves. He double locked the front door.

The air was crisp and cold. He filled his lungs with it. Was he crazy? What had he accomplished this morning? And at what cost? He walked down the steps and crossed the lawn. The children were waiting. He looked back at the house for a long moment before getting into the car with them. Jane's house. The house she'd found and made her own. Maybe some part of her had left it now, the part locked up in the car trunk, in those trash bags at the curb. The part, perhaps, that haunted him still. He'd find out. Can you lay a ghost to rest by taking her clothes away? Her perfume? Her nail polish?

He pulled out of the driveway and turned on the radio. Music filled the car, loud and bright. He began to hum. He drove to the church on Fort Hamilton Parkway, not far away. Next to the rectory, at the curb, there was a green dumpster he'd passed so many times. He pulled in next to it. Society of St. Vincent de Paul was stenciled on it in white letters. He opened each suitcase carefully, dumping the clothes in. Kneeling on the sidewalk, he zipped the suitcases closed and put them back into the trunk of the car.

He felt strong now, and ravenously hungry. He got back into the car. "I could eat a wolf," he said. "Two wolves and a bear." He started the car and drove off. "Anybody hungry back there?" On the radio Sinatra sang an up-tempo tune.

Whistling along with Old Blue Eyes, he turned the car down the avenue, heading for McDonald's.

PART
TWO

PART

TWO

10

A FALSE SPRING.

Only the end of February and Mother Nature was offering a taste of what was to come. Temperature in the fifties, a sharp yellow sun, a breeze that felt warm on the skin. Leaving the house that morning, Paul had stopped to sniff the air. Crocuses bloomed at the edge of the lawn, yellow bells, tiny white dwarfs, delicate purples. Green and red shoots of emerging daffs and tulips and hyacinths dotted the chocolate-brown earth under the rhododendrons. One more gift Jane the gardener had left behind. In April and May blooms would brighten the front of the house, a legacy of Myron the gardening maven down the street. Myron Levy, the man who had bought the house directly behind his own, had it knocked down and carted away, and on that large plot constructed a garden of such beauty it had been featured in many house and garden magazines. Myron the Maven, who had dragged a willing Jane to secret garden stores where only the best bulbs were good enough. Jane, laughing at Paul's amazed look when she purchased six hundred twenty-five bulbs at one shot. That was the funny part; actually getting down on her knees to plant six hundred and twenty-five bulbs was the hard part. Years later they still bloomed, daff shoots sprouting green like scallion tops.

Life goes on. Even without Jane.

It was warm and stuffy in the office, so he kept the window open, putting up with the hum of car traffic on the bridge and the ripe aroma of fish. Down in Florida baseball teams played in the Grapefruit League, preparing to come north. Was it possible that the season would begin in little more than a month?

Paul went to the window and looked at the flowing river. The weather had gotten into his blood. He wanted to run swiftly on bright green meadows, hold up a gloved hand and judge a flyball against a blue sky. Summer games. The whoosh of surf, the sweet tang of salt air, a hot sandy beach. Jesus, he deserved it after this cold and lonely winter.

Flu had come and gone in serial. Bobby with a temperature of a hundred and three, rosy cheeks against pale green complexion, those sweet eyes glazed by the fever. In the kitchen at two A.M., Paul made sugary tea for the boy. Each day he squeezed fresh oranges for juice. And in the mornings during that siege of a week he waited for steadfast Gemma to come trudging along snowy sidewalks. Not one moment did Bobby spend in the house alone. Not his son, not when he was so sick. Handing over to Gemma for the day—you have the con—aye, aye, sir. And then Hilary came down with the flu, not as severe, thank God. The complication was that Gemma had it as well. Brave captain at the helm, Paul stayed home for three days nursing Hilary, this bedraggled kitten whose long unwashed hair lay as limp as she was. Chicken soup from a can—thank you, Mother Swanson, you'll have to do. Jane's soup would have had flecks of carrot and celery, soft white pieces of real chicken meat. Sue me, he told his daughter, trying to cheer her into a smile. I'm not a real Jewish Mother.

No sooner was Hilary off to school again than Paul went weak in the knees himself. Headaches, nausea, runny nose, stuffed sinuses, and a high temperature he did not want to take for fear of what it was. Unshaved, unwashed and uncaring, he stayed anchored in bed for four days. Weeks later, his nose still ran.

A great winter for masochists. In late January the heating went on the fritz. When the alarm went off Paul awakened to a house chilled to a snappy fifty degrees. Two days until the idiot repair man could finally set it right. One look at the bill and Paul changed his opinion; the repair man was smart, he was the idiot who had to pay. He packed the kids off to Phyllis Berg down the street. Nanook of the North stayed at home in the igloo keeping watch. Longjohns to sleep in, under the down comforter, only his face felt freezing until he found Bobby's knitted wool balaclava and somehow stretched it over his much larger head. Thank you, Jane.

Soon he'd be in Chicago and Minneapolis. Ready or not, here I come. Restless, he wanted to pace the office. Instead he buckled down to a solid two hours of work. He called Fischetti in Chicago, Carter in Minneapolis, laying final plans for his swing to their cities; wine tastings in hotels, selling visits to key retailers, a couple of appearances on local television shows. Paul could feel his juices stirring. He was ready to hit the road again.

The intercom buzzed. "There's a Marion Gerber on the line for you," Lillian Lerner told him.

Marion Gerber, mid-forties, divorced for several years, was one of Jane's friends from the neighborhood. He hadn't heard from Marion in months, not since the last time she'd had all three of them over to dinner.

"Paul? I didn't have your office number, so I called information."

"You got me. Is everything all right, Marion?"

"Oh, yes. I just wanted to know how you are, and the kids, how you're getting along. . . ."

"We're scraping by, I guess." He waited for Marion to go on.

"I was thinking of you today, that's really why I called. You know it's bake-sale time again in school. Jane and I always worked on it together. And . . . I don't know . . . I just felt so blue thinking about Jane I thought I'd call and see how you were getting on."

The P.T.A. bake sale, of course. Jane would be getting the whole thing organized now.

"I haven't upset you by calling, have I?" Marion asked.

"No," Paul replied, "I'm fine."

"How's Bobby doing in the new school?"

"Okay. He's even gotten used to the trip."

"I'd really like to have all three of you over to dinner soon."

"Accepted," Paul said at once. "I have no shame about scrounging dinner anywhere, any time."

"How is next week for you?"

"Good for the kids, but I'll be on the road for two weeks. It would be a help for Hilary and Bobby, though. If you don't mind, Marion."

"It's fine, Paul," she said. "I've really been a stinker. I should have had you over more often, I'm sorry."

"You've had us a few times. No need to apologize."

"No, I should have been doing more. I'll make it up. I feel I've almost been a stranger. Please forgive me, Paul."

"Marion, stop apologizing," he said. "You were always our friend, and you still are. How are your kids?"

"Fine. The boys are back in school. Jeff started Cornell this fall, you know. And the girls are fine." Paul heard Marion cough a couple of times. She smoked too much, Jane had always been going on about it with Marion. She'd become a very nervous woman after kicking Phil out of the house. "All right, then," Marion said. "I'll have the kids for dinner while you're away. And after you come back I expect to see you."

"You've got a deal," Paul said.

"Come on, Bob-o," Paul was saying as he looked at the clock above the pizzeria's door, "we've got to get moving. The play starts at eight."

Bobby stuffed a large chunk of pizza in his mouth and chewed silently. There was a smudge of pizza sauce on the boy's chin, another small fleck of red on his cheek. Paul took a napkin from the dispenser and reached across the table to wipe the boy's face, but Bobby pulled his head away. "You haven't answered me yet," the boy said.

"I'm thinking about it," Paul said. He put the napkin in front of Bobby. "Your chin and on your cheek. Sauce."

"Why am I the only one?" the boy asked. "You stopped seeing Dr. Wirtz. Hilary stopped. Why can't I quit going too?"

"Wirtz says he still wants to see you."

"Well, I don't want to see him."

"He's a doctor."

"He sucks, Dad. I really don't like him. And I don't think he likes me."

"Of course he likes you," Paul said. He lit a cigarette, took a long drag. "You're his patient, he's trying to help you."

"How? By sitting back in that stupid swivel chair and never saying anything? The guy is weird, Dad, I mean it." Bobby picked up the napkin and rubbed his chin.

"Dr. Wirtz is a psychiatrist. His job is to listen to your troubles, find out what's bugging you. Most of what he does is listen."

"Most of what he does is stupid," the boy said vehemently. "He keeps twisting everything I say. It's hard to talk to somebody like that."

"Why is it hard?"

The boy rolled up his eyes. "That's just what *he* does," he said.

"What is?"

"Jesus!" Bobby said, raising his voice, "you did it again."

"I'm sorry." A family of four went out the front door of the pizzeria.

"He turns everything into a question. I want to quit going there, Dad."

"I'll talk to him about it, okay? Look, we'd better get out of here and into school." Paul slid out of the booth and Bobby followed. There was still a spot of sauce on the boy's cheek. Paul took a napkin and wet a corner with his mouth, then wiped the smudge away.

They crossed the street behind Hilary's school and walked toward the entrance. "How much do you pay Dr. Wirtz?" Bobby asked. "I'll bet it's a lot."

"Don't worry about it, chum." Near the school entrance they took their place in a short line, and followed the crowd along a wide corridor. Glass cases set into the wall displayed photographs of students engaged in school activities. They were given programs as they entered the auditorium and found seats together a few rows from the stage. Paul helped Bobby get settled in his seat, making the boy remove his sweater because the auditorium was so warm. He folded his own coat onto his lap and settled back with the program. *"You're a Good Man, Charlie Brown,"* the program read, "directed by Eugene Bodian." That would be the famous Mr. Bodian Hilary had been talking about for months. Hilary was playing the part of Lucy Van Pelt, charter member of the Peanuts gang, and her name was listed last among the players.

The overture began; it sounded like a small group led by a piano, and Bobby whispered in Paul's ear: "That's Peter playing guitar."

"Hilary's Peter?"

"Yep."

The curtain rose on a stage almost bare except for a few low benches and something that was probably Snoopy's doghouse. When Hilary came marching out during the opening number, Paul's mouth flew open. *She was so beautiful!* Her face upthrust, her strong chin and high cheekbones outlined in the bright stage lighting, she no longer looked like his baby girl but like a confident young woman. "Look at her!" he hissed to Bobby. "She's gorgeous!" And then Paul realized why the transformation was so shocking: It was a long time since he'd seen Hilary in a dress, the first time he could remember seeing makeup and lipstick on her pale face. His heart swelled with a mixture of pride and sorrow.

Now everybody was applauding the opening number, which ended with Hilary down front, a wide smile on her glowing face. Bobby put two fingers in his mouth and whistled loudly; Paul clapped his hands together until they hurt.

A short while later, Hilary was singing a song to Schroeder, her heartthrob, while he played Beethoven's "Moonlight Sonata" and paid absolutely no attention to her. It was a comic moment, and all about Paul the audience began to laugh. Even Bobby, beside him, was laughing. But he found himself on the edge of tears. Jane, he thought. Jane should be here to share the pride he felt at this moment.

It wasn't until the second act that Paul could lose himself in the play. Hilary was Lucy to the life, her crabby voice, her sneering yet cheery contempt for poor Charlie Brown. She was giving a wonderful performance, doing more than holding her own against the others in the cast. In Paul's eyes she was the best performer on the stage, and her voice was pleasant and strong.

After the finale, and prolonged applause from the audience, Mr. Bodian, a tall man with a trim chestnut beard, was brought out for his bow. Onstage, Hilary had found Paul and Bobby. She winked at them. Paul found himself grinning in return.

Taking their coats, Paul and Bobby made their way through the side door and into a corridor that led backstage. They found a large classroom rapidly filling with friends and parents, a crowd of performers and stage crew milling about, laughing and shouting. A table was set up under a blackboard and on it were large bottles of Coke and paper cups. When Paul caught sight of Hilary she was in the grasp of Eugene Bodian, who was hugging her. Holding Bobby's hand, for he was afraid of losing him in the crush, Paul pushed his way to Hilary. She kissed his cheek, squeezed Bobby, and introduced both of them to Mr. Bodian. "Wasn't she just perfect?" the bearded teacher said. "My angel."

Hilary's face wore a permanent grin. "I'm going to marry him," she said to Paul, indicating Gene Bodian with a toss of her head.

"What about Peter?" Bobby asked.

"I'll marry him, too!" Hilary said, laughing.

"Not until next Friday, please," Bodian said. "First, four more perfect performances."

Hilary took a large slug of soda. "Peter!" she suddenly shouted as she caught sight of her boyfriend across the room. Then she was gone in the crowd.

"What a girl," Bodian said, wagging his bearded head. "Pure delight. And she has the makings of a damn fine actress, too."

"Thank you," Paul said. "You did a good job. All the kids were great."

"I knew your Jane," Bodian said. "Years ago, my God, in another life it seems. When I was working out of the board of ed. We served on a curriculum-enrichment committee for a couple of years, when the city had money for that. Hilary reminds me of her. Her eyes, I think, and when she smiles. She has Jane's dedication, too.''

"Sometimes," Paul said.

"Don't worry about Hilary," Bodian said, putting a hand on Paul's shoulder. "Have you thought about college for her yet?"

"No, not really. She still has a year of high school left."

Bodian smiled through his beard. "You'll be surprised how fast it goes. I'd like to see Hilary in a good school, someplace she'd be challenged. She's a kid with a lot of potential, a good writer, an excellent math student, too. She could go either way, sciences or humanities."

Hilary in a science lab, among test tubes and beakers? Paul was surprised by the thought, grinning inwardly as he pictured a staff of clean-cut, white-coated scientists gathered about his daughter, who would be wearing a stained and torn lab coat missing a button. "I wish she dressed better," he found himself confessing.

Bodian laughed. "She *is* slightly off the wall in the clothes department. All part of her personality, I suppose. Still, you ought to count your blessings. She's not a druggy, or a punk-rock freak. And she's as honest as they come."

"Sometimes *too* honest," Bobby said.

"She can be a real pain, eh?" Bodian asked the boy.

Bobby nodded. "Sometimes."

"I know what you mean," the teacher said. He shook Paul's hand. "I have to circulate," he said. "Harvard, Yale, Columbia . . . Hilary could go to any one of those schools. She's special, you know."

"I'll think about it. And thanks."

Bodian pushed off through the crowd, looking for cast members and their parents. Paul took Bobby's hand and started searching for Hilary. They found her in a corner of the room with Peter Block and his parents.

"Here's my daddy!" Hilary announced, as if the Blocks had never met Paul before.

"They were all wonderful," Mimi Block said. "Your girl especially."

"Thank you."

Mrs. Block drew Paul aside, leading him a few steps away in the crush. She was a heavy-set woman, wearing a dark mink coat and a fur hat. Paul had only a nodding acquaintance with her, from local parties and meetings they'd attended. "So are you the father of the bride?" she said to him, smiling. "Our kids seem to be crazy about each other."

"A little too much, perhaps," Paul said.

"Who can stop them? Peter doesn't make a move without consulting Hilary. I have to tell you, she's been very good for him. He's cleaned up his act a lot."

Paul nodded, half smiling. He couldn't think of a way to reply.

"Let me ask you something," Mimi Block said. "Have you forbidden Hilary to have dinner at my house?"

"Forbidden? No, not at all."

Mimi Block nodded to herself, pursing her lips. "You know, I've asked her to join us a hundred times, but she always refuses. She says you want her to be home, with you and Bobby, that it's one of your rules. That's why I haven't pushed."

Paul was touched at Hilary's sense of duty and loyalty. "I didn't know anything about it," he said, "honestly."

"I think it would be nice for her to have dinner with us once in a while. Hilary's such a delight to have around. And I'd keep an eye on them, of course."

"I'd have no objections," Paul said.

"Good." She smiled at him in a questioning way. "And how about you? How are you getting along?"

"Fine," Paul said.

"You could have dinner with us, too, you know. Any time you like."

"Thank you, that's very kind."

"Are you seeing people yet?" There was a light in her eye that was puzzling, almost a glint of invitation.

"Seeing who?"

"Women, I mean. Are you dating?"

Oh, God. Now he knew what this woman, whom he barely knew, was driving at. "No," he said.

"You should start looking, you know. You're a very handsome man. I'm sure you'll find plenty of women out there."

"Sometime maybe, not now."

"Did you know that Saul is my second husband? That's why I

feel I can talk to you this way. I also lost a mate. Of course, we were married only a short time, three years. Believe me, the faster you put yourself back on the market, the better off you'll be."

On the market? Paul felt a spark of anger. What was he, a piece of meat, a used car? "Not yet," he said in a controlled way, feeling trapped by the crush of the crowd and this pushy woman whom he did not want to offend.

"Whenever you're ready," Mrs. Block said. "I have a cousin, a lovely woman, recently widowed with a ten-year-old boy. I'll have the both of you to dinner. Either with the kids or without, whatever you say."

What a nervy bore of a mink-clad *yenta* she was. If anything could make Paul think better of Peter Block, it was understanding what the kid's mother was like. Somehow, Peter had survived her. The boy was a miracle, no question.

"Don't underestimate sex," Mimi Block said, nodding sagely. "It happens to be a very important part of life." Leaning forward to whisper she added, "Especially for a man."

He wanted to laugh, but checked himself. What if he ripped the mink coat off this butterball and had her right here on the floor? Sex is important, baby, especially for a man. Couldn't help myself, sex-starved widower confesses after high-school orgy. *National Enquirer* please copy. "I've got to go," Paul said, turning.

"You think about it," said Mimi Block. "My cousin's available. Any time."

Paul fought his way back to Hilary, who was hugging another girl from the show. "We're going out to celebrate opening night, Dad, all the cast members. I'll get a lift home. Okay?"

"Not too late now," he said, "there's school tomorrow." When Hilary broke away from her friend, he hugged her himself. "You were sensational," he told her. She kissed his cheek.

Halfway home in the car with Bobby, he felt compelled to start a conversation with the silent boy. He reached out and squeezed Bobby's arm. "Great show, wasn't it?"

Bobby shrugged. "Okay," he said.

"I thought they did it well."

"Fair," Bobby said.

"But Hilary was wonderful, wasn't she?"

"Actually, I've seen her do it better at home."

Paul laughed, which made Bobby turn to stare at him.

"What's so funny?"

"Nothing. You're a helluva critic, you know."

"Well, I'll say this about it. It was okay, but not as funny as *M*A*S*H.*"

11

THE 727 JINKED in the sky over Staten Island and turned north, heading up the Hudson River past an illuminated Manhattan that looked like an architect's model. Somewhere out there, past the dark green of the park, was home. Thirteen days on the road. Chicago and Minneapolis. Good hard work that had paid off, fences mended, Paul was back in the swing again. What's more, he'd enjoyed it. Away from home, working hard, the fears and problems fading with distance.

He couldn't wait to see the kids.

On the telephone they'd sounded fine, managing like a pair of troupers with help from Gemma, and with Phyllis Berg poking her pretty nose in once in a while. Phyllis had given them dinner three times, Gemma had cooked things and left them, and Marion Gerber, true to her word, had the kids over not once but twice. And Hilary had managed in the morning, getting them both off to school with a minimum of grousing from Bobby.

* * *

The house was waiting for him when he returned. The taxi driver came into the neighborhood through the broad avenue of Albemarle Road with its center island mall of trees and plantings. The tulips had broken ground in the round flower circles, and the forsythia had begun to turn yellow. The lights were on, golden against the dusk. When he rang the doorbell, the kids came jumping downstairs in a pounding rush. He kissed Hilary and then Bobby, the boy all but leaping on to his neck in his excitement. "Good heavens," Paul said. "I'll have to go away more often if this is the greeting I get."

They'd waited dinner for him, all of it prepared with their own hands. He sat at the head of the table, a king returned from the wars, while they served him. Later they helped Paul unpack his bags, chattering away happily, and after he had tucked Bobby into bed, he had time for a private conversation with Hilary. She was concerned about her brother. "He goes into a funk, sometimes," she said, "and he was weird when you were away."

"Weird how?"

"He cried a few times, alone in his room."

"He's been that way right along, babe."

"I know," the girl said. "But it seems to be getting worse, not better. A couple of times he couldn't sleep. I heard him going downstairs to watch TV. That's not normal, Dad."

Later, alone in the quiet kitchen, he settled down to handling two weeks' worth of mail. He sorted bills, threw away the huge assortment of junk mail, and looked through two seed catalogs addressed to Jane. He'd have to get to the garden soon, making order of the matted brown jungle out there. One of the catalogs he leafed through had page after page of tomatoes. Which ones had Jane always bought? Big Boys? Supersonics? Myron the Maven, down the street, would know. And if Paul couldn't recreate the garden exactly the way Jane would, perhaps he would come close.

Alone in the big bed, her pillow tucked against his chest, he drifted into a dream-filled sleep. He stood at the end of a long and dark subway platform, waiting for Jane. Far off down the black tunnel came the noise of a train approaching. Where was Jane? Why was she late? Why was there not another person on this subway platform? The rumble of the approaching train filled the cavern with noise. Far away he saw a pair of legs coming down the stairs, then a skirt, Jane's tweed skirt he loved so much; then he saw that it was Jane but she looked so different, wearing sunglasses in this dark subway station. He called out to her, but the rushing roaring noise of the train drowned out his voice. *"Jane!"* She walked to the edge of the platform, hands extended like a blind person, as if she could not see. *"Jane!"* The train was entering the station, headlights gleaming bright, the noise growing in volume, Jane on the very edge of the platform. He saw himself begin to run toward her, saw her teetering on the edge of the drop to the tracks; he was screaming now, *"Jane! Stop!"* as the train rushed toward her, the rumble and roar pounding in his ears.

A dream.

He sat up in bed, staring at the blackness. Somewhere in the house there was a metallic rumble. Not the low rumble of a subway train passing in the night; the noise was in the house, upstairs in one of the small rooms on the third floor.

The hallway was black, the doors to the children's rooms closed. A glow came from the hallway light on the top floor. Slowly, Paul went up the stairs, the noise growing louder. On the top-floor landing he saw that the light was on in the small room directly above his bedroom. The train room. The small room where long ago Paul had created a model railroad of H-O trains on a big plywood board for Bobby.

The boy sat cross-legged on the floor in his pajamas, the controls before him. The freight train rounded a curve and crossed over to the inside track. The dim overhead light made dark circles under Bobby's eyes.

"Bob-o."

"I couldn't sleep."

"I see that. Babe, it's the middle of the night."

"I know," the boy said.

Paul felt a chill on his feet; there was no heat on the top floor. Bobby brought the freight train to a halt, began backing it up to the crossing.

"How long have you been here? It's cold. You ought to have socks on, a robe."

"I'm not cold." When the small Union Pacific freight cleared the crossing, the boy switched it to the curving outer track. Paul watched, saying nothing. "There's no school tomorrow," Bobby said. "I can sleep all day if I want to. And all day Sunday, too."

"But you won't," Paul said. "Listen, chum, how about we go down to the kitchen and I'll make you some warm milk. It might help you fall asleep."

"I hate warm milk."

"Right. Some cocoa then? How about we both have a cup of cocoa?"

Bobby shrugged, concentrating on the train which he now sent along the outer track at an ever-increasing speed. Once, then twice, the train circled the outer perimeter of the eight-foot-square board. "You never painted the board," Bobby said. "Remember when we put it together? How you were going to paint the board green and then we were going to make a station, and add a siding, and get those little trees and houses and stuff? You never did that, like you said."

"I'm sorry."

"I kept asking you and you kept saying you would, but you never did. It's just the way we put it together when we first got the trains. For my eighth birthday. And we never got that car with the logs on it, either."

"I kept forgetting," Paul said. "And then you stopped playing with it."

"Yeah," Bobby said. He brought the train to a halt. "Trains are stupid anyway. They just go around and around."

"Bob-o, I think you should try to sleep. Just tuck in and close your eyes and give it a try."

The boy shrugged, sitting and staring at the train for a long while. Then he switched the power off but did not get up. "She really loved me, didn't she?" he said in a low voice.

"Mom? Of course she did. From the minute you were born."

"Was I sick a lot when I was a baby?"

"Some, yes. Well, maybe a lot. There was some trouble with your formula, I remember. We kept switching it around. You had lots of bellyaches, and croup, and you had trouble with your ears. She walked the floor plenty with you, and so did I. But she loved you, even when you were sick."

"She went back to work though, didn't she? When I was little?"

"Subbing, yes, not every day. Then the next fall full-time."

"And how long did she stay home with Hilary?"

"Longer. But Hilary was the first. By the time you were born, we knew a lot more."

"And Margaret took care of me when Mom worked, right? And she watched Hilary, too."

"Yes. And Grandma came over a lot in those days, too."

"What happened to Margaret?"

"She moved to Pennsylvania. You were five then, almost ready for school."

"I remember being home alone. Mom was in school and I was watching cartoons."

"We *never* left you alone, Bob."

"But I *remember* being in the house alone. No one was here and I was in the living room watching TV."

"Perhaps you're mixing it up with something that happened later, when you were older."

"No. I was alone."

"We never left you alone, not once. Margaret was here, or Grandma, or Mom. Maybe you're remembering a moment when Margaret was upstairs or on the porch, or something like that."

The smile on Bobby's face made Paul go cold. It looked somehow cunning and wise, a mask that isolated him from his father. "I'm not wrong. I was alone." The boy stood up and stretched his arms, yawning. "I'll try to sleep now," he said, "I think I feel tired."

Paul followed Bobby down the stairs, switching lights off behind them. He tucked the blanket in tight, then ruffled the boy's hair. Even in the dim glow of the night light, he could see the flicker of Bobby's eyelashes. "She loved you very much, Bob-o," Paul said. "She always loved you."

Now sleep, kiddo, go ahead, I dare you.

He sat up smoking in the club chair, listening as the boy tossed in his bed, Bobby's arm or knee thumping against the wall. Hilary had always been easy, Bobby the one they worried about. Even now that had not changed. Second-born, the boy had fought for attention, including those summers when Hilary had been away in camp and Bobby was the only child in the house.

Did the boy really think that Jane loved Hilary more? How could he? Bobby had always been Jane's baby, the one she specially nurtured and looked after, the little boy she loved to make laugh. More serious than his big sister, afraid of all the little things Hilary had taken in stride, Bobby had walked later than Hilary, began speaking later, and even now insisted on a night light in his room.

After four o'clock, Paul got into bed. Mercifully, sleep came fast.

On Sunday, Phyllis Berg stopped by to invite them all to dinner on the following Friday evening. "You're always having us," Paul said. "I'm beginning to feel like a boarder."

"Don't worry about it."

"Someday we'll invite you back."

"Whatever," Phyllis said. "I'm also inviting a friend who works with Dave, I hope you don't mind."

"Why should I mind?" Paul shrugged.

"She's a radiologist. Single."

"Fine."

"I don't want you to think I'm matchmaking, Paul."

"Aren't you?" he twitted her.

"No." Behind the owl glasses, Phyllis's eyes went myopic. "Well, maybe I am, a little. She's a terrific gal. You're sure you don't mind?"

"Not as long as you don't make stuffed cabbage."

Alice Freed was in her early thirties, quietly attractive, with a cropped head of prematurely gray hair. She'd seen half the world, it seemed, traveling on the cheap and mostly by herself. Medicine, travel, and racquetball were what she wanted to talk about, and when for a time the children at the table took over the conversation, her lack of interest showed all too clearly. A curtain came down for Paul. She ceased being as attractive as she had been before. Love me, love my kids, he thought to himself as they chatted over coffee; they were a package deal. And they did not come as cheap as the week on the Costa del Sol Alice Freed would soon be off to.

Later, after seeing the children into the house, Paul drove Alice home. They had little to say to each other, speaking mostly about Phyllis and Dave Berg and how sweet they were. At her door, Alice sat for a moment before getting out of the Buick. "Lovely meeting you," she said.

"Same here," he lied. "Have a nice time on your trip."

"Thank you. Perhaps, when I get back, we can get together. Would you like to try racquetball?"

"Perhaps."

She opened the car door and got out, waving good night. He watched until she safely entered the door of her brownstone, feeling somehow sad. No chemistry. Not a spark of interest. He hoped she wouldn't send him a postcard from Spain.

The children had cleared the dishes from Marion Gerber's elegant oak dining table and had gone upstairs. Marion's girls, Susie and Joy, were younger than Hilary and doted on her. "More coffee?" Marion asked.

"Love it, thanks." Paul settled back in his chair and watched Marion go to the kitchen. It was a handsome dining room, built in an unusual oval shape with crosshatched oak beams across the ceiling. Years ago, when Phil was still living here, he and Jane had come to many dinner parties in this room. Marion and Phil had been one of the couples in the neighborhood theater-party, dinner-party, fund-raising P.T.A. group. Jane and Marion had been friendly, not close but chummy, and Jane had taught two of Marion's four kids in the local school. Husband Phil had always been a bore, a nasty cynical accountant, and when Marion had finally chased him from their home, not many in the neighborhood had been surprised. Jane had even tried matchmaking on Marion's behalf, inviting her to dinner on several occasions to meet eligible men.

Marion came back from the kitchen and poured coffee from a carafe. Poor Marion, Paul thought, as she lit her tenth after-dinner cigarette. There was something so sad in her small brown eyes, a perpetual hangdog expression. She'd gone blond some time after the divorce but she didn't look as if she was having more fun. "The kids look fine," she said to him. "You should go away more often."

"Confession time," he said. "I enjoyed it."

"Why not? It's allowed."

"I took clients to fancy restaurants, drank too much, ate too much, and all in all had a good time. Thanks for having the kids over to dinner." Marion made a gesture of dismissal. "We're hanging together," he went on. "Still some problems but we're healing, I think. And how are you doing, Marion?"

"Shitty, now that you ask," she said with a mirthless smile. "Phil's being an absolute bastard about the support payments, falling behind, making me call my lawyer and actually go into court a few times. In the end he always pays, but not before he's ground my guts a little. But why should I be surprised? He was always a bastard at home, too."

"You're well rid of him," Paul said.

"You're telling me. He had a nasty little hobby, Phil did. He liked to screw young girls." She stubbed out her cigarette in the littered ashtray. "Some men collect stamps. Phil collected teeny-boppers. When I think of how long it took me to catch on . . . God, what an idiot I was."

"Are you seeing anyone in particular?" Paul asked.

"Not at the moment," she said. "I had a thing with a very nice guy, but . . ." She paused to light another cigarette. "And how about you, Paul? Are you dating?"

"Me? God, no."

"You should start thinking about it, you know."

"Oh, I *think* about it, but that's about all. It scares me, Marion. I don't think I'd know what to do on a date."

Marion smiled. "You'll be surprised how it all comes back, Paul. The first time I dated, after Phil, almost a disaster. The poor guy took me back to his apartment and when we got into bed I began to weep like a maniac. Har!" Marion's laugh sounded like a bark. "But it gets better. You'll get married again, I'm sure of it."

Paul felt the bitter edge of anger begin. He took a sip of coffee to mask it. "Why do you say that?" he asked.

"Statistics, Paul. There are a helluva lot more of me out there than you. Plus you're good-looking, charming, and a pretty nice guy. And living alone with kids isn't easy, as you already know. You'll be surprised at how many women will be coming after you."

"Not so far."

"Listen, some advice. Let your friends know you're available, that's important. And there's a group called Parents Without Partners. You could try them."

"Have you?"

"Yes."

"And?"

"I met a few nice men with children and we sat around talking about our kids' problems. I think I finally decided I had enough problems with my own kids, I didn't need any others."

"I don't think I'm there yet," Paul said. "No black book anymore. Not for eighteen years."

"Listen," Marion said. "I've been thinking about you. No," she added, seeing the look on his face, "don't get excited, not that way. But I do think that we're both parents alone, we know each other, living only two blocks away, and we could become friends. Without lovey-dovey stuff, Paul, I mean that. But we could see a movie once in a while, or have dinner . . . without the kids. No strings, just as friends."

"I don't know," Paul said.

"Look, I'm too old for you by six or seven years, so don't worry about that. And God knows I'm not sexy enough by half."

"Marion," he interrupted, "you're still a good-looking woman."

"Har! You think about it, Paul. I'd like to have you as a friend."

"Thanks," Paul said. "I'll think about it."

Hilary's seventeenth birthday. Paul took the kids out to dinner to celebrate, and as a special favor to Hilary invited Peter Block to join them. Hilary picked the place, a cheap Indian restaurant in Greenwich Village where she and Peter had often dined before going to concerts and movies. "But we always have the two-dollar special," she explained. "Tonight we can splurge." To please Paul, Hilary had worn a skirt and blouse. She looked very grown-up, much more mature than Peter in his blazer with the too-short sleeves. The restaurant smelled sharply of cheap deodorant and strange spices. Paul suffered along with Bobby, the two of them filling up on exotic breads because the dishes Hilary ordered for them were alternately hot, pungent, or covered with a spicy grease.

He gave Hilary the ten-speed bicycle she had been hinting about and a cashmere sweater from Bloomingdale's. Bobby gave her a box of chocolates which the two of them devoured almost instantly. The last present for Hilary arrived one afternoon a week later. When Paul came home that evening, Hilary was down the stairs in a flash and hugging him. "What a sweetie you are!" she exclaimed, taking him by the hand and dragging him upstairs to her room. The telephone was baby blue: "A Princess to match my princess," he said, smiling.

"But you haven't seen the best part," she said. Behind her wicker nightstand, where the telephone had been installed, Paul saw what looked like a mile of flat telephone cord. "Watch this," Hilary said, picking up the phone and marching the fifteen feet from her nightstand and out into the hall. "Follow me." He followed, she marched ten feet down the hall to the kids' bathroom door. "I had the telephone man put it in. It doesn't cost anything extra."

"How long is that cord?"

"Aha!" Grinning, she disappeared into the bathroom. When he looked, she was sitting on the pot, telephone to her ear. "Isn't that terrific? I get some of my best ideas in here."

Later that evening he was not laughing.

"I've made an appointment," Hilary told him when he came into her room to say good night. She was wearing a pair of old flannel pajamas, sitting cross-legged on her bed, her long hair still wet from the shower. "Planned Parenthood, this Thursday afternoon."

He sank into a chair.

"I wanted to let you know, Daddy."

"Of course," he said.

"I'm seventeen now," she said. "You asked me to wait and I did."

"And I thank you for that," he said. They looked at each other for a long moment, neither knowing what to say.

"I've saved my allowance," the girl said. "I can pay for it myself."

"I'll pay for it," Paul said. He cleared a frog from his throat. "How much is it?"

"About thirty-five dollars . . . for the examination and the . . . the things."

"I'll give you a check," he said.

"Thank you." She smiled briefly, her head erect on her beautiful swan neck, his little girl who looked at him with such womanly dignity. "I love you, Daddy," she said.

"I know that, sugar."

"I'll be very careful," she said.

"I know you will." His throat was heavy again. He felt he had to say something, to give her advice, but the words seemed elusive. "This is very difficult for me," he said. "Damn, I wish your mother were here."

"We talked about this a couple of times, Mom and me. Years ago."

"Good. I'm glad."

"I don't plan on being promiscuous. Or cheap."

"No, you're too special for that." He smiled at her. "I keep thinking I ought to make a speech, but maybe I don't know how. My code is from my time. But I do remember what we boys used to think of girls who were easy, who had a reputation, and I don't think that part of it has changed. Just remember who you are, sugar, what you came from. Remember your own worth, the kind of woman I hope you'll grow up to be. Don't ever do anything you don't want to, that doesn't seem natural, that scares you. You have a lot of good sense. And I trust you to use it."

"I will."

He got out of the chair and went to her. Leaning down, he kissed her cheek and was surprised by a hug from Hilary that was fierce and lasting.

Later that night, before he fell asleep, he wondered: Was it the last hug of childhood?

He had the feeling that time was speeding up, events coming one on top of another through the spring. Last July the hands of the clock had frozen in place, turning days into weeks, each moment an agony to struggle through somehow. Now the days went speeding swiftly by.

Down in Fort Lauderdale, Jane's mother was feeling better. Sylvia called each weekend, at the cheap telephone rates, saying hello to Paul and speaking to the kids. One Saturday, after speaking to Hilary at length, Sylvia called him back to the telephone. "What are you doing about the unveiling?" she asked. "What's the date, I want to come in for it."

Paul was taken aback. It was one subject he'd avoided thinking about and now, thanks to Sylvia, it was upon him. "No unveiling," he said without thinking.

Sylvia was shocked. "You have to have an unveiling, Paul. It's expected, it's tradition."

"Send out invitations?" he rasped. "Invite friends? Have it catered, perhaps? *No.*" He'd been to too many in his lifetime. One year after the death of a loved one, family and friends gathered in the cemetery; black cloth was draped around the headstone, a rabbi none of the bereaved had ever met before or would meet again intoned some Hebrew words, the cloth was undraped, revealing the words carved on the stone and into the hearts of the mourners. Then, to show you had been there, you put a pebble on the headstone and went away. No, there would be no unveiling for Jane, no public ceremony. He'd been to the cemetery once this winter alone; the headstone was already in place and carved, "Jane Klein, Beloved Wife." Cold and freezing in the rain he'd stood there and wept. No, no unveiling.

"You must," Sylvia insisted from sunny Florida, "for her friends, for the family. Show some respect, Paul."

Respect.

The black cloud of grief he'd fought off stood once more over his head. Outside the bedroom window a jay screamed in the pine tree. "Sylvia, no. We're not going to go through all that. Not me, and especially not the kids."

Sylvia had begun to cry. "So fast you want to forget? So fast?"

"Don't ever say that!" he shouted into the phone.

She called again the following day. To mollify her, he promised to take the children to the cemetery one day, but there would be no formal ceremony. As a peace offering to Sylvia, he put Hilary and Bobby on a plane to Florida in late April, at the beginning of their spring school vacation. They'd spend a week in her condo in the sun, splashing in the pool, being shown off to Sylvia's friends, ultimately being bored and glad to come home.

Paul took the opportunity to slip off to Cleveland for two days, working with his salesman there. When he came home, he called Marion Gerber and asked her out to see a movie that was playing in the neighborhood. Afterward they had coffee in a local diner. Marion talked about the film for a while, then turned the conversation to her ex-husband. Her supply of venom toward Phil was inexhaustible. "Two kids we had to save our marriage, would you believe? Susie and Joy. But at least I've got them. That's my generation, you know, stick together no matter what. Dumb as a door post."

Driving home in the Buick, she carried on the diatribe, telling Paul details of their married life he had no wish to hear. When he pulled up in front of her house, she was still talking. Paul put a hand on her arm to stop her, saying, "Marion, good night." In reply she clasped his head with both hands and gave him a fervent closed-mouth kiss.

"Hello," he said. "What was that?"

"I don't know," she said. "Just a feeling."

"Helluva feeling." He looked at her in the half-dark of the streetlight, suddenly worried that a neighbor would walk by and see them.

"You're a good man," she said. "I like talking to you. You listen." She got out of the car then, walking around to his window to say good night. "Forget I did that," she said before turning away.

Fat chance.

A week later, with the kids back from Florida and settled once more into their school routine, he called Marion and invited her out to dinner. Alone. Not kidding himself, he knew what was on his mind. Seduction, plain and simple. That Marion had somehow announced she was available was plain, but it did not turn out to be so simple.

They ate seafood in a noisy barn of a restaurant down by the bay. Marion had dressed colorfully though casually for the occasion, eschewing her usual basic black. And for once, thank heaven, she forgot about Phil, chattering away happily about her kids and passing on neighborhood gossip. Afterward he drove the Buick to a quiet street that fronted the water. When he shut off the motor and turned to her, she was in his arms.

Like schoolkids they necked chastely, no hands, no groping. Coming up for air, Marion lit a cigarette. They both looked at the lights dancing on the water. Finally, Marion spoke. "Do you feel funny about this?"

"Yes, a little."

126

"So do I."

"It's almost . . . incestuous," Paul said. "We've known each other a long time, Marion."

"You're Jane's husband," Marion said, "that's how I still think of you. And Jane was my friend."

"And I think of you sitting and drinking coffee with Jane in the kitchen. The lady who ran the bake sale. And had to put up with Phil. He was such a didactic, boring son of a bitch. God! I always avoided him at parties, you know."

Marion giggled nervously. She lit another cigarette. "So what do you want to do?" she asked.

"I don't know, Marty," he cracked, "what do you want to do?"

"The situation is kind of ridiculous," she said. "I'm too old to neck in a car."

"Same here," Paul said, laughing. "A hotel?"

"Oh, God! That's too scary," Marion said. "Besides, I told the kids I'd be home by eleven."

"And I don't have any idea of a hotel to go to, anyway."

"And I have to be up at seven to get the girls off to school."

He drove Marion home.

On Sunday Marion invited him for brunch without the kids. When he walked in and found Marion's girls were off visiting their father for the day, he got the idea.

She fed him bagels and lox, eating almost nothing herself. Smoking nonstop, Marion sipped coffee, giving off an aura of nerves more than desire. Watching her, Paul thought her sad eyes could shed tears at any moment. "Relax," he said, "you look like a scared bird about to take off." He took her hand in his and squeezed it gently.

"I don't know why I'm so nervous," she said.

"We could forget about it, Marion. I can go home . . ."

"No, no," she said, gamely smiling. "It's why I invited you here."

"I'm the one who should be nervous," he said. "It's been a long time for me."

"It's like riding a bicycle, you don't forget." She stubbed her cigarette out in the ashtray and took Paul's hand. "All right, come on then."

In Paul's ears, it sounded like "Let's get it over with." He followed her up the stairs, one hand on her waist. When would desire come, he wondered? Perhaps daylight was a mistake. He saw the crow's feet around her eyes so clearly, the brown roots under her bleached blond hair. Perhaps it was he, not Marion. Maybe he wouldn't be able to perform, she'd be disappointed in him, laugh at him. *Coraggio!*

At the door to her pink bedroom she turned to him. "Promise you won't laugh at me," she said.

"Marion, you're a lovely woman. I'd never laugh at you."

She kissed his temple. "I have very heavy thighs," she confessed, "and a fat little belly."

"I'll love them," he promised, wondering whether he would.

Leaving him standing in the doorway, she flitted off to the master bath, closing the door with such a bang it made Paul jump. He walked into the bedroom, a memory coming back to him of a dinner party when he'd come up here to leave his coat and Jane's on the bed. Jane's short camel coat with the furry collar. *Stop it!* His eyes went to the windows; even with closed venetian blinds and drawn curtains he still felt prying neighborhood eyes. What was he doing here and why? Getting laid, kimosabe, even nice people did it.

He undressed quickly and got under the bedclothes. He heard Marion flush the toilet in the bathroom. She was taking a long time. Had she changed her mind? Relax. Should he confess to her that she would be the only woman in eighteen years besides Jane, that he had always been faithful? What for? Do you want a medal? Mr. Marvelous, Old Faithful, what good did it do? Your wife still died.

The bathroom door opened, Marion's head appeared. "Would you turn around while I get in? Please?"

He looked away, hearing her quick footsteps on the carpet, wondering if what they were about to do was right or wrong.

They did it right, but it was wrong. Mechanical and joyless for both of them. And worse, they knew it. Afterward they lay beside each other, smoking cigarettes, Marion covered to the neck under the sheet, unwilling to let him see the body she had just surrendered. "I'm sorry," Paul said.

"Don't be. It was me."

"No report cards," Paul said, using Jane's old phrase for after-sex conversation. "I'm amazed it hadn't rusted and fallen off," he said.

"Har! You were fine. I just couldn't help thinking of Jane," Marion said. "This was a mistake."

"Yes."

Marion sighed, a puff of smoke rising in the air. "So much for my great plans," she said, finding his hand under the sheet and clasping it. "I had it all figured out. We'd get to be friends, lovers, neighborhood buddies. Your kids and mine would get along. And then . . ."

He smiled at her, seeing her plan clearly because it had occurred to him as well. "Thanks," he said, "it's the best offer I've had in a long time. But I don't think I'm ready. And after Jane, I don't know if any woman will ever measure up. Even someone as sweet as you are, Marion."

"The offer still goes," she said. "I'll be here."

"Who knows?" Paul said. "Maybe you'll meet someone."

"There's always hope. Look—I'm sorry if I led you on. Because I did, you know."

"Please. I'm grateful, Marion. It's just . . . well, we found out we weren't meant to be lovers, I guess."

"I guess not," she said soberly. "Har!" she barked, "the thing is, I hope this won't interfere with our friendship."

If anything, it brought them closer.

In the weeks and months that followed Paul could touch Marion, kiss her good night, give her a friendly hug without feeling constrained. They began to confide in each other, Marion about some of the men she was dating, Paul asking her advice about the kids. Marion had all the Kleins to dinner more often and Paul asked her girls along when he took Hilary and Bobby to a movie or a ball game.

Paul hadn't had lunch with his partner in almost six weeks. Freshly back from a tiring buying trip in Europe, Michael Bradie looked tanned, fit, and about to tell a joke. "So Goldberg and this Chinese fella are sitting at the bar, drinking and talking. When all of a sudden Goldberg hauls off and socks the Chinese guy right in the snoot, knocks him clean off the bar stool." Eyebrows dancing in delight, Michael paused to take a sip of his vodka gimlet. "The Chinese guy picks himself up, and says to Goldberg: 'What the hell was that for?' And Goldberg says: 'That was for Pearl Harbor.'

" 'Pearl Harbor?' the Chinese guy says. 'I'm *Chinese*, not Japanese!'

" 'Chinese, Japanese, what's the difference?' Goldberg says, and they go on drinking. A little while later, out of the clear blue, the Chinese guy hauls off and smacks Goldberg right in the chops, down he goes to the floor. Well, Goldberg gets up and he says to the Chinese guy: 'What'd you do that for?'

" 'That was for sinking the *Titanic*,' says the Chinese guy.

" 'The *Titanic!* That was sunk by an iceberg,' Goldberg says.

" 'Iceberg, *Gold*berg, *what's the difference?*' "

Paul laughed so loud some of the other diners looked in his direction. Michael's leprechaun face beamed. "*Boychick*," he said, "you look good. Did you miss me?"

"No."

"Same here," Michael grinned.

"Why do you look so tanned?"

"I sneaked a weekend in Marbella early in the trip, then later, from Turin, I hopped over to see my *paisanos* in Lake Como."

"Sounds better than sunny Cleveland."

"Work, work, work," Michael said, winking. After so many years together, Paul could see that Michael had good news to tell him. Knowing Michael's flair for the dramatic, he waited. With the coffee, and after lighting a cigar, Michael was ready. "I saved the best news for last. It seems that the firm of Bradie and Klein, Incorporated, is not exactly unknown on the other side of the pond. Word has gotten around, Paul, that we have a pretty solid organization. Let me tell you, it's a nice feeling to have people approach us, instead of always running around knocking on doors. A very nice feeling." Michael took a long pull on his cigar, looking pleased. "We're about to get into the big time, Paul."

"The Asti spumante deal came through?"

"That's one of them," Michael said, smiling, "and a sangria." He named the brands involved. "They're perfect for us. No conflicts with any of the lines we handle. Good products. Smart shippers, who've already been on television, and want to go that way even stronger.''

"Television advertising," Paul said, "like the big boys."

"That's right. The sangria in the summer, the spumante in the fall and around the holidays. And every TV commercial is going to say, 'Imported by Bradie and Klein.' Which is going to make our distributors and our salesmen very, very happy. It's volume business, like we've always wanted, and it just fell into our lap.''

"Mike, that's fantastic."

"No more than we deserve. Remember, they came to us. Because they know what kind of a job we can do. We're about to get very big, and without working a helluva lot harder. How about that?''

Paul reached across the table to shake hands with Michael, holding his hand in a firm grip. "I love it, Mike."

"Here's to us," Michael said, raising his coffee cup in a toast. "So, marketing man, time to get on your horse. We need an advertising agency, and fast. Good commercials, not like the ones they've been doing up to now, running in good places and at the right time. Do you know anything about choosing an ad agency?''

"No," Paul said. "But it sure sounds like fun."

12

SPRING HURT.

Full spring now with hot sunny days and balmy evenings, azaleas shouting red and white through the neighborhood, yellow and white tulips tall and graceful and no one to see them with, remark upon, no hand-holding slow walks through the scented streets with Jane. He filled his days and nights as well as he could, but the center of him held the pain, the empty place.

He wanted to send the children away for the summer and he wanted them close by. He wanted others to see to them, care for them, and he would yield to no one in his desire to do this himself. He wanted freedom, a breathing space, and he desperately wanted their company. He wanted, he wanted . . .

Jane.

They did the garden at last, three of them now where once Jane alone had cleared, spaded, weeded, planted. Myron the Maven came and advised, going off to bring back flats of tomato plants, peppers, zucchini, eggplant. A damp cold spell killed off a number of the spindly plants, leaving gaps. Foolishly, Paul transplanted to fill in the rows, killing still more. Not Jane's garden anymore; he hated looking out on it from his kitchen chair, wondering what secret touch she had to make those tiny plants flourish.

His anodyne was work and now it blossomed, too.

People in the advertising business were crazy. When word got out that Paul was seeking the services of an agency, he was besieged. Phone calls, telegrams, letters came in a flood. Packages arrived bearing calling cards, agency brochures, proofs of ads. One day a messenger in a gorilla suit stood growling in front of Lillian Lerner's desk, demanding to see Paul. When Paul came rushing out in answer to her urgent summons, the gorilla launched into a song and dance to the effect that business was a jungle, but Gaffney, Furgang & Ross knew the territory better than anyone else. Paul and an astonished Lillian had a good laugh before throwing the gorilla out.

Michael had dumped the responsibility on him, saying only that he would like to meet with the agency Paul selected so he could give them the benefit of his expertise. Paul narrowed the number of agencies seeking permission to solicit his business down to ten. He had lunch meetings, breakfast meetings, trying to save the bulk of the day to conduct normal business. He shied away from the big agencies, recognizing that with less than two million dollars to spend on advertising, his account would be lost among the giants.

Paul winnowed out half the agencies seeking his business, then cut the list to a final three. It was amazing how much work these advertising people would do for nothing. He sat through elaborate presentations—"dog and pony shows," one adman called them—with charts and graphics and long-winded recitations of agency triumphs. One small shop actually produced a thirty-second color commercial on videotape, featuring the sangria. Paul was amazed that a business so small it employed only seven people would spend several thousand dollars just in the hope of gaining his account. It was a foolish, not to say *desperate*, gesture, and he crossed the agency off his list.

Of the three remaining, Paul had a warm feeling toward the agency called Golden/Chan. The principals of the shop were a Jewish copywriter and a Chinese-American art director. Their offices were in a modern office building just off Third Avenue, amply though simply furnished, and without the brassy knock-your-eye-out decoration he had seen up and down Madison Avenue. He met them first for breakfast, a no-nonsense coffee and Danish session.

"We don't believe in a lot of flash," Ruth Golden told him. "We're selling our brains, not breakfast." The Golden of Golden/Chan was a tall, shapely woman; in her mid-thirties, Paul judged. Miss Golden's hair was not golden but rather a dark blond, cut into bangs across her forehead and hanging straight to her shoulders. Her eyes were green, her coloring fair, and her generous mouth always seemed to be on the verge of a smile. She was easy to talk to, and when after an hour she reached for another half Danish, groaning that breakfast meetings always played hob with her diet, Paul felt sympathetic.

Her partner, George Chan, was a small, slight man with horn-rimmed glasses. He let Ruth Golden do almost all the talking for them, sipping coffee and listening while doodling on a sketchpad. Golden/Chan had been in business for only three years, and although they hadn't boomed like some agencies, they were doing well. "We believe in staying lean," Ruth Golden said, "although I personally can't seem to manage it." Paul counted twelve employees when they gave him a tour of their offices, and he liked the work they had done for their clients. It had a fresh, offbeat quality, but was solidly based on marketing realities and not just someone's idea of a joke.

A week later he met with Golden/Chan again, to hear their thinking on the Asti spumante and sangria advertising. They showed him only a few rough sketches of commercials they might do, nothing elaborate, but he responded well to their ideas. It made it more difficult when, a few days later, and having seen ideas from the other two agencies in competition for his account, he had to cross them off his list. His decision was based strictly on business. Golden/Chan was too small, had no experience in wines and spirits, had no marketing department to exchange ideas with, and their media department consisted of one bright young man only a few years out of college. Too bad. He liked Ruth Golden; she had a very sharp head on her shapely shoulders.

He called her to break the news.

"Always a bridesmaid," she sighed.

"I like your shop, though," Paul said. "I think you'll go far. But you're just not right for us."

"I understand," Ruth said. "I hate it, but I understand. We would have done a helluva job for you."

"I think so, too."

"Would you tell me exactly why you're turning us down? I think it would be helpful, especially for George, who tends to throw things against the wall when we lose a pitch. Sometimes *me.*"

Paul laughed, and explained about the marketing and the media departments, or rather the lack of them.

"Well, thanks for being honest," she said before hanging up. "It would have been fun to work with you."

Saturday morning he walked around the kitchen, making a shopping list. With the windows open he could hear the *pong* of a tennis ball banging against the front porch steps.

Paul went upstairs to take cash out of the book in the bedroom. As he passed Bobby's room, he saw the boy had not made his bed and his pajamas were on the floor, lying on top of a scattered group of cards from his Stratomatic baseball board game. He walked into the room. On the desk in the corner was a blue bound album, one of the six photo albums Jane had so scrupulously kept up to date. Paul turned the pages, coming to one that was blank. The notations were there: "Labor Day Barbecue," "Jane and Bobby," "Bergs' Backyard, 1975," "At the Beach, 1976"; but the photos had been removed.

Paul put on a light jacket and went outside. Bobby was still throwing the ball against the steps. "Shopping time," Paul said lightly.

"I'm not going."

"Okay," Paul said. He watched Bobby retrieve a ground ball. "How about lunch? Don't you want to have pizza at Guido's?"

The boy did not answer. He threw the ball again.

"Come on, chum. We always go shopping on Saturday and have pizza and stuff."

"I don't want to, okay?" Bobby said, his voice rising. "Why the hell don't you leave me alone!"

Even under the shade of his cap, Paul could see that Bobby's eyes were angry. He met the youngster's stare. "You didn't make your bed this morning. What's that about?"

"You don't really care if I make my bed," Bobby said. "Only Mom cared about that, not you. So I'm not making it anymore. It's stupid, anyway."

"It's not stupid," Paul said. "Your room looks like hell."

Across the street the Dawsons' front door opened. Pippy, their black poodle, came bounding out. He ran to Bobby and sniffed his sneakers.

"I want you to make your bed," Paul said.

"I heard you. And you want me to go shopping and behave myself and do what you say and be one big happy family. Shit!" Kneeling down, Bobby began to fondle the dog.

"Get in the house," Paul said. "Go on inside and clean up your room. And wait for me to come back from shopping."

Sullenly, Bobby retreated inside, turning back to stare into Paul's eyes. Paul hurried through the shopping, barely concentrating, worrying over what might come next if the child had turned to mutiny, and how could he handle it. By the time his weekly order was totaled, he had calmed down. He walked across the street to Guido's pizzeria. "Three slices to go, Guido," he said.

Guido wrapped the slices in paper. "Where's your boy?" he asked. "He's not sick or nothin'?"

"No. He's fine."

"Good." When Guido smiled, his thick moustache thinned across his pale face. "I set my clock by you guys," he said. "Every Saturday. I remember when he was little and your wife used to bring him in here. He's grown a lot."

"Yep. He's getting big."

Guido handed the package over the counter. "My son," Guido said, "fifteen now and he knows everything, you understand? Fresh kid. They get a certain age, they want to make it hard for the old man." He gave Paul his change. "Enjoy 'em while they're young and sweet. After that, you got nothin' but heartache."

Back in the house, Paul set out plates at Bobby's place and his own, setting a glass half-filled with ice cubes at the boy's. Bobby came into the kitchen and went silently to his chair.

"I brought us back some pizza," Paul said.

Bobby nodded.

"Guido says hello." Paul stared into the wall oven, waiting for the pizza to warm. "Did you clean up your room?"

Bobby let out a long sigh. "Yes." His voice was barely audible.

"Make your bed?"

"Yes."

They ate in silence, the air charged between them. A bee hummed on the window screen. "Do you want to talk about it?" Paul said at last.

"No."

"Bob-o, I can't stand this," Paul said. "I have to know that things are okay between us."

"I'm not mad at you," the boy said. "It's just—" He broke off, groping for words, frown lines across his small forehead. "I mean, what's the use of it? What's the point? We just go on doing the same stupid things day after day, week after week. I get up, I go to school, I come home, I go to sleep. On Saturday, I make my bed and go to the supermarket with you. It's all just so . . . stupid."

"It's called living, babe, how we get from day to day."

"But why?"

"Because," Paul said, "because that's the way it is. Because we're trying to get through a bad time, all of us. Because we're lonely now, and hurt."

"Hilary's not lonely," Bobby said, a bitter edge to his voice. "And neither are you."

"How do you know how lonely we are? Maybe we show it less than you do."

"I know," the boy said. "Don't think I don't know."

"If you think we've forgotten your mother, you're wrong."

Bobby's small mouth held a thin smirk. "Maybe."

"And while we're at it, I saw that some pictures were missing from one of the photo albums. Do you have them?"

Bobby looked at Paul, then out the window. One hand played with the edge of the cloth place mat, rolling, unrolling, then smoothing it down again. "They're in my pocket."

Outside the window a dove swooped down and lighted on the basketball hoop. "You carry them around with you?"

To Paul's eyes, the boy looked on the edge of tears. He remembered one of the snapshots now in Bobby's pocket; he'd taken that one as he'd taken most of them on the beach that day, Jane kneeling down on the sand, her arms around the boy in swimming trunks and a Mickey Mouse sweatshirt, her eyes hidden behind sunglasses and Bobby's eyes squinting in the sun, Jane's brilliant smile lighting her face with tenderness as she hugged the boy.

"I look at them sometimes," Bobby said. "In school. Sometimes before I go to sleep."

"That's okay," Paul said.

"I won't hurt them, really. I keep them in my train-pass case, so they won't get crushed."

"Good."

"You don't mind, do you?" The anxiety on the boy's face made Paul's breath catch. "I don't have to put them back in the album, do I?"

"No," Paul said. "It's all right."

"Good."

Steady, kimosabe, do not start bawling. "She loved you a lot, Bob-o. A lot."

"But not as much as I loved her," the boy said.

The trouble was, now that there were only two agencies left in the race for his account, Paul found it difficult to make a choice. He wrestled with the problem, aware that time was passing and the need was immediate. Michael listened sympathetically, then suggested he flip a coin. "Either sounds fine with me, so pick one."

Paul had a better idea. He telephoned Ruth Golden.

"Don't tell me," she said, "we're back in the running."

"No."

"The other agencies turned you down, fat chance, and now you're coming crawling and begging back to us."

"No," he said, "I need help," and then explained why. "It's Tweedledum and Tweedledee, you see. Can we discuss it? Will you help me?"

"Why should I help you?" she asked. "You've just killed our Christmas bonus."

"Because I'm a nice fella and you're nice, too. Besides being much smarter than I am."

"I noticed that, too," she teased.

"Can I buy you lunch today?"

"I usually eat at my desk. We're too busy for long lunch hours. Can I order up a sandwich for you?"

"I'm too rich to eat sandwiches," Paul said, making Ruth laugh. "How about Madrigal? It's nearby."

"Oh, God! You know what that place does to a waistline? Just touching the menu puts on three pounds."

"How about Italian food? Giambelli is near you."

"That's worse," she said. "Wait a minute. There's a health-food place just up the street. We can be in and out in under an hour."

Ruth was waiting outside the restaurant—her head tilted back, enjoying the sun—when he lighted from his cab. "The outside world," she said. "I haven't seen it much lately. George usually keeps me chained to my desk."

Standing side by side, Paul was surprised by how tall she was. Almost eye to eye with him in her heels. She was wearing denim jeans and a green silk blouse, a long rope of pearls about her neck. "I'm not exactly dressed for Madrigal, as you can see," she said, leading him inside. They stood in a line of people that passed slowly in front of a long counter. "You pick the things you want," she explained, "then they bring them to your table. Great salads, soups, and the bread is exceptional." She selected a large salad and dark bread, and Paul did the same.

When they had been seated, the food placed before them, Ruth broke a piece of bread in half. "First of all," she said, "let me tell you I think you have a helluva nerve doing this. I'm really sore."

"I'm sorry."

"The hell with that. Look, if I'm smart enough to help you choose an agency, I'm smart enough to do your advertising."

"I told you the reasons why I was turning down your shop."

"Yes, I heard them, and I even believe you mean it. But you're wrong. You're an expert in the wine business, who could know it better than you do? You don't need some muckymuck marketing guy with a Ph.D. in being a grind to go out and bring back answers you already know. With your knowledge and my brains, we could really sell some wine."

"I thought we'd settled this," Paul said.

"And I thought, have lunch with the guy, it's another chance to change his mind. Look, let me tell you about our media man. He's

139

young, but he's terrific. And very shrewd. For instance," she said, launching into a long and complicated story of how her man had saved a good deal of money for one of her clients. Paul began to eat his salad, listening to her musical voice, watching the color rise in her pale cheeks, seeing the light catch in her green eyes. Her fervor reminded him of himself when he had been a young salesman trying to build a business. When the customer said no, that's when you *really* started selling. "So you see," she said, "experience doesn't mean beans if it's the wrong kind of experience."

"I understand," Paul said, as sympathetically as he could, "but I'm afraid my mind is made up."

"Right," she nodded, "but I'm giving you another chance to change it."

"Look, Miss Golden," he began.

"Call me Ruth, for God's sake!" she said impatiently. "If I'm going to holler at you, call me by my first name."

"Are you going to holler at me?"

"Hell, yes. Shout and kick and scream, too. I'm a tiger when I get started."

"I noticed that."

"I'm very competitive. And a sore loser. Now tell me again why we can't have your account."

"Besides the media and marketing departments you don't have? Lack of a track record, mainly. You've only been in business three years."

"Oh, hell! That's crapola and you know it. George and me, we're in our prime. You saw our work, terrific, right? We're on a roll, Klein, *we're hot*. You'd be stupid to go anywhere else." She picked up the knife beside her plate and for one brief instant Paul thought she might plunge it into his breast. She plunged it into the butter instead, smeared a thick chunk onto a small piece of bread, and thrust it into her mouth. "Look what you've made me do," she said between bites. *"Butter!* Now I'll have to run three miles tonight, instead of two."

"You're a jogger?"

"Runner," she corrected, "and I swim and go to exercise class or I'd have a shape like a refrigerator. Jesus, you're an upsetting man."

"Don't worry about your shape," Paul said. "It suits you."

"A lot you know," she scoffed, "and *don't* change the subject. Look, you asked me to help you, right? Why?"

"Well, I liked you," Paul said. "I was impressed with your work."

"What else?"

"I think you're levelheaded. And honest. There are a lot of phonies in your business."

"In *every* business. Any more reasons?"

Paul considered. "Yes. I sensed that we were simpatico, in a way. We can speak freely, and I respect your opinion."

"Same here," Ruth said. "But listen to what you just said. I'm honest, levelheaded, do good work, not a phony, and we get along. Now, do you *really* want to take your business elsewhere? Don't you think that's kind of dumb?"

Paul grinned. "Don't you *ever* give up?"

"You'd be our prime account. You'd get special attention. George is a *fantastic* visual man. Hell, we're made for each other!"

"Look, Ruth," he said mildly, "can we set this aside for a moment? Let me tell you about these other two agencies, okay. You said you'd help me."

"I'm still deciding that. Jesus, it's like choosing your own method of execution. Either way, I'm dead."

"Next time it'll be you," he said.

Ruth Golden's eyes flashed. "That's it," she said. She brushed her lips with her napkin and placed it on the table. Reaching down, she found her handbag.

"Wait a minute."

"What for?" She thrust her hand across the table and found his, picking it up and shaking it. "Good-bye, Klein. I hope you and your new agency will be very happy."

Paul held onto her hand. "Come on, Ruth, sit down." She tugged at his hand, trying to remove her own from his grasp.

"Leggo my hand or I'll call a cop," she said, wrenching it free, then turned and marched off through the restaurant. Paul watched her go, astonished that she would leave him sitting here. He began to get up to follow her, then sat down again. She was like a tidal wave stomping toward the door, then she was outside and gone.

He finished his lunch, then left to hail a cab. Two doors away from the restaurant, a florist had moved half his shop outside in the sunlight. On an impulse he decided to send her flowers, then had a better idea. He found a large flowering cactus in a beautiful bowl, and he wrote a note to go with it. "Sorry about that, but you were right. The bread *was* exceptional!"

He signed it "Klein."

The following morning, she was on the telephone. "Klein? What the hell is this *cactus* doing in my office?"

"Flowering, I hope."

"What's the big idea?"

"It reminded me of you, so I sent it."

"Is that how you see me? A *cactus?*"

"Yep. Tough, spiny, thorns to prick your finger. But with a beautiful flower on top."

Her laugh had a lilt to it. "Thank you. It's very nice."

"I wanted to thank you for one of the most remarkable lunch dates I almost had. I think you owe me one."

"You're a funny guy, Klein."

"Who, me? Nah, very serious."

"Oh, hell," she said, sighing. "Tell me about the two other agencies. I couldn't *stand* it if you went to a really bad shop."

Five miles away downtown, Paul was grinning into the telephone. He named the agencies and told her most of what they had proposed to him.

"No contest," Ruth said, telling him which one she would choose in his place, and why. "And listen," she added, "when it's time to shoot your commercials, don't let them give you a hosing. Make them get you prices from Boston, Toronto, and the facility in North Carolina. We've saved a lot of money for our clients shooting out of New York."

"Thanks, Ruth."

"*De nada.* You really should've come to us, but so it goes. And I'm sorry about yesterday's lunch. I have a hang-up about people telling me 'next time.' It just *gravels* me."

"Thanks again. I appreciate it."

"See you in the funny papers, Klein."

Sylvia came in from Florida and promptly began driving them all crazy. Paul and Bobby picked her up at the airport: a small, bony woman whose skin had become excessively wrinkled from the tropical sun. Right from her opening greeting—"Where's Hilary?"—she spread guilt through the household as if from an aerosol dispenser. Love, too, lots of hugs and kisses, lots of cheek pinching and hair stroking, cries of "gorgeous" and "beautiful" and long heart-to-hearts with the kids. She bedded down in the second-floor guest bedroom and promptly complained that the house was cold. In May, then, Paul turned up the heat—forget about conserving energy—and Sylvia walked around the place wearing a heavy sweater while the rest of them sweltered.

She found every dirty corner, greasy pot, dusty picture frame. A spy passing on military secrets, she whispered to Paul of Gemma's incompetence. As if he didn't know all of it already, having chosen between perfect cleanliness and a friend for the children. "How much do you pay her?" Sylvia wanted to know. When he told her, those eyes so like Jane's rolled up to heaven. When she offered to find someone who knew how to get down on her knees with a scrub brush, Paul politely declined.

"Only two weeks," he reassured a suffering Gemma, "hang on."

Sylvia took a large portion of guilt for herself, having brought it up from Florida by the gross, and plunged into an orgy of cooking all the old-time favorites for the kids. But years of cooking for one, eating in cheap restaurants, had diminished her skills. Not that Sylvia had ever put Julia Child in jeopardy; Paul remembered her overcooked and much too salty touch from his courting days. The children smiled and chewed, doing the best they could, happy at least that the fourth chair at the table was filled again. That is, when they could make Sylvia sit down and join them, not just stand and watch. Peter was given the grandmotherly once-over more than once, and Friday night Sylvia sat up watching anything on the living room TV until Hilary returned from her late-night concert.

On Sunday they drove out to the cemetery, Hilary for once in a dress, Bobby in his blazer jacket; there was not one needle Sylvia neglected to jab into Paul on the hot, slow, traffic-filled ride out to Long Island. There should have been a formal unveiling, yes. There should have been a crowd of invited friends and relatives, yes. They should have prepared a collation back at the house for close friends afterward, yes. Tears too, just a few, on the Long Island Expressway. When Sylvia cried it was never privately. She let them all know, groaning, "She was so young, so young."

Mount Hebron was jammed with cars and people, long black limousines and hearses driving by in processions for which they made way. Paul parked the car at the end of a lane and they walked a long distance to the grave. He walked holding Bobby's hand, anxiety etched all too clearly on the boy's face. With all the preparation and explaining he had done beforehand, it was still a shock for the children when they caught sight of the gray marble headstone. Bobby buried his head in Paul's jacket and wept; me strong like fodder summoned reserves of strength to keep his own emotions in check.

The grave was well kept, thank God, with a covering of grass and dark ivy. Not at all the dark brown earthen scar of last July. Pain dwelt here, though covered with grass. His parents' twin headstone alongside Jane's, one by one he had seen them to their rest, parts and pieces torn from him and buried alongside them. Sylvia spoke suddenly, bringing him back. "We need one of those men. To say the prayers."

Yes, a man, like the stranger who had said the words over Jane while he stood here wondering why the world had been broken apart. "Sylvia," he heard himself saying, "I don't want that. It's meaningless."

"You can't deny me this," she said, a look of passion in her eyes so scorching he averted his gaze to the earth. "If you don't find one of those men, I will."

She would, too, and started to walk away from the grave before he stopped her. Ritual, yes, she would have it and so would they all. He put Bobby into Sylvia's grasp and walked back to the lane. A rabbi, any rabbi, to speak the prayers in a language he had long since forgotten, a language Jane would hear and not understand. You could be a Jew and not speak those words, Paul knew, as he also knew he could not shuck off his heritage and tradition, could not deny the blood of Moses and Abraham that flowed in his veins, would not forget that in his bones were the scars of generations who had lived beyond the Pale, listening fearfully for the sound of Cossacks riding by in the night, who fled from despotism to find a new life here.

On a bench in the shade a young, pale man in a black suit looked up at him. "You need a rabbi?" Behind the steel-rimmed glasses, his eyes were a watery blue.

"Yes," Paul said, wondering at the man's youth, certainly not yet twenty.

They walked back together, the young man reaching into his pocket and pulling out a skullcap. "Your loved one?" the young man asked.

"My wife."

"Ah!" an explosion of breath. "And the others?" head tilted toward the group that stood and waited.

"My children, and my wife's mother."

"Ah, yes. I will say prayers for each of them. Do you wish a 'Woman of Valor'?" he added, in Hebrew.

"I don't understand."

"It's a special prayer we say for a woman."

Paul nodded, "Yes, say that too. But rabbi—you are a rabbi?"

A gold tooth shone in the young man's smile. "Oh, yes."

"Is there any way you could translate for us? I would like very much if you could do that."

The young man opened the leather-bound volume he carried in his hand. He handed small pamphlets to Paul. "The translation is already here, you see? I will show you where to find it."

So Sylvia had her ritual, and Paul had what he was seeking. They read along as the rabbi chanted; a prayer for a child, a mother, a wife. And the special prayer for Jane, which began: "A woman of valor, who can find her? For her price is far above rubies."

Now he was thanking the young man and slipping a bill into his hands. The children were remarkable, dry-eyed and composed now, braver than he thought they could be. Sylvia's eyes were streaming tears; she blew her nose into a delicate handkerchief. Kneeling down, Sylvia picked up a small pebble and placed it atop the slab of polished marble; a small anguished cry came from her lips. Paul walked away, going to his parents' headstone. Stooping, he located a stone, a calling card in a graveyard, and silently put it in place. Rest in peace, Edith and Herman Klein, I miss you.

Turning back, he watched as first Hilary, then Bobby put small pebbles atop Jane's headstone. As Paul placed his pebble beside theirs the boy looked up at him. "I know why we do this," Bobby said. "It's a way to tell Mommy that we were here, that we remember her."

Yes, Paul nodded, stricken now, the "Mommy" on his son's lips breaking the scar tissue that had healed on his heart. He turned his back and covered his eyes, weeping silently, and the child he had comforted so long and so well now comforted him, thin arms clinging about his father's waist, his small head between Paul's shoulder blades. "It's all right, Daddy," Bobby said. "It's all right to cry."

13

HIS BIRTHDAY CAME at the end of May. He had no wish to commemorate the worst year of his life, but the children would not let him forget. He found a card on the kitchen table that morning when he came down to prepare breakfast, and with it a box containing a cardigan sweater. Hilary's doing, of course, but most of the money had come from Bobby's carefully saved allowance. Bobby was the Scrooge of the family, using his weekly three dollars only to buy the occasional candy bar. Hilary's money went quickly on concert tickets and records. After dinner the lights in the kitchen went out and in came Hilary with a birthday cake she'd bought and two lighted candles. Luckily, he had remembered to make coffee.

Work and worry filled his days and some of his nights. The new agency took a lot of his time. Why did advertising people love meetings so, he wondered as he trekked uptown on the subway. He was plunged into marketing meetings, media meetings; budgets were thrown back and forth like frisbees. On top of this he had to do his own work downtown, keeping distributors happy, pushing salesmen to perform, slipping off for a fast three days in Cincinnati and St. Louis, which only contributed to the backlog of papers on his desk.

Ruth Golden. She had found a place in his mind and stuck there. As he sat through advertising meetings with the people from the agency, he found himself thinking about her, wondering how it would have been to work with her instead of them. He thought of calling her but held back. To say what? "Hello there, how about a date?" It seemed a big step, a Rubicon he could not yet cross for fear of a crushing no.

Lunching with Michael, a chance remark gave him pause. "I see you've made a choice," Michael was saying. "You're going to live the rest of your life as a Jewish monk." When he demurred, Michael grinned his leprechaun smile. "You've got to get your feet wet, pal, not to say other parts of your anatomy."

Marion Gerber was after him as well. One night, the remains of a huge bucket of Kentucky Fried Chicken on the table and the kids upstairs, she chided him. "She sounds nice, this Ruth. Why don't you see her?"

"Fear."

"Of what?"

"Rejection."

"Isn't that silly, Paul?"

"It's ridiculous, actually. I feel like a sixteen-year-old afraid to call that pretty girl in his math class. Getting older doesn't seem to have changed that."

"Call her. All she can do is say no."

"Ah. But then I lose my dreams and illusions, you see. For all I know she may be living with someone."

Marion shook her head, her sad eyes laughed at him.

"I'm a bit afraid of her, Marion. She's so unlike the women we know. I have no idea what she'd say if I asked her for a date."

"There are other women, Paul."

"Where?"

The storyboards of the first two commercials were presented to him. He liked them very much, but reserved judgment, taking photostats back to his office to discuss with Michael. When he reached his desk the following morning, they stared up at him. Paul picked up the telephone and called Ruth.

"Klein, don't tell me. You've thrown those bums out and decided to hire us."

"Hello, Ruth."

"Can't do without us, eh? I knew it."

"I have storyboards of our first two commercials. I'd like you to take a look at them."

"What on earth for?"

"I value your opinion. I think they're good, but I'd like to hear what you say."

"What am I, your *consultant?* At these prices?"

"I still owe you a lunch, how about it?"

"Whoa, boy, slow down there. First of all, I'm up to my ears in work. Secondly, I don't know if it's such a good idea. I'd hate to have someone looking over *my* shoulder, judging my work when I'm not around to defend it. And look—how do you know I won't tell you I hate your storyboards just to louse up your agency? I'd still like to have you as a client."

"You wouldn't sabotage anyone, Ruth. You're too honest."

He heard her sigh. "Okay, one o'clock up here, we're staying in and ordering up. Bring your own sandwich. That's my best offer."

He arrived carrying a roast beef sandwich and a black coffee. Ruth was eating a sandwich and typing on yellow copy paper. The trouble was, George Chan was having lunch in Ruth's office, too. Sheets of George's tissue-paper drawings were on the floor, the chairs, the desk, and half the floor. "Just find yourself a place to settle," Ruth said, "if that's possible."

Paul found a broad window ledge and had his lunch there. All the while George and Ruth kept exchanging ideas and copy lines, ignoring him. After half an hour she turned to him. "Okay, you've got about ten minutes. Let's see those *awful* commercials."

Ruth looked closely at Paul's photostats, with her partner observing over her shoulder. He saw a look pass between Ruth and George. "Not bad," she said. "In fact, okay." She looked at George. "Do you want to tell him?"

George grunted. "You tell him."

"The label on the sangria bottle," she said, "it's from the last century. Sangria is bought by people in their twenties. Get your agency to spiff it up, make it look glitzy, maybe include some pictures of fruit.''

"Good idea." It was a very good idea in fact. No doubt it would make the product look better on television and on store shelves, where it counted.

"Of course it's a good idea," Ruth said, "it's ours."

"Thank you."

"We'll send you a bill." Paul looked at her. "Only kidding," she grinned. "Now scram, Klein, and for God's sake don't tell your agency where you got the idea."

He was dismissed, although he remained in the office for ten minutes more. When Golden/Chan worked, they *worked.* There was no way for him to say anything personal to Ruth, not while George was there. Because they ignored him, he could look at her as she worked. She was wearing jeans again, this time with an ivory shirt that seemed to lighten her blond hair. No makeup, except for lipstick, gold bangle earrings. Why did he want to smile just looking at her?

They didn't seem to notice when he left.

That night, before bed, he gave himself the once-over in the bathroom mirror. Was he too old for her? Would she laugh at him? *Coraggio,* he told himself. You have your teeth and hair, no old-age home yet. And Marion Gerber didn't think you were over the hill. But Marion was no kid herself. And neither is Ruth Golden. He checked the lines in his face. Character, he decided, not age. What was he so worried about? You are what you are. Suppose Ruth was a disco fanatic? She could be. The last dance he had learned was the mambo. He couldn't see himself boogying.

Relax.

It took him a couple of days to work up his *coraggio.* Direct assault, no more shilly-shallying. Just telephone and ask for a date. The only thing you have to fear . . . so why was his hand shaking as he dialed her office number?

"Klein?"

"Good morning, Ruth. How are you?"

"Hassled and weary, client meetings all damn morning. How's yourself?"

"Fine."

"What's your problem?"

"No problem." Come on, say it! Why was his mouth cottony? "How's the cactus doing?" Oh, great, you idiot, the *cactus?*

"Still blooming."

"Listen, Ruth. I'd like to see you."

"About what?"

"Oh, not about anything. I mean a date." He held his breath.

"Did you say you want a date?"

"That's the general idea. Yes."

"Wow," she said, "that's a surprise. A whole new thought, in fact. Aren't you married?"

"No."

"That's funny. I thought you mentioned something about having a couple of kids. You did, and a house, right?"

"Right. My wife died about a year ago."

"Oh. I'm sorry."

"That's all right. Ruth, I think you're terrific. I'd like to get to know you better."

"I see," she said. "It's funny. I have you filed away in my head as a prospective client, I'm having trouble switching gears."

"I'm a man, too."

"I noticed that."

"I don't want to talk business. I'd like to take you out to dinner. I have the feeling we'd hit it off. You're very attractive."

"Well," she said, "you're not so bad yourself. Okay, why not?"

"Wonderful!"

"The world is full of surprises," she said.

During a business meeting that day, Michael looked over at Paul. "What's up?" he asked. "You've had a smile on your face all afternoon."

"Iceberg, Goldberg," Paul said, "what's the difference?"

"Come on, pal, I've known you a long time."

"If you must know, I've got a date."

"Glory hallelujah. Who with?"

"A woman."

"Even better. When, if I may ask?"

"Saturday night."

"Are you going to keep smiling till then? I don't think I can stand it."

His step was light when he came home that evening. In the kitchen, preparing dinner, he found himself humming, joking more than usual with Hilary and Bobby. "Someone seems happy," Hilary said.

"I am."

"Any particular reason?"

"What are your plans for Saturday night?" he asked her.

"Are we going someplace?" Bobby wanted to know.

"No. I am."

"I'm going to a party with Peter," Hilary said.

"Uh huh. That means you'll be home alone, Bob-o. Shall we see if you can sleep at Marion's, or the Bergs' house?"

"No."

"You're sure?"

"I stayed alone before. I'm not a baby."

"Are you going away on a trip?" Hilary asked.

"No," Paul said. "I have a date."

It took a moment for the word to sink in. "You mean, with a girl?" the boy said.

"A woman, yes. I met her in business. Her name is Ruth Golden and she runs a small advertising agency. She's nice."

"Are you in love with her?" Bobby said.

"Bobby!" Hilary said sharply, "don't be stupid."

"It's not stupid," Paul said, "and I'm not in love with her. It's just a date, don't make too much of it. At this point, I have no idea if she even likes me or not."

"Of course she does," Hilary said.

"Oh? How do you know?" Paul asked.

"You're terrific," she said. "She has to."

Paul laughed. "Thank you."

"You're handsome," Hilary sailed on, "intelligent, easy to talk to, and *très charmant.*"

Saturday evening, Paul put dinner on the table for the boy, then went off to shower and get dressed. He was fixing his hair, looking in the misty mirror in the bathroom, when Bobby appeared. "Did you clear away the dishes, chum?"

"Of course."

In his underwear, Paul went to his closet. All day he'd thought about what he would wear tonight; now it was time to decide. He took a blue button-down shirt from its hanger and slipped it on. Dark gray pinstripe suit, three-piece navy suit, or something else? He took both suits out of the closet and laid them side by side on the bed. "Which do you like?" he asked the boy.

"The dark blue one."

"You don't think maybe it's a bit too formal?"

Bobby shrugged. "You look nice in it."

"Nope, I'm going younger," Paul decided, picking up both suits and hanging them back in the closet. Charcoal gray slacks and navy blazer, younger and zippier. He sat down on the bed and put on his navy socks.

"How old is this lady?" Bobby asked.

"Hard to tell. Mid-thirties, somewhere in there."

"Didn't you ask her?"

"Nope."

"Why not?"

"Ladies are funny about that. Older ladies especially."

"Grandma Sylvia is sixty-seven. She doesn't care if people know."

"Well, some older ladies care. You have to be careful and know your lady. Most times, if she wants you to know she'll tell you." He took his black loafers from the closet and slipped them on.

"Daddy, can I ask you something? Are you going to get married again?"

Standing in front of his tie rack, Paul shrugged. "Someday, maybe." He picked out a bright striped tie and moved to the mirror above Jane's dresser to put it on.

"Would we still live here then?" Bobby asked.

"Of course we would."

"Good."

He put the blazer on and buttoned it, checking himself in the mirror. "How do I look?"

"Nice."

"Only nice?"

"Very nice."

"Good."

"I don't want to move away from here, Dad," Bobby said. "I like this house too much. It's a good place."

153

"It's a *great* place," Paul said, "and I love it here, too." He went to the bathroom shelf and sprayed some cologne on his hair, then playfully sprayed a shot of it on Bobby's arm. "I'm off. Come on downstairs with me and double lock the front door. And don't stay up too late, okay?"

"I won't."

In the front hallway he stooped to kiss the boy, but Bobby turned his head away. "I wish you weren't going out," Bobby said.

Taken aback, Paul paused. Bobby had that distant look on his face. "What's the matter?"

"Couldn't you stay home?"

"Bob-o," Paul said gently, "we talked about this."

"Why do you have to go out? We could watch TV, or play Stratego."

"I'll play Stratego with you tomorrow. Tonight I'm going out. Come on, chum, be reasonable. I can't stay home all the time."

But Bobby had turned away into the living room. The boy went to the TV and switched it on. "Bobby," Paul said to his back, "don't be this way. Please."

"Go ahead," the boy said without turning around, "enjoy yourself."

Paul left, double locking the front door from the outside with his key.

Ruth lived in the East Seventies, but had insisted on meeting him at the restaurant. Paul put the Buick in a garage, a comfortable ten minutes early as he'd wanted to be. The restaurant was French and very elegant, a place he'd taken Jane on special occasions. He confirmed his reservation with the maître d' and asked to be seated at a quiet banquette for two.

"I'll try, monsieur," the man said.

Paul slipped a bill into the man's hand. "Please do. I'll be at the bar."

It had been a long time since he'd sat in a restaurant waiting for a date to arrive. Jane had been the last one, a blind date arranged by a mutual friend who now lived in Seattle. He remembered it well. Summertime and hot, at Nick's in Greenwich Village, Pee Wee Russell playing clarinet in the group on the bandstand. Jane had come through the door in a white scoop-neck dress, her collarbones so delicate and fragile; a small girl with small white gloves, holding a red pocketbook. The place was loud with talk and music, they could hardly hear each other all evening. It wasn't until he'd taken her home and they sat in the car that they could talk. The one kiss she'd given him before saying good night, sudden and intense.

"I'll call you," he told her.

"Will you?" Those soft brown eyes shining in the dim light, her small hand on his cheek.

"Why is this man drinking alone?" Ruth materialized at his elbow, green eyes looking down at him as he sat on the bar stool. "You looked as if you were off somewhere," she said.

"Hello. You look smashing," he said. She was wearing a black tailored suit, a heavy strand of pink pearls about her throat. Her hair was the color of champagne in the rosy light.

"My girly things." She grinned at him. "Look." One pink polished fingertip pointed at her eyes. "Green eye shadow, eye liner, mascara, the works. Sexy, no?"

"Sexy, yes. And now I know all your secrets."

"Not all of them."

"Would you like a drink here first?"

"No, I think you'd better feed me. I'm famished."

He took her elbow and led her to the maître d', who turned them over to the captain, who led them down three carpeted stairs and across the floor to a banquette in the far corner. As he followed in Ruth's wake, Paul was aware of heads turning, men looking up from their soup to stare first at Ruth and then at him. It pleased him.

"I have a confession to make," she said when they were seated. "I realized that you've only seen me in my working clothes before. Which is why I'm dressed to kill. I always wear jeans in the office, except when I have a client meeting."

"And I realized you've only seen me in business suits. Which is why I'm wearing this." He smiled at her, which was easy to do.

"One more confession," she said, "my last, I hope. After your first visit to the office I lost your business card. That's why I kept calling you Klein—I'd forgotten your first name, Paul."

"You've learned it now, I see."

"I called your secretary. She must have thought I was a loon."

"She never said a word to me."

155

"Good woman."

"Calling me Klein is one of the things I liked about you."

Ruth's green eyes danced with tiny gold flecks when she smiled. "Shall we dine . . . Klein?"

They did, and very well. Oysters, a smooth lobster bisque the restaurant was well known for, striped bass Livornese. Paul showed off for her, ordering a 1970 Taittinger Brut Blanc de Blanc: "One of the greatest years for champagne," and went on about *remuage* and *dégorgement* until Ruth said, "I may not know champagne, but I know what I like."

Relaxed and obviously enjoying his company, she told Paul a good deal about herself. Her father was a urologist with a practice in Westchester, where she'd grown up. She'd gone to Wellesley, but graduated from Cornell with a degree in English literature "and a letter in field hockey, of all things. I was a jock with a hockey stick in those days." She'd drifted into advertising because it was one of the fields where gender didn't matter.

"And I'd discovered by then that I wasn't ever going to write the great American novel. Oh, yes, I really thought that was what I was cut out to do. I found a cheap walk-up in Greenwich Village, set up my portable typewriter on a folding table, bought plenty of typing paper, and found out I couldn't cut it. I wrote the most outrageous claptrap, really awful stuff. And suffered in the cause of art. Very romantic and very stupid. My mother was practically in mourning because of the way I was living. Every time she came calling she brought roach powder. And my father was angry at me because I was waiting on tables to support myself, he hated that, and I kept turning down the money he was offering to help me out. I had to suffer, you see, and live by my wits like the great artist I was going to be. It was a great comedown to discover I didn't have the talent. Devastating, in fact."

"How old were you then?"

"Twenty-three and very angry at myself. A schoolmate talked me into taking this junior-junior copywriter job at J. Walter Thompson, which saved my life as it turned out. Because everything just seemed to gel when I began writing ads. I was very good at it. It was easy for me, fun and all that. There's a knack to making ads and commercials and apparently I had it. I stayed at J. Walter for three years, moving up the ladder step by step. The trouble

was, it was a very tall ladder and I wasn't anywhere near the top."
She took a sip of her espresso. "I told you I was very competitive.
There was Mary Wells, making millions, and I thought I was just
as good as she was, if not better."

"Anyway, it was right then that I got a good piece of advice
from a man I was having a thing with. An account man at the
agency, married, of course—I thought I really loved him, fool that
I was. Later I found out that I was just one in a long string of love
affairs Charlie always seemed to have going. A wife and three kids
in Stamford and a girl in the city. But Charlie did know the business, I'll give him that. He told me to find a really *bad* agency and
go to work for them, where I'd stand out."

"Like cream rising to the top," Paul said.

"Exactly. Oh, it was really funny. The agency was run by a
bunch of fuddy-duddies who were afraid of any idea that hadn't
been done a thousand times before. And here I came along, doing
my tough young creative genius act, being *outrageous,* insisting on
selling my ideas directly to the client, never budging from doing
only terrific work, and being a woman, besides. I tell you, Paul,
they'd *never* seen anyone like me. Most of them wanted to fire me,
there was always a cabal going to throw me óut, but the clients
thought I was God's gift to advertising, so they couldn't let me go.
Instead they kept promoting me, shoveling money at me and more
responsibility. They made me creative director inside a year and a
half. That's where I met George Chan, by the way, where we became a team."

The waiter brought more espresso and poured for them.

"George was a very unhappy art director when we began working together. Unhappy because nobody up there let him do the kind
of work he wanted to do. I remember the meeting when I came to
love George and knew I wanted to keep working with him. We
were making a presentation to a *cement* company, a new client
pitch. We had ten ads pinned up on the wall and I did most of the
talking, selling the copy and the ideas, you know.

"Well, one of the cement guys got up, the ad manager, and he
said that he didn't like George's layout, that the picture was too
large, that the headline ought to be smaller, things like that. All
wrong, of course. And then he turned to George, who hadn't said
anything till then, and he asked George how the ad would look if it

were changed the way he'd suggested. And George just looked at the guy and said: 'It would look, sir, like a turd in the gutter. Better *you* stick to making cement, and *I'll* make the ads.' "

Paul laughed. "You didn't get that account, I'll bet."

"The hell we didn't. At lunch they seated me next to the president of the company and I leveled with him. 'Look,' I said, 'let's not kid each other, this campaign isn't about selling cement, it's about making the company look smart in Wall Street, right? So maybe you can push the price of your stock up and float loans when you need them and sell bonds. Cement is cement, and probably yours isn't any better than the next guy's. Now if that bubblehead ad manager is going to get in our hair every time we send a photographer out to take glitzy pictures of some dam or high-rise condo made with your cement, we'll be wasting our time and your money.' "

Paul shook his head. "You didn't really say all that?"

Ruth laughed. "Sure I did! Common sense, that's all. They wanted fancy ads in *Fortune* and *Business Week,* and I was letting them know they'd come to the right place."

"You're really a pistol, kiddo."

"Thirty-eight caliber, minus a couple of years. They kicked the ad manager upstairs, put in a young guy we could work with, and we changed the whole image of that company and won a lot of awards, too. Advertising may have more awards than show business, I think. Anyway, George and I ran the creative side of the agency for about two years, and as we became known in the business some very good agencies started coming after us. We were finally hired by a top creative shop who paid us an *unbelievable* amount of money to do the kind of work we liked. It was like a permanent party at that shop. We had gigantic offices, secretaries, couches and thick carpeting, a bar, the works. Creative *heaven,* all of it, lots of fun and good times. If we decided we had to shoot a commercial on the beach in Hawaii, off we went. The best hotels, expense accounts, everything. I mean, we were *stars*. They really pampered us. Sometimes I think we should never have left."

"Why did you?" Paul asked. He poured more espresso into her cup.

"It's a long story."

"We're not going anywhere."

Ruth sipped her coffee thoughtfully. "I guess it's George's doing. And in a way, Sam's."

"Aha! And who is Sam?"

Ruth grinned wryly. "Who *was* Sam, you mean. A very darling man. Sam Aaron. We lived together for about three years. Sam directed Off-Broadway, at the Manhattan Theater Club, for Joe Papp, lots of places. He's a good director. Comedies, especially. About four years ago George started *hocking* me to go into business for ourselves. That was always George's dream, to have an agency with his name on the door. I wasn't so sure that was what I wanted, but George is a determined guy. Anyway, he convinced me. Or almost convinced me. Meanwhile, Sam had started working in television, directing soaps and comedy sit-coms that were shot here or on the Coast. He got an agent out in L.A. and his career in TV began to take off. A pilot he directed for CBS was picked up for a series, and he wanted us to move to Hollywood. For Sam, the future was on the Coast. He wanted to get into TV movies, and then features."

"And you didn't want to go."

"I didn't *know* what I wanted. No, that's wrong. What I really wanted was for things to stay exactly the same. To live with Sam and keep working with George. But I couldn't have that. Sam wanted to get married and move to L.A., for us to have kids and for me to become a Beverly Hills housewife. I couldn't see myself not working anymore. I knew I'd be very unhappy if I did that. So I chose George instead of Sam and threw myself into opening our own agency. And here we are."

"So in a way," Paul said, "you're married to George."

"And George has a wife and two kids in New Jersey he goes home to every night."

"Are you sorry?"

"About what?"

"Sam."

"Sometimes. Not too often anymore. He took a long time to get over. But sometimes . . . yes. Rainy Sundays when I stomp around the apartment and end up talking to the cat. Sometimes when I'm standing in line to see a movie alone. Coming home with big news and no one to tell it to who'd understand. Yeah, I'm lonely sometimes. But you can't look back, can you?''

There was a long silence between them. Paul wanted to reach out and touch her hand, to tell this lovely woman that she could call him when she was lonely, that he would listen to her big news and be a friend. Instead, he nodded at the hovering waiter and accepted the check. After studying it, he reached inside his wallet and took out a credit card.

"Can we split that?" Ruth asked.

Paul was taken aback. "Certainly not."

"We should go dutch," Ruth said. "How much is it?" She reached down and opened her handbag.

"Wait a minute. I asked *you* out, remember?"

"That's silly," she said. "We've both enjoyed it, why shouldn't I pay half the check?"

"Next time."

He saw Ruth's nostrils flare. "Klein, do me a favor, okay? Don't tell me 'next time.' "

"Take it easy, Ruth. You can take me out to dinner and pay the check, if that makes you happy. But this one I'm paying. And if we're going to have an argument, let's have it over something more important than money."

"Okay, okay," she said, but to Paul she still looked upset.

"All right, Miss Golden, if you insist. You owe me exactly sixty-two dollars and forty cents," he said.

"Wow!" she said. "That *is* expensive."

"Good restaurant, champagne, what'd you expect? I'm not charging you for my company," he added, "because that's priceless, of course."

Ruth had her handbag on the table. "Will you take a check?"

"Oh, absolutely. And we'll figure my parking fee and the cab you took to get here are a wash, agreed?"

"Agreed." Ruth's checkbook was covered in dark alligator. She found a ballpoint in her leather handbag and wrote the check, then handed it over. "I feel like a kept man," Paul said, accepting the check and putting it in his pocket.

"I'm not charging you for that," she said in a teasing way, "because that's priceless, of course."

Paul laughed. "Touché. And just to show you I'm nice, I won't charge you for the gasoline I use when I drive you home."

"That's fair," Ruth agreed. "And to show you I'm a sport, I won't charge you for the coffee I'm going to serve back in my apartment."

"Oh? Am I going back to your apartment?"

"What the hell," Ruth said. "What the hell."

14

SHE LIVED IN a huge high-rise with a circular drive to park in out front and a doorman to let them in. Twelve floors up, a long ride in the elevator with Muzak to keep them company. Why wasn't he nervous? He felt comfortable with her. "One of my fantasies," Ruth said, "is stepping into this elevator to find Fred Astaire and Ginger Rogers dancing to the music. I keep hoping it'll happen."

When she opened the door to her apartment a marmalade cat sat in the foyer, staring at them. "Marmaduke, meet Klein," Ruth said as the cat stalked off. "Don't be offended, he's not a friendly cat."

Ruth showed him through the apartment, one bedroom, living room and dining alcove combined, and a small kitchen. "Very nice," he said. "Neat."

"It should be. I spent all morning cleaning it." She slipped off her pumps and began padding off to the kitchen. "Make yourself comfortable. I'll put the coffee on."

He glanced at his watch. It was almost midnight. "Ruth? Could I use the telephone?"

"Sure. In here." She looked at him strangely. "Do you have a late date, or what?"

"Hardly." He dialed home and waited through three rings, aware that Ruth was watching him.

"Yankee Stadium," Bobby said.

"Hello, nut, it's your father. What's happening?"

"Saturday Night Live."

"Any good?"

"Stupid as usual. Are you going to be late?"

"A little, yeah, so you'd better not wait up. Are you in your pj's?"

"Yes. When is Hilary going to be home?"

"The concert ends at one, so it won't be soon. Tuck in when the show's over, okay, and don't forget to brush your teeth and wash your face."

"How is she?"

"How's who?"

"Your lady. Is she nice?"

Paul laughed. Ruth turned around from putting a kettle of water on the stove. "My son wants to know if you're nice."

"Checking up on me, eh?" she said in a funny voice. She began putting coffee beans into a small electric grinder.

"She's nice," Paul said. "Very nice," he added when Ruth made a face. "She's making coffee at the moment. We're going to talk for a while."

Paul heard a strange low laugh that didn't at all sound like the Bobby he knew. "What's so funny?"

"Talk?" the boy said before he hung up.

Paul stared at the phone in disbelief. "My son has a dirty mind," he said to Ruth.

She grinned at him as she put the ground coffee into a filter pot. "Tell me about him."

He began talking about Bobby and continued as Ruth brought the freshly brewed coffee to the Parsons table in the dining alcove. When he finished with Bobby, he told her about Hilary.

"She sounds like me," Ruth said, "very much like me when I

163

was at home. Especially the dressing up part. God, how I hated it.''

"Look at you now," Paul said.

"You get older, you learn. But it was always a test of wills between my mother and me. I was the rebel in the family, the younger daughter. My sister, Diane, of course, was always perfect. She's three years older than I am and has never in her life had a hair out of place.''

"A tough act to follow."

"*Impossible.* So I went the opposite way. I wouldn't wear the preppy clothes Diane did. She's also beautiful, by the way.''

"She couldn't be better-looking than you are."

"Thanks, but I'm only ordinary. Diane was *gorgeous. And* obedient. And went to Wellesley and loved it, *and* married a doctor, and has a home in Mamaroneck and three kids. If you wanted to find a perfect daughter, Diane would be it. And didn't my father know it. Every Sunday afternoon we went for a drive in the car and then out to dinner. And every Sunday afternoon *Diane* sat in the front seat with my father and I sat in the back with Mom.''

"I was an only child," Paul said, "so I got all the love they could give me. It must have been tough for you."

"Let me tell you about 'next time,' my father's favorite words. When Diane got roller skates and I wanted them too, it was 'next time.' Or a doll, or a bike, or almost anything. Then of course when I wanted to go to U.C.L.A., it had to be Wellesley, preppy heaven. And when I wanted to switch to N.Y.U. and live in Greenwich Village, they wouldn't let me. It's a wonder we're still talking to each other, let alone friends. But they're nice. They're just not me, that's all. And my father is still practicing, and they still take a ride on Sunday afternoons and go out to dinner.''

"And their daughter," Paul said, "is the terror of the advertising world."

"This is true," she grinned. "My poor mother. It's been hard for her to accept the fact that I'll probably never marry and give her more grandchildren.''

"You never know," Paul shrugged.

"I'll be thirty-six in a couple of months, Paul. And I'm running a business. I can't see shooting commercials while nursing a baby."

"You're not against marriage though, are you?"

"I had my chance and I blew it," she said.

"And if another chance came along?"

"Who knows?"

Their eyes met for a long moment. Paul looked away and when he glanced at his watch saw that it was almost three A.M. "It's that time," he said. "I should be going."

"You poor guy," she said. "I've barely let you get a word in edgewise."

"Then we'll just have to do this again."

"Why not." She walked with him to the foyer.

"You're terrific, you know," he said.

"You're not exactly chopped liver yourself." As he turned, her face was very close. "This is where you get to kiss the girl," she said.

He took her in his arms for a moment and cradled her head to his. Then he found her lips and she responded, her arms hugging him tight. "I've been thinking about this for weeks," he confessed, then kissed her again.

"Klein, go home," she said as she drew herself from his embrace.

He opened the door to the hall. "I could stay," he said.

Gently and playfully, she pushed him into the hall. "Next time." She grinned at him as she began to close the door.

Going down in the elevator, he two-stepped to the music.

Sunday came up sunny and beautiful, a perfect spring day. When he woke at noon, Paul could hear the sound of Bobby shooting baskets in the driveway. Hilary was reading the newspaper when he came down to the kitchen. "My wandering father," she said. "What time did you come home?"

He grunted at her and poured himself a glass of orange juice.

"I got home after two and the car wasn't back yet. You must have painted the town."

"Hardly. We had dinner and went back to her place for coffee." He split an English muffin and put it into the toaster.

"Was she nice?"

Paul took eggs and butter from the refrigerator and put a frying pan on the stove. "Very." As he broke an egg into the bubbling butter in the pan, Hilary giggled. The yolk of the egg ran over the edge of white. "What's so funny?" he grumbled. Hilary had a knowing look on her face, too knowing he decided. "Not what you're thinking," he said. He managed to get the second egg into the pan without breaking it.

"I didn't say anything," the girl said, an angelic look on her face.

"Two dirty minds," he said, "you and your brother. It's not always sex, you know. Adults can have a perfectly nice evening just talking."

The lightly browned muffin popped out of the toaster. Hilary got up and went over to butter it. "You must have had a lot to talk about," she said. He could see that she was having a hard time holding back the giggles.

"Look," he said as he put his eggs onto a plate, "I am not John Forsythe and this is not *Bachelor Father*, okay? Lay off." He cleared the Sunday newspapers from his part of the table and sat down.

"Would you like coffee?"

"Forgot it again. Yes, please, and thanks."

"Are you going to see her again?" Hilary asked.

"Probably," he said through a mouthful of egg and muffin. Hell, yes, he was thinking. He could see Ruth serving him coffee at this very table, coffee like they'd had last night, hot and strong. Then she would sit down next to him and they would have breakfast and read the papers, the way he and Jane did on all the Sundays of their married life, talking only now and then, reading things to each other, laughing about stupid fashions and Russell Baker and . . . Slow down, you are way ahead of yourself. Yes. But it was possible. She was available, he was attracted to her, and he was not exactly chopped liver.

Possible.

Hilary was putting a mug of coffee on the table. "I'm going to wash my hair, and then I have a paper to write. Are we going out to dinner?"

"Sure," he nodded. "I thought maybe Chinatown."

Later, outside in the garden, he tied tomato plants to stakes; little green nubbins of fruit were just beginning from the yellow flowers. In the green watering can he dumped two measures of Myron the Maven's secret formula for happy vegetables, then filled the can from the hose and gave the tomato plants a drink. At four o'clock he poured himself a Jack Daniels and read the book review section of the paper. But concentration was far away. He imagined Ruth sitting on the white upholstered couch near the window in her living room, the cat beside her, reading the same book reviews. He heard the *tap-tap* of Hilary's typewriter from the open window. In the living room, a sound of cheering from the TV as Bobby watched the Yankees. He picked up the telephone and called her.

"I'm thinking about you," he said.

"That's nice."

"What are you doing?"

"Thinking about getting dressed."

"What are you wearing?"

"Hmm. An old shortie nightgown and a light cotton robe."

"Are you on the couch?"

"At the table. Deciding if I have the energy to go out and take a walk."

"Next Saturday?"

"Sure."

"Same time, same station?"

"We'll talk."

"I may not live till then."

Her laugh was different, more of a giggle.

"You wouldn't want to have dinner in Chinatown tonight, would you? With the three flying Kleins?"

"Nope."

"I didn't think so. Hey, Ruth—why am I thinking about you?"

"Because I'm irresistible."

That evening he sat on Bobby's bed and waited for the boy to finish his gargling symphony in the bathroom. They went through Bobby's going-to-bed rituals together. First Bobby, in his favorite purple print too-short cotton pajamas, lined up the digital clock on his dresser so it directly faced his pillow on the bed. Next, the items on top of his yellow toy chest—Peanuts paperbacks, two metal racing cars, and pencils—had to be lined up in one neat pile so they wouldn't cast scary shadows when the night light was put on. When Bobby climbed into bed Paul had to reach over and tightly tuck in the light quilt on the wall side of the bed, then the room side was tucked as tight as a drum. Hands out of sight below the quilt, only Bobby's shiny just-washed face looked up at his father. "Okay, chum?"

"Sure."

"Good day?"

"Fine."

"Another good one tomorrow, okay?"

"Why not?"

But there was something not forthcoming in the boy's eyes. "You want to talk about last night?" Paul asked.

He could see the curtain come down. "There's nothing to talk about."

"Bob-o, don't kid a kidder, okay? You don't like the idea of my dating, do you?"

The boy looked at him for a long moment. "I don't. No."

"Do you know why?"

A shrug. A blinking of those beautiful eyes.

"Is it something to do with Mom?" Very careful here, his inner voice said. "Honey, men get lonely. Spending time with a woman, talking and things, it helps. But just because I do that . . . it doesn't mean I love you less."

"Could we not talk about it anymore?" The boy's voice was close to breaking.

"Sure."

A kiss then, on the boy's forehead, a squeeze of shoulder under the quilt. A kiss from Bobby on his cheek, then closing the door securely so it would not rattle when the breeze blew in from the open windows.

In the soft night he sat on the front porch. Across the way the Dawsons' bedroom window danced with flickering blue light from a television set. It was so quiet on the street that Paul could hear the click and buzz as the traffic signals on the corner flicked from red to green. He lit a cigarette, thinking about Ruth Golden.

Energy. She was charged with it. He felt so alive when he was with her, or even spoke to her on the telephone. She had all the qualities he admired: verve, determination, a willingness to take the bumps and keep on fighting. She was only six years younger than he, but she made him feel young.

The way her hair moved when she walked. The way she tossed her head when she laughed. The gesture she had of placing the back of her hand under her chin when she listened to him.

Was it too soon? Was there some calendar to live your life by, some clock of custom and conscience that would say when? Unlike wine, loneliness did not improve with age.

And how would she be with the children? Could she take them on, too? He could see Bobby enfolded in Ruth's long arms, hugged tight against her. He saw Hilary watching Ruth brush her long hair, the two women smiling as they spoke words he could not hear.

Alone on the porch, he smiled to himself. And on this Sunday night he fell asleep in bed easily and quickly, and had dreams he did not remember.

On the way to work the next morning he stopped off at a florist and sent a bouquet to her apartment. He had difficulty with the card, standing a long time, pen poised, unable to think of what to write. "Thank you for a lovely evening" was too banal; a simple "I love you" too forward, too soon, too much. Smiling, he wrote, "It's a long way until Saturday."

The next morning she called him. "Klein? You're a little crazy, you know that?"

"You're welcome," he said.

"How rich are you, anyway? Those flowers must have cost a fortune."

"When am I going to see you?" he asked.

"Saturday," she said, and he groaned. "Unless you die on me," she added.

"I just may."

"Control yourself."

The next afternoon, from the office, he phoned her. "I've been thinking about you all day," he said.

"Oh, God, you again. I've got a desk full of work, a grumpy partner, the coffee from the container spilled on my sandwich, and now you."

"Talk to me."

"I'm talking, I'm talking. You know what a *wet* tunafish sandwich tastes like? I am not in the happiest of moods, Klein."

"How about dinner? I could meet you at seven-thirty."

"At seven-thirty I am still going to be typing this *stupid* copy for a stupid brochure about laxatives. Sound like fun to you? Amazing what people will take if they don't have a good crap every day. Did you ever hear about laxative rebound, Klein? Your body gets used to this foreign substance that sends you to the toilet and then it can't function normally without it. Pleasant, isn't it? American ingenuity at its best. Millions of people convinced that if they don't have a *doo-doo* every day it's illegal, immoral, and un-American."

"We could see a movie. There's a new Truffaut at the Paris."

"I'm talking shit and he's giving me movies."

"We could eat popcorn, hold hands."

"No time. If I don't send this copy out to be set tonight my client will be very unhappy."

"And I was going to let you take advantage of me, too. Oh, well."

A wet and dreary Thursday morning. He called Ruth, but the receptionist told him she was at a client's office. Late in the afternoon she called him back. "Success!" she declared. "The world has been preserved from constipation."

"At last. Children may sleep safe in their beds. You sound terrific."

"Merely elated. They loved the brochure, *loved* it! Genius time!"

"Can we celebrate? Where do you go to celebrate a laxative triumph? The Potty Theater? John's Restaurant?"

"The Baronet Theater at six o'clock. Do you like Woody Allen?"

"As what?"

"No jokes, please. I'll meet you there at six and I'll buy the tickets. After that you can buy me a hamburger."

She was waiting under the marquee in a pouring rain, wearing a green pants suit, a bright yellow print scarf tied about her hair. She looked so adorable his heart jumped when he saw her. Dripping wet from his mad dash from the parking lot around the corner, he wanted to hug her right there and then. Instead he grinned stupidly

170

and let her lead him inside. They sat in the smoking section and held hands, her touch making it difficult to concentrate on the film.

He bought her a rare hamburger in a loud café on Third Avenue, hold the French fries. He ordered the deluxe burger that came with the works. As Ruth ate she kept sneaking French fries from his plate with her fingers, delighting him, shaking her head at herself as she finished half the fries on his plate. He felt content to be here with her, listening to her, a part of himself sitting on his shoulder looking down on the two of them. He realized he was off in his own world when she asked him something and waited for a reply. "The kids," she repeated, "what did you do about them?"

"I'm sorry," he said. "What about the kids?"

"What do they do about dinner when you don't come home?"

"Oh." He explained about ordering a pizza that Guido would deliver, and the house money in the book upstairs. "Probably Bobby will make salad for the two of them. He's gotten very good at it. And they'll have salad while waiting for Guido to deliver, which on a night like this will be an hour, most likely. Hilary will preheat the oven and serve half the pizza when it comes and slap the rest of it in to keep warm. Then Bobby will clear and Hilary will do the dishes, and Bobby will take out the garbage, remembering to lock the back door when he comes in. I hope."

"They sound so self-reliant."

"They've learned. We've all learned." He lit a cigarette. Outside the streaky windows, the rain pelted down. "For a long time the most important thing seemed to be having milk and bread in the house. Just living day to day, trying to hold on to each other. It's gotten better. Bobby is still the one I worry about. Of the three of us, he's the one who's still in mourning."

"He's so young," she said.

"He'll be okay. We all will. As long as we're there for each other." He made a face. "That sounds so pompous. We're doing the best we can, that's about it. Tonight, of course," he added, "I'm doing a helluva lot better." He took her hand in his and squeezed it. "You're looking particularly gorgeous tonight."

"I've been trying to decide what I like about you," she said. "Charm. Lots of charm."

"Four years of charm school."

"And you always manage to say the right thing."

"You'll notice I haven't mentioned constipation once tonight."

She laughed, her teeth flashing white, little laugh lines at the corners of her mouth. "There's work tomorrow, Klein. I think you'd better take me home."

He made her wait under the awning in front and ran through the rain to bring the car around. When he reached her apartment building, he found a place to park in the half-circle of drive. "No," she said as he turned to her, "you're not coming up." She leaned toward him to give him a chaste pecking kiss, but he put his arms about her to hold her close. Her mouth opened and her tongue excited him. When their lips parted, she looked at him. "The guy buys me a hamburger and then tries to squeeze it out of me."

He stilled her with another lingering kiss.

"I hope my doorman doesn't see this," she said. Then she turned aggressor, thrusting herself upon him so that he was pushed back against the door and window, her large body pressing into him as she held his head and kissed him passionately. "That's in case you don't think I care," she said. "Saturday night. Don't make any other plans."

"I won't," he said, grinning. "I'm crazy about you, Ruth."

"Shhh," she said, putting a finger to his lips. "All in good time, Klein." She opened the car door.

"I'll call you," he said as she slammed the door shut and ran for the shelter of the portico.

Friday afternoon a curious Lillian Lerner brought a floral delivery to his desk. He unwrapped the package to find a large potted philodendron in a handsome brass bowl. The card read: "How I see you: good-looking, sturdy, dependable, but needs a lot of care." It was signed, "The Cactus Lady."

"From a customer?" Lillian asked. "That would be a first."

"No, an admirer." He couldn't help grinning.

"Male or female?"

"Very female."

Twenty minutes later Michael Bradie was in Paul's office, inspecting the philodendron which now occupied a rather too-narrow perch on the windowsill. "There's a rumor going around that a female admirer sent you this."

"True."

"Ah. The advertising lady, or some other, may I ask?"

"Ruth Golden."

"A woman sending you a present," Michael said with a sly look. "You must have performed a service she appreciates."

"Michael, control yourself."

Those bushy eyebrows danced. "Oh, I have perfect control. You, on the other hand, apparently do not. Congratulations." All of which reminded Michael of several dirty stories, all of which he told.

When he cleared out of the office, Paul called Ruth. "A philodendron?" he teased her. "And here I saw myself as a tiger lily."

"You're lucky they didn't have skunk cabbage," she said.

The lights in the buildings of lower Manhattan were glowing gold as he drove under the promenade in the Heights. Above the dark river he soared on Mr. Roebling's bridge, ten thousand shining wires surrounding him, the towers of Manhattan magnificent against the blue dusk.

The doorman having rung upstairs to announce him, Ruth was waiting in the doorway of her apartment. She was wearing a long caftan of blue silk spun with threads that matched her tawny hair. "Hello," she said softly, almost shyly as she closed the door behind him. She reached up and laid a warm hand on his cheek, then kissed him gently. "Hello," Paul said as they stood holding each other.

"I thought we'd have dinner and stay in," she said.

"Fine." At the end of the living room the dining table was set, two candles lit and glowing. With his hand about her waist, they walked across the room.

"I'm not much of a cook," she said.

"That's all right."

"I mean, I don't want to give you the wrong impression. I have

173

vichyssoise, a quiche I have to pop in the oven, and an apple tart. All of it from a wonderful take-out place on Second Avenue.''

"Sounds fine."

"The only thing I made was the salad." Ruth's voice was quiet, without her usual verve. "And not too well."

"Stop apologizing." He put his arms about her from behind, smelling the sweet fragrance of her hair, his cheek against hers.

"I'll make coffee later," she said in a whisper. "I'm very good at coffee."

"Ruth," he said huskily, his heart beating in his ears. She turned to him then, holding him tight; he felt her shiver. They kissed, deep and satisfying, and drew apart still holding each other. She nodded, smiling, "Yes, oh yes." Were those tears that made her eyes glow in the candlelight? A surge of strength flowed through him. Reaching behind her legs, he swept her up into his arms, walked to the bedroom, and across the bare floor to the large bed, one dim lamp near the door making a large shadow. He put her down gently.

"Hurry," she whispered.

He threw clothes off, not caring where they flew. Naked, he found the zipper at the top of her gown and pulled it all the way. Her breasts were large and round and pink-tipped. With shaking hands he pulled blue bikini panties down and off as her arms reached out for him. He kissed her lips, her chin, the hollow of her throat, then all of her as she moaned his name. Not Klein here, not now, a cry of "Paul, oh Paul," as she arched to meet him and he entered her, thrusting deep and deeper still, the hurrying tempo increasing as their need grew stronger until with a quivering cry, *"Paul!"* she reached her zenith an instant before him.

A fallen warrior, he lay still in her arms, his head upon her breast. Later, when he thought to shift his weight, she held him fast, a gentle kiss on the top of his head. Thus commanded, he obeyed, no thoughts except of wonder for his good fortune, her smooth warm hand rubbing care away from between his shoulders and down his back. "Well," a giggle from her, "what *else* would you like to do tonight?"

Laughing, he showed her.

New candles then, to dine by, the first having melted to stubs. Long after midnight the quiche was burned in the overheated oven that had stayed on, the soup ignored, a few bites of food and wine to sip, drinking each other in with their eyes, hands touching on the dainty tablecloth, Ruth shivering as he stroked the golden hairs on her forearm. "Your hands," she said. "They make me crazy."

"All *I* have to do is look at you."

Gold flecks in her eyes reflecting the candlelight. A girl now, no woman surely, the heavy feeling in his throat as she smiled. "Ruth, I love you."

"This is so crazy," she said. "Crazy and very fast."

"Never too fast." Heart on his sleeve and on his lips. "I love you, Ruth Golden. And I want to marry you and take you home and have you love me and my children and live happily ever after." Except he, of all people, already knew there was no ever after.

"One step at a time," she said, fondling his hand across the table.

"Yes," Paul said. "I think you owe me a step, then."

"Can't you tell, Mr. Klein?"

"Say it, woman."

"Oh," she said, pretending to be casual, but giving it away with her smile. "Oh, I guess I love you a little." She giggled then, began babbling. "Jesus, I'm nuts about you, totally wacked-out if you want it all. I want to take care of you, cook and sew and all that, except I can't cook and I can't sew, but you get the idea. Is this making any sense? When you look at me like that I get goosepimply."

"You're doing fine so far."

"Why do I feel like a teenager all of a sudden? Oh, Paul, I want you to crush me, kiss me, hold me in your arms forever." A sudden realization brought her fingertips to her lips. "Ohmigod! I'm going to be a mother!"

Paul began to laugh, which made her glare at him, which made him laugh even more. "Well, I am," she said. "Holy Toledo, two kids, and at my age."

"Stepmother," he managed to say.

"Oh no, not that!" she said. "Stepmothers are always wicked old crones. Beating up on kids, making them sweep the fireplace. Do you have a fireplace in your house? Wait a minute, where *is* your house? I'll have to move in, won't I? Do you have furniture?

175

What a stupid question. Of course, you must have furniture and everything. I have a lease here, but I can get out of it. And the *business!* George will be so mad at me, we'll never get time for a honeymoon, maybe a weekend, you won't mind that, will you? Oh, I'm so happy! The kids, what are their names again? Hilary and Bobby. I love them already. Oh, Paul, what if they don't like me?''

"One step at a time," he said, his heart full.

"They're kids, they could hate me." She came around the table and plopped herself in his lap, covering his face with kisses small as pearls.

"How could they not love you?" he said, holding her tight.

15

THEY EITHER MET or spoke once a day, sometimes five or six times a day. But once face to face they couldn't keep their hands off each other. Some lunchtimes Paul would rush uptown by Buick, Ruth by subway or cab, meeting in her apartment for a furious encounter. Pure flame when they touched, the heat of passion matching the rising temperature of early summer. "Noonsies," Ruth called it, a term not unknown in the advertising business. Paul hated the word, calling it cheap. "We're making love," he said, "not having 'noonsies.' There's a big difference." The big naked lady on the bed laughed at him. "Loosen up, Klein, we're *fucking* is what we're doing. Good old Anglo-Saxon word, that. Why does it hang you up?" Now the copywriter gave him instructions in the use of language, not letting him touch her until he said the dreaded word. "Say it, come on!" Rolling away, she made him chase her, two naked people playing romantic tag. Laughing, he said it, and catching her, did it. "Jane never said 'fuck,' " he told her afterward. "Never." "Fuck that nonsense," she said. "I'm me, not Jane."

That she was, and he loved her for it.

She was unpredictable, given to quicksilver changes of mood, a loose and free spirit. And there was so much of her to love. Five feet and nine inches of solid woman, with strength in her arms, long delicious legs, a body kept firm by exercise classes and running. No cuddle-toy against his chest like Jane, this big woman somehow made Paul feel bigger, stronger. On her bed the world was far away, no problems of business, the children not in his mind. Love was here for him, in this place, and he gave himself to it.

Ruth wanted to meet his children and see the house she would someday call home. Here Paul was cautious. He wanted her first meeting with the children to go right, wanted Hilary and Bobby to love Ruth as he did. And with the tempo of his business affairs rising, he put it off week after week.

Not since the early days had he worked so hard, when he was newly married and scrambling around the country building a business by sheer dint of will and persuasion. Introducing two new products would have been work enough; the television schedule and the advertising agency seemed to double it. With Ruth looking over his shoulder and advising, he poked, prodded, and pushed the agency to compare production costs for the commercials in every facility on the East Coast and two in California. Wilmington, North Carolina, won, as Ruth suspected it might, and Paul had a new city on his itinerary. Three grand and glorious days in a surprisingly modern studio, chalking up yet another Ramada Inn in his growing Baedeker of places never to come back to if he could help it.

Producing a new label for the sangria could easily have turned into a year's project if he had permitted it. The agency did splendid work, no question, but how they hated to be hurried. All he wanted was a good design, no more, but the research wallahs and bearded art directors treated it as a new canvas to be displayed someday in the Museum of Modern Art. Research plumped for surveys. "Tickle them in the ribs and see if they laugh," one tweedy Ph.D. actually said. "We never put a pencil to paper without some idea of what the great unwashed expects," the man told him. Groaning inwardly, but keeping his cool, he pushed. His guide was the three G's: by Guess, by Guts, and by God. And by June fifteenth he had

178

his design. Which was only the beginning. Printed in Switzerland, by the same firm that had done countless labels for Bradie & Klein, Inc., they were affixed to the bottles in Barcelona, an international balancing act of terror-filled coordination.

But love gave him energy, and he spent it all.

Frantic and frenetic, he was everywhere, *run do not walk* the order of the day. Flying trips to distributors to hammer out television schedules in person. The greedy grasped and demanded more. Open the treasure trove of TV advertising and the lame and halt will somehow spring to their feet and tap dance.

One evening, when they were scrounging yet another dinner at Marion Gerber's, he waited until the kids had gone off and then told Marion about Ruth.

"Never married and no kids," Marion said, "a single lady with a business. Not what I thought you'd end up with, Paul."

"She's wonderful."

"A lot to handle, I'll bet."

"When I get to handle her," Paul grinned. "I don't know if I'm coming or going these days."

"Coming is the good part. Har! Has she met your kids?"

Bingo! Marion hit his worry head-on. "Not yet, Marion. I want it to be right when the kids meet her. And I sense a lack of enthusiasm at my dating again. Mostly from Bobby."

Over her coffee cup, Marion looked at him. "It's not surprising, Paul. Think about it. If you fall in love with somebody, that's less love for him. Never mind all the permutations and combinations of bringing a second woman—a stepmother—into the house." She took a sip of her coffee, wiping her mouth daintily with a napkin. "My girls hate it when I go out. They're still hoping that Phil will make a comeback, as if I'd have anything to do with that bastard again. Kids are like that, Paul, little dreamers. Listen to them and you'll stay home and single. Permanent Daddy-Paul, always there for them at home. As if you're not entitled to a life of your own. As if they won't run off and leave you when their time comes."

"I think I'm afraid of bringing Ruth home," he confessed.

"Jesus, why?"

"If they don't hit it off, what then?"

"Trouble in River City. But you can get over that, too."

"I don't know. I'm trying to stage-manage the whole thing, finding the right time, the right place."

"Just do it," she said. "They don't want to marry her, you do. And Paul, there's never a right time. Just do it."

He took Marion's advice and took the plunge, a Sunday at home. He would barbecue hamburgers on the grill in the backyard. Ruth would bring dessert from Manhattan. "Gooey and chocolate," he told her; both kids would kill for chocolate.

A family conference first, to set it all up. Casual, cool, a Friday night at the local trattoria, Bobby putting away a huge bowl of Luigi's linguine and red clam sauce, Hilary picking at a veal cutlet. Paul tried to ignore the hole in the knee of her jeans. Nor did he comment on the fire-engine-red laces in her sneakers—more anti-fashion freak show—and the work shirt with the Magic Marker smudge, worn over braless breasts. He told them about Sunday, the barbecue, a long time since they'd had one. "And we're going to have a guest, Ruth Golden."

Hilary nodded, she took a sip of her Coke. "Can Peter come?"

"I'd rather not, if you don't mind, babe. I'd like you both to have a good chance to get to know Ruth. She's been anxious to meet you. I think you'll like her."

"Do we have a choice?" Bobby asked.

"What do you mean?" he said. "Of course you do. But give her a chance, Bob-o."

"So why can't Peter come, too?" Hilary was asking. "We usually see each other on Sundays now that school is over. He won't get in the way, Daddy."

"Okay," Paul retreated. "But no going off alone, the two of you. Ruth will be our guest and we should treat her like one."

"What do we need *her* for?" Bobby sucked a strand of linguine into his mouth. "We've been doing good lately. Except that you're hardly home anymore."

"You know why I've been working so hard," Paul said.

"You're only home for dinner maybe once a week," the boy exaggerated, "because you're always seeing Ruth. We've only seen one Yankee game so far this summer. And we haven't even been to the beach once."

"I never took you to the beach during the week," Paul said.

"Your mother did. Remember? I'd leave her the car and go to work by subway."

"You could take a day off and do it," Bobby said, his lower lip projecting in a challenge. "Or we could go on a weekend."

"We'll talk about it," Paul promised. "After Sunday."

He sat waiting for her with the Sunday magazine section, trying to read but looking up so often to the corner she'd turn coming from the subway that he couldn't even track through Russell Baker. Sunny, hot and beautiful; the block gleamed as if newly painted. Bobby shot baskets down the drive, the sun now over the yardarm putting the half-court in cooler shadow. Inside, Hilary pounded the piano in a show-off "Maple Leaf Rag" with Peter Block, his guitar and his orchestra, plunking away to keep up with her. A small piece of Sunday sweetness, this, *recherche du temps perdu*, very past indeed and yet he had never shifted Jane's chair from its place alongside his facing out to the street. One flickering thought of wasted but so lovely late Sundays here with Jane, kids off somewhere, just the two of them sharing the newspaper and early gin and tonics, ice tinkling in the cool shade under the overhang of the porch roof, waving a hello to neighbors in cars slowing down for the traffic light on the corner.

On the corner. Here she came, rounding the Troutmans' high green hedge, a tall lady striding as if she owned the world, cake box in hand, shoulder bag tucked under the other arm, sneakers and jeans and a blue chambray shirt filled with breasts he couldn't get enough of, dark sunglasses against her fair face, hair yellow as butter in the sun. He went off down the street to meet her, not running but wanting to, wanting to kiss her, too, but holding back because the Dawsons were sitting out and they could make their own gossip without help, thank you. "Hello," she smiled, taking him in and the green street as well. "What a beautiful place this is. Which house is yours?"

He pointed, looking at it with her eyes. Yellow shingles above yellow brick, the color of her hair now, brown trim around the shutters and the porch. "Very Victorian," she pronounced. "The stained-glass windows!" catching sight of his three-in-a-row along the driveway. Bobby drove in for a lay-up, missed, collared the rebound against the garage, at seventy feet a small figure in cutoff jeans and white Hershey's T-shirt. "That's Bobby," waving to the boy and being ignored as the kid spun and dribbled. "Come and sit on the porch awhile. How was your trip?"

"Almost an hour," her eyes taking in the lawn, purple rhododendrons in flower just in time to greet her. "Lovely," she said, buoying him to bursting. "Just lovely. I can see why you don't want to part with this place. But that subway is murder."

On the porch, behind the tall Doric columns, he squeezed a handful of denim-covered ass. Sex-crazed widower assaults blonde beauty on front porch. Down, boy. She handed him the cake box for the fridge. "The kids can o.d. on that one," she said. "Chocolate fudge and buttercream about two inches high on top. If I even *look* at that later, stop me."

"A drink? Gin and tonic?"

"With a wedge of lime, lovely." Instinctively, she sat herself in *his* chair, the better sited of the two.

The dreamer stood admiring her for a second before ducking inside the door. This tall sexy woman in Papa Bear's chair, long red-capped fingers dropping her bag to the floor, mysterious eyes hidden behind the sunglasses. Why is this man smiling? Cake box in hand he called out to the piano player and her consort guitarist, "Ruth's here!" and shuffled off to the kitchen to put away the cake and fetch the drinks.

Yes there were limes in the refrigerator, because Jane used to say that gin and tonic without lime tasted like medicine, so when you bought tonic you always bought limes. The good tall glasses, too, not the Welch's jelly glass he had taken to using. He made the drinks quickly, added Cokes for the kids, a wedge of Jarlsberg on a wooden cutting board, a cheese knife, a bowl of crackers, and put everything on a tray. Eighteen years of marriage, he thought, you learn how to host. Jane would have had water biscuits instead of Ritz crackers, but . . . *napkins!*

He went to the open kitchen window to call Bobby, just in time to hear and see the boy dribbling down the mythical N.B.A. court saying, "He drives, he shoots, he *scores!*" As he picked up the tray he heard from the living room the sound of four hands playing piano, "Heart and Soul," the old duet. Ruth, her sunglasses perched prettily atop her hair, sat cheek-to-cheek on the piano bench with Hilary, pounding out the bass part. She grinned at him. "Twelve years of piano lessons."

Why had he worried about Ruth fitting in? In five minutes she had impressed Hilary, that much was evident, and tall Peter Block was eyeing Ruth with a slack-mouth grin. Paul set the drinks tray down on the coffee table and joined the party, happy to stand and listen as Hilary sang, happy to have noise and life back in this beautiful room again.

Bobby came in and met Ruth, shaking her hand very correctly, then trailing in her wake as Paul and Hilary escorted her on a guided tour. Paul recited the history of the house: built in 1905 by a Mr. Lopez of Colombia, a coffee merchant; home to the Bailey family from 1910 to 1945 (the Baileys built boats); then the Friedbergers until the Kleins moved in thirteen years ago. And they knew all this because when the neighborhood was given landmark status the city researched it and issued a pamphlet.

"And we met one of the Baileys," Hilary put in, "a grandson of the original Baileys who came here one day to show his daughter the place. Remember, Dad?"

"Yes, and he told us how the house had been changed over the years. This wall once had a fireplace, and that ceiling beam shows where a wall used to be that was knocked down to make the living room larger."

"I didn't know places so huge existed in New York," Ruth said. "The height of these ceilings!"

"Twelve feet. Tough to heat, but lots of room to breathe."

"It's a palace!"

"We like it," Bobby said, ever so casually, making his father smile. On the second floor Hilary took over, insisting on taking Ruth upstairs to the top floor, which Paul knew Gemma hardly ever cleaned. Following Ruth, he let his daughter lead on to the small rooms above, the storage room with neatly stacked and labeled cartons, the room with a dusty Ping-Pong table the kids almost never used, the tiny room with Bobby's model electric trains, the room that stored the family's suitcases.

"You've got rooms on top of rooms," Ruth said.

Downstairs, they lingered in the kitchen. Paul took the meat from the refrigerator, holding the door for Bobby, who removed the salad vegetables from the chiller bin down below. Gemma had done them proud. The copper range-hood gleamed, four large clean windows let in the afternoon sun, and the wood cabinets seemed to glow under a coat of shiny wax. Ruth stood in the breakfast nook, looking at the shelves. "How many cookbooks do you have? My God!"

"Lots," Paul said. "They just accumulated somehow."

"Jane must have been a good cook," she said.

"She was a *great* cook," Bobby said. He was opening a cabinet, taking out the big salad bowl used only when company came.

"I'm just about a dead loss in the kitchen," Ruth confessed. "All I know about food is how to eat it." She walked over to the chopping block, where Bobby was tearing bibb and romaine lettuce and tossing it into the spin-washer. "Can I help? Salads I can make." Picking up a knife, she began to slice tomatoes.

"Uh, Ruth," Bobby began. He shot a questioning look at Paul. "Ruth, we kind of *chunk* the tomatoes for salad, not slice them."

"Oops! Sorry. Yes, of course." She looked in dismay at her error. "What do I do now?" she asked.

"If you cut those slices in four they'd be okay," Bobby said.

She did, then reached for a cucumber. "Bobby," she asked before using the knife, "how shall I do the cucumber?"

"Skins off, seeds out, cut in half, and then slice not too thin."

"Easy for you to say," she cracked. Using the knife, she began to peel the cucumber. Without speaking, Bobby opened the utility drawer next to the chopping block and handed her a vegetable peeler. "This is easier," he said.

"Thanks." She began to use the peeler, taking off too much cucumber meat with each stroke. Paul went outside to begin the fire.

Bobby was cleaning and seeding a green pepper under the faucet in the sink. "Leave some cucumber, Ruth," he said. "You're peeling too deep."

"Stupid me," she sighed.

"Just go very lightly," Bobby said, watching her try it. "Leave it," he said after a moment. "I'll do it."

"No," she said. "I'll get the hang of it." With a careless stroke she nicked the edge of her thumb—"Ouch!"—then put the grazed member in her mouth. Sucking her thumb, she stood looking into Bobby's disapproving stare. "Food is not my best subject," she said.

The barbecue was served on the terrazzo deck under the shade of the tall pine tree. Talk was desultory and strained, with Paul doing most of it. The children, he supposed, were a bit reserved in front of Ruth. But the gooey cake she'd brought was fallen upon with sheer greed, even Ruth had a small slice, promising to hate herself later. Peter Block, sometimes called Silent Sam by Paul, left early, so that when Paul and Bobby did the washing up, Hilary and Ruth had time to slip off to the living room for some woman talk.

He drove Ruth home before nine o'clock, mindful of how long the round trip to Manhattan would take, detouring at first to drive slowly through the neighborhood to show it off. "I'm amazed such a sweet place exists right in the city," Ruth said. "I grew up in a place like this, in Westchester, on a quiet street with big trees and green lawns."

"You should see it when it snows," he said. "Right out of Currier and Ives."

"It's lovely, Paul, but a helluva long way from the office."

"Not a bad trip," Paul said, a defensive tone in his voice. "Maybe forty-five minutes by subway."

"If the wind is right. How long is Bobby's trip to school?"

"Over an hour."

"Isn't that tough on him?"

"He's used to it now."

Paul brought the Buick over the bridge to Manhattan and circled onto the northbound drive. "So tell me about my kids," he said.

"Oh, Paul, they're so *dear*. And so . . . *mature*. Bobby's a fine boy. God, those eyelashes! I wanted to grab him and start hugging and squeezing."

"Someday you will," he said. "Let him get to know you."

"I hope he'll let me," she said. "And Hilary is seventeen going on thirty, but a little girl, too. She reminds me of *me* when I was her age . . . sophisticated and immature, a little mixed-up, a little crazy, trying so hard to be different. We talked about college. I told

185

her not to go to Wellesley under any circumstances. She needs a big, *lively* school.''

"By God, I feel good," Paul said. "It's such a relief, having you to talk to about the kids. Like a load has been lifted from my back.''

Ruth was silent, her expression so wistful when he glanced over at her that he had to ask what was wrong. "A little scary," she said, "all of it. Your kids, that great big beautiful house, marrying you, a whole new way of life. Just a little scary, Paul.''

"It's going to be wonderful, babe," he said, believing it. "Not to worry. The day you move in is the day I'll be happy. You'll see, it's going to be just fine.''

The children were awake and waiting for him when he returned. He found Hilary in her room, drying her long hair with a towel. "She's nice," Hilary said, "but how old is she? She seems so young." Bobby's nightly gargling song came from the bathroom.

"She's old enough," Paul said.

"She's not what I expected," the girl said. "She's . . . I don't know. Different.''

"From what?''

Hilary shrugged. "She's not quiet, like Mom was. Not loud, exactly, but peppier, or something. You like her a lot, don't you?''

"Yes. A lot.''

"She's got a good sense of humor," the girl said, "like you." She looked at her father. "You want to marry her, don't you?''

"Yes," Paul said. He sensed an unasked question in Hilary's face. "I love her, sugar, and that's the truth. She's not your mother, though. Your mother was very special. Ruth is different. She's kind and decent and halfway to loving you already. She's a very sharp, very smart lady.''

Behind Paul, Bobby poked his head through the doorway. "Who is?''

"Ruth," Hilary said.

"What's so smart about her?" Bobby asked. "Did you see the way she holds a knife? She can chop her fingers off. The first thing

186

Mom showed me was to hold your other hand *above* the knife, not under it. That's just stupid.''

"She can learn," Paul said. "It's not the most important thing."

"You like her, don't you?" Bobby said.

"Yes I do."

"You gonna see her again?"

"Uh huh. Probably a lot."

Bobby considered, his face thoughtful. "And what if I don't like her?''

"Give her a chance," Paul said, his heart sinking. "She likes you a lot."

"And what if I *still* don't like her?"

"I'm hoping you will," Paul said.

"Uh huh," Bobby said, nodding. "You know what? She's too big for you. When you stand next to her, you look funny together."

"Not like your mother, you mean," Paul said.

"Not like Mommy at all."

They just needed time, Paul thought. Sooner or later, please God, make it sooner, Ruth would win over the children on her own terms. The thing was to keep her in their lives, widen the circle, make Ruth become part of them, to make that *them* into an *us*.

The children were spending the summer at home because Paul couldn't bear to send them away. When Hilary insisted she wanted to find a job, Paul gave her one: keeping an eye on Bobby.

With Ruth, they became a foursome. Paul played Papa at restaurants, movies, weekends at home and in Manhattan. To please Bobby, he and Ruth began to take Fridays off from work and they went to Jones Beach. The first time, Ruth brought a picnic lunch from an elegant uptown brasserie: poached chicken, cheese, French bread, a cold quiche. Bobby was scandalized. "Where are the tuna sandwiches?" he wanted to know, and he sulked all day. From then on, Paul was in charge of beach lunches.

Ruth, the uptown kid, dragged them through museums and art galleries, to weekend movies on Third Avenue; with her, they sampled the joy and utter chaos of a Saturday shopping spree at

Bloomingdale's, where, praise be, Hilary was talked into buying a skirt and blouse that were not blue denim. Score one for Ruth's influence.

Her apartment became a stopping-off place for them on expeditions into Manhattan. Bobby made friends with Marmaduke, Ruth's cat, and wanted to know why they'd never had a pet at home. Hilary knew why, as did Paul, both having fought the good fight with Jane when Hilary was five. Jane had been allergic to cat fur and dander, she'd had a deep-rooted fear of dogs as well.

One rainy Sunday Marmaduke was transported in his travel box and spent the day *chez* Klein. If Ruth was still in awe of the big house, the cat loved it, wandering from room to room and floor to floor until, when it was time to leave, Marmaduke could not be found. A search party was dispatched, thirteen rooms to look through, countless nooks and crannies. Under the dust ruffle on Hilary's bed Marmaduke was finally found, happily chewing on Remus, the teddy bear.

The summer sizzled, and with the television advertising for the sangria finally running and doing well, Paul could cut his business trips and stay close to home. Yet, in that small space at the back of his mind where problems accumulated, something nagged. Hilary and Bobby were friendly to Ruth when they were with her, yet Paul knew they had not given her their hearts. Time would break down that barrier. And yet it bothered him when he chose to think about it.

His love for Ruth grew week by week through the busy, running-around summer. Her fair skin was turned light gold by the sun; in his eyes she blossomed. He showed her off at dinner parties, reveling in the look Michael gave her when she walked into his house wearing a revealing green shift. Those busy eyebrows of Michael's didn't stop dancing all evening. "A lot of woman," he said in a quiet moment when Kathleen was off showing Ruth the Bradie house. "And brainy, too? More than you deserve, pal."

"Every bit of what I deserve," Paul said.

"She's not a bit like Jane, you know. Complete antithesis. How does she get on with the kids?"

"Okay. Better with Hilary than Bobby, but she's gaining on him."

"December, you said? Getting married around Christmas."

"That's the plan, God willing. I wish it were sooner."

Michael took a long pull on his cigar, his face glowing red from the lighted tip. "I was thinking about Jane during dinner. Years ago, remember, how the girls would come down to see her, in their little nightgowns, hair in braids, and after kissing Kathleen and me they'd let Jane kiss them good night, too. They loved her so much, we all loved her so much." Michael rubbed his eyes with the back of his hand.

"That long weekend in Rufina, Paul, remember? When Enzo invited us for the harvest and we took the girls along? Four thousand miles for a weekend."

"We were much younger then," Paul said.

"Babies. That luncheon party Enzo gave in his villa up on the mountain. With the old guy playing accordion, and all of us drunk on the wine, out in the garden, with the reflecting pool and the cypresses, hot and dusty but beautiful too."

"The dance," Paul said.

"The tarantella. Kathleen and Jane, in their long summer dresses, wearing those big picture hats. They were so gorgeous that afternoon."

"That's when they became friends. That day."

"Yes. Dancing together, remember? Stepping into the reflecting pool, lifting their skirts, the sun so strong and yellow, one hand on their hats, one hand holding their skirts above the water, dancing and laughing in the pool while we all watched and applauded in time to the music. The loveliest day I've ever spent, Paul, the best."

"We were so afraid they wouldn't get along, Kathleen and Jane."

"They didn't, until then. Oh, man, what a day that was." Michael sighed, his small hand found Paul's shoulder. "Good luck with Ruth, Paul. I hope you'll be happy again. I hope we all live to be a hundred and twenty."

"Thanks, Mike."

"A good woman, that's it, isn't it? What makes us tick inside, what makes it all worthwhile. A good woman, Paul."

* * *

Dave and Phyllis Berg had a cookout in Ruth's honor, and invited half the neighborhood to meet her. "The night of a thousand eyes," Ruth called it when he took her home later that evening.

"It's only natural, babe," Paul said. "They all knew Jane very well. Are you upset?"

"A little. I felt like a prize petunia, with everyone coming up to look and sniff."

"You did very well."

"Who the hell cares?" Ruth said angrily. "I don't need the approval of the neighborhood to marry you. Christ, they did everything but take out a scale and weigh me. 'You're taller than Jane,' " Ruth said in a singsong voice. " 'You're much bigger than Jane,' 'Oh, Jane was so different from you,' 'I hope you can bake like Jane, her chocolate cake was always a hit at the bake sale.' "

"Easy, babe."

"I am not Jane, Paul, and I am not going to be like Jane. You better know that now. Sure, those people are your friends—"

"Only some of them," he put in.

"But I am not going to be buddy-buddy with them like she was. I'll be polite and friendly with the Bergs, sure, they're okay. But please keep those other types away from me."

That he promised to do, one of the many promises he was making each week to her, scattering them like dandelion seeds on the summer wind. "When they were married," those promises began, and ended always with his assurance that when they were tucked in together in the same house everything would be better. *When they were married,* the magic words that carried Ruth and himself through a time of short-tempered turmoil. They would have no formal period of engagement, they decided, so in effect this summer was it.

One Saturday he packed the kids into the Buick, picked up Ruth, and they traveled to Tarrytown to meet Ruth's parents. It was Paul's turn to be inspected. While Ruth's mother took the children outside to swim in the huge pool, Jesse Golden grilled Paul on his lifestyle, his business prospects, the general size of his bank account. Dr. Golden was a tall, spare man with thinning hair swept back to cover his scalp. Ruth's eyes came directly from him, gold flecks Paul found disconcerting when the doctor stared at him so directly.

"Good luck," Jesse Golden said as he shook Paul's hand. "I hope you'll make my Ruthie happy."

"I'll try," Paul said, pumping the bony surgeon's fingers.

"God knows she wasn't happy with us," Jesse Golden said. "She always wanted something we couldn't give her. It's strange to think that *you're* that something. And with two kids." He shook his head, smiling a shadow of Ruth's smile. "Don't give in to every little thing she wants, Paul. Ruthie can be very selfish sometimes. Hell, most times. A whim of iron, her mother calls it. Be careful."

Paul was shocked, but concealed his feelings until he could tell Ruth about it later that evening by telephone, with his children out of earshot. Ruth laughed, but without amusement. "You saw the Mercedes and the pool, right? The way they live? Would it amaze you to know that I had to fight for everything I got in that house? While my sister got anything she wanted. That's my daddy, and he still hasn't changed. You know what we're going to get for a wedding present from him? A sigh of relief."

Paul pressed her to set a date for their wedding, but Ruth kept putting him off. December was a good time, she had decided; they'd be married during Christmas week when her business was in a lull. The kids could be sent off to Sylvia in Florida; she and Paul could take a week for a real honeymoon in the Caribbean. "We'll both be wrecks by then," Paul told her. "This yo-yoing from your place to mine is killing me. I want you in my arms all night. I want to wake up and see you beside me."

"Do you think those kids are ready for me?"

The sixty-four-dollar question. "You know they like you, babe. They show it every time you're with them."

"Bobby loves Marmaduke," Ruth said. "You don't see his eyes, I do. Let's wait until Christmas."

"October."

"Paul, there are so many things *to do!* Subletting my apartment. Deciding about my furniture. Working out free time with George and my clients. Christmas."

The more he was with her, the more he hungered for her physically. He wanted to take her away with him for a week, a weekend, just the two of them. In his mind's eye he saw a cabin isolated far off in the woods; he and Ruth making love before a crackling fire. In reality, he wanted to stay just one night in her bed, forget the kids for one day, find time to be alone with her. Behind this wish came a wave of guilt: They were *his* children. How could he not want to be with them?

Back from the beach one Friday evening, sandy and tired, he persuaded Ruth to stay the night, saving him the round trip to Manhattan and back. He was sitting in the club chair in his bedroom when she emerged from the shower, wrapped in a long pink bath sheet of Jane's. Pure lust filled his heart. Disregarding Bobby's singing in the shower just across the hall, the music coming from Hilary's stereo on the far side of the bathroom wall, he wrapped Ruth in his arms, then tried to peel the towel away from her.

"The kids!" she hissed, fighting him off like a virgin. "Paul, no!"

He groaned and kissed her breasts, then fell down on the bed, alone. That night Ruth slept chastely in the guest room down the hall, while Paul tossed and turned alone in the big bed, debating the propriety of sneaking out of his room to join her. What if Hilary awakened, or Bobby had one of his post-midnight rambles? Frustrated, Paul fell asleep after two in the morning. The three Kleins were sitting at the breakfast table when Ruth appeared, looking fresh and beautiful in yesterday's clothing. "Sorry I'm late." Ruth smiled. "That bed is very comfortable." She went to the cabinet above the sink and took out a coffee mug for herself. The brown mug with a hairline crack down the inside, Jane's mug. Paul's mouth opened in surprise; he began to say no, but stopped himself as Ruth poured coffee into the mug and sat down at Jane's place at the table.

He saw the look that passed between the children, the shock. Paul felt a loss of breath at the sight of this woman sitting in his wife's place, drinking coffee from her mug.

He said nothing to Ruth when he took her home, but when he returned to the house that day he secretly took Jane's old mug and threw it away in the trash.

The second week in August, Ruth was away in California on

business, and returned on Friday night. He'd missed her terribly, even though he'd spoken to her by telephone three times during the week. They arranged an early dinner on Saturday, just the two of them, and a long evening at her place. Hilary and Peter Block were off to a late show at a Village club, which left Bobby alone. The boy was surly about it, but by now Paul had learned to harden his heart. He double locked the front door with his key and fled from Bobby's hard stare.

The California sun had deepened Ruth's tan. Stunning in a white dress, she met him at the little Greek restaurant. Hands joined across the table; underneath it knees touched. They couldn't wait to get back to her apartment and fall upon each other.

Two A.M. It couldn't be that late, he thought, then realized they had fallen asleep. He disengaged his leg from under the sleeping goddess and hastily got dressed, letting himself out quietly. It was almost three when he put his key in the front-door lock and turned it. *Twice?* It was unlike Hilary to double lock the door when she came home before him. Surely she'd seen the car was not in the drive.

Paul went quietly upstairs, standing for a moment in the dimly lit hall outside Hilary's closed door. When he opened it and peered in, he could see that her bed was still crisply made. Not home yet. Three A.M.

Easy, kiddo, the hair prickled on the back of his neck. Subways break down, shows can run overtime with many encores, Hilary and Peter could have stopped someplace for ice cream. He hung his tie and jacket away in the closet, then sat smoking a cigarette in the club chair. He decided he'd wait until three-thirty. He wandered downstairs to the kitchen and sat listening to the all-news station on the radio. Incidents were happening in the Middle East, but not on the subways. Where the hell had Hilary gone off to? Why hadn't he listened more carefully when she'd told him? Ruth was why, of course. Your mind was someplace else tonight, face it.

He tiptoed into Bobby's room, looking down for a moment at the sleeping boy, then waking him gently. "Don't get up, Bob-o. It's only me." He brushed a strand of damp hair from the boy's forehead. A warm night and the boy had the quilt tucked up to his ears. "What club did Hilary go to? Do you remember?"

"Oh . . . the Bottom Line."

"You're sure?"

"Uh huh." A big yawn interrupted. "Is anything wrong?"

"Go back to sleep. Everything's fine."

Downstairs he heard the rumble of a subway train pulling into the station nearby. Perhaps that's it, the train Hilary and Peter were on. In about two minutes they'd come walking up to the front door. He adjusted the venetian blind in the living room window that looked out to the street corner. A figure walked slowly past, coming from the direction of the subway station. Not Hilary.

The traffic lights turned from red to green and back again as he stood waiting and watching. With a sinking feeling, he went to the telephone in the kitchen, got information, dialed the number of the club. Eight rings at the other end. Nine. She's been in an accident. That sweet, young girl was injured somewhere. *No, don't think that!* Twelve rings and then a voice: "Yello?" in a Puerto Rican accent.

"Is this the Bottom Line?"

"Who is dis pliz?"

"You had a late show tonight. What time did it end?"

"I'm just de cleaner, man. Nobody here to talk to."

"Do you know when the show let out? When everyone left?"

"Is closed, ju know? The boss not here, man. Evveybody they go home a long time already. One o'clock."

Too long ago, much too long ago. He stood staring out into the garden. Where was she? Where the hell was she? Call the police, find out now. A seventeen-year-old girl, long brown hair, wearing jeans and a green E.R.A. T-shirt.

He lit a cigarette with trembling hands, his throat going dry. *Think!* She could be hurt, in a hospital, maybe dead. It doesn't take this long to get home, even if she and Peter stopped off someplace. Oh, please God, not dead! Should he call the Blocks' house to see if by some chance Peter was home? No, he'd go there himself, it wasn't far. He went out the front door, not double locking it behind him but running across the lawn to the car. Pulling out of the drive in haste, he stalled the Buick, cursed at it, then rolled to the corner and turned toward the subway station. He'd wait for one more train. Stupid kids, they could have stopped off with friends; they could have let time slip away without thinking.

The subway clerk was listening to disco music inside his booth. The clock above the turnstiles said two minutes to four. "Are . . . are the trains running okay?" Frog in his throat; Paul cleared it with a cough.

"Sure. Fine." The young moustachioed clerk's head bounced with the beat of the music. "Next one's due anytime now. From Manhattan, right?"

He nodded and walked away, lighting another cigarette. Far off, he could hear the clatter on the tracks below.

"That's it coming now," the clerk called out to him.

"Were there any tie-ups this morning?"

"Nope."

"Since one or two o'clock?"

"Everything's on time," the clerk said, "for once."

Please, please let them be on this train, he was thinking as it rolled into the station below. A well-dressed young couple came up the stairs from the platform, followed by a bearded teenager in jeans. No one else.

Paul left the station behind them, his heart pounding. He drove the few streets to the Blocks' house, parking out front. The house was dark, the porch light on, no car stood in the driveway. He rang the bell, hearing chimes inside the house in the quiet night. A dog barked next door. A few moments later he rang again, leaning on the bell this time and letting the chimes go on and on. Wake up, Blocks! Your son and my daughter are lost somewhere in this jungle of a city. Wake up! Was there no one home? He pushed the bell again. A light came on inside, the glow reflecting through the living room window. Paul heard feet padding toward the door. "Who's there?" asked a voice. *It was Peter!*

"Paul Klein," he said. "Peter?"

The door opened slowly, the front foyer light came on. Peter Block was standing there in jeans and nothing else, his face gone pale. "Where's Hilary?" Paul asked in a rush. "How come you're home? Did you drop her off somewhere? Peter!"

The boy stared, then backed a step away inside the house.

"Where is Hilary?!"

Paul heard the sound of footsteps coming down the stairs. Sneakers with red laces, jeans. "Daddy?" Hilary, in one piece, thank God, her eyes wide open, looking scared. "Daddy?"

A sound came from him then, a rush of tension letting go, of relief, and behind it a growl as he felt the heat of anger. "Where the hell have you been?" he snapped at them.

Peter backed away as Paul stepped inside the house. The boy looked at Hilary and blinked. "How long have you been home?" Paul asked.

"Daddy," Hilary began, then she stared at the floor.

"Where are your parents?" Paul said.

Peter shrugged, moving sideways a step so he stood behind Hilary.

"They're away for the weekend," Hilary said. "We fell asleep upstairs and—"

"Did you even *go* to the concert!" he roared at her, stepping forward so quickly she flinched backward a half-step.

"Daddy, listen—"

"Your parents away, an empty house," he spat at Peter. "It's after four in the morning, damn it! I thought she was hurt, or dead. Instead you were here all the time, weren't you?" They stared, silent. *"Weren't you?"*

"I'm sorry," Peter said, shame in his eyes. "We did fall asleep, Mr. Klein."

"You were lying to me!" he shouted at Hilary. "There never was any damn concert!"

Hilary's head turned slowly from side to side. The one word, "no," fell like a heavy weight from her lips. Paul's rage overflowed, his hands balled into fists, one arm moving back as if ready to strike Hilary. Instead that hand grasped her roughly by the arm and jerked her forward. "Get in the car," he said. He pulled her toward the door, then watched her descend the front steps. "And you, snot nose," he said, turning back to Peter, "your parents will hear about this. And stay away from my house!" Paul slammed the door shut and walked down the steps.

Hilary was sitting in the front seat of the Buick when he got in. He fumbled for the car keys in his pocket, glaring at her.

"I'm sorry," she said quietly. "I'm really sorry. It was a mistake."

He looked at her in the dim light that shone through the overarching trees, beyond anger now, feeling the relief of seeing her alive and not hurt.

"I didn't mean for this to happen," she said.

"I came home and you weren't there," he said. "I saw you dead a hundred times."

Hilary began to cry, one balled fist wiping angrily at her eyes.

"I don't want you to see him again," Paul said.

Hilary sobbed once, her hand to her mouth. "It's not just him. It's me, too."

His arms went around her, hugging her tight, loving her but not forgiving. "You lied," he said. "That's what hurts."

"You're not listening anymore," she said. "You're always someplace else since you met her."

He let her go then and started the engine, not driving away but looking at her.

"Everything's Ruth," Hilary said. "That's all you think about."

"That's not true."

"Isn't it? Isn't it where you were tonight? Ruth, Ruth, your darling Ruth!"

"Hilary, stop it! Just cut it out!"

"You're like a different person since you met her."

"Hogwash," Paul said. "I'm doing everything for you and getting nothing back. I give you freedom and understanding and you lie to me."

The hard look on the girl's face chilled his heart. "You think your precious Miss Perfect doesn't lie?" Hilary said bitterly. "All she wants is you. She doesn't give a damn about Bobby and me."

"What's bugging you? That I can love someone else? Does it hurt you so much?"

"She's a phony, and you're the only one who doesn't see it. Ask Bobby, he'll say the same."

"You're grounded," Paul said. "You don't leave the house until school starts. And if Peter comes around, so help me I'll kill him. You got that?"

"Yeah," Hilary said, turning away from him to stare into the dark street. They sat for a moment in charged silence, the anger between them like a wall. Paul wanted to hit her, he wanted to hug her, he wanted the words she'd said to go out of his mind.

"Marry her," Hilary said quietly. "That's all you care about, so marry her."

"If you knew how much she loved you, how much Ruth cares about you," he said. "She's the one holding back, not me. All she wants is a little love and understanding from you."

"Marry her," the girl said.

Ruth saw the look on his face when he came to her apartment the next afternoon, heard the tension in his voice when he brushed aside her offer of coffee or a drink. "Marry me," Paul said. "I can't wait any longer."

"Paul . . ."

"We're falling apart without you, Ruth. Falling into little pieces."

"I thought we'd agreed on Christmas week. Time for—"

"September," he interrupted. "Sometime in September."

"Paul, that's impossible."

The hard look in his eyes frightened her. "Nothing's impossible if you want it bad enough. I need you. Now. So do the kids." He told her about the events of the early morning, anger in his voice each time he said Hilary's name. He did not tell her what Hilary had said. "What's your schedule in September?"

"The same as always, impossible. Not to mention the apartment, my furniture—"

"Details. I'll pay to store the furniture, and I'll have my attorney handle your lease. That's only money. It's you I need." He pulled her into his arms, looking into her gold-flecked green eyes. "September. The kids will be back in school, settled down. You pick the date. As long as it's not Friday the thirteenth."

She kissed his cheek. "You're rushing me, Paul."

"That's right. I am."

"You're rushing the kids, too."

"Right again. September."

"They don't know me, they don't trust me yet."

"September."

"Be reasonable, Paul. Rushing is only going—"

"To get you home with me fast." He put a grin on his face, the one that stirred her. "September," he said, "or tomorrow, take your pick."

"Oh, Paul," she said, feeling his arms tight against her.

"That's my last and final word."

"It's foolish," she said.

"We're in love, babe. It's okay to be foolish."

Her arms went about him then, her body tight against his and fitting perfectly. "September, then, you crazy man," she whispered in his ear, kissing his cheek. "I love you so much," she said before he kissed her lips.

Holding her close, he realized she had begun to cry softly. Home and dry, he thought, everything is going to work out just fine.

One tiny tear wet his cheek.

PART
THREE

16

HERE IS RUTH on the subway coming home to Jane's house: She is standing in the middle of a crowded car hanging on to a pole for dear life as the train jolts around a curve. A tall woman in jeans, raincoat, and cowboy hat, she towers over the Hispanic man standing next to her who is admiring her out of the corner of his eye; she looks out through the grimy window at culvert walls gray with rain, then checks her reflection in the same window. Mrs. Klein, she thinks. It does have a ring to it. Third finger left-hand ring, in fact, of antique gold, there on the hand that holds the pole in the middle of this smelly car.

Paul had told her all about the subway, but the son of a bitch should have warned her. People did this twice a day, amazing. Crammed in like olives in a jar. Fifty-five minutes she'd traveled thus far from the station near her office uptown, changing trains once to catch this decaying graffitied local. How romantic Paul had made this very subway line seem, telling her with relish how a man who had lived down his very street had built it as a posh railroad to carry important people from lower Manhattan to the track and beach resort in Coney Island. Now it was a subway, and a lousy one. But that was Paul—confidence man, supersalesman. He could tell her anything and she'd believe him. All he had to do was smile, show her those crinkly lines at the corner of his dark eyes, touch her with those big hands, call her babe. She grinned, thinking about Paul, missing him but knowing he'd call tonight.

"Love conquers all, babe. Believe it." Yes.

The local screeched to a grinding halt at the station and she fought her way out of the crowded car, stepping into cold driving rain. She followed the crowd to the stairs, juggling her heavy shoulder bag and her attaché case from hand to hand. Late again, five minutes to seven and—shit!—she'd forgotten to take something out of the freezer for dinner that morning. Six weeks a bride and a stepmother and she was still fucking up. And Paul down in Miami was probably stepping off the warm, sunlit beach at this very moment.

She paused at the station door upstairs, then stepped into a gust of wind that blew icy spray into her face. How could it be so cold and still rain? Forget it. Run, baby, run. She broke into a fast jog, reminding herself that she hadn't gone to exercise class or been running since a week before the wedding. How the hell could she find the time for it now? Up at the crack of dawn to get the boy ready for school, then Hilary, then a fast shower, and off to work so she could get at least *something* done by the time the damn telephones started ringing.

What I did for love, she thought, not singing it.

George was making those funny faces at her again, rolling his almond-shaped eyes when she left the office for home, as he did tonight. There wasn't enough time in the day for them, never had been before, and it was worse now. Dear loyal, lovely George. She'd left him with copy for six ads; he'd be there until ten or eleven tonight doing layouts. Alone. Not like just two months ago when she would stay and work with him, not contributing a lot, but at least being there. That's what partners were for.

At the corner, waiting for the traffic light to change, she was wheezing. Ten years of running like a maniac to stay in shape and she'd blown it in six weeks of sloth. Tonight, after dinner, after Bobby went to bed, after she did the work she'd brought home with her, she'd get into her sweat clothes and the nylon running jacket and do a slow two miles.

The hell she would.

She'd collapse into the big empty bed, hug Paul's pillow to her, and try to fall asleep. And maybe tonight she'd remember to set the clock-radio alarm for that ungodly hour. There was nothing worse than waking up late, realizing the alarm hadn't gone off, waking the boy under panic conditions ("seven o'clock, Bobby, I'm sorry, we'd better hurry"), and getting him dressed, breakfasted, and off to school with a lunch in his knapsack. That was a time to go back to bed in a state of shock, not go off to the office.

She climbed the front steps and got under the porch roof and out of the rain. Black night in early October and no porch lights on. The house looked dark and uninhabited. Just once she'd like to come home to find both kids waiting for her. Or one of them. Just a friendly face at the door to open it for her, to smile and say hello.

Once inside, she put her attaché case down with relief, thinking of the work she'd brought home. How do you create a fresh, provocative thirty-second TV spot for jeans after all the hype that had gone down in the past couple of years? How, baby? They should never have taken the account. The company was second-rate; guttersnipe Seventh Avenue rag merchants looking to cash in and be trendy, but just too damn late. And too damn cheap. Class, they wanted, pronounced "kless."

"Hello, up there!" Ruth called. "I'm home!" There was no response. "Hold the applause," she added.

She brushed wet hair away from her forehead and went into the foyer bathroom to wash and make herself halfway human after the rain and the foul subway.

Bobby was waiting for her in the kitchen, sitting on top of the chopping block. "What's for dinner?"

"Hello to you, too," Ruth said.

"Oh, hello. How are you?"

"Lousy. That subway is inhuman. How do you stand it twice a day?"

The boy shrugged. "It's not too bad."

"Not too bad for what? Goats?"

"It's not too crowded when I go, in the morning. And coming home it's empty."

"Lucky you." She went to the liquor cabinet in the dining room and brought back a bottle of Dewar's. When she put tap water into the drink the surface was covered with a white foam. She took a sip, made a face to coax a grin from the boy who was watching her. We are not amused, she thought.

"Homework all done?"

Bobby nodded.

"You never forget, do you?"

"Nope," he said. "And you always ask me anyway."

"Sorry about that."

"Look, Ruth, I always do my homework. Even when my mother died, I did it then. And I fed Marmaduke, which is your next question, right?"

"Am I that predictable?" she asked.

"How did things go in school today?" Bobby asked in a fair imitation of her voice. "Fine," he answered himself, "just fine."

She stared at him over the lip of her drink, wanting to hug him or slug him. Ignore it, she told herself. Give it time. "Where is Marmaduke, by the way? He's my cat, you'd think he'd show his face once in a while when I'm around."

"He's up in my room, playing with a tennis ball. He likes me."

"I noticed that."

"I feed him, maybe that's why. And I clean his litter box."

"And maybe he likes you just because you're a nice kid," Ruth said. "Did you ever think of that?"

Bobby shrugged.

"You should feel honored, you know. Marmaduke is a snooty cat, he doesn't like everyone." Stepping forward, she put her arms around Bobby, seeing his gaze fall even as she approached. She hugged him as he sat on the counter; he turned his face to avoid her breasts, a block of stone in her arms. She let him go. "Speaking of dinner," she said, "we've got a problem."

"You forgot again."

"Bingo."

She watched his eyes roll up to heaven and back down again, the mocking grin begin at the corners of his mouth, Paul's grin in miniature. "All is not lost, however," she went on, as gaily as she could. "From my vast repertoire of culinary miracles, and always

206

providing we have the ingredients in the house, I offer you the following delicious choices.''

"Not French toast and not homemade pizza on English muffins," Bobby said.

"Okay."

"Guido's pizza is so much better," the boy said, "and I don't like French toast the way you make it."

"And here I thought it was a gourmet's delight."

"It's dry, and it has that yucky white stuff on the edges."

"How descriptive," she said drily. "Scrambled eggs?"

Bobby shook his head. "I'll have the Japanese soup." He jumped down from the chopping block and turned toward the pantry. "I can make it. Do we have scallions in the house?"

"Of course," Ruth said, hoping it was true. Did she remember to buy them last Saturday? "I'll make it for you."

"Never mind," the boy said. "We have sesame oil, I know that." He took the rectangular package from the pantry, put it on the counter.

Ruth opened the refrigerator. Kneeling down to the chiller compartment at the bottom she searched through lettuce, celery, packaged carrots. Thank heavens. "Scallions!" she announced. "I can make the soup for you, Bob."

"That's okay." He pounded the soup package with a hard karate chop. The package split and a white spray of curly noodles covered the counter top. "Shit!" the boy said. He stared at the littered counter.

"It's okay," Ruth said. "We can save it."

"It's not okay. Look what I did. Stupid!" His voice was close to a shout.

"Don't sweat it," she said. Quickly, she got a pot from under the stove, went to the counter, and began brushing the noodles off the edge and into the pot.

"What are you doing?" Bobby said. "That won't work. You have to boil water first, *then* put the noodles in."

"Oh. Well, I'll put up some water to boil in another pot, and then I'll put the noodles in. How much water?"

"Jesus," Bobby said.

"How much water?" She turned to get another pot.

"I can't believe this," Bobby said. "You don't even know how to make Jap soup. You can't even cook as good as my *father.*"

"This is true," she said.

"He's twice as good as you are. So is Hilary."

"I'm not as good a cook as your mother. Isn't that what you're trying to say?"

The boy blinked at her, mouth turning down. *"Nobody is as good a cook as my mother."*

"And especially not me. Right?"

"That's right, especially not you."

"Good," she said, getting up. "So we know where we stand. Now, how much water for the soup?"

The boy turned away, began walking from the kitchen.

"Bobby? Hey!"

"Screw the soup," he said. "I won't eat." He kept walking.

With quick strides, still holding the pot, she pursued, catching him in the front hall. "Don't give me crap, pal, okay?" she said. "Let's at least act like human beings to each other. Like it or not, you're stuck with me. And I don't care if we all eat bread sandwiches, we'll have dinner together, you, me, and Hilary."

"What if I don't want to eat?" he said, scowling.

"Then you'll sit there and keep us company."

"And what if I don't want to?"

"You'll do it anyway, because I say so. When your father's away, I'm in charge here. And I don't give a damn whether you like it or not." She met his hot eyes with fire in her own and stared him down. "Now, go upstairs and tell your sister to get her sweet ass down here."

"Ass?" The boy's eyes widened.

"You heard me. There's nothing wrong with ass. You can say it and I won't even be offended."

"I wish you'd get your sweet ass out of this house," Bobby said.

"Sorry, pal, I'm here to stay."

"I wish my father'd never married you."

"Yeah, I noticed that, too. Call your sister."

His eyes flashed, but he turned and headed upstairs. Ruth followed to the landing to make sure he did as she'd asked. She watched as he opened Hilary's door without knocking and went in.

The door slammed shut behind him, rattling the pictures on the wall.

Christ, she thought, the wicked stepmother comes home and all is chaos. Soap opera time, except it was too damn real. The little squirt had the charm of an ayatollah; his sister had the warmth of an icicle. The dynamic duo versus Wonder Woman, one hell of a match-up except for the players in the game.

She stood for a moment, looking up at the photographs on the wall. Small dark-haired Jane in her bridal veil looked down on her. They're your kids, lady, you made them, Ruth thought. And neither of them wants me here.

And, I get the feeling, neither do you.

She'd worn a cocktail dress of beige silk at the wedding, bought in ten minutes at a boutique around the corner from her office. A nifty-swifty wedding, she called it, although it turned out fine, thanks to Kathleen Bradie. Kathleen had insisted on having Paul and Ruth married in the Bradies' big house in Short Hills. "So much nicer than a judge's study, Ruth, and no trouble at all. And if you say one more word, I'll slug you, so help me."

Help *me,* Ruth almost said. I need all the help I can get.

All her lovely furniture carted off and into storage. Her sweet little apartment, home for five years and *at last* the way she wanted it, taken apart before her very eyes. Just a few things went to the house on Rugby Road. Her cocktail table, sleek chrome and glass, to replace the nicked and scarred wooden one in front of Paul's couch. Miraculously, it fit in. Her typing stand and I.B.M. Selectric, copywriter's tools, set up in the guest room, which would become her office at home. One lamp from her living room to Paul's, and another that didn't look quite right in the guest room, but she couldn't bear to part with it. Her beautiful white couch, so perfect for lounging, stuck away in a storage vault. It couldn't be helped.

She felt like a space invader, landing on a foreign planet.

Putting her clothing into that old triple dresser in Paul's bedroom, so spooky. Her bedroom now, *theirs*. Now her clothing would smell from Jane's lavender sachets. The hell it would. On the sly she removed them, hiding them in her handbag until she could dump them later on at home. Home no longer. The lease was set to rights, Paul's attorney handled it, and if money had changed hands (likely) she didn't know about it. And a hundred *schlepping* trips back and forth to Paul's place. *Hers!* Why couldn't she ever say it right, Dr. Freud?

The nifty-swifty bride.

Golden/Chan took it on the chin. All those wedding plans, thousands of phone calls, and the bride-to-be had to take care of business, too. Poor George. "You sure you can't get married in the office, Ruthie?" he asked her one night, grinning. "We'll just push these layouts aside, plenty of room. And that way we can keep working."

"Shut up and draw, wise guy, or we'll never get out of here."

She picked the wedding date, Friday afternoon, September tenth, in a toss-up between two appointments for commercial shoots and her regular-as-clockwork menstrual cycle. Push that bank commercial back a week; she'd be damned if she'd have the curse on her honeymoon. Honeymoon? A long weekend somewhere, Friday night to Tuesday. Back in the office on Wednesday. Paul arranged their trip, but he wouldn't tell her where they were going. About the only surprise the nifty-swifty bride would have.

They were all being so *wonderful* toward her. Michael supplied the judge, Alfred B. Rosman, a friend who lived just down the road. Kathleen thought of all the little things Ruth had forgotten. The Bergs would take the kids for the weekend, not to worry. And Paul. Mostly Paul. Always and forever Paul, the reason for it all. When she got hysterical, he calmed her. When her quick temper boiled over, he rode with it. She hoped he wouldn't invite the whole neighborhood, and he didn't. Only the Bergs and Marion Gerber. Plus a couple of people from his office. Grandma Sylvia was not coming. *"Thank God,"* Paul said.

She kept the list from her side short as well. Her parents, of course; her sister, Diane, and husband, Gary; George and Grace Chan; a couple of women friends from agencies she'd worked for; one friend with husband; plus two old girl friends from college and one from Westchester, her oldest friend, Susie.

Now the guests were all gathered downstairs in the big Bradie living room, which was overflowing with flowers. Pouring rain, but it didn't matter. She looked at herself in Kathleen's dressing-table mirror and smiled. Happy's the bride 'cause the sun shines on today, even if it's raining. Don't get sentimental now, she cautioned herself, that's not your style.

"All ready downstairs," Kathleen announced, coming into the room to escort her downstairs like a good matron of honor. "And not one of them drunk yet."

"Including my husband?"

"Especially not your husband. He's holding on to Bobby and Hilary for dear life. Your sister, Diane, is it? She's stunning."

"Always was."

Kathleen smiled at her in the mirror. "But not as gorgeous as you, Ruth. Not today." Kathleen took up a hairbrush and lightly stroked the back of Ruth's long hair. "I'm surprised you didn't put it up, or have it set differently. For today, I mean."

"Not one pin or roller gets into this mop, not ever," Ruth said. "For tonight, I meant."

"Why is this night different from any other night?" Ruth said, winking. She saw Kathleen's pink cheeks color. "Sorry. Did I shock you?"

"Of course not," Kathleen said. "We're all grown-ups these days."

"There will be something different," Ruth said. "Paul won't be getting up to go home."

Kathleen laughed. "I'm glad you both saved *something*, anyway."

"Tell me about Jane, Kath," Ruth said.

"She was a wonderful friend, like I hope you'll be."

"I think we will be friends. Was Jane a confidante?"

"After some years. But finally, yes."

"Was there anything you didn't like about her? She scares me a little. A tough act to follow."

"Don't worry about Jane," Kathleen said. "You're not a bit like her, you know."

"I know. She was perfect, like my sister, Diane."

"Not perfect," Kathleen said. "Too quiet, sometimes, reserved. Like when Mike told a bawdy joke and I boomed out my big laugh, I'd look at her and she'd be barely smiling. Made me feel a bit coarse to be laughing, if you take my meaning."

"That's not much."

"She was like that. She could be prim and proper. Schoolteacherish. But we loved her for it. You know, always trying to get a rise out of her, for fun. And she could be didactic, too. Her way was the best. She read this and so and knew this and such. That could be a bit much, sometimes.''

"And with the kids?"

"I could never be so patient, let me tell you. I'd shush them or swat them, but she never did.''

"Saint Jane."

"Not really. Ah, but listen, this isn't for you to be worrying about five minutes before your wedding. You're a gift from God, Ruth, for Paul and those kids.''

"The kids sure don't think so."

"They will. Just give it a bit, they'll come around."

"When I'm old and gray, probably."

"My money's on you, kid. Just be you, Ruth, not Jane. You'll be fine. You're tougher than both those kids put together.''

"We should have waited until December."

"Well," Kathleen said with a smile, "if you want to back out, now's the time, my girl.''

"Not a chance."

"The kids will be gone faster than you think. Hilary to college next year, Bobby a few years later. It goes quickly, Ruth, too damn quickly.''

"I'll tell you something else that scares me, Kath. That house. It's her house, you know, her taste, her touch all over it. And starting next week, I'll be living there. Sleeping in her bed, sitting in her chair, fluffing up her needlepoint pillows.''

"Redecorate, then," Kathleen said. "Not right away, though. That wouldn't be a good idea. But maybe next spring or summer. Make the house yours.''

"And do I take her picture down from the wall?"

Bending over, Kathleen brushed the top of Ruth's head with a phantom kiss. "Speaking of down, I think we should be going. We've kept them waiting just long enough. Let me check you out.''

Ruth rose and turned slowly under Kathleen's smiling gaze. "You'll do, I suppose," she grinned. "Something old?"

"These shoes. They even match the dress."

"And the dress is new, of course."

"What do I borrow?"

"The family Bible on the dressing table, there. I did remember to bring it up from the living room this morning. You can carry it in your hand during the ceremony. Something blue?"

"Bikini panties, with a little rip in the seat. You won't tell Paul, will you?"

"Hell, no," Kathleen said. "Let him find out for himself."

Ruth and Bobby were sitting in the living room, watching a *M*A*S*H* rerun, when later that evening Paul telephoned from Florida. Bobby picked up the phone in the pantry and called out to her: "It's Dad!" then dashed off to the intercom in the kitchen to call Hilary. "Howdy, stranger," Paul said to her. "How's it going?"

"Fine," she said, before she heard two extensions click and the kids were saying hello.

"It was seventy-five and sunny down here," Paul said. "Beautiful. I understand you had some rain."

"And cold," Ruth said. "It's drafty in this big house."

"Put a sweater on," Paul said. "How are things with you, Hil?"

"Okay, Daddy," the girl said.

"Good. And you, Bob-o?"

"I'm fine, Dad."

"Everybody getting along?" Paul asked.

There was an instant of hesitation, at least it seemed so to Ruth, and then both kids chorused yes.

"Ruth forgot to defrost dinner again," Bobby said.

Paul laughed. "I've been there."

Ruth waited for Bobby to go on, to tell his father about his nose-to-nose confrontation with her, but the boy didn't mention it.

The children talked with Paul for a while as Ruth listened, then he said good night to them and asked to speak to Ruth alone. They both waited for the kids to click off the line. "I miss you, babe," Paul said.

"Same here."

"How's it *really* going?"

Before she could answer, Bobby was coming past her from the

213

kitchen. He stopped a few feet away and looked at her. "Well," she said, "not exactly terrific." Her eyes met the boy's.

"What happened?"

She met Bobby's cool stare and did not speak.

"Is someone listening?" Paul asked.

"You got it, buster."

"Bobby?"

"Yep."

She heard Paul sigh. "This too shall pass," he said. "I wish he'd loosen up and give you a break."

"That makes two of us."

"Why don't you shoo him off?" Paul asked. "Tell him to scoot."

"I'd rather not do that right now," she said. "I'm in enough trouble as it is."

"Oh, babe, I wish he'd see what you are. He's really a very sweet kid."

"I know that."

"Nuts," Paul said. "I'll see you Friday, then. My days are filled with Chilean exporters, none of whom is as pretty as you. And if Michael hadn't dashed off to France on such short notice, I'd be home with you now. *Caramba!* That's my big Spanish word for today. How about I call you later when the kids are asleep and we'll talk dirty?"

"Then I'll never get to sleep. Klein, good-bye."

"And good night to you, Mrs. Klein. And doesn't that sound good!" He clicked off.

Ruth put down the telephone, her smile fading as Bobby's rose. "That isn't a very nice thing to do," she said, "listening in on a private conversation."

"I wanted to hear if you were going to tell Dad about tonight."

"You heard. I didn't say much."

"Thanks." The boy stood very still as he gazed at her, long lashes blinking under the overhead light. "I'm sorry about the soup," he said at last.

"And I'm sorry I lost my temper," Ruth said.

"Sometimes I get very mad."

"Me too. When my Irish comes up, look out." She looked at his serious expression and smiled. "Level with me, Bob. What's going on? Ever since I moved in here you've been different."

The boy shrugged.

"Strong silent type, eh? Look—I really thought we'd be friends. Right from the day you taught me how to make salad, remember? But lately . . . Have I done something wrong, Bobby?"

"Ruth," he said, then stopped. The sad look in his eyes made Ruth's heart lurch. Bobby shrugged. "I have to take a shower," he said, then turned away and went upstairs.

The boy was in bed at last and now she could work. No tucking-in ritual for the stepmother, oh no. That was reserved for Big Daddy alone. Only he could tuck those covers in tight, kiss that brow, ruffle that little head of hair. It hurt, that withholding of affection. She was a physical person, as Paul was. When she was alone with Bobby at bedtime, like tonight, all she got was a cold brow to plant a kiss on. Her job was to see to the night light and close the door after the boy was in bed. It left her with a need unfulfilled.

The boy had even taken her cat. Marmaduke was asleep on Bobby's bed, the unfaithful wretch. She could use Marmaduke right now, as she sat in the rocker in the guest room and tried to come up with a jeans campaign. A smooth feline to pet and stroke as she thought, a warm body to hold in her lap.

The door opened and Hilary's head appeared. "Ruth, can I talk to you?"

"Sure. Come on in. I'm not getting much work done, anyway."

The girl seated herself on a corner of the studio couch. "I've got a slight problem," she began.

"I'm listening."

"Well, there's this boy in my trig class. He's been after me ever since school began. Mark Becker, he's on the swim team, but he's not like a jock or anything. Very smart and really nice."

"Uh huh."

"He passes me these notes in class. They're very funny. You know, comments on Mr. Glass, the trig teacher, who's a complete idiot."

"What about Peter?"

"Oh. Well, that's mostly over. He's still a friend, but not the way we were. Not since I've been grounded. We talked it over and decided we should see other people. Except since I can't go out at night I haven't been able to see anyone."

"Has Peter?"

"Not yet. He's really very shy, you see, so it's not easy for him."

"So what's your problem?"

"Well, there's this swim meet in school on Friday night. Mark wants me to come and root for him, then afterward we would go out for a Coke or something, and he would bring me home after that. I wouldn't be home late, Ruth, before twelve o'clock for sure."

"But you're grounded, Hil," Ruth said.

The girl's smile was cautious. "I thought perhaps you could let me go."

Ruth thought about that for a moment. "You spoke to Paul tonight, when he called. Why didn't you ask him about it?"

"Never mind," Hilary said. She got up from the couch, her face a mask.

"Wait. Let's talk about it."

"I should have known what you'd say."

"Hil," Ruth said, "that's a little unfair, isn't it?"

"Is it? I don't think so. You're not on my side. Anything my father says is okay with you, right?"

"Your *father* grounded you, Hil, not me. It's up to him to unground you."

"Sometime next year," the girl said.

"Not that long. I'm sure."

"How do you know?" Hilary said with some heat. "I'm not on his mind anymore, or didn't you notice? He doesn't give a rat's ass about me, or about Bobby anymore."

"That's not true."

Hilary stood in the doorway. "Good night," she said, but made no move to go.

"I don't like what's happening between us," Ruth said. "I know you resent my marrying your father. And it's not easy for you to accept another woman in the house after your mother. I understand all that, Hil, but give me a chance. Let's get to know each other. We haven't had one decent conversation since the wedding. Am I such a terrible person?''

The girl said nothing.

Later that evening, when Hilary's light had been out for an hour, Ruth went downstairs to use the kitchen phone to call Paul. She told him about her conversation with Hilary, and some of what had happened with Bobby, but not all of it.

''Don't be upset,'' Paul said. ''It's only the old whipsaw game, that's all, honey. They did it with Jane and me, lots of times. Jane was always the one who said no, and I was Mister Softie. So they'd come to me all the time to get me to work on Jane.''

''How did I get in the middle?''

''You did that by marrying me, remember?'' Paul said, laughing. ''Hey, relax, it's not serious, babe.''

''So why do I feel like the Wicked Witch of the West?''

''They'll get over it. Just give it time and let me be the heavy, okay? I'm the father, I make the rules. You stay out of it.''

''I love you.''

''I wish you were here to prove it. Get some sleep, okay? And don't worry.''

She tossed about in the big bed for an hour, but sleep would not come. There were noises in this big old house, spooky noises at one o'clock in the morning without a man around. That bang from behind the dresser, for instance, which was probably Bobby thrashing about in his sleep and hitting the wall. The wind rattling the windows. The gurgling outside the bedroom wall as rain ran off the roof and down the leader pipe.

She heard the heating system kick on far below and the sigh of forced air coming through the registers. That entailed a whole catalog of other noises. Paul had explained most of them to her. Something about tin ducts expanding and contracting as the heat passed through them. Even so, each metallic *ping* was scary.

Ruth put on a robe and went down to the kitchen. Should have put on socks, too, she thought as she felt a draft. She sat at the Papa Bear's place, waiting for her tea to steep. Jane's house. A wall of wicker breadbaskets behind the stove. The plants on the windowsills, she'd have to get to at least know the *names* of them. Two woks, no waiting. Nice wallpaper that looked like tile and a vinyl floor like brick. All in good taste, Jane, can't fault you there. She took a small loose-leaf notebook from the shelf behind her and opened it. Recipes, some clipped from newspapers and magazines, others in small, neat handwriting. "Special Brownies," "Sylvia's Meat Loaf." *Jane D. Klein,* a very neat signature on the inside of the blue cover. Small, organized, and very buttoned-up, Ruth thought, another Miss Perfect in whose footsteps I'm supposed to follow.

Did anything ever scare you, Jane, she wondered? Did anything ever come along that was too big and too difficult for you to handle? Were you ever disappointed in yourself? Superwife, Supermom. Did you have faults, were you human?

Deep inside, Ruth felt an ache of fear and dread. She'd gotten off on the wrong foot with the kids. The house made her feel uncomfortable. And no matter how much that sweet, handsome, smart, and totally lovable man said not to worry, she was worried.

She was not alone. Jane was still here somehow, in this house, and no one could measure up to her standards.

Below her the heat came on again. Cold air coming before the warm surged through the register near the floor and chilled her feet. In the quiet kitchen it sounded like a moan.

17

"You know what?" George Chan was saying as he filled in the dancing figures on his television storyboard. "This is a hell of an idea. I think it's going to work."

"Of course it's going to work," Ruth said. "I thought of it, didn't I?"

George grinned at her. "You're a bloody genius."

"This is true," she said, *"and* extremely modest. The poster will work, too, just the way you've sketched it."

"A Lautrec campaign for blue jeans," George said. "Crazy."

"Like a fox. They want different, we'll give them different." She held up George's poster sketch and looked at it through squinted eyes, letting the total effect fill her vision while the details went fuzzy. It was one of her little tricks, learned through years in the business; look away from the trees and see the forest. George's sketch was a loose rendering of a Toulouse-Lautrec cabaret poster, capturing the same line and mood. Except that the figure in the foreground and all the smaller ones dancing behind her were wearing jeans instead of the flowing dresses of turn-of-the-century Paris.

"I hope we don't catch hell, fiddling with Lautrec."

"We should be so lucky," Ruth said. "Controversy would be a plus. And after all, George, the jeans are French. Look—there isn't a damn thing we can say about these jeans that hasn't been said before, and on much bigger budgets than we have to work with. And I've been wearing the stupid jeans ever since we got the account." She made a face at her partner. "What can I tell you? They're jeans, that's all. No better or worse than anyone else's jeans. So we've got to give them flash to stand out."

"Oh, it'll stand out all right." George took a bite of the hamburger that he had unwrapped a long time ago, before they had sparked to the work in front of them. "You want a cold hamburger?"

"No thanks." Ruth speared some of her salad and chewed on it thoughtfully.

"Do you have a copy line for the poster?" he asked her.

"A few," she said. "One I really like." She cleared her throat with a dramatic flourish. "Are you ready? I kind of like . . . *Never too tight, never Toulouse.*"

George looked at her, then laughed out loud, covering his mouth with his hand as if to apologize. "You wouldn't."

"Why the hell not? It's just crazy enough to work."

"Never Toulouse," George said, shaking his head and grinning. "Do I have to be there when you spring it on the client?"

"Never mind the client. I'll murder him if he doesn't buy it." She took a sip of the coffee in the Styrofoam cup at the edge of George's drawing board. "Cold. To go with your hamburger."

"Rabbit food again?" George said. "What's with you, Ruthie? It's too cold to eat salads all the time."

"A woman is supposed to have a waistline," she said. Ruth stretched, then got up to walk a few paces around the office, twisting her neck to loosen the tension there.

"I don't run anymore, or go to exercise class. And I've fallen into a family of eaters. I've got to watch it, George, or I'll turn into a fat hausfrau."

"You? Fat?"

"I can just about get into these jeans, buster."

"I don't think Paul would mind if you put on a few pounds," George said.

"You mean the king?" Ruth said, smiling. "No, he's pretty happy these days. But I'd mind."

"Oh, before I forget," George said, "a friend of mine called. There's supposed to be a watch account looking for a new agency, and he has an inside track. So we might get to make a pitch."

"Good, good," Ruth said, hardly listening. She looked out the window for a few moments as George went on. Far below on Third Avenue the streets were jammed with people on their lunch break. "Tell me about kids, George," she said.

"Well, they're small, they cry a lot, and some of them are cute."

"What would you do if your kids didn't like you?" she asked.

"Drown them, I guess," George said. He looked at his partner, who stood unmoving before the window. "Are they still cool, Ruthie?"

"Cold is more like it."

"Damn," he growled. "How could they not like you? Hit 'em with a two-by-four."

"That's Paul's department. And he won't lay a glove on them."

"Well," George said, "to tell you the truth, I don't see my kids anymore. I've got this bug-out partner who runs away at five o'clock and leaves me with a deskful of work every night. So I've forgotten about kids."

Ruth made a face at him.

"Kids," he said. "Well, let's see. You've got your carrot and you've got your stick. Bribery works, sometimes, you could try that. I remember when Timmy wouldn't let himself be potty trained, he was driving Grace bananas. Grace's mother came to stay with us. A pretty smart old bird, that lady. It was Easter, and she brought all these chocolate bunnies for the kids, and she told Timmy that she'd give him a chocolate bunny every time he went and made on the potty. That was it, Ruthie. Timmy kept running and sitting on the potty whether he had to go or not. In two days he was trained, no more diapers. Plain old bribery did the trick."

"Bribery, huh?" Ruth said, turning the idea over in her mind. It was certainly worth a try. She ruffled George's thick black hair. "Thanks. I'm off."

"Wait a minute," George said as she turned to leave his office. "Ruth, where are you going?"

"Bloomingdale's."

"But we've got work. Ruth?" he called after her, but the nifty-swifty bride was gone.

She came sweeping into the house that evening, ringing the doorbell because she knew Paul was already home and would come to the door. "Look at you!" he cried, pulling her into his arms before she had a chance to take off her coat or drop the attaché case and the big Bloomingdale's bag she carried. "Easy." She laughed as he squeezed her tight. "Don't break the merchandise."

"Some merchandise," he said, kissing her cheek. How could he have been lucky enough to find a woman so beautiful and wonderful and filled with life? Was it God's way of making up? He helped her doff her raincoat, grinning at the boy-styled Irish tweed cap rakishly tilted on her golden hair, secretly wanting her to keep it on for the evening so he could just look at the happy picture she made in it. Bridegroom seduces second wife in front hall; children shocked. Down, boy.

In the kitchen he gave her a scotch to match the bourbon he'd already started, taking care to make the drink light and watery, the way Ruth preferred it. "I haven't given dinner one thought," she said airily as she toasted him.

"I'd already figured that out," he grinned, indicating with a nod the grocery package that stood on the chopping block. "Wokking tonight on the old camp grounds. You are not to do a thing except look gorgeous."

"That's easy."

"And tell me what a wonderful cook I am, which is true, of course."

"Of course," Ruth said. "Where are the kids?"

Paul shrugged. "Upstairs. What's in the Bloomie's bag?"

She ignored him and brought the bag to the table, distributed gift-wrapped packages at each place except her own, then called the kids on the intercom. As they waited for the children, she grinned at the perplexed look on Paul's face but refused to say more.

"Isn't it early for dinner?" Hilary said, then caught sight of the packages on the table. "Presents?"

"The mystery woman strikes," Paul said to her.

"Patience, patience," Ruth said as they waited for Bobby.

"What's going on?" the boy asked when he walked into the kitchen to find everyone staring at him.

"It's a holiday," Ruth said. "I, Ruth Klein, née Golden, have declared a holiday." She grinned at the blank faces surrounding her. "It's just a whim, but the presents are real. Don't look so amazed. I'm happy, that's all, and I thought I'd surprise you." Bobby was staring at her as if she had gone mad. "Open 'em, go on," she said. "Didn't you ever get a present for no reason before?"

Hilary acted first, whooping with delight as she held up a bulky sweater that fastened down the front with oversize wooden buttons. "I love it!" she cried, throwing her arms about Ruth and hugging her.

"It's Peruvian," Ruth said. "The minute I saw it, it just said Hilary to me."

"It's great! Can I wear it to school?"

"Of course," Ruth said. "Wear it any time you want."

Bobby held up a new book about his favorite baseball player, Ron Guidry. "Hey, terrific," he said, grinning at her. "Thanks. But I still don't know why we're getting presents."

"Because it's Thursday," Ruth said. "Enjoy it."

Paul was taking a handsome plaid sweater from its box. "Wow!" he said, holding it against himself. "Nobody's going to miss seeing me in this."

"Exactly," Ruth said. "I'll make a spiffy guy out of you yet."

"And how about you?" Paul wanted to know. "Did you buy something for yourself, I hope?"

"Is the pope Catholic?" Ruth said, smiling. "It's in the bag."

"Let's see it," Paul said. "What is it?"

"An item of lingerie," Ruth said in a matter-of-fact way. "And you will get to see it in the fullness of time," she said, winking at him. The look on his face made her laugh out loud. "Cook, do your stuff," she said. "I'm starving."

* * *

Bobby was curled up in bed when Ruth came upstairs, the baseball book hiding his face. Instead of making a left turn into her bedroom, she walked into the boy's room and seated herself on his bed. "How's the book?"

"Good," Bobby said. "How did you know I liked Ron Guidry?"

"I have my sources," she said.

"Dad?"

"Got it in one. I also happen to be an ace baseball fan."

"You are?"

"Ask me who has the highest lifetime batting average. Ty Cobb, Detroit Tigers," she sailed on without waiting. "Three sixty-seven. Ask me who made the last unassisted triple play in a World Series."

"Who?"

"Bill Wambsgans, Cleveland, in the 1920 Series against Brooklyn. How about how many homers Babe Ruth hit?"

"How many?"

"Seven hundred and fourteen."

Bobby nodded agreement.

"What'd I tell you?" she said. "Impressive, isn't it?"

"How many homers did Hank Aaron hit?" the boy asked.

"Uh-oh," Ruth said. "I know he broke the Babe's record."

"That's right so far." He looked at her, grinning. "How many?"

"Could you give me a hint?"

"Less than seven hundred sixty."

"Seven hundred fifty?" she guessed.

"Fifty-five," Bobby said.

"Well, I was close," she said.

"Close only counts in horseshoes," Bobby said. "Some expert."

"You're still the champ," she smiled. "But I do like baseball. Next summer, how about we go to some games?"

"I wouldn't mind," Bobby said, not able to conceal his pleasure.

"I'll work on your old man," she said, getting up.

"Ruth," the boy said as she headed for the door, making her stop. "Thanks for the book."

* * *

Paul was propped up in bed, one eye on the late evening TV news and the other on Ruth as she undressed for bed. A scrap of memory came to him, of watching Jane in this situation. How different each woman was. Modest Jane, his virgin bride; she had never really outgrown an innate shyness about her body. Even after eighteen years of marriage, Jane had been reluctant to show herself off to him, turning her back to take off her bra, slipping her nightgown over her head and all the way down before she stepped out of her pantyhose. And here was Ruth, naked as a newborn, looking at him looking at her and carrying on a normal conversation. His own X-rated late show, blonde beauty before the dresser, and he looked forward to it every night.

Ruth put her Bloomingdale's package into the middle drawer of the dresser. "What sort of lingerie is it?" he asked.

"A nightgown," she said.

"Sexy?"

"Outrageous."

They smiled at each other. "Care to put it on?" he said casually.

"Not tonight, Josephine. I'm saving it."

"For what?"

She shrugged. "Our first dirty weekend, something like that. Or when your morale needs lifting."

"My morale's already lifted."

"So I've noticed," Ruth said. On her way to the bathroom she paused in front of his dresser, staring at the framed needlepoint that hung above it on the wall. "You know what?" she said. "I hate that picture. And the other one above the TV."

"The needlepoints?"

"*Jane's* needlepoints," Ruth said. "What would you say if I replaced them with a couple of my museum prints . . . the ones we put away up in the attic."

"What's wrong with them? They've been in this room for ten years."

"*But I haven't*," Ruth said. She came and sat on the foot of the bed. "Paul, they're not me. I miss my Renoir print of the two girls at the piano. It'd be perfect right there. And we can find another picture to go in the corner." Ruth watched his face, not wanting to hurt him. "Are you worried about what the kids would say?"

"A little."

225

"It's not their room, Klein. It's ours."

"Sure," he said, "whatever you want," and with that he took her hand. "I remember Jane working on those pictures, her needlepoint passion, First she covered every piece of furniture with needlepoint pillows until there wasn't a chair safe to sit on, then she went into pictures. Whenever we watched TV she'd do needlepoint. We used to kid her and say for her TV was radio. She hardly ever looked up . . . I'm sorry, babe," he went on. "Of course you can change anything you want."

"Your wedding picture on the staircase," Ruth said. "That has to go."

"You don't kid around, do you?"

"Nope. I've got George's wedding pictures of us standing in front of Michael's fireplace. There's one nice one I'd like to enlarge so it will fit into the same frame."

"Okay," Paul said.

"I've been thinking about it awhile."

"And I haven't given it a single thought. I'm sorry. I drag you away from your apartment, almost kicking and screaming, and plop you down in the middle of another woman's house to live. I guess I think you're strong enough to do anything. That's why I never worry about you."

"Now that you mention it, I do feel like a kidnap victim at times. Putting my clothes in Jane's closet, sleeping in her bed, on her sheets, with her husband. But none of that's really important, Paul. Not if we stay tuned in to each other. And I can get the kids to accept me as I am, and not some shadow of Jane's."

"They will."

"Maybe," she said.

"Is that what the present business was about?"

"You got it. Did you see Hilary's reaction? I think that was genuine. And I had my first pleasant conversation with Bobby in weeks. I'll win them over, one way or another, even if I have to bribe them to do it."

"Hell, you've won *me* over," Paul said.

"You?" Ruth said, laughing. "You were a pushover."

"What's all this about going shopping?" Paul was saying the following Saturday afternoon.

"For shoes, Daddy," Hilary said. She didn't look happy to Paul. "It's Ruth's idea. For my college interviews. I'm supposed to look preppy, or something."

"Not preppy," Ruth said, coming into the kitchen, "just neat. She needs an undressy dressy shoe to go with the skirt and blouse she's going to wear."

"An undressy dressy shoe," Paul repeated. "Is that some sort of code?"

"Car keys, please," Ruth said, putting out her hand. Paul handed them over. "We're going to the shopping center in Mill Basin. I've never been there, but Hilary knows the way. If we're not back in three hours, send a search party."

"Drive carefully," Paul said.

"That's what my father always said when he gave me the car keys," Ruth said.

"I don't know why I can't wear my Chinese shoes," Hilary said.

"They're fine with jeans," Ruth said, "but you have to be Chinese to think they look good with a skirt. Let's go."

The shopping center was crowded on this late fall afternoon, and Ruth had to circle up and down parking levels until finally finding a space on the roof. They took the escalator down to the main shopping floor and looked through half-a-dozen jammed shoe stores without success. Ruth knew exactly what she was searching for, a plain low-heeled pump to match Hilary's navy skirt, but finding it was not easy. Nor was Hilary's reluctant attitude toward the whole idea. If she rolls her eyes one more time, Ruth thought, I'll swat her. She didn't, of course, nor did she say anything, not wanting to provoke open warfare. She'd given Hilary one victory already by not insisting she wear the skirt to go shopping, which was a mistake. And then there was the matter of the unshaven hairy legs Hilary would be showing off under her skirt.

"It's a sexist thing," Hilary was saying as they sat waiting for a shoe clerk to notice them. "Men make us shave our legs and underarms, and like fools, we do it."

"I don't know," Ruth said. "I think silky smooth legs are more sexy than sexist. I can't see myself with hairy armpits, frankly."

"I am not shaving my legs or armpits for a college interview," Hilary insisted. "No way."

"I don't think the Yale interviewer will actually go so far as to inspect your armpits," Ruth said, making Hilary smile. "About Brown, I'm not so sure."

"It's the advertising-media-male-chauvinist machine that sells us on shaving, don't you see that?" The girl looked at Ruth with the thin smile of the utterly convinced for her lesser sisters. "I didn't expect you to understand," she said smugly.

"Just a second there, buster," Ruth said hotly. "I really don't give a damn whether your legs and armpits are shaved or look like the Black Forest. Just remember that I've been on my own since I was twenty-one, fighting my own battles in the advertising world, and I won't let anyone question my credentials. I've paid my feminist dues, Hil, believe me I have."

Ruth called out as the harried shoe salesman passed their way, but the man only threw her a crazed look and disappeared into the stockroom. "I don't think we'll ever get waited on here," Ruth said, getting up. "Would you like a soda? I'm parched."

They found their way to the fountain restaurant in the mall's large department store and slid into a booth. "This was a mistake," Ruth said. "If you'd met me in Manhattan after school, we'd have found your shoes in about five minutes."

Hilary nodded, brushing hair away from her face with the back of her hand. "I hate shopping for clothes," she said.

"Some women spend their lives that way," Ruth said.

"Disgusting. Sometimes I think we ought to be issued uniforms and made to wear them. Then maybe we could judge people by what they *are* instead of how they look."

"Just my luck I'd get a blue uniform," Ruth said. "I look like hell in blue." Ruth caught the waiter's eye and ordered their drinks. "I used to think clothes were a bother when I was your age," she went on. "Of course, I had an older sister who was born to wear good clothes. Now I like to dress up."

"I'll never like it," Hilary said.

The waiter brought their drinks and set them down. Ruth's coffee was too steaming to drink. She stirred it with a spoon. "Can I ask you a straight question, Hil? Are you pissed off at *me,* or just the world in general?"

Hilary's almond eyes narrowed. "What do you mean?"

228

"You've had a chip on your shoulder ever since I moved into the house. Is it just the situation, or have I done something wrong?"

"I don't have a chip on my shoulder," Hilary said. She lowered her eyes to her Coke and sipped through the straw.

"Be honest," Ruth said. "You're not exactly thrilled to have me in the house, are you? Nor is Bobby, for that matter."

"Bobby's screwed-up," Hilary said, not looking up. "I don't hate you, if that's what you mean."

A silence hung between them for a few moments. Hilary would not meet Ruth's eyes. "I don't know what you want from me," the girl said at last. "You've got my father . . . isn't that enough?"

"Oh, Hil," Ruth said. Her cheeks stung as if they'd been slapped.

"What am I supposed to do," Hilary said, her eyes on Ruth now and angry. "Give you some bullshit about being a friend? You're not *my* friend. You're *his* friend, and Bobby and I are just part of the deal that goes along with him. Isn't that the way it is?"

"No, it's not."

"You're the one who said to be honest. You wouldn't even know me if you hadn't met him. How can I think you care about me? How can I even be sure you love my father?"

"I love him," Ruth said. "How could anyone not? You can be sure of that. Why else would I change my life so completely to marry him, Hil? For the great thrill of living on Rugby Road? And I love you and Bobby, too, because you're part of him. You can believe that or not. But ever since I moved in, and even before, I've had the hand of friendship extended toward you. And what have you done? Spit on it."

Hilary toyed with the straw in her glass, twirling it to make the ice spin around.

"I really thought we could get along," Ruth said. "I look at you sometimes and I see me when I was your age. I know you think I'm establishment, but in my own heart I'm still a rebel. Like you. Listen, I grew up unhappy at home, in a bad situation, arguing with my parents. I couldn't wait to get away. I think I understand you a little, and what you've gone through."

"You don't," the girl said flatly. "I think we were starting to be all right and then *you* came along. And now I don't know where we are. That's what I think. I took all the feeling I had for my mom and gave it to Daddy and now he's turned to you." The girl stared down at the table. "I don't know what I think anymore. I thought I loved Peter and now when I see him I wonder how I could have ever thought that. I don't want to love anybody for a while, understand? I want a fucking vacation from loving. I want to graduate from school and go off to college on my own and just be left alone. I'm not giving myself again, not so easy, Ruth. I'm just going to look out for me, okay?"

The vehemence of Hilary's voice was so great it made Ruth speak quietly. "Yes," she said. "You should look out for you."

"I wish you weren't so good-looking, or so funny, or so young," Hilary said. "I wish he'd found some plain dumb older woman to marry, so I could see it was just to keep house and take care of him. I could live with that."

"What should I do, Hil? Try to grow pimples? Wear sackcloth and ashes?"

"He'd still love you," the girl said.

"And you'd still resent it."

"Yes." The straw was in Hilary's fingers, being rolled and unrolled on the table.

"What do we do now?" Ruth said.

"I don't know." Hilary shrugged.

"Hil, I can't live with an enemy in the house. In business, okay, I can handle that. But not at home."

"I don't want to be your enemy," the girl said. "I just want to be out of it."

"But you're in it, Hil, we all are. And it's a long time until you go away to college. Is there some way we can declare a truce, do you think?"

"I don't know," Hilary said. "It depends on how much I can trust you. Like . . . I'm wondering if you're going to run back home now and tell Daddy every word of what I said."

"Nope, not a word."

"How do I know that's straight?"

"Try me. I'm always straight. I don't bullshit anyone."

Hilary thought for a moment. The straw began to shred and break apart. "Okay," she said. "With a big *maybe* attached. I'll have to see."

"And you be straight with me, too, okay? No secret plots, no whispering in corners behind my back. You be up-front with me and I'll be the same way with you.''

Hilary nodded, as if she had decided something. For a long time she did not say anything, then she asked: "Tell me again why I have to get a dressy shoe?"

"To go with your skirt, to make you look like you know what's appropriate, and to show off your gorgeous legs.''

A brief smile flickered across Hilary's face. "Then let's go get the stupid things,'' she said, getting up.

An overnighter in Philadelphia, and all because the distributor demanded a whole day from Paul, beginning promptly at eight o'clock in the morning. Curse all people who take him from this bed, Ruth said to herself. She looked at the clock again. Only ten minutes had passed since the last time she'd looked.

There was a thumping sound from behind Paul's closet. The hairs on her arms prickled. It was nothing, another sound from the old house. Still, she was listening a little more carefully to the night.

Was that a groan?

A high keening sound, it came again. Suddenly the darkness of the bedroom was frightening. Sitting up, she put on the night-table lamp, slipped into her mules, and walked a few paces from the bed. She stood there, listening, feeling the chill of the sixty-degree air. Yes, a sound again, from Bobby's room.

She threw on her robe and went down the hallway, listening outside his door. "No," she heard the boy say. "No!" She opened the door carefully and walked in, looking down at him in the dim glow of the night light. His head and shoulders were out from beneath the tight quilt and still now, but as she watched he rolled in bed, an arm striking the wall. The boy's face contorted as if in pain, one sightless eye regarded her, he cried out: "No!"

Ruth sat on the bed. She put her hand on his damp forehead, another on his shoulder, gently shaking him awake. "Bob . . . Bob-o . . .''

She felt his body stiffen then go slack. His eyes fluttered open, wide with fright. "A bad dream, Bobby. That's all, honey.''

"Ruth," he said, and began to whimper.

"Shh," she whispered. "Only a dream, baby, that's all it is.''

She petted his shoulder gently. At the foot of the bed, Marmaduke purred in his sleep. "Just a bad dream," she repeated. "You're all right now."

Slowly, the boy became calm. "I'm sorry," he said. "It was bad."

"Yes."

"They were . . ." he began, then stopped. "I couldn't do anything," he said.

To Ruth's eyes he still looked frightened, and half asleep. "Do you want to talk about it?" she asked.

"No," Bobby said.

"But you know it was only a dream and not real?"

"Yes." He looked at her and shivered. "I have to go to the bathroom," he said.

Ruth stood up and helped him out from beneath the quilt. Bobby found his slippers and padded off to the hall. The bathroom light came on, then off as the boy closed the door behind him.

Ruth's throat was tight with pity for the boy. What terrors lurked in his mind, coming in darkness to disturb his sleep? She flicked on the reading lamp above the bed, then reached over and tucked the quilt tight against the wall. As she picked up Bobby's pillow to plump it, she caught a quick glance of six tombstones underneath. No, not tombstones, photographs laid neatly in a row.

Leaning down, she studied them. A gap-toothed young Bobby smiled in the arms of Jane. Jane in sunglasses smiling, holding the skinny boy in her arms. Jane and Bobby, Bobby and Jane, snapshot after snapshot. This is how he sleeps, she thought, with her pictures under his pillow, and still the nightmares come.

In the bathroom the toilet flushed, the doorknob clicked. Quickly, she replaced the pillow, hiding the photographs once again. Bobby came padding slowly back into the room.

"Are you okay?" she asked him.

"I think so." He got back into bed, pulling the quilt to his neck. He almost smiled at her and she leaned down quickly and kissed his brow. "Ruth," he said, "thanks."

"For what? If you need me, kiddo, I'm here." She tucked the quilt again.

"I'm sorry I got you up," he said.

"I wasn't sleeping anyway." She snapped off his bed lamp. "Do you want me to sit in here while you fall asleep?"

"You don't have to."

"I think I want to, okay?"

"Sure. Good night, Ruth."

She sat in the chair by his desk and waited. In less time than she thought possible his breathing was slow and regular. When she looked down at him before leaving, he was fast asleep.

She thought about him for a long time before falling asleep herself.

18

"'WE'RE OFF ON the road to Morocco,'" Paul sang in the front seat as the Buick zipped up I-95 toward Connecticut. From the back seat Hilary and Bobby joined in. "'We're off to have loads of good fun.'" Paul looked at Ruth. "Join in, kid."

"Don't know it."

"'Like Webster's dictionary, we're Morocco-bound!'" the three Kleins sang, with Paul trying a quasiharmony ending that fell flat. "Surely, you jest," he said to Ruth. "How could you not know that song?"

"I know what it is," she said, "but not the words."

"It's kind of a tradition with us," Paul said.

"Whenever we start a trip somewhere we sing that song," Bobby said.

"Always," Hilary said.

"Not always," Paul said. "Sometimes we forget."

At this early-morning hour, traffic was light. Paul hummed a few bars of the song to himself.

"I'll confess something," Ruth said. "I never thought those

Road pictures were so great. I never became a Hope and Crosby fan. To me, funny is the Marx Brothers. That is real craziness.'' She put on a Groucho voice. ''This morning I shot an elephant in my pajamas . . .''

Bobby chimed in: ''How he got into my pajamas, I'll never know.''

Ruth grinned at the boy. ''We've got some movie experts here, I see.''

''Years of dragging them off to revival houses,'' Paul said. ''You ought to see Bobby do his famous Chaplin walk. Fabulous!'' He looked at the boy in the rearview mirror. ''Come to think of it, Bob-o, you haven't done that in a while. And I haven't heard your W.C. Fields voice, either.''

''Hilary,'' Ruth said, ''you look a little green back there. Are you all right?''

''Fine,'' the girl said in a small voice.

''Nervous?''

''Yes.''

''It's only an interview,'' Ruth said. ''They'll look at your high school grades, your teacher recommendations, your record of service.''

''But it's *Yale*,'' Hilary said. ''And they won't get my records and my application until January. I'm going to make an idiot of myself, I know it.''

''Relax,'' Ruth said. ''I was so snotty at my Wellesley interview. I hated the whole idea of going there and they took me anyway. So don't worry. Just be yourself, Hil, that's the important thing.''

''That's why I'm worried,'' the girl said. ''I don't know *which* me to be.''

The day was cold but sunny, a Saturday on campus with not too much activity going on. They waited for Hilary to reappear, walking along with coats buttoned up, Paul's arm about Ruth's waist and a bored Bobby trailing in their wake. Hilary's last look back at them before she went up the steps and into the gray building was that of a condemned woman going to the gallows. They'll love Hilary, he told himself, everyone did when they spent a little time with her.

After an hour, the girl reappeared from the building, waving and running down the stone steps two at a time, her skirt flying out from under her peacoat. She looked so happy, running across the green quad to join them. "What a neat guy!" she said, grinning. "You know what he does when he's not interviewing? He's part of a *mime* troupe! Can you believe that?"

"It went well?" Paul asked.

"What a man, Daddy! You'd love him. He was so great, and I wasn't nervous at all." Impulsively, she leaped up and put her arms about Paul. He didn't mind it at all. "Look at this place!" Hilary gushed. "Can you see me going to school here? It's so beautiful!"

"I can see it," Paul grinned. "My daughter a Yalie."

"On to Brown University," Hilary said. "I'm going to kill them at Brown."

They checked out Wesleyan in Middletown, on the way to Providence and Hilary's next interview. After a solid two hours of driving, Paul pulled in for a rest stop at a small hamburger stand. Ruth and Hilary ran off to find the bathroom. Paul brought Cokes and stood with the boy near the steamy windows as they sipped them. Bobby's finger traced a tic-tac-toe game on the clouded glass.

"Is the motel nice?" the boy asked. "The one we're staying at tonight?"

"I think so," Paul said. "Back near Mystic Seaport."

"Will it have miniature golf?"

"Golf? Bob-o, it's freezing. Too cold for golf."

"We could wear our coats," Bobby said.

"And it'll be dark when we get there."

The boy looked at the caravan of cars scudding along the highway. "Remember that motel in Santa Barbara? On our California trip? That was a great place."

"I remember. With the miniature golf."

"Just down the road." The boy took a sip of his drink. "That was the last vacation we ever had together. With Mom."

"Yes."

Bobby looked up at him, a sweet smile on his lips. "Remember we had sides for miniature golf? Mom and me against you and Hilary. We beat you, remember?"

"Yes, you did. And the two of you talked about it for the rest of the trip, as I recall."

"Yes. That was a great vacation." He wiped his lips with the back of his hand. Paul thought the boy was about to cry. "She was fun to be with, wasn't she?"

"Oh, yes." He put his hand on the boy's shoulder. "Lots of fun."

"She could be so silly. You know, to make us laugh. Those funny faces she'd make." Bobby turned away from Paul, looking at the girl flipping hamburgers on the grill. "I'm not going to cry," he said. "I can think of Mom now and not cry, you know."

"Me too."

"Do you still think of her a lot?"

"Yes," Paul said. "Yes, I do."

"I was thinking before of what we did in the car, how she always made up games with license plates and signs and stuff. And on long drives she'd come and sit in the back with me and I'd fall asleep sometimes with her holding me. She had a nice smell. Soap and flowers and Jergen's Lotion. I liked to cuddle up against her in the back seat even when I didn't fall asleep. The way she petted me. It was a good feeling."

"Yes," Paul croaked through a throat suddenly tight.

"Dad," Bobby said, his serious face looking up at him, "there was a bad thing I had for a long time. About Mom dying. I was very ashamed and I felt really bad. Because I thought it was my fault, that I must have done something bad and that was why. . . . It was stupid. I couldn't even tell Dr. Wirtz about it because it was so stupid."

"Nothing is stupid when it hurts, Bob-o."

"Yeah. But this was dumb." He put his arm about Paul and hugged him. "I'm glad I've got you, Dad," the boy said. "And I hope you never, never die."

"Not for ages and ages," Paul said. "Not for a very long time."

Hilary did well at her Brown interview, she thought, although not quite as well as she'd done at Yale. They left Providence in late afternoon, the setting sun in Paul's eyes as they headed south. After checking into the large motel, two rooms side by side though not connected, they found a local steak house and had dinner. Hilary was in high spirits, relieved that she had risen in the face of what she thought would be a disaster. Paul ordered a fine burgundy he found on the wine list and had the waiter bring a wineglass for Hilary. He made a ceremony out of Hilary's first sip, waiting for her judgment. "Dry," she pronounced solemnly, "and an excellent year, no doubt."

Hilary seemed to be glowing in Paul's eyes. She chattered on about the colleges they'd seen. Yes, she could be happy at Yale, if they'd have her. It wasn't as scary a place as she'd thought. She could see herself going there, fitting in. She was smart enough, and if she wanted to go on to Yale drama school, it was a good place to be. Wesleyan was a problem. She didn't know if she'd apply there. Just driving through, looking at the buildings, she couldn't tell. The setting was nice, though, a real small college town. Brown, she declared, looked thoroughly seedy, but seedy with a kind of charm. "I'd be a bum there," she said, "living in one of those houses, but their drama department is excellent." On the other hand, she might major in philosophy. She was thinking about that, philosophy instead of drama perhaps, but it was something she didn't have to decide for a while yet, thank heaven.

"Enjoying the wine?" Paul asked, wondering if it hadn't gone to Hilary's head, she was so animated. He refilled the girl's glass.

"Loving it," Hilary said. "One of yours?" She took a large sip of her wine.

"No. Julius Wile."

"I should really go to Reed College," Hilary said. "That's what I really should do."

"No way," Paul said. They'd talked about Reed a few times. "It rains all the time out there."

"It does not. And it's a very good school."

"Name one person you've heard of who went to Reed," he challenged. "You see, and it's way to hell and gone in Oregon."

"Is that bad?" Hilary asked. She took a sip of wine, her eyes on Paul. "I'd probably not come back for those small breaks. And maybe I'd be invited to stay with someone for midyear, too. I'm sure Ruth wouldn't mind that."

"Hilary—" Paul began, but Ruth interrupted.

"The idea is to be happy in school, Hil, wherever you go. And I do like having you around, in spite of what you think."

"I'm not letting you apply to Reed, so that's that," Paul said.

"Democracy at work," Hilary said, in a sarcastic tone.

"No," said Paul. "Just the power of the veto, and I think you've had too much wine, my girl."

"In vino veritas," Hilary said. "Is that the way you say it? Anyway, I meant it."

"Then I think you owe Ruth an apology," Paul said to the girl.

"No," Ruth interjected. "She's just speaking her mind."

"That's right, Ruth, I'm just speaking the truth. You *will* feel better with me away, I know that, and so will you, Daddy. Even though you won't admit it. No," she added, holding up a hand, palm out, "don't try to shut me up. I understand what I'm saying. Really. I'll feel better, too. A fresh start, a new place. I'm going to be *terrific* in college. Oh, yes, I will. And out of your hair. And I'll be so *happy* to be away from you. Oops! That didn't come out right. I mean . . . I've been in your *pocket*, Dad, since Mom died. You've been smothering me, been on top of me. And if Mom was here I'd be fighting to get away from her also. But she isn't, and now Ruth is here, and she's on top of me too and I resent it. Because she isn't my mother, see, and that's worse . . . Am I getting mixed up? Do you understand?"

"Some of it," Paul said.

"Too old for high school and too young for college," Hilary said. "And raring to get away. Sorry, folks, that's the way it is."

"I hear you loud and clear," Ruth said. "You're just being straight."

"Give the lady a big cigar," Hilary said. She tipped her wineglass back and finished the lot. "Very dry," she said.

"Should we arrange a wake-up call for tomorrow?" Ruth was sitting on the edge of the big double bed in the motel, doing a little tweezing while Paul fiddled with the TV set.

"No," he said, switching off the TV. "We'll sleep late. Or as late as the kids let us. Then we'll have breakfast, check out, and catch Mystic Seaport on the way home." He unzipped the small overnight bag Ruth had packed and found his pajamas. He also found the Bloomie's nightgown Ruth had been saving, a short, gauzy number in see-through black chiffon. "Wow!" He held the

239

nightgown to himself. "You must be serious," he said, grinning wickedly.

Ruth looked over at him. "Ah, it's captured your attention, I see."

"I'm getting excited just holding this thing," he said.

"I'll probably freeze my ass off, but what the hell."

He brought the nightgown over and sat down beside her on the bed, watching her concentration as she plucked. "That's absolutely barbaric, you know. Pulling hairs from your body."

"The things we do for beauty," Ruth said.

"I'd love you even with bushy eyebrows."

"But I wouldn't."

He put a hand on her blue-jeaned behind. "When do you actually put on the nightgown?"

"Patience, patience. Why don't you go brush your teeth or something."

Groaning a little, he got up and plopped himself down in the fake leather chair, then took his shoes off. "Are you upset about what Hilary said, babe?"

"Nope." Ruth put the mirror on the night table. "Hil was just being truthful. She *will* feel better when she gets away. I have a feeling she's beginning to trust me a little, and that's a start. Now if I could only get Bobby on my side."

"That'll come," Paul said. "I see some improvement in him."

"I hope so. But sometimes he just looks so lost."

There was a quiet knock on the door. "Daddy?" Bobby called from outside. Paul looked at Ruth, then got up and walked across the carpet. "What's up?" he asked as the boy came into the room.

"I can't find my pajamas. Or my slippers."

"Are you sure?" Paul asked.

"Yes. I looked in the bag, and then Hilary did. No pj's."

Paul turned to look at Ruth. "I must have forgotten to pack them," she said.

Bobby looked up at Paul. "So what do I do?"

"Sleep in your underwear, what else?"

Bobby thought about that for a second. "Oh. Okay." He had a confused look on his face. "Today's underwear, or tomorrow's?"

Paul snorted. "Today's. Then put on your fresh underwear tomorrow."

"Right," the boy said. "And I'll go barefoot. There's carpet, anyway, it doesn't matter."

"You do have fresh underwear for tomorrow?" Paul asked.

"Yes," Ruth answered from behind him. "I packed fresh underwear and another shirt, in case he got this one dirty."

Bobby looked across at her. "I never had to sleep in my underwear before."

"There's always a first time," Paul said.

"She should have made a list," Bobby said to Paul, as if Ruth were not there. "Mom always made a list and then she didn't forget anything."

"It's no big deal," Paul said. "Now go tuck in, Bob-o, and you and Hil try to sleep late, okay? And when it's time for breakfast, call us on the telephone."

"Would you come and tuck me in?" Bobby asked. He saw the look on Paul's face and added, "Please?"

Paul sighed. "All right." He turned away from the door and went to the small overnight bag near the dresser, taking out his shaving kit, Ruth's makeup case, a sweater. "No slippers," he said to Ruth, turning over the bag and emptying it. "You forgot my slippers, too."

"Sorry."

"It's not important," he said. He slipped into his shoes and accompanied Bobby next door.

When he returned, a few minutes later, Ruth was sitting on the couch, hugging her knees to her chest. He could see that she was angry. "Miss Stepmother fucks up again," she said when he'd closed the door.

"It's nothing, Ruth, forget it."

"You can be damn sure Bobby won't," she said. "Shit! Seven o'clock in the morning, even before coffee, I just threw stuff into their bag and ours and we took off. You should have checked me."

"I wasn't thinking," he said.

Ruth took a cigarette from his pack on the night table and lit one with trembling hands.

"What's this? You don't smoke, babe."

"A pack a year," Ruth said, "when I'm totally pissed-off."

"Easy," he said, sitting down beside her.

"Did Jane really make a list for everything?"

"Yes."

"Jesus. She should have been *President.*"

Paul put a hand on Ruth's knee, noticing how she ignored it. "Come on, it's nothing. Don't let it spoil our evening."

"It ain't easy, Klein," she said. "New life, new house, husband, kids. What I don't understand is screwing up so much. Damn it, I never worried about coping before."

"You're great."

"The week you were away, disaster. And it's not much better with you home. You guys have rules and ways of doing things I know nothing about. Hell, sometimes I think you're talking code. Little secrets, inside words, punch lines to jokes I never heard. And bad as it is at home, it's worse in the office. We're so behind. God, we can just manage to get out the work for clients we *do* have, never mind pitching others. Because I don't stay late anymore, I hardly work weekends, and my head is in sixteen places at once."

As Ruth stubbed out her cigarette, Paul lit one of his own. "Ever think about quitting?"

"Klein!" Her eyes were blazing. "It's not a job, it's a business. I've got four years of blood and sweat invested in it."

"You could pack it in and take a job, couldn't you? One that wouldn't demand so much of your time."

"Not on your life, Klein. I've got a partner, remember, a dozen employees? I won't walk away from that . . . to do what? Stay home and be Mommy?"

"Okay."

"Besides which, you'd probably be better at home than me. God knows, you're a better cook and a better housekeeper."

Paul laughed. "Okay, okay . . . I get the message." He kissed her gently on her forehead. She responded by throwing her arms about him and squeezing hard, then kissing him fully, her tongue teasing his lips as she withdrew. "That's one thing you do well," he whispered.

"There are others," she said as she unbuckled his belt.

She didn't get to wear the sexy nightgown until much later, when the lights were out and they were ready for sleep. Ruth snuggled under the blankets, fitting herself to the curve of his back. "I'm a happy man," he said, reaching back to pat her flank.

"You should be," she giggled. Her fingers played with the curly wisps of hair at the nape of his neck. "Tell me about Jane," she said.

"Tell you *what* about Jane?"

"Was she always perfect?"

"No."

"In which ways wasn't she?"

Paul groaned. He turned in bed, settling on his back. "She was a human being. She had her faults. Too strict with the kids, maybe. Too hard on Hilary, that's for sure. Bobby could get away with almost anything. But Jane wasn't perfect. She made mistakes."

"And how was she with you?"

"Ruth, this isn't right," he said.

"Did she love you?"

"That's a stupid question."

"*Did* she?"

"Yes," he hissed at her. "Always. Eighteen years, start to finish, there wasn't a moment I didn't know how much she loved me." He sat up in bed and fumbled for his cigarettes on the night table. He lit one and smoked for a few moments, Ruth watching as the red glow lit his serious face.

"And did you love her that much?"

"Yes," he said at once.

"Did you ever fight?"

Paul laughed low in his throat. "Twice, I think. Once about sex, and once about money. She won both times, as I remember. She couldn't stand arguing or shouting. Whenever the kids acted up the first thing she'd say was, 'Lower your voice.' That was her way."

"And how was she in bed?"

Paul exhaled smoke, sighing through it. "Let it rest, babe."

"I'm just asking." She stroked his naked chest gently, his hair soft under her fingers, watching the expression in his eyes as his face was lit by the glowing cigarette and trying to tell what he was thinking. Why am I so curious, she wondered, what sort of cheap victory do I want and why do I need it so much?

"Not as good as you," Paul said flatly. "Isn't that the answer you want?"

"If it's the truth."

"This isn't like you."

"I know."

"Are you so insecure?"

"A little shaky around the edges, yes."

"You? Shaky?" He laughed.

"I know it's hard to believe," she said, laughing herself.

"Give her a place to stand and she'll move the world." He squeezed her shoulder gently.

"Are you ready for this?" she asked. "I hate the house. *Hate* it."

"Come on," he said, as if she were joking.

"It's not my house, Paul, it's Jane's. I haven't felt at home there since the day I moved in. We ought to have a place of our own."

"That's out of the question," he said. "Bobby was born there. It's the only place he knows. It's his home. And Hilary—"

"I know," she interrupted. "You guys *all* belong there, but I don't. That's the hell of it. And if you say, 'Give it time' again, so help me I'll slug you."

"Oh, hell," Paul said. He stubbed out the cigarette in the ashtray. "Listen—to move the kids away after all they've been through . . . It's terribly wrong, Ruth. I'm sorry, but that's the way I feel. I know you haven't really settled in yet, but you will. And you'll love it. Let's just get through the winter. In the spring, when the weather turns, it'll be different. We'll do the garden. We'll fix up. We'll take the kids away someplace nice for spring vacation. We'll sit outside on the porch after dinner and drink our coffee. You'll be happy there, I promise you."

"Like Jane was, right?" she said. "And I'll do all the homemaker things she did to make you happy."

"Unfair," he said.

"Living in her house . . . it's like I'm living in her *clothes*, Paul."

"You think I don't know how different you are? How wonderful, how strong, how alive? I love you for you, for what you are. How can you doubt that?" He took her roughly in his arms and held her close. *"Coraggio,"* he said. "Believe."

His kiss was warm upon her mouth. "And am I really a better lover?" she whispered as he tasted her shoulder. She took his face in her hands and looked into his eyes in the dark. "Am I?"

"Is an apple better than an orange?" he whispered, then stilled her lips with his own.

She lay at peace in the warm nest of his arms, his breath sweet on her shoulder. Yes, she thought, it *will* work out, because we're too smart and too much in love for it not to. She'd find her place in the house, she'd win the children over completely. She was a competitor, a fighter. She thought of Bobby, sleeping in the room next door, so thin and fragile and in need of mothering. Someday he'd permit her to hold him, to share his hurts and fears, and nestle in her arms as she did in his father's. Someday, no matter how mean and unbending he was to her. You give love and keep on giving it until you get it back. In spite of sharp words and hurting looks. The wound inside the child was deep, her presence a constant reminder of the mother he had lost. But in the end, with patience and kindness, she would win him over.

Someday.

19

SHE BEGAN A love campaign. The boy didn't even notice, or if he did, he said nothing about it.

She made a point of calling home each afternoon, when Bobby was back from school. Sometimes he wouldn't even come to the phone, calling out to Gemma or Hilary that he was too involved with his homework to speak to Ruth. And when he did speak to her, she did all the talking:

"How was school?"

"Fine."

"Any problems?"

"No."

"Did you have a glass of milk and a cookie?"

"Yes."

In the supermarket one Saturday, she bought a six-pack of Hershey bars and slipped one each day into his lunch bag. Bobby said nothing about it. After three days she couldn't stand it. "Are you enjoying the Hershey bars?" she asked as she helped him on with his knapsack. "They're good," he said as he made ready to go out the door, "but I really like them without almonds."

Thanks for nothing, she thought, watching him go down to the corner and wait for the traffic light to change. A grown woman, and a little kid has me going in circles.

She stopped off at a fancy French bakery near her office and brought home a pair of gooey chocolate squares for the boy and Hilary. His eyes lit up when she trotted them out for dessert, but he took one taste and pushed the plate away. "Rum," he said. "I hate rum."

She finished the little cake, then kicked herself as she thought of what it would do to her waistline.

On a day when Bobby had only a half-day of school, she suggested he come up to her office and they would have lunch together. She gave him subway instructions, waited anxiously when he was fifteen minutes late. He showed up at her office door, complaining about the stupid trains and why couldn't they run right? He had no idea where he wanted to go to eat, merely shrugging while she went through her childproof list of restaurants. When he said he wanted only a hamburger, she took him to McDonald's to please him, watching him pick at his Big Mac while she made all the conversation.

Afterward she dragged him off to Bloomingdale's to shop for clothes. A big mistake, she realized when he turned sullen after trying on his fifth pair of jeans. Boys are not girls, she berated herself; Bobby doesn't give a damn what he wears. When she spotted a display of football team sweatshirts he was too angry with her to try on even one. She held the New York Giants sweatshirt against him, ignoring the murderous look he was giving her, and bought it for him. One size too small, it turned out, at least it was after one of Gemma's washings. More evidence of her incompetence as a mother, the sweatshirt lay folded in a corner of Bobby's shirt drawer where she could see it each morning when she picked out his clothes for the day.

One afternoon she let the boy goad her into losing her temper while talking to him on the telephone. "What do you care?" he said after a series of monosyllabic answers to her questions.

"I care, I care!" she yelled at him.

"You're not my mother, Ruth."

247

"But I love you like one!" she cried. "Give me a break!"

"You're trying too hard," Bobby said and hung up.

She heard the click and dial tone and slammed the phone back onto its cradle, yelling an epithet. When George poked his head into the doorway to see what the noise was about, she had tears of frustration in her eyes.

"Not a client, I hope?" George asked.

"No! A fucking kid!"

"So," Michael asked one day at lunch, "how's the bridegroom?"

Paul's grin was an answer in itself.

"And besides that, how's Ruth?"

"Terrific. She and Hilary are getting along better. I'm in hog heaven. Bobby's the problem. But hell, two out of three ain't bad."

There were some shocks. Sometimes in the morning, lying in bed while Ruth was in the kitchen, hearing the scrape of chairs from down below, he would think it was years ago and Jane was still there. It still gave him a funny feeling to see Ruth stepping into Jane's closet. One morning when he was just on the edge of awakening from sleep, hearing the shower running but not hearing it, he opened his eyes at the squeak of the bathroom door and was startled when Ruth emerged wrapped in a bath towel. He had expected to see Jane, his eyes had even looked automatically at the level of Jane's head, Ruth's breasts.

At dinner two weeks before Thanksgiving, Paul answered a phone call from Phyllis Berg. "Of course," Ruth heard him say, "I think it's a great idea. Sure, just the way we always used to do it."

"Guess what?" Paul said, after hanging up the phone. "We're going home-and-home with the Bergs again this year."

Hilary beamed. "Great."

"Just like the old days," Paul said.

"Not exactly," Bobby said.

"That was Phyllis Berg," Paul explained to Ruth. "She's invited us to have Thanksgiving dinner with them. And I invited them to have dinner here on Christmas."

"That's very sweet," Ruth said, although she felt some terror at the prospect.

"We used to do it every year," Paul said. "If they came here for Thanksgiving, we went there for Christmas. And vice versa. Ever since we moved in here."

"We'll use the dining room again," Hilary said. "And the good china."

"You'll get together with Phyllis," Paul said to Ruth. "Usually when we went there, we brought only dessert. But maybe there are some other things we could do."

"There's not a lot I can do," Ruth said. "What sort of dessert?"

"Pumpkin pie, of course," Bobby said. "And Mom always made an apple pie, too."

"Oh, God," Hilary said. "Mom's pumpkin pie. Wasn't it the best?"

"None better," Paul said.

"The apple pie wasn't too shabby, either," Bobby said. "That's what I always had—à la mode—and you always wondered how I could eat it after such a big dinner, remember?"

"Yes," Paul said. "Jane always said you ate enough at Thanksgiving to hold you till Christmas. And enough at Christmas to last till New Year's."

"This family is always thinking about food," Ruth said.

"Or eating it," said Paul.

"I'll buy a couple of pies to bring the Bergs. There's a very nice bakery in my old neighborhood." Ruth could not help notice the silence with which her offer was greeted. "Really," she added, "they make very good pies."

"That'll be fine," Paul said.

Ruth felt uncomfortable looking at Bobby and Hilary. She knew what they were thinking, what they seemed to feel, whom they wanted sitting at this table instead of her.

Hilary went to the cookbook shelf. She took down Jane's little blue loose-leaf notebook and sat down at her place again. "Here's her recipe," Hilary said, after turning a few pages. "And here's the apple pie recipe, too." She read to herself, with the others looking on.

"We could try to make them," Hilary said. "It doesn't look too hard."

"I'd help," Bobby said.

"You?" Paul began to laugh.

"I can skin apples," Bobby said. "It's easy."

"I'll help, too," Hilary said. "Can we, Dad? Say yes. I know we can do it! *Please.*"

"It wouldn't be easy," Paul said, but looking at the kids, seeing the excitement in their faces, he changed his mind. "Okay." He grinned. "And I'll help, too. What can happen? We'll ruin a couple of pies."

Hilary leaped up and flung her arms about Paul's neck. Neither of them noticed Ruth as she left the table.

Later that evening, Paul opened the door to the guest room and poked his head inside. Ruth was sitting with her back to him, scribbling furiously on a yellow pad. "Hon? Are you coming to bed?"

"Soon," Ruth said, not turning around.

Paul watched her for a moment. She'd been upstairs all evening. He got the sense that she was upset at something. "I'll be watching the news," he said. When she didn't reply, he closed the door and went to the bedroom, undressed, watched the eleven o'clock TV news, and got into bed.

It was after midnight when he heard her come quietly into the bedroom, take her nightgown from the dresser, and go into the bathroom. He lay in the dark, waiting for her.

"Are you all right?" he asked as she came to bed.

"Fine," she said. She got under the down comforter, turning her back to him.

"Ruth, what's wrong?" He put a hand on her back, rubbing gently.

"Nothing."

"You've been locked up all evening. Something's bothering you."

"Only everything," she said. "That's all." She shrugged her shoulders under his hand, as if to tell him not to touch her. They lay for a while, not sleeping, the night sounds of the old house magnified in the silence.

"How could you do that to me?" Ruth said quietly.

"Do what?"

"The pies," she said. "Didn't you see my face? Didn't you hear me say I'd buy them?"

He was nonplussed. "What's wrong with making pies?"

He heard a low laugh; the one that meant she was not amused. "What do they want, Paul, a kind of test? 'See if you can make these pies like my mother, Ruth? We dare you.' As if I could compete with Jane in her own kitchen."

"Is that what you thought?"

"Why didn't you cut them off at the pass? I said I'd buy the stupid pies."

"Ruth, you're wrong."

"Then why do I feel so hurt?"

"You're being ultrasensitive, babe."

"Am I? Didn't you see what was going on? Let's bring Mama Jane back for Thanksgiving by making her pies. Another guest at the feast, the Supermom of all time. And you *encouraged* them."

"I can't believe you're saying this," Paul said. "Did you see their faces? Did you see how excited they were? How could I throw cold water on that?"

"By agreeing with me," she said. "Or weren't you listening? So what happens now? Am I supposed to learn how to whip up a spectacular pie crust by Thursday? Should I take lessons?"

"The kids want to do it, Ruth. This has nothing to do with you."

"It has *everything* to do with me."

"They'll make the pies and I'll help them, I suppose. You don't have to get involved. Unless you want to."

"Be sure to leave me the part that screws everything up," she said bitterly.

Paul began to say something, but Ruth cut him off. "I don't want to talk about it. The alarm goes off at six-thirty." She turned away and plumped her pillow, then settled down.

That was the first time Paul let his nifty-swifty bride go to sleep angry with him.

A few evenings later, Ruth called Phyllis Berg to coordinate their Thanksgiving meal. Phyllis insisted that Ruth come right down the street and join her for coffee. "Show your face," Phyllis said. "I haven't seen you in weeks."

Once outside the house, strolling in the crisp cold air, Ruth felt her spirits rise. She'd forgotten how often she'd gone for a walk in the evening in Manhattan. Or a run, she remembered ruefully. It always made her feel better; it cut problems down to size.

Phyllis met her at the front door, led her into the kitchen, where she gave Ruth a cup of freshly brewed coffee. Phyllis sat down beside her at the oval oak table, looking critically at Ruth through her thick eyeglasses. "You look sallow, Ruth, a little peaky. Do you take vitamins?"

"No."

"You should. I'll bet you're not eating right." Phyllis put a spoonful of sugar into her coffee, stirring it thoughtfully. "You've got problems, haven't you? I can see it in your face. Is it Paul?"

"Paul is fine."

"The kids?"

Ruth sighed. "The kids, the house, the office, my *life* . . . nothing serious," she said, smiling.

"I don't envy what you've taken on, Ruth. I'm sure it's a load. Is Bobby acting up?"

"How did you know?"

"It figures." Phyllis took a sip of her coffee and offered Ruth a cookie from the cut-glass tray on the table. When Ruth declined, Phyllis took one. "He hasn't gotten over it yet, the poor lamb. Who knows if he ever will? Bobby and my Billy, they used to be pals. But ever since Jane died, Bobby's been different. We don't see his face around here very often."

"No one sees Bobby very often," Ruth said. "He spends more time with my cat than he does with me. And he resents me very much. He doesn't even try to hide it."

"Of course," Phyllis nodded. "You're not Jane. She was Bobby's whole world, you know: the sun, moon, and stars. 'Jane's shadow,' I used to call him; he was her baby. I don't think it's possible for a mother and child to be closer than those two were. Which wouldn't have been such a bad thing except that she died."

"I can't get through to him, Phyllis."

"Ruth, let me tell you something: I worry about all three of them. After Jane died, because we were so close, I was in and out of there every day, and they were here for dinner two or three times a week. But then something happened, darned if I know what. They stopped coming so often. They got awfully tight. That's one of the reasons I wanted to make sure we continued our holiday get-togethers. We always were the best of friends, and our kids got along so well. We did a lot of porch sitting together, a lot of barbecueing, movies, going out to dinner. Very close. But not anymore. If they hadn't gone through such a tragedy, I'd be hurt by it.''

"You knew Jane very well, didn't you?''

"Sorority sisters,'' Phyllis said. She munched another cookie. "I found their house for them. Jane was my best friend.''

"Was she as perfect as everyone says?''

Phyllis giggled. "Almost. But you know, that was her main flaw. It was very difficult to be really close to someone whose standards were so high. I mean, Jane's house was always spotless, her children immaculate, her garden perfect, her cooking the best. And while she knew everyone in the neighborhood—she was a teacher, after all—she didn't have a lot of friends. Me, Marion Gerber, Mickey Schaeffer, who taught with her, and Kathleen Bradie. That's it. She could be very high and mighty sometimes, and that's hard to take. You know, everyone liked a film, Jane criticized it. We ate in a great restaurant, she'd find fault with it. You could say she was a snob, except that she was usually right. I couldn't go shopping for clothes with her, I'll tell you that. Because she'd find some little fault in everything I tried on. I don't think I ever bought a dress when Jane was along.''

Ruth mentioned the upcoming Thanksgiving meal, and what had happened with the pies.

"I don't know where Paul's brains are sometimes,'' Phyllis said. "That's awful.''

"And I'm right in the middle.''

"Stay out of it,'' Phyllis said.

"I'm trying to.''

"I know about Jane's recipes. Whenever I made one of them, it never came out as well as when she made it. I don't know why that is, but it's so. I guarantee those pies won't taste anything like Jane's. And who cares, anyway? The idea is sharing, not what we eat.''

"I agree,'' Ruth said. She was very happy to see that Phyllis Berg was a sane and rational woman. "Is there anything more I can do for you? For Thanksgiving?''

Phyllis looked at her speculatively. "Can you cook at all?''

"Nope.''

Phyllis laughed heartily. "Right. Then don't worry about it. Just show up."

Ruth laughed along with Phyllis. "Thanks. There is one thing that does worry me, though. How am I going to manage Christmas dinner for everyone?"

"I'll help you," Phyllis said at once. "You just do the turkey. And maybe a plain bread stuffing. Oh, don't look so rattled. Just cook the bird with a lot of butter, about an hour less than they tell you on the wrapping. And the stuffing is the easiest thing in the world, as long as you cook it in a pan and not in the bird. Don't worry, Ruth, I'll help. Come down here Thursday afternoon, when I'm cooking, and I'll show you how to do everything."

"You're on," Ruth said. "And thanks." She felt so good at that moment, she took a cookie and munched it. "I hope we'll be friends, Phyllis."

"I expect we will," Phyllis said. "You look like you could use a friend."

It worked out perfectly for Ruth. While Paul and the kids were hard at work in the kitchen—peeling apples, cooking a ripe pumpkin in the oven, and generally making a mess—she slipped down the street and spent two hours in Phyllis Berg's big kitchen. Phyllis was a good teacher. The turkey was already cooking when Ruth arrived, but Phyllis took her through the preparation anyway, spelling out all the steps.

Ruth looked into the glass door of the wall oven. "How big is that beast?"

"Twenty-four pounds. A frozen bird. You'll have to let yours defrost, for Christmas dinner, but I'll call and remind you. And I'll give you the cooking time, too. Now, let's make stuffing."

She led Ruth through it, standing aside and letting Ruth do the work. In a short time, the cubed bread stuffing was oven-ready. "That's really not too hard," Ruth said.

"You see? You can do it. In fact, you did it." Phyllis showed Ruth how to make gravy, putting the giblets into a pot with water to cook, and then she let Ruth make the gravy when the turkey was done.

"I think I can do it now," Ruth said.

"Of course you can." She told Ruth to buy a large package of frozen vegetables for Christmas dinner. "And cranberry sauce. Jane always made it from scratch, but I don't." She showed Ruth the brand of cranberry sauce she was using. "Just put it into a nice glass bowl and they'll never know the difference."

"It's really not so difficult," Ruth said.

"If you know what you're doing."

"Then why am I so scared? My God, I feel like a bride."

"You are, honey," Phyllis laughed. "You are."

When Ruth went back down the block to dress for dinner, she found all three Kleins in the kitchen, watching two pies cooling on a rack. The smell of cinnamon, apples, and burnt dough filled the air. No one had attempted to clean up. Apple skins and flour littered the chopping block and counter; a batch of measuring implements and mixing bowls filled the sink. "How'd you all do?" she asked.

"Not terrific," Paul said. "I think we overcooked the pumpkin pie. It's much browner than I remember."

"The apple pie exploded," Hilary said.

"No it didn't," Bobby said. "It just overflowed."

"We forgot to cut a hole in the top," Paul said, "and the juice leaked out. I hope it's edible."

"It's Thanksgiving," Ruth said. "It's not what we eat, it's being together." She couldn't help smiling to herself as she cleaned up the messy kitchen.

Thanksgiving dinner was a happy time for everyone. Paul and the kids were enjoying the familiar surroundings and company, and to Ruth's eyes even Bobby looked as if he was having a good time. She couldn't help feeling that she was more relaxed in Phyllis Berg's home than in her own just down the street. When everyone had been served, and were overeating, another Thanksgiving tradition of the Bergs' and Kleins', Phyllis slyly announced that the stuffing and the gravy had been made by Ruth. "Terrific, honey," Paul said between mouthfuls. Ruth ignored the surprised look in his eyes. "I had a good teacher," she said.

Afterward she followed Phyllis into the kitchen to help her with the cleanup, but Phyllis wouldn't permit it. "I don't clean up in your house, and you don't clean up in mine. That's the deal."

"Sold."

"And the rest of the deal is not sharing leftovers. My gang'll be eating turkey for a week, like it or not."

Paul was waiting for Ruth when she came to bed that night. She could see that his pajamas were on the club chair, and even though the comforter was up to his neck, his shoulders were bare. "You're not still mad at me, are you?" he asked.

"I never was," she lied.

"You've been very cool this past week. Distant."

"I'm sorry, darling. There's been a lot on my mind. The office is going crazy. Impossible."

He smiled at her, holding back the covers so she could see his naked body. "I'm going crazy, too," Paul said. "Get under these covers or I'll come out and get you."

When Paul came down to breakfast the following morning, he found Ruth on the telephone, speaking to George Chan. He poured himself a cup of the coffee she had made. Bobby was sitting on the floor in the corner, playing with Marmaduke.

"Okay, George," Ruth said. "I'll meet you there in about an hour." She put down the telephone. "Good morning," she said to Paul. "We just got a real break. I'm so excited! There's this big watch account." She mentioned the name. "Through a connection, George got us an invitation to pitch. They're known for ladies' watches, but they've come out with a line of men's watches now. That's the one that's up for grabs. Isn't that great?" Impulsively, she leaned over and kissed Paul's cheek.

"Sounds good," Paul said.

"If we got the men's watches, it'd be a foot in the door for the rest of the account. The only problem is, we have to be ready by Monday."

"You're kidding."

"I wish I was," she said. "I'm meeting George in the office. He's going to try and round up as many of our people as he can reach."

"It's Thanksgiving weekend, babe."

"I'm sorry," she said, getting up.

"Wait a minute," Paul said. "We were going to eat dinner out and see a movie in Manhattan. And we have tickets for a matinee on Sunday."

"Honey, I know that. What can I do? This is a real opportunity."

"How long have you known about this?" Paul asked in an angry tone.

"George has been working on it for weeks. But it wasn't *confirmed* until just now."

"Damn it! Why didn't you tell me?"

"Don't raise your voice," Ruth hissed, nodding her head at the boy across the room. "Honey, I'm going to work," she continued. "I'm sorry but I must. I'll call you."

"Thanks a lot," Paul said bitterly. "We'll manage without you. Go on!"

"Have some coffee," she said, "you'll feel better."

"I'm awake. I don't need coffee to see things clearly. Ruth, your business is getting in the way."

"I knew you'd say that," she snapped at him. "You're being totally unreasonable, and I don't have time to discuss it right now." She turned on her heel and hurried from the room.

Upstairs she fumed as she dressed, trying not to let herself get even more upset. How could he treat her so unfairly? She didn't *want* to run off on this weekend and spend it working in the office. Couldn't he see that? *His* business came first, of course. Why didn't he understand how hard she was working, juggling the office and the home front and making mistakes in both places? There wasn't time enough in the day. And when something had to give, why was *she* the one who had to give it? She'd been cheating George—and herself—from the very day she'd come back from her honeymoon. They were a team, she and George, they had to work *together*. Scribbling ideas and copy lines at home didn't work. She needed George's input, his clear cold eye.

She came downstairs in a hurry, looking through the front door in the foyer to judge the weather. It looked sunny.

"Ruth?"

Bobby was standing behind her, holding Marmaduke in his arms. "Ruth, can I talk to you about Dukie?"

"Oh, Bobby, not now."

"Why is he only an inside cat?"

She answered him as she took her short jacket from the closet.

257

"He's had his front claws removed. So if he went outside, he couldn't defend himself."

"Against what?"

"Bobby, I've got to run," she said. "Can we talk about this later?"

Paul came into earshot through the dining room doorway.

"Don't bother Ruth, Bob-o," he said in an icy tone. "Can't you see she's in a hurry?"

Putting aside her need to leave, she forced herself to answer Bobby calmly. "Because Marmaduke's been declawed, Bob, he's defenseless against another animal. A squirrel, a dog, or even another cat. You see?"

"But why can't I play with him outside? In the backyard. I would watch him, Ruth. I wouldn't let anyone hurt him."

"It's not a good idea."

"We play this tennis-ball game," Bobby said. "I bounce it and Dukie catches it in his mouth. Couldn't I take him out into the backyard?"

"Bobby, no," she said. "He could run away. He's never been outside."

"*Please*, Ruth," the boy pleaded. "We have a fence and a gate. Dukie wouldn't run away from me."

"You heard Ruth," Paul said. "The answer is no. Marmaduke is her cat."

Ruth could not let that remark pass. "He's *our* cat now," she said, "and Bobby's most of all."

"Ah," Paul said, "if that's so, why don't you give the kid a break? He's responsible, Ruth. He'd take care of Dukie."

That's right, Ruth thought, take Bobby's side. As if we don't have enough to separate us. "He doesn't have a flea collar," she said.

"I can get one," Paul said.

She hated the smile on Paul's face. He was getting back at her, she knew, but how terrible to use the boy this way.

"Please," Bobby said.

"Okay," she said, defeated by Bobby's look of gratitude, which was directed at his father. Two against one, as usual. She took her shoulder bag and turned to the door. Paul did not say good-bye.

The air was crisp, but not cold. There was no wind. At the corner she waited for the traffic light to change so she could cross the street. She would have to forget about her hurt, her worry. She had to have a clear mind to work effectively.

She looked back at the house, at the yellow tower rising in the bright sun. The red-shingled porch roof, the dormer windows thrusting from the roof. So big, so roomy, and no place in it for her.

20

THE FILM-COMPANY LIMOUSINE dropped Ruth off at the Beverly Wilshire just before five in the afternoon. She checked for messages at the front desk. There were none, the clerk said, and handed over a key to her room in the old wing of the hotel. She headed upstairs.

What she wanted was a hot shower and a drink. She was exhausted. An early wake-up time after a nighttime flight to the Coast was a sure recipe for the jet-lag blues. It had been terribly hot out at the ranch, at the mock western town where they'd shot most of the watch commercial. A long, tedious day in the sun.

She looked at herself in the mirror over the white enamel dresser. Who was that woman? Her hair was lanky and grubby, dark rings showed under her eyes. You are not a happy girl, she said to herself.

It should have been a day of triumph.

They'd won the watch company account on the strength of the commercial she and George had come up with that Thanksgiving weekend. The watch people'd bought it with lots of enthusiasm and mutterings in the background of how this was the kind of work they wanted from their other agency, the one that had the biggest part of their business. No promises made, of course, but the writing was on the wall. If this commercial scored big for the men's watch line, the ladies' watch account would be theirs for the asking.

Genius time.

The commercial would work, she had no doubt about that. Then why didn't she feel like cheering?

Paul thought she'd come out here on purpose, to get away from home. He didn't give a damn about her business. "It's a western street, Paul," she'd told him, "a standing set in Hollywood. I have to shoot it out there, don't you see?"

He saw only what he wanted to see these days.

She called room service and ordered a gin and tonic, swinging her feet onto the bed and lying down to wait for it. Not enough energy to take a shower. She could call home soon. After eight, they'd probably still be sitting in the kitchen. Doing whatever they do when I'm not around to spoil it. Four of them, actually, in that house. Because Jane was still there. She was with them, old perfect Jane, in their hearts, in their minds, in their memories. In every floorboard and wall, every room, every piece of furniture. And you, girl, are not now nor can you ever be like old Janie.

There was a knock on the door. The room-service waiter brought in gin and tonic. She took a long sip of the icy drink and sat down by the telephone. She called the airline and reconfirmed her flight for the following afternoon. Three hours in the sound studio in the morning for the voice-overs, plenty of time if everything went right to catch a two P.M. plane back. By rights she should have allowed an extra day out here, just in case something went wrong. But she couldn't afford it. Paul wouldn't understand.

Why in the hell should she feel so guilty?

Guilty about what? Doing her job? Functioning in the world, using all the expertise and skills she'd acquired? Why guilt?

She put through the call to home, waiting through clicks and beeps until she heard the ring of her home telephone. "Hello," Paul said.

"Hello there, honey. It's me." Cheery, cheery.

261

"The lady in California," Paul said, his voice cool. "We know you, don't we?"

"I should hope so. How is everybody?"

"Fine. Bobby has a few sniffles, but nothing serious. We're managing very well."

Without you went on the end of that sentence. Ruth heard it clearly, although Paul had not said it. She waited for him to ask how the shooting had gone, but he did not. She filled in the short silence by telling him all about it.

"Good," Paul said when she'd finished. "I'm glad. Are you still on the same flight home?"

"Yes."

"Then I'll see you tomorrow."

There was a long silence. She wanted to scream at him for being so cool and detached. "What's wrong?" she asked. "You don't sound right."

"I'm fine," he said.

"Don't be angry with me, Paul. I love you."

"I love you, too," he said. "You're imagining things. I just hate your being away, that's all. I'll feel better when I see you."

"Same here," she said.

"Well . . . until tomorrow," Paul said. "Good-bye."

She held the phone to her ear, hearing the click as the connection was broken. When she put the receiver back in its cradle, she began to cry.

"Okay, chum, time for lights out," Paul said. He secured the winter quilt one more time under the boy's chin, tucking it tight. Marmaduke was curled up under Bobby's desk, watching with yellow eyes. During the night the cat would sleep on the bed, at Bobby's feet, which was where Paul had found him that morning.

"I've got a new game with Dukie now," Bobby said. "We play with the trains upstairs. Dukie goes in the middle and hops over the tracks while the train goes around. Sometimes he knocks the locomotive off the tracks."

"That cat surely does love you," Paul said.

"He's so funny, Dad. Do you know if I slowly bring a tennis ball up to his nose he goes cross-eyed? You should see it."

"I can't wait," Paul said. He kissed the boy's forehead. "And now good night."

"Daddy, can I ask you a question?"

"Yes."

"Why did you marry Ruth?"

"Because," he said slowly, "I loved her. I wanted to be with her. And it was the best way to get her to come and live with us, so you and Hilary could love her too."

Bobby thought about this for a moment. "Do you still love her?"

"Yes I do. Very much. And she loves you very much. You know that, don't you?"

Bobby nodded. "Dad, do you still love Mom?"

"Yes, baby, yes I do."

"Then how can you love Ruth?"

"It's allowed, Bob-o. You can love a lot of people. I love you and Hil and Ruth and Grandma Sylvia. And your mother, too."

"But you still think about Mom?"

"Sometimes. Yes."

"I think about her all the time," Bobby said. "I don't want to ever forget her."

Paul squeezed the boy's shoulder beneath the quilt. "I know you'll never forget her. But Mom is a part of your past, Bob-o. She'll always be with you. But you should be able to open up and love others, too. It doesn't mean you're forgetting Mom if you do that."

"I love you," the boy said. "And Hil and Grandma, too. And Dukie, of course."

Paul waited a moment, but the boy would not say more. "Try to love Ruth, Bob-o."

Bobby shrugged, the gesture he used when he did not want to disagree. "She's not like Mom," he said. "She couldn't be like Mom in a million years."

Downstairs again, showered and changed, Ruth felt better. She poked her head into Hernando's Hideaway, took one look at the mariachi band tooting away, and left. Across the street she found a Hamburger Hamlet. She sat at the counter and ate a mushroom burger, not tasting it. She felt restless and lonely. She wished Paul were here to make her laugh.

She walked up Rodeo Drive in the deepening twilight. The stores were closed, not too many people on the street. She window shopped, amused by the warmth of the air and the Christmas decorations in every shop. Christmas in Beverly Hills. At these prices, they should have imported snow to cover the streets. She worried again about Christmas dinner, then checked herself. They'd eat it and like it, or else. When you do your best, you can't worry about it.

Had it all been a mistake, she asked herself. Why had she fallen for that darling, funny man? You were lonely, she knew in her deepest heart, lonely and vulnerable. And he *is* wonderful. But the package deal was what she didn't know about, hadn't really been prepared for. One boy, one girl, one house, one ghost.

On an impulse, she hailed a passing taxi and went to Westwood Village. A movie was a good idea, any movie. Two hours of no-think. She found a Burt Reynolds film at a triplex and watched cars crash and dumb policemen chase Burt's Camaro. But even during the film, when the sparse crowd all about her was laughing, she was still thinking.

What would have happened if she'd married Sam Aaron when he wanted her to? She'd be a mother by now, somewhere close by, living mostly through Sam's career. And you'd be unhappy, she told herself, and arguing with Sam about taking a job in an L.A. ad agency.

Back in her room at the Beverly Wilshire, she watched TV then turned it off. Sam Aaron. She hadn't thought about him in a long while. A nice man, easy to get along with, except where his career was concerned. That came first, always.

He couldn't hold a candle to Paul. Not in tenderness, in feeling, in understanding, the things that really counted. Why couldn't Paul understand her need to work and build something? Jane had worked, why wasn't he used to a working wife by now? And why couldn't he see how much Bobby resented her?

She took the telephone directory from under the night table and looked up Aaron. There were two, but only one Sam, living on a street in Beverly Hills. She'd been right about that. On an impulse she called his number.

"Ruth? My God, it's good to hear from you!" He sounded happy to hear her voice.

Sam wanted to know what she was doing out in L.A. and she told him. "And what about you?" she asked.

"Married, but you knew that, and we have two little boys." And then Sam began to talk about working out here, how different it was from New York. He'd shot one feature, a comedy; now if the damned studio would only release it maybe something would happen. And the TV work she knew about, but he went on to tell her anyway. Sam, Sam, she thought, you really haven't changed.

After about ten minutes, when she thought she'd scream if she heard one more story about a lousy producer, Sam finally got around to her. "You got married. I heard it through the grapevine. Tell me about him."

"He's wonderful. Handsome and funny, and very nice. His name's Paul; he's in the wine business, a widower with a couple of kids and a big old house."

"Kids?" Sam laughed. "You, a stepmother? Oh, Ruthie, that's funny." He laughed again.

"Not that funny," she said.

"It is to me."

"Are you happy, Sam?" she asked. She heard the suddenly defensive tone in his reply.

"Yeah, I'm happy . . . sure, I'm happy. You know . . . married is different. A lot different from what we had. Not so many highs, or lows, but richer, if you know what I mean. Real life, Ruthie, not playing house like we did. Having children does that, kids settle you down. Hey! I'd sure like to see you. Can we have lunch tomorrow? I'll take you to the Polo Lounge, for laughs. How about it?"

She told him about her schedule, her two o'clock flight home. He sounded disappointed. "You're at the Beverly Wilshire, right? I can be there in five minutes."

"Sam, it's late, and I have to be up early tomorrow."

"I can get out, no problem. One drink, Ruthie. I'd like to see you again. Touch you . . ."

"Oh, Sam," she said, "don't."

"I miss you sometimes," he said. "Even after all these years.

265

You were the best, baby, the best,'' he added, his voice going low and husky.

"We'd better say good-bye."

"Wait! Don't hang up. Can I call you when I get to New York? I come in sometimes. Would you have lunch with me?"

"I don't think so."

"Ruthie, come on. What would it mean if we got together again? For old times' sake. You're still on the pill, aren't you?"

"This was a mistake," she said. "I'm hanging up."

"Don't! Ruthie, come on. Why not, for God's sake?"

"Because," she said before cutting the connection, "because I'm a happily married woman."

"There's an on-the-job training for being a mother," Phyllis Berg was saying, "and you missed it, Ruth. When you watch them grow up you learn a lot of things along the way, including when to give them a good swat if they need it." It was Christmas weekend, two days before the holiday, which fell on a Monday this year. Paul and the children were out shopping for last-minute gifts, and Phyllis had come to drop off a number of items Ruth would need for Christmas dinner.

"You don't really hit your kids, do you?" Ruth asked.

"Oh, sure I do," Phyllis said. "Well, once or twice . . . when they were little. What Bobby needs is a swift boot in the ass, except you're not the one who should give it to him."

"Paul would never do that."

"More's the pity."

"I kiss him, Phyllis, and he wipes it right off. Doesn't even bother not to let me see it."

"He's a hard case," Phyllis said, "but don't give up on him. Now, let's see. The turkey's in your freezer. Let's take a look at it." She opened the freezer compartment door and pulled out the Butterball. "Twenty pounds, I see. Cook it fifteen minutes a pound. That's about five hours."

"And lots of butter and remember to baste," Ruth said.

"You're catching on," Phyllis grinned. "What are you making for firsts?"

"Shrimp cocktail."

"For this crowd? Wow."

"I buy cleaned shrimp and open a jar of sauce."

"It'll cost a *fortune*," Phyllis said.

"Hell, I'm a sporty kid."

"And Marion Gerber's coming, I heard, with her gang."

"Yes. Paul invited them. Of course, I'd like to have been consulted beforehand, but . . ."

"You'll manage. The dining room table seats thirteen easily. So I'll bring candied sweets, and cole slaw, and dessert, of course. The *coffee*. I almost forgot."

"Coffee I can make, Phyllis. It's my best thing."

"Good, then you're set. And I'll come early to help, don't worry."

"What, me worry?" Ruth grinned. "My knees are shaking, that's all. Dinner for thirteen people, my God! I hope I don't mess up, that's all."

"You'll be fine. Ooops! Rolls, butter, veggies?"

Ruth unfolded a long piece of foolscap. "I have a menu plan, and a step-by-step list of what to do and when."

"Jane," Phyllis said in a shaky voice. "That's Jane's list."

"Yes," Ruth nodded. "I found it in the back of her recipe book."

Phyllis stared. "And you're going to use it?"

"Why not?" Ruth said. "It's her kitchen, isn't it?"

Paul was determined to make it a happy Christmas. The bitter taste of last year still lay on his tongue. Three mourners then, grieving in a world rejoicing, the air filled with carols that only deepened their somber mood. No more of that.

He spent money as if he were minting it. If it were possible to purchase joy he would buy a carload. Business was unbelievable, the best year Bradie & Klein had ever had. The Asti spumante advertising was running on TV in twenty markets and doing fine, despite the fact that Ruth thought it only fair. And next year would be even better.

He took time off from the office, slipping away to shop for the kids. Christmas was always for the kids; he and Jane never exchanged gifts.

In a toy shop on Fifth Avenue, Paul purchased a model train car that held logs, a crane car to remove them, more track and grade crossings, small trees, a tunnel, and a depot. He had not forgotten the promise made long ago that was never kept. And now that Bobby was once again playing with the trains upstairs, completing the setup was even more meaningful.

He had casually asked Hilary which rock groups she currently favored, and the next day got back a list numbered one through twenty, ranked in descending order of need. He purchased the first half-dozen on the list, and a book about the Beatles. He left it to Ruth to shop for clothing gifts for Hilary, reminding her how much the girl liked coat sweaters. That was last year, darling, she told him. Don't worry, I have Hilary's number. Nothing that smacks of mass fashion would appeal to Hilary, Ruth knew. It either had to be so avant-garde as to look ridiculous, or a back number that smacked of thrift shop. Ruth bought Bobby's clothing presents as well, warm shirts for school and a brilliant red Shetland sweater.

The woman's touch, one that Jane had had in abundance.

It was only partly there in Ruth, he felt. He worried about her relationship with the kids. Why couldn't she find a common ground with Bobby? The boy was as hungry for love as a puppy, hanging around Paul's neck the moment he came through the door. Not so with Ruth. It was worrisome, as were his own feelings toward her. He had expected Ruth to bring love with her into the house, and she had. For him. And even there, with her impossible dedication to work, there had begun crosscurrents and undertones he didn't like. She was not fitting in somehow. There was an uneasiness in the house you could almost feel sometimes. "My Ruthie can be very selfish," her own father had told him. Was it true?

It was going to be the longest, toughest day of her life. Ruth was sitting on the high kitchen stool, mashing stuffing cubes, eggs, and canned chicken soup with her hands. And a Merry Christmas to you, too, baby. Her hands were clammy and covered with gunk. Time for a break. It was about noon. The turkey was cooking, the stuffing was ready to be put in its glass pan, to go into the oven later. The happy homemaker. She cleaned her hands in the sink, then found the scotch, and poured herself a healthy shot over ice in Paul's jelly glass. Just a single sip made her feel warmer.

How did she get here, she asked herself? Right now, if she hadn't met Paul, she'd be home in her apartment, probably still sleeping. But alone, mustn't forget that, all alone with only a cat for company.

Christmas morning had begun for her at precisely six-thirty. There was Bobby, knocking on their bedroom door. "What's that?" she nudged Paul and asked. "Time to get up, babe, and go downstairs to watch the kids open their presents." She was incredulous, and sleepy, and nervous enough over all the cooking she had to do today. "We always do it that way," Paul said. Of course, why hadn't she known? Another Klein tradition. Anything the three of them had done together for twenty minutes was a tradition. He could have told her about this morning, warned her, advised, something. Another failure of communication. One of many. Somehow they weren't talking as they used to.

She basted the turkey. Another twenty minutes and she'd have to turn the huge beast over. She checked Jane's long foolscap list just to make sure. Yep. Thank you, Saint Jane.

You've made your bed, now lie in it. Correction. Jane made the bed, picked it out of a furniture showroom eons ago, and now you have to lie in it, girl.

Hilary came into the kitchen, carrying one of the gifts she had opened this morning. "Do you have a minute?" she asked. "I just wanted to tell you I *love* the jacket you bought me."

"I thought you would," Ruth said, grinning. She felt a warm glow as the girl kissed her cheek. "You're easy to shop for, Hil. I just look and look until I see something *outrageous* . . . and then I say to myself, 'That's for Hilary,' and it usually is."

Hilary giggled. "Maybe you do understand me."

"A little," Ruth said.

Hilary nodded. "Do you need help down here? Is there something I can do?"

"No, I'm fine. Where are the men in this family?"

"Up in the train room, putting Bobby's new things together. Do you want them?"

"Later. I could use some help setting the table," Ruth said.

"Oh, that's my job," the girl said, "and Bobby helps. We'll use the good china, the silver." Hilary's eyes widened. "Did you remember to polish the silver?"

"Yes. I had Gemma do it all on Friday." Ruth nodded her head

269

in the direction of the long list posted on the corkboard near the oven. "I have a little list."

Hilary glanced in the direction of the corkboard, saw the list, and went closer to read it. Ruth saw her shoulders slump, and when Hilary turned, her face was twisted. "Mom's list," she said. "Her Christmas dinner list."

Ruth stood very still at the sink, looking at Hilary.

"She was the best, Ruth . . . this used to be such a special day."

"Hilary," Ruth said, and stepped forward to take the girl in her arms, but as she did so, Hilary turned and fled. "I'm sorry," Ruth called after her, then wondered what she was sorry for.

Five minutes later, she heard heavy footsteps pounding down the stairs. Paul's face was angry in a way she had never seen. He strode to the corkboard and looked at the list. "How could you!" he said and ripped the list from the board, crumpling it into a ball in his fist. He threw it into the garbage pail, letting the lid fall closed with a clang. "Are you crazy?" he demanded. "Don't you have a brain in your head?"

Shocked beyond words, she stared openmouthed.

"Didn't you realize what that would do to the kids? Are you too stupid to realize how sensitive they are about her?"

"Wait a minute," she said. "It's only a piece of paper."

"I'm glad Bobby didn't see it," he snapped at her. "We don't need reminders, Ruth. Keep out of her things."

"Hold it right there," she said, fighting back. "What about the pie business? That was her thing, and you even *encouraged* them then."

"Have some understanding," he said harshly. "That was different. It made them happy. Can't you see that?"

"No!" she exploded, not holding back her voice. "I don't understand *anything* in this damn house! Is it only you guys who can talk about her? Am I supposed to never mention her name? Tell me, Klein, so I'll know. What are the rules around here? Once and for all let's get it straight. I'm supposed to cook like her but not *be* like her, is that it? Or be *me* but only like *her*. What the hell am I supposed to do?"

"Lower your voice."

270

"Oh, yes, Jane was always a lady," she said cuttingly. "I'm sorry, when I get mad I start to yell. She never did that, did she?"

"And don't use her against me," Paul said. "It's stupid and it's wrong."

"Another rule," she spat back at him. "What do you do, make them up as you go along? Don't you see that I can never win, that I can never be right? That I'm going slightly nuts trying to live in this house?"

Paul's face was cold now, the anger gone, replaced by a look of weary resignation. He turned away. "We'll talk about this later," he said. "You're not thinking straight."

She pursued him through the pantry and into the dining room. "Don't run away from me!" she cried out.

"For God's sake keep your voice down," he said. "Do you want the kids to hear us arguing?"

She stood looking at him as he walked up the stairs. For an instant she was tempted to take her coat from the closet and flee, just walk away from this house and never come back. Tears came to her eyes. She wiped at them angrily with the dish towel she was holding in her hands. It was all coming apart, everything was going wrong. The one strong link that held her here was her love for Paul. And now she was seeing that beginning to break.

When she smelled the turkey she began to run toward the kitchen.

The dinner was a smashing success, but all of it was spoiled for her. The turkey was perfectly roasted, her stuffing drew compliments from Phyllis and Marion Gerber. But their words sounded hollow in her ears. Paul was at the head of the table, playing *pater-familias* and carving the big bird. Ruth picked at the food on her plate, not tasting it.

A few hours later she was in the kitchen, cleaning up at the sink. She felt a hand on her shoulder. "A great dinner, kid," Phyllis Berg was saying. "You'll be a cook yet, mark my words."

"Thanks," Ruth said.

"What's wrong? You haven't been yourself all evening, Ruth."

"Nothing's wrong," Ruth said.

Phyllis took a dish towel from the rack and began drying a pot.

"Come on," she said. "You've looked grim since the minute we came in."

"What are you doing? I thought we didn't help each other clean up, wasn't that the deal?"

"Never mind the deal," Phyllis said. "Did you have a fight with one of the kids?"

"Nope, with the big boss himself."

"Your first fight?" Phyllis said. "Congratulations. There'll be plenty more."

"I don't think so, not like this one." She stared out the kitchen window into the darkness. "I don't know what they expect of me, I don't know how to make it any better. I'm losing a little more ground every day. And now I'm beginning to think they're right."

"Right about what?"

"I don't belong in this house."

21

JANUARY IS THE cruelest month, Paul was thinking, never mind April. Only January puts thirty-one consecutive freezing days together without a holiday to break it up. And if Mr. Eliot had had to heat the big house on Rugby Road and pay the fuel bills, perhaps he would have agreed.

He was worried about the nifty-swifty bride. She didn't look right, act right, and he knew she didn't feel right. A little nagging cold, nothing to be concerned about, but the tip of Ruth's nose was red, her voice cracked sometimes, and she had a persistent cough that wouldn't go away. She'd be awakened in the night sometimes by a fit of coughing. Most times he slept through it, not always. "Babe? What is it?" She was sitting up, her feet off the bed.

"Shh. Sleep, honey, I'm okay." She cleared her throat, then began to cough again. Getting up, she put on her robe. "I'm going downstairs. A cup of tea might help."

"Want company?" he mumbled, not getting up.

"No. You sleep. I'll be all right."

But she wasn't. The stupid cold hung on. Paul didn't like the

273

way she looked. Dark smudges under her eyes from lack of sleep, the hacking cough. "Listen to you," he said when she was coughing one night after dinner. "You sound like the last act of *Camille.*"

"It's nothing," she managed to say.

"And you look like hell."

"Thanks a lot," she said, smiling.

"I have a thought. A week in the sun would do you good. And I know just the place. St. Thomas."

"Don't be silly," she said. "Look—it's not pneumonia. Dave Berg listened to my chest—"

"Lucky Dave."

"And he said I was fine. Besides, how do I get away for a week?"

"Well," Paul said, "you buy an airline ticket, make a reservation . . ." He saw the look on her face and backed off. By now he had learned to tread lightly when it came to Ruth's working so hard and long. It was her way, just as being home every afternoon after school had been Jane's way.

The next morning, he called George Chan and told him he was worried about Ruth.

"Same here. She looks lousy, Paul."

"George, please hear me out, okay? I want her to get away for a week with me. To someplace warm where she can sit in the sun and shake that cold. Do you think your business will utterly collapse if she did that?"

"No," George said, "not entirely."

"Could you lean on her a little for me, George? I'd appreciate it."

"You think she listens to me any more than to you?" George said. "But okay, I'll try."

That afternoon, right after lunch, Ruth was on the telephone. "What is this, Klein, a conspiracy? All of a sudden everybody wants to ship me off to a tropical isle?"

Paul pretended ignorance, but she wouldn't let him hide. "George can't keep a secret from me," she said. "It's one of the things I love about him."

"So how about it? A warm beach, a tropical sun, a piña colada, and me. Romantic nights under the stars, sleeping till noon."

He heard Ruth groan. "God, that sounds good."

"I'll buy the tickets."

"No, we'll talk about it some more. Tonight."

She was worried about leaving the children alone for a week. The business part worried her, too, but she could overcome that anxiety by working twice as hard when she came back. "I don't know how the kids will manage on their own, honey."

"They'll do fine," he assured her. "Hilary's a big girl. Phyllis Berg will look out for them. Not to worry."

"I'm worried, I'm worried." She blew her runny nose into a tissue. "Do you think they'll resent it? You take me off for a vacation while they freeze back here alone?"

Paul was taken aback. "Why should *that* worry you?"

"It does."

"Isn't that silly?"

"My credit is not too terrific with them," she said. "Of course I worry about it."

Paul started to say something, but an idea crossed his mind. "Got it! Grandma Sylvia. I'll bet she'd love to stay with the kids for a week. Especially if I'm paying the freight."

"Can she handle it?" Ruth asked. "I don't know anything about her."

"I've saved you from that," Paul grinned. "And she can handle anything, including me. Why didn't I think of it before? Sylvia, of course."

"Okay, I guess," Ruth said. "I'll feel better about going if she's here with the kids. Do you think she'll come?"

"You leave that to your Uncle Dudley. Sylvia comes. We go. Okay?"

Her smile warmed his heart. "Klein, you got a deal."

Polyester must grow in Florida, like oranges, Paul was thinking as he watched the crowd of sun-tanned doubleknits come off the airplane. Here came Sylvia carrying a huge knitting bag; when he took her in an embrace she turned her head away. "Used to be you'd bring the kids down to see me," she said, even before a hello. "Now you make me risk pneumonia in your cold house just to see my kidlets."

Down at the luggage carousel, Paul retrieved two large suitcases and got them into the trunk of the Buick. Sylvia had brought enough clothes for a month, he thought, and immediately began worrying about snowstorms closing the airports, about Sylvia staying until March or April. He knew she was angry with him. Sylvia didn't bother to hide her feelings. Although she called the kids each weekend, he'd hardly spoken to her since the day he'd phoned her from the office to tell her he was marrying Ruth. "So fast?" she spat at him. "You didn't wait long, did you?" Like Bobby, she was another guardian of Jane's memory.

"The kids are fine," he said, trying to make conversation as they rode home.

"A lot you know," she said mysteriously. "Tell me about your big blondie."

"Her name is Ruth."

Sylvia nodded, looking pleased for some reason. "And she's always working, she can't even boil water, and doesn't get along with the kids."

"Not true, Sylvia," Paul said.

"Who says? You forget, I have my own conversations with those kids. I hear a lot of things you wish you knew about, Paulie."

Angered, but trying to maintain his balance, Paul lit a cigarette from the dashboard lighter. "She's doing fine," he said, "but, you know . . . a new house, the kids, settling in . . . it hasn't been easy for her."

"So who has it been easy for?" Sylvia said, always the scorekeeper of grief. "Was there ever anyone like my Janie? Hah? So good, so fine, such a mother? You think those kids are going to forget about her so fast?"

Paul groaned. "Sylvia, lay off," he snapped. "You've never even spoken to Ruth. She's terrific."

"I'll bet," Sylvia said.

"*Sylvia!* One more word, damn it, and I'll turn the car around and send you back where you came from."

"What'd I say?" Jane's mother said blandly and folded her hands over her knitting bag.

They didn't exchange another word all the way home. Paul brought in her suitcases, caught one sorrowful look from Gemma, and fled to the office.

Jane's pot roast was on the table when Paul reached home. There was a tablecloth on the dining room table, instead of the more efficient place mats, the good china they hadn't used since Christmas, and Jane's silver gravy boat, polished to perfection. Ruth was going to be late, thank heavens. The less time she spent with Sylvia the better.

The kids ate greedily, pushed along by Grandma Sylvia's huge portions. When they had staggered upstairs, Paul sat over a second cup of coffee while Sylvia cleared the table.

"You've been a busy girl," Paul said amiably.

"This house," Sylvia said, rolling her eyes. "Your Ruth doesn't seem to care about cleaning. And Gemma . . . *well.*"

"We don't worry about that too much these days."

"Obviously. This place will be shipshape when you get back. Miss Gemma is going to learn what a scrub brush is for, believe me."

"Take it easy on Gemma, will you? She's doing fine."

"The carpet in Bobby's room is filthy," Sylvia declared. "I'm going to have a man in to deep-clean it, if you don't mind. And if you do mind I'll pay for it myself. Listen—you raise a kid in filth and that's all he's used to. My Jane knew that."

Paul heard footsteps on the porch and the outer door opening. He met Ruth in the foyer while Sylvia cleared his coffee cup to the kitchen. "We're on vacation," Ruth said happily. "Look—no attaché case. George said forget about the office, and for once I will."

Paul took her in a hug before she could remove her coat. "The Dragon Lady is here," he whispered in her ear. "Beware."

Ruth looked puzzled by Paul's expression.

"Hates you from the last picture," he mumbled, then followed Ruth into the kitchen.

"Well, well," Sylvia was saying with her best smile. "So this is who my son-in-law married." She took Ruth's hand cordially and then, standing on tiptoe, pecked Ruth's cheek. "So tall," she went on, "and so beautiful. Why didn't you tell me she was gorgeous, Paulie? Like a picture."

Ruth declined Sylvia's offer of reheated pot roast and made herself only toast and tea. "Don't you worry about a thing now,"

Sylvia told Ruth. "Just enjoy yourself. My kids will be in good hands this week."

If Ruth caught the venom in Sylvia's words she showed no sign of it, but once upstairs and alone with Paul, she shook her head. "Why do I get the feeling Sylvia might sneak in here tonight and pour poison in my ear?" she asked.

"Because it's true."

"What a woman," Ruth said. "And that's Jane's mother? My name is going to be zilch around here when we get back, you know that, don't you?"

"Don't think about it. Tomorrow we'll be wiggling our toes in the warm Caribbean. Seven whole days of sun and sand, and thou beside me . . ."

"Coughing in the wilderness," Ruth finished it. "You're right, I won't think about Sylvia."

Nothing stays the same, Paul was thinking as they lay side by side on chaise longues in the shade of a tall palm. Ruth was dozing, her hands tucked up under her chin, her paperback book in the sand. Why hadn't he had the sense to choose another beach club instead of this one, where he had come with Jane? But when the travel agent began making excuses about short notice, how heavily booked most places were, and then had mentioned Coconut Bay as one of the places they *might* get into, he had agreed at once. Was it a kind of test for Ruth, for himself? How foolish. You can't go back, kimosabe.

The hotel showed its age. The furniture in their room needed refurbishing, rust spots appeared on the concrete buildings, and the whole place had taken on a look of faded elegance. How many years ago had he sat here with Jane? Too many years to think about. The kids were babies then; Sam and Sylvia, the loving grandparents who happily babysat when they got away. Nobody dead then, nobody scarred, the future bright as the sun above. Jane the organizer would have him up early, not to miss the cool hours before the sun got too hot, wearing one of the three bathing suits she always brought because she was in and out of the water so much, playing tennis, snorkeling, making sure they got their money's worth out of every moment. How different Ruth was.

She'd come here to sleep and rest and that's what she did.

Rereading *Pride and Prejudice,* which she said she did every year, sleeping late each morning and napping in the afternoon. And not much more. Ruth hadn't been in the warm turquoise water more than once or twice, even after her cold had gone. She still looked tired under her suntan, especially after her runs along the beach in the late afternoon. "Out of shape," she said ruefully each time she came back to their room. "A mile and I'm winded, Klein." And she was not eating well, either, worrying about the few pounds she'd put on. Where those mysterious pounds were he couldn't tell, she looked the same to him. She had only pineapple and black coffee for breakfast, a small salad at lunch. "It is written," she told him, "that what thou eatest shall cometh upon thy waistline and stay with thee always."

"You're no fatted calf, babe," he said. "You're perfect." It made her laugh.

Restless, he left the sleeping Ruth and walked along the edge of the broad-armed bay, sun-splashed silver spray at his feet. Nothing stays the same. The champagne he had surprised Ruth with the second day they were here. Why had he tried to recreate that perfect and tender moment he had once had with Jane? Stupid. It had been a joke to Ruth. "Champagne? Why, Mr. Klein, I do believe you have intentions of seducing me this fine afternoon; you know how champagne makes my head swim." Sexy and teasing, not tenderly loving. It was Ruth's way.

Why did he still think of Jane so much? Why hadn't Ruth swept her memory away like the tide at his feet?

"Hon, are you okay?" Ruth was beside him.

"I'm fine," he said.

"You look funny. Sad, sort of."

"It's a perfect day for bananafish," he said, smiling. "I'm fine. Maybe a nap up in the room before dinner. Not to worry."

They walked back toward their cottage, his arm about her waist.

His sleep was shallow and restless, filled with bits and pieces of dim memory. That small girl in the bikini whose smile could lift his heart. The day in the channel when he feared she was gone. Jane . . . her small belly swollen huge with Hilary inside. . . . He woke to find Ruth watching him: "Are you okay? You were mumbling in your sleep."

Sitting up, he lit a cigarette, then walked to the window to look out. An iron bar hung from his shoulders, weighing him down. He had to clear his tight throat before he could speak. "The world is so fine, Ruthie, it makes you think it will go on forever," he said. "And then you grow up and find out that it can go away, that everything has an end."

He knew Ruth was looking at him from the bed, but at this moment he did not want to see her.

"The possibility of loss," he said. "The first time I ever truly realized that Jane could die . . . that *I* could, that everything could end. . . . Like Wiley Coyote running off a cliff in a cartoon, running on in the air, still confident and without fear. And then he looks back and sees where he is, and falls. It's only when he *sees* it, when he knows where he is and that it's impossible, that he falls. The terrible moment when you understand the possibility. . . ." He took a long drag on his cigarette. "Am I making any sense?" he asked.

"You still miss her," Ruth said.

"God help me, Ruth, I do."

The slope of his shoulders, the pain on his face, stirred Ruth's heart. She came to where he stood in the window and put her arms about him.

"The most beautiful place on earth and I'm sad," he said.

"I love you," she said.

"Oh, I know that. And I know how lucky I am to have found you. Maybe too much luck for one lifetime."

"Shhh," she said in his ear. "You mustn't question luck or it goes away."

"I really thought she was gone," he said. "For a long time, from the time I met you . . . I thought you'd finished her." He shook his head slowly. "I'm sorry."

"We'll live through it," Ruth said. "If we love each other and just hang on."

"Sure we will," he said, turning to take her in his arms. "Sure we will."

They sat at a table under the stars while a small combo played island tunes. As if on cue, a crescent moon rose over the headland and made a silver pathway on the sea. It had been a quiet dinner, with Ruth making most of the conversation. Paul was withdrawn, keeping his secrets, drinking too much. She looked at his strong face; a light breeze ruffled his hair. She wished he could open up and share his sorrow, that she could do something to help him throw off the memories that haunted. Reaching across the table, she took his hand.

"A penny for them," she said.

Paul sipped his bourbon. "They're not worth that much."

"Would you like to dance?"

Paul looked at Ruth and remembered how small and fragile Jane was in his arms when they danced, how her head tucked so neatly under his chin, how strong and protective it always made him feel. He shook his head.

On the bandstand, the combo swung into yet another version of "Yellow Bird," steel drums taking the lead. From behind her, Ruth could hear the quiet swish of surf. "Babe," she said, "let me help you."

His eyes glinted sharply at her over the rim of his glass. "How?" he said. "Ruthie, I don't even know what's going on myself . . ."

"Drinking won't help."

"Couldn't hurt," he said. Ruth wasn't smiling. "That's a joke, the punch line to a joke."

"I don't know it," she said.

"Obviously," Paul said in a tone so derisive it made her shiver. "Cold?" he asked.

"No," Ruth said. "Someone just walked over my grave, I think."

"Or vice versa," Paul said.

"Don't," Ruth said, taking her hand from his, "don't wallow in it, Paul. Do something. Howl at the moon, throw your glass on the floor, hit me. But don't wallow in self-pity."

"One little wallow," he said, taking another drink, "couldn't hurt."

Ruth closed her eyes for a moment. When she opened them, he was grinning at her. "What happened to my white knight?" she said. "My demon lover who came courting and wouldn't let me go?"

"He got married," Paul said, "haven't you heard?"

"And that's the end of him? I don't think I like that story."

"There's courtship and there's marriage. Two different things. Take it from an old married man," Paul said. "The guy's got the big house, kids, backyard patio, the works." He tossed off the rest of his drink and raised his hand to signal the waiter who was watching them from the bar.

"Paul, please don't," she said.

"Got to do it," he answered, slurring the phrase. "The white knight needs another drink. How about his faithful Indian companion, huh? Does she?"

"No thanks."

"Right," Paul said. "Can't give firewater to the redskin, can we? Wrong thing to do." He gave the waiter a smile and picked up the fresh drink he had brought. *"Salut!"* he said, toasting Ruth.

"I think the white knight's a little drunk."

"More than a little," Paul said. "And the name's Klein, lady."

"How about bed, Klein?"

Paul giggled. "Sex is very important," he announced gravely, "especially for a man."

"For a woman, too," Ruth said.

"Yep," he agreed, nodding his head. "Lissen—gonna say something stupid now, but you listen, okay? I think sometimes— God, this is stupid . . . but a baby would be good now, I think, for you and me. . . . And don't look so sad, I know I can't be a father. But still . . . maybe not so stupid, huh?"

"Maybes don't help anyone."

"Right," Paul said, grinning. "Right as usual. That's my smart Ruthie, *Je ne regrette rien.* But that vasectomy . . . that made a vas difference. Which is a joke, only not too funny because you're not laughing. Okay, but sometimes I regret more than a little *rien."*

"Stop it, Paul."

"Ah . . . humor me, babe, come on. Wanna talk about a pregnant lady I knew named Janie . . . little thing, maybe a hundred pounds soaking wet . . . and she looked so damn beautiful with a big belly . . . like a flower in bloom. Round cheeks, face all pink, and big breasts for once . . . God, Ruthie, it was the sweetest time. We used to lie in bed and I'd listen to that big belly, feeling the kicks, saying, 'Hello in there, kid, it's your Daddy' . . . Jesus, the sweetest time." He looked at Ruth, grinning foolishly, a windblown wisp of hair down across his forehead.

The other diners had left the terrace, drifting beyond the bar to where the combo was setting up for dancing. A single waiter stood watching them, smoking a cigarette he kept cupped in his hand.

"The sweetest wife a man could have," Paul said. "Did every damn thing for me and did it right. Ran the house, raised the kids, cooked and cleaned and took care of business. The best, Ruthie. I never had a shirt without a button, never worried about paying bills, never worried, period. I could fly off and run around and I never had to think about a thing, because she was there."

"Do you want to hurt me?" Ruth said. "Is that what this is about?"

"Everybody hurts, Ruthie," he said. "Rule of life."

"I can't be like her, Paul. I told you that a long time ago."

"I know that," he said. "Hell, nobody can be like her. That's why I'm so fucked-up, don't you see?"

Ruth started to take her hand from his but he held it fast. "Baby," she said, "let me take you back and put you to sleep."

"Soon, soon," he said. He began twisting the gold band on her finger, humming to himself, staring at the bay and the moonlight shining upon it. "Most beautiful spot in the whole damn world."

"Yes."

"And only one more day here. A pity."

"I wish we could stay another week," Ruth said. "I think we have things to talk about."

"Why the hell not," Paul said. "I'll call Michael right now and tell'm to hold the fort. Whaddya say, kiddo?"

"I wish it were that easy."

"You just call old Georgie-porgie and tell him to fuck off. You're down here with the white knight and you ain't coming back."

"Nope. Can't do that, Klein."

"Well, shit. I thought you were a free and liberated lady. Why not?"

"You know why not."

"Q.E.D.," Paul said, "I rest my case. You won't stay here, won't stay home either. Aye-aye, sir," he said, raising hand to brow in a mock salute.

"You don't have to be drunk to say those things."

"Ah, you're no fun, letting a guy drink alone. Who needs you?"

"I think *you* do."

He grinned at her. "Working girl."

"That's right."

"Married to me and Georgie, too."

Ruth signaled the waiter, who approached the table with a check. "One more drink," Paul said, but Ruth ignored him. She signed the check, then rose. "Paul, let's go." He smiled at her through half-closed eyes. When he was halfway to his feet he lurched against her; she caught him under the arms and felt his weight. "Drunk as a skunk," he whispered in her ear.

"Do you need help, missy?" the waiter asked.

Leaning against Ruth, Paul began walking across the terrace. "No," she said, "I think I can handle him myself."

What followed was silence and embarrassment until they returned home; Ruth would have preferred revelation and honesty. Hungover, Paul spent most of their final full day in paradise sleeping in the shade. When Ruth attempted to talk about what he'd said the night before, Paul brushed it off. He was drunk, he said, he was being foolish and brooding, he was sorry. The chilling part was that he made no jokes. A dead-serious Paul who would not speak was a new companion.

Ruth read Jane Austen while Paul slept and Jane Klein watched from behind a palm tree. Her ghost had not been laid; how foolish she'd been to think that, Ruth realized. Glorious and perfect wife, Jane lived on in Paul's heart. They had traveled thousands of miles, crossed oceans and seas, only to find the shade here before them. The small type in the paperback swam before Ruth's eyes. She put her finger in the book and stared out to sea, thinking that she could be filled with a sense of dread here under the sun as well as in the large, cold house back in New York. It seemed the chill came from the inside, not out. "The sweetest wife a man could have," he'd said. "There's nothing better than perfect, is there?" No, nothing. Especially not a large blond ad woman who can't sew a button and doesn't know anything about mothering.

How I spent my winter vacation, Ruth thought, watching my marriage melting in the sun.

* * *

The children must have been standing watch inside the front door. When the airport taxi pulled up in front of the house, Bobby and Hilary came flying down the front steps and out into the freezing evening, coatless of course, jumping on Paul even before he had a chance to pay the taxi driver. "Easy," Paul said, loving it. "Down, you crazy kids."

Ruth stood on the sidewalk, waiting for a hello that did not come, then took the small suitcase and went up the front steps alone. Sylvia watched from inside the door, bundled into two sweaters, grinning at the scene still being played on the sidewalk. "Look at those two," she said. "They sure love their father."

"Yes," Ruth said, "and he loves them."

She avoided Sylvia all evening; thank God the woman was leaving the following morning. There was a price she'd have to pay for Jane's mother's spending a week with the kids. She could see the difference in their attitude in the way they looked at her, the way Bobby avoided her in the same way she steered clear of Sylvia. Hilary came in to say good night, a small victory, but turned her face away when Ruth tried to kiss her, mumbling that she had a cold.

At midnight Ruth was in the kitchen, calming herself with a cup of tea. She heard clumping footsteps coming down the stairs; no place to run or hide now. Dressed in a heavy robe and wearing socks, Sylvia came into the kitchen. "I wanted to say good-bye," she said. "I didn't know if I'd see you in the morning." She seated herself in Paul's place at the table.

"I hope you didn't mind staying here," Ruth said.

"Who, me? Listen, I loved it. And so did the kiddies. I made them all the things they've been missing. Noodle pudding, brisket, chicken and soup. All the oldies but goodies, the favorites my Janie made them. Where do you think those recipes came from? From me, that's where. Jane wasn't born a cook, you know." She drummed her fingers on the table. "And you," she said, "you're not from the cooks I hear."

"No."

"You could learn. It's not hard if you really want to. I'm sure you could learn to make things the way Janie did."

"Sylvia, the kids are not undernourished," Ruth said.

Sylvia's eyes blinked once, twice. "Oh, I don't mean that," she

285

said. She nodded, as if the subject was closed. "All the recipes are in Jane's blue notebook on the shelf. If you change your mind, that is. . . . And I'm leaving you a clean house. You should watch Gemma like a hawk. And tell her what to do. All the venetians are washed, the bookshelves have been sponged, and I made her take down all the books and dust them. It's a crying shame what this house looked like."

"Thank you," Ruth said, almost choking.

"You've got to keep on top of it," Sylvia said. "Jane always had a plan, you know. Windows washed on a schedule, the stove and the oven cleaned every other week, sponging the woodwork. You know what—the mattresses hadn't been turned in a year."

"I'll get to all that," Ruth said. Why was she so defensive? Why didn't she tell the old busybody to fuck off?

"I'm sure," Sylvia said; her face belied her words. "It's a big house, you've got to keep after it. And it's time to start redecorating, too. Jane was going to last fall. The living room first. The carpet is shot, you know, so she was going to have it taken up. The floor underneath is good, it just has to be scraped and finished, and then a nice area rug, maybe an Oriental. Now the club chairs—"

"Sylvia, I really don't want to hear what Jane would have done," Ruth interrupted.

"Why not?"

"Because I have my own ideas."

"What could it hurt to listen? The club chairs are still good, you only need to recover them."

"Sylvia," Ruth said, "I don't care."

A wispy smile played on the older woman's lips. "That I know. I know how much you care by the filthy house I found here. Big fancy lady in business, doesn't even know how to dust a table."

"I'm not going to turn this house into a shrine," Ruth said. "Sooner or later, I'll make it my house, not Jane's."

"Oh, will you?" Sylvia said mockingly. "So far you're not doing so good. You should hear what those kids say about you."

Ruth stood up, taking her tea to the sink and setting the mug down. "We don't have anything further to say to each other," she said.

"They're not forgetting my Janie so fast," Sylvia spat at her.

"Not with you around," Ruth said.

286

"Or you!" Sylvia said.

Ruth's anger rushed to her throat, choking her words. She wanted to fly at Jane's mother, wanted to tear at her silver-gray hair. Most of all, she didn't want Sylvia to see her so upset. She turned on her heel and fled, Sylvia's final words burning in her ears. "Six months! You'll be gone, lady. *I give you six months!*"

22

HER HEART WAS as cold as the February wind.

Day by day Ruth felt more alone and isolated in the big house. There were a few sharp, flaring arguments with Paul. Small storms that quickly came and went. Staying late at the office one night, she'd forgotten to call home. One Saturday she'd missed buying a couple of items in the supermarket that Paul had counted on for a Chinese dinner. Trivial things, certainly, but they brought sharp words that lingered on and festered in her mind.

She cursed Jane silently for spoiling Paul. It must have been easier when you came home early every day, when you didn't have to juggle a dozen demanding clients who wanted their work *now*.

Some evenings she'd come down from working in her guest-room office to find the three of them huddled together on the couch, watching TV. Her place was on the club chair, only five feet away, but the gap between them was much larger.

"A dozen for a dollar," Hilary remarked one evening at dinner when Paul was talking about buying a new stereo for her. It began an argument between Hilary and Paul while a bewildered Ruth sat by and wondered why Paul had taken offense at such a meaningless remark. Paul explained it to her later that evening, telling her the story about Herman and the socks with no toes. She still felt left out.

Midway through the month, Bobby woke up with a scratchy throat. When Ruth took his temperature, it was a touch over a hundred degrees, just enough to play safe and keep Bobby home from school for the day. She gave the boy an aspirin and told him to roll over and try to get back to sleep. Later, dressed and ready to leave for the office, she woke Paul and told him about Bobby. Half-asleep, he looked at her. "And you're going to the office?" he asked.

"Of course."

"I suppose you wouldn't dream of staying home, would you?" His nasty tone surprised her.

"Gemma will be here by ten o'clock," she said, sounding defensive in spite of her anger. "I told Hilary to come directly home from school. Bobby won't be alone."

"Go on, then," Paul said, rolling off the bed and heading for the bathroom. "Have a nice fucking day," he snapped as he closed the door.

Ruth went slowly downstairs, but instead of heading for the coat closet, she went to the kitchen and sat down at the table. What would Jane do in a situation like this? That was what Paul expected her to do. You've screwed-up again, girl, she thought. Every time you think you've got her measure, old Bigfoot Jane's shoes just get harder and harder to fill.

She'd stay home then.

Early-bird George was at his post when she telephoned. "Sure, sure," he told her. "We'll manage."

Paul was surprised to find her in the kitchen, even more surprised when she slid two fried eggs onto a plate and set it down before him with toast and coffee. "You're staying home?"

"Yes."

"Good. You're doing the right thing, babe."

Jane's thing, she thought, not mine.

She watched as Paul ate his breakfast and read the newspaper. How easy it would be to do this every morning if she quit working. After breakfast she'd clear the kitchen, straighten up the house, do the laundry. Plenty of time to experiment with cooking. She wasn't a complete dummy, sooner or later she could turn out a pot roast they'd all like.

And sooner or later she'd start climbing the walls. In six months she'd slash her wrists.

She sat in the kitchen even after Paul left for his office, until she heard a toilet flush upstairs and the sound of Bobby moving about in his bedroom. She made him a cup of sugary tea, toast with his favorite apple jelly, and put it on a tray. Bobby looked frightened. "I heard footsteps," he said. "I got scared."

"Only me, Bob-o. I can't leave a sick boy all alone. How are you feeling?"

"My throat hurts when I swallow."

Before he could say more she popped a thermometer in his mouth. The reading was down a degree. "I think the aspirin is working," she told the boy, who was picking at his toast. He managed to eat only half a slice, but drank the tea.

"I think I feel a little better," Bobby said.

"Good. Can I bring you anything?"

"Maybe some apple juice. I like to drink that when I'm sick."

"With an ice cube?"

The boy smiled at her. "Yes, please. And maybe the sports section of the paper."

"Coming right up, sir," she kidded him as she cleared the tray.

"Ruth," Bobby said, "you didn't have to stay home. I'm okay."

When she brought up the juice and the newspaper, Bobby busied himself reading. Ruth sat in the boy's desk chair, across the room. After he'd finished the paper and put it down, folding it neatly first, she asked: "What do we do now? Would you like to play a board game?"

The boy shook his head.

"Do you want to play cards?"

"No thanks."

There was a long silence between them. What happens now, she wondered, do we stare at each other all day? "What did your Mother do when you were sick, Bob-o?" Please, she silently pleaded, please don't say *I'm not your Mother*.

"She put me in her bed, so I could watch TV in her room."

290

"Then let's do that."

"You don't mind?" He seemed surprised.

"Of course not." The boy's smile came and went in an instant. She installed him in the big bed, propped pillows behind his back, then turned on the television set for him. "I like game shows," Bobby said. "They're so dumb."

Ruth sat in the club chair. The small boy looked lost in the big bed, a cork adrift in a sea of blankets and pillows, but he seemed content. They watched a television show in which people dressed up as vegetables were hoodwinked by a toothy emcee while the audience went wild. From downstairs there was the sound of the front door slamming shut. Still in her coat, Gemma appeared in the doorway. "Somebody's not feeling well," she said.

"I'm okay," Bobby said.

"If you're okay, how come you're home?" Gemma asked.

"He had a little fever," Ruth said.

"You can go now," Bobby said. "Gemma can take care of me. Really, Ruth, you don't have to stay home."

Ruth leaned over the boy and kissed his forehead, checking for fever. His expression was as cool as his brow. "Not warm," she told him.

"One aspirin every four hours," Bobby said, "and drink lots of juice. I've been sick before, Ruth."

"I'm going then." When Ruth looked back from the doorway, Bobby was smiling at Gemma in a way he'd never smiled at her. She fled to the office.

At midday, Paul was on the telephone. "Couldn't stay home one day, eh?" he teased her. "Too boring?"

"He's fine, and Gemma came along. It was senseless to stay."

"Right," Paul said. He didn't sound convinced.

"And Bobby himself wanted me to go. Honestly." Why did she feel she was being judged?

"See you at home," Paul said. "And call if you're going to be late," he added before hanging up.

Wrong again, Ruth thought bitterly: wrong if she stayed, wrong if she went. No way to win. Perhaps the three Flying Kleins would be better off without her. What had moving in and playing Mommy accomplished? How had she improved the quality of their lives? She remembered Paul boasting of how the three of them had supported each other in the bad times after Jane's death. Where was the support for her?

One day, later that month, George insisted on taking her out to lunch. "A real lunch, Ruthie, with drinks and everything. What the hell, we deserve it."

In the small French restaurant around the corner from the office, he took a sip of his drink, then said what he'd taken her away from the office to say. "You look like hell, Ruthie. What's eating you? Have I done something wrong?"

She began to laugh.

"The tan doesn't hide the dark rings under your eyes," George said, "and you've been losing weight. Are you worried about the business? Hell, we're doing fine. What is it, Ruth?"

"Not you, George," she reassured him. "I wish everyone was as straight as you are. It's home," she said, the word burning on her tongue.

"Is Paul beating you up?"

"Don't I wish," she said with a laugh. "I'd knock his block off, the big stiff. I'm fighting shadows, George. Dirty looks behind my back, a feeling I'm giving my best and it's not good enough. They're a closed corporation, the three of them, and I'm still the outsider in the house. And then, a minute later, I'm sure it's not true, that I'm being paranoid about everything."

"You're working well," George said. "Our stuff is good."

"If you knew how happy I am to get to the office. And how rotten it is to go home."

"And what are you going to do about it? Ruth, you can't keep eating yourself up like you've been doing. We're in an ulcer business anyway, you know that. The way you are, you're going to come apart at the seams."

"I know," she said. "Right now, George, I hate my life."

"So do something. Make a move. If it's so bad, yelling and screaming won't make it worse. Try it."

"I don't want to hurt them. They've gone through a lot."

"Is this my Ruthie talking?" Deadpan George Chan gave her one of his rare smiles. "Whatever happened to that tough lady I knew? The one who never backed down from a fight?"

"She's thinking she made a helluva mistake," Ruth said, "and she doesn't know how to get out of it."

Several miles downtown, Michael Bradie was holding forth to his partner at Sweets Restaurant. "So the women in this old-age home are very pissed off because the men pay them absolutely no attention. Every night after dinner, the men go off to play cards and that's it. So Becky tells Sadie, 'Tonight we're going to get a little attention around here. What we're going to do, Sadie, is we're going to take all our clothes off and streak through the card room.' Naturally, it takes some doing, there's a hullabaloo and so on, but Becky convinces Sadie, and the two of them get undressed after dinner sure enough and streak right through the card room. Jake and Sam, playing pinochle, don't turn a hair. But after a minute, Jake says to Sam, 'Sam, did you see what I think I saw?' And Sam nods and says, 'Needs pressing!' "

Michael laughed heartily, as he always did at his own jokes, but this time much more than Paul. "No like?" He shrugged. "*I* thought it was funny."

"Is that what we think of women?" Paul said. "Is it only their bodies that make us interested? That and what they can do for us?"

Michael's eyebrows danced. "Philosophy yet, and before lunch. What's happening, partner? You don't sound like you."

Paul took a sip of his Jack Daniels. "I guess I'm just not in a funny mood."

"We haven't seen much of you and Ruth lately. Is everything all right?"

Be honest, Paul thought, but something held him back. What could he tell Michael? That there was tension at home, a sense of things not fitting together? That he never knew what Ruth would do or say? They were four bodies in motion within an enclosed universe, with collisions, near misses, no fixed orbits. Somehow they couldn't make it run smooth. "Everything's peachy-keen," he said. "Don't I wish."

Michael waited, and when Paul did not go on, prompted him. "You don't have to talk about it."

"I don't really want to, Michael. How's Kathleen?"

Michael grinned his leprechaun smile. "Sassy as ever, giving me and the girls a hard time. One more year and she'll graduate.

The oldest scrub nurse in the O.R., that's her ambition. I tell you, Paul, she's going to be a pistol.''

"She's always been that.''

"She's been watching *General Hospital* too much, that's what it is.''

"I'll bet she hates it when you tell her that.''

"Hell, yes. Well, you know Kathleen. Thinks nothing of pulling what little hair I've got left. That's how I lost it all, you know, from her pulling it out. That and worrying she was *going* to pull it out.''

"Kidding aside,'' Paul said, "you and Kathleen have always had fights, haven't you?''

"The day isn't complete without a good argument. But then the making up is so sweet, you see.'' Michael drained his glass and, catching Jesse's eye, signaled for another round.

"Jane and I never fought, you know that. I guess I got used to it. But with Ruth . . .'' He made a face.

"Scrapping, huh?'' Michael said. "And you're worried about it.''

"Among other things.''

"And do you always make it up, Paul?''

"Not always. And she has run-ins with the kids. And it's just not too terrific at home right now, Mike.''

Michael's fingertips drummed on the white tablecloth. "She's a heckuva gal, your Ruth. Strong lady.''

"Maybe too much,'' Paul said.

"And after Jane,'' Michael said, and shrugged. "Fighting isn't always bad, Paul,'' he went on. "It's the making up you have to do. Kathleen and me, we're almost playing *roles* now, if you take my meaning. I make a male chauvinist remark, she picks it up, and we slip right into an argument. Hell''—he grinned—"I think we *enjoy* it most of the time.''

"I'm not enjoying it, and neither is Ruth.''

"You haven't practiced enough,'' Michael said dryly. "What are you fighting *about*, if I may ask?''

"The usual,'' Paul sighed. "The kids, her work, not spending time together, her feeling that she doesn't fit in, that we're all against her, that Bobby hates her, that she doesn't do things right—I mean—the way we're used to . . .''

Michael looked at his partner. "Sure you haven't left anything out?"

"It does sound like a lot, doesn't it?" Paul said. "Here's the latest trivial example. Ruth left a dress to be cleaned. Since I'm the one with the car, I've always taken things to the dry cleaners. Anyway, she left it on the footstool near our bed, the place where Jane always left her dresses for Gemma to wash and iron."

"Don't tell me," Michael said. "Gemma washed the dress."

"Ruined it."

"Good old dopey Gemma."

"I can't lay this off on Gemma, Michael, she does her best. Ruth told me about the dress for the cleaners but I forgot. My fault. But you see, Jane left her dry-cleaning stuff in the corner near my dresser, where I couldn't miss it. And when I told that to Ruth, she blew up."

"And when she gets weary," Michael sang, "buy her another shabby dress."

"Michael," Paul said, "I'm still not laughing."

It was all over in a few seconds, but its effect went on and on. Ruth was scribbling some copy in the upstairs guest room, her door closed, wondering what the next line should say. Distracted, her mind still on her work, she decided to wash her ink-stained hands. Paul was in the master bathroom, the door closed. Without thinking about it, Ruth headed for the kids' bathroom in the hallway and opened the door without seeing that the light was on inside. Bobby, stark naked and just out of the shower, stared at her. "Hey!" the boy cried out, turning swiftly around to put his back to her.

"I'm sorry," Ruth mumbled, embarrassed for herself and the boy.

"Get out!" Bobby shrieked.

Ruth retreated, closing the bathroom door. Down the hall, Hilary's head appeared in the doorway of her room. "What's happening?" she asked.

"She just walked right in!" Bobby yelled from inside the bathroom before Ruth could answer. Hilary's head disappeared back inside her room. Her door clicked shut. "Don't you knock?" Bobby demanded, opening the bathroom door to face Ruth. Still wet from the shower, he was wrapped in a bath towel, his face clear and shiny. His thin bony shoulders looked so beautiful that Ruth wanted to throw her arms about him. "There's still privacy around here," he said, and slammed the door shut in her face.

"What's happening?" came Paul's muffled voice from within the master bath.

"I'm sorry," Ruth said to Bobby through the closed door.

"Just get out of here!" Bobby shouted back.

Something inside Ruth gave way at that moment. The weight she'd been lugging around in her chest seemed to pull her down. "I'll go downstairs," she said, her voice so low only she could hear it. As she washed her hands in the downstairs bathroom, she thought, Why am I so upset over something so silly? Because he can scream at you and you can't reciprocate. Because you walk on eggs in this house, afraid to make a mistake. Because you can never win.

She looked in the mirror, seeing the anger etched into her face. This has to be the end, she realized. When you can't yell at a kid or be yourself, you are finished.

She could not stand another moment in this house. She needed air, light, space. On impulse, she took her furry jacket and warm gloves from the closet across the foyer. And Hilary's black woolen watch-cap, dirty though it was. She stood for a moment at the base of the stairs and called up the stairwell. "I'm going out . . . for a walk." There was no answer.

She plunged out the door, slamming it shut behind her, and walked swiftly to the corner, feeling she had to get away—they would come after her if she didn't move quickly, they would somehow drag her back against her will. Only after walking several blocks did she realize how cold it was; tiny flakes of snow began to fall in the night. She pulled Hilary's cap lower about her ears and walked on, the inner voices in her head blotting everything else out.

Finished and a failure. Failure. They didn't care about her, not a damn. They looked at her and saw Jane, and because she was not Jane they hated her for it.

Clustered about the father. Hanging on for dear life. Not letting go. The circle closed against her from the start.

Give it up. They didn't need her, not really. Bobby had even said so to her face. Let them go back to the way they were. Papa Bear and the two baby bears. And the hell with Goldilocks.

So many mistakes. It could have worked. Should have worked. If they'd just given her a chance, bent a little.

You almost got through to Hilary. So close, but no cigar. Because Hilary wanted out, to get away and not be involved. And she stood by and watched me fail.

You'll never get to mother Bobby. Never squeeze him, kiss that sweet face. Even now, even after taking so much crap and spite from him, that was still what she wanted to do. That's what cut the deepest.

She began to cry then, tears streaming down her cheeks as she walked blindly on, the wetness blending with the snowflakes that melted on her face. Walking on, not knowing or caring where, except away. The snow was beginning to stick to the grass and the tops of cars. She came to a shopping street and crossed it, walking down a street of row houses.

Damn that little boy. She had been putty in his hands ever since the day she met him. *"Uh, Ruth, we kind of chunk tomatoes, not slice them."* Her heart had melted when he said that, when he showed her things about the kitchen and the house, when he was eager as a puppy to be near her. What happened? What the hell had happened between them? The boy was so sweet, so lovable, and in so much pain. The tender way he took care of Marmaduke. No boy who loves a cat can be all bad.

"You're not my mother." Never was. One mama to a customer, kid. Not me. But we could have been pals, could have come close if you'd only given me half a chance. Too late now.

Paul hadn't helped. Not one bit. He was all over them, on top of both kids, guarding them with his life. From day one the kids were *his.* Stay away, Ruthie, I'll do it. I'm in your pocket, Dad, Hilary had said. So how could the kids turn to her, how trust her? Papa Bear was doing everything. What she said didn't count for much. Didn't count at all, be truthful. He was the Supreme Court, the Pres, the whole shebang. And I was only the new wife. Period. And a klutz. Can't cook. Doesn't know how *we* do things.

Continuity. Doctor what's-his-face and his famous phrase. Going crazy here, but lots of continuity. Continue with what? The ghostest with the mostest, old baby Jane. Now you're talking, the gal who never put a foot wrong, would not say shit if she had a mouthful. She never sat down on a toilet, not Jane. Her crap did not stink. Made love, she did, never fucked. The ghost who still lived in the house had done her in finally. Jane's house, now and forever, the house and Jane looking on from on high, criticizing, judging. Never had a chance against the father, the son, the daughter, and the holy ghost.

Go now. Pull a disappearing act, make a getaway. But go where, how? What was that travel promotion George suggested for the jeans people? *Pack a bag and go.* Exactly. Throw some clothes in a bag and get out. Lots of hotels near the office. Get the rest of your things later. You can look for an apartment, plenty of time, but get away before you go nuts.

Alone again. Yes, that too. You've done it before and lived through it. Right now alone sounds good. Peace and privacy, plenty of time to work. Are you going to be an old lady who lives alone? Is that why you held on to Paul? No . . . you loved the guy, fell head over heels and bought the whole deal. Do you still love him? Do you?

She stopped walking then, crossed her arms against a lamp post, and cried bitter tears. The snow began to fall a little more heavily, soft fat flakes swirling down.

Her feet were freezing in the tennis sneakers she was wearing. She'd run out of the house so fast. The street did not look familiar. She began walking again, not a soul on the streets in the snow. There was a signpost on the corner. Glenwood Road and Nostrand Avenue. How could she get back to the house? Where was she? Out in the snow and lost. She walked down the street toward an intersection of stores. Light from their windows spilled out and illuminated the falling snow. She walked into a candy store. Call a cab. Get away. When she reached into her pockets she found they were empty. No money, no wallet.

Behind the counter, an old man sat reading the *Daily News.*

"Mister?"

The old man looked up.

"I've done a foolish thing," she said, "gone out walking and left all my money at home." She tried a smile that was hard coming.

"In this weather you were walking?" He looked at her as if she were a maniac.

"I need a dime to call my husband. I'm sure he'll come and pick me up and I'll return—"

The cash register rang open. The man put a dime on the glass counter.

"Thank you . . . I . . ."

"Over there," the man said with a tilt of his head. He went back to his newspaper.

She dialed home and heard Paul pick up on the first half-ring. "Ruth?"

"Yes."

"Where are you? Where did you go?" His voice roared in her ear.

She told him where she was. "Please . . . don't be angry."

"Do you know how worried I am? Just walking out, not telling anyone."

"I'm sorry," she said, cowed by his anger. "I took a walk . . . I needed to get out."

"I'll be there in five minutes," Paul said and hung up.

She put the phone down, feeling drained, and rested her head against the metal telephone box. She banged her head . . . once, twice . . . against the metal.

"Lady? Are you all right?"

She turned to face the old man, who stared at her from above his newspaper. "He's coming for me . . . my husband."

The old man's eyes narrowed. "Is he . . . ah . . . he's not going to hurt you, is he?"

"What?" She wasn't sure she'd heard right.

"Your husband, is he mad at you? You had a fight?"

A nervous giggle escaped her lips. "No. We didn't have a fight. You'll get your dime back."

"Who's worried about the dime? I just don't want, you know, he should walk in here and start a fight."

"He's not a violent man."

"Famous last words," the old man said. He made a clucking sound. "People today, you never know. You say *boo* and they can stick a knife in you. You watch television news?"

"Yes."

"Then you know. I stay open till ten, for the evening papers, and I never know who's going to walk in here." He clucked again, looking at her. "If you don't mind my saying, you don't look too good. You want a glass of water?"

"No, I'm all right," she said, adding a thank you.

"You been married long?"

"A few months."

"Is that all? I would of thought longer. And you ran out? In the snow and everything?"

Ruth said nothing.

"It's hard in the beginning, but you get used to it. Married thirty-two and a half years, I know what I'm saying. The trouble today is everybody wants to have the last word. You know what the last word is? A curse, usually."

"Ruth?" Paul came walking through the door, wearing a fur-collared storm coat, pajama legs showing underneath. "What happened? How'd you get all the way down here?"

"Will you give this nice man a dime, please?" she said.

Paul looked at her, then did as she said. He took her arm. "You've been crying." He led her to the door and outside, opening the door of the Buick for her and helping her in. The sidewalk was covered with a thin white coating and black tracks of automobiles ran down the street. Paul got in his side of the car and pulled away from the curb. "We didn't know where you were," he said. "We looked everywhere, even the basement. You picked a helluva time to go for a walk."

Say it, she told herself; but the words wouldn't come. She stared out the windshield straight ahead. Snowflakes danced in the headlights.

"What happened?" He glanced at her, driving slowly on the slippery pavement. "You had a fight with Bobby, right? I could only hear a few words. Is he giving you a hard time again? I'll kill that kid."

"It's not Bobby, it's me. It's just getting worse."

He came up slowly on a red light, braking gently. "You're upset, babe. Take it easy. We'll get home, have a cup of tea . . ."

"You don't need me," she said. "That's the hell of it."

"What are you saying? Of course we need you. *I* need you, we

300

all need you. What happened tonight? Between you and Bobby? Is that what made you pull this crazy stunt?''

"I'm leaving," she said flatly.

"Don't be silly," he said.

"I'll sleep in the guest room tonight. Tomorrow, I'll pack a bag and go to a hotel.''

"Come on, babe, simmer down. It'll all seem so trivial in the morning.''

"I wish to hell you hadn't made me sell so much of my furniture," she said.

"Hey, I love you," he said, putting a hand on her arm. "You're talking crazy, Ruth.''

"Thinking I could live in *her* house, *that* was crazy.''

He turned the Buick down their street, pulling up in the driveway. The snow was falling more gently, but the wind had kicked up, swirling the thin covering on the ground. Paul killed the engine, extinguished the headlights, but made no move to get out of the car. "You can't leave," he said. "I won't let you leave. Whatever's bothering you, we'll solve it, whatever's hurting you, we'll fix it. I adore you," he said, in a husky voice. "You know that. You're my wife.''

She opened the car door and got out, not wanting to talk anymore, not to hurt him further. She ran across the white-dappled grass, snow crunching under her sneakers, and up the front steps. Reaching into the pocket of her jeans, she felt for her keys to open the door and slip inside without him, and only then remembered she had left them behind, too, in her quick escape from the house. She waited for Paul, not looking at him.

He opened the door silently, stepping aside to let her pass, then following her to the closet to hang up his coat after she'd doffed hers. "We have to talk," he said, putting a hand on her arm and guiding her toward the kitchen. She felt weak and used up, without strength to protest. Sinking into the chair at the head of the table, his chair, she put her head in her hands. She heard Paul open a cabinet to take out a pot, the sound of water running in the sink.

He put the teakettle on the stove and lit the burner. Words came to him but he did not trust his voice. He opened the cabinet above the stove and took down the package of tea bags. The sight of her golden hair under the hanging light filled his heart to breaking.

Sighing, she looked out into the garden. A few tiny flakes filtered down, the floodlights bright against the white garage doors; a dead brown leaf looped toward the ground. "I was never happy here," she said.

"It will get better," Paul said. "Just hang on."

"No," she said with a shake of her head, "I wasn't meant to live in this house. It's not my house."

They both heard the sound of footsteps coming down the stairs. Hilary came into the kitchen, Bobby behind her. "Ruth!" Hilary said. "Where were you? We were so worried."

"She took a walk," Paul said before Ruth could speak. "Everything's all right."

"It was snowing," Bobby said.

"Yes," Ruth said, "but it's stopped now." She glanced at the children, standing together across the kitchen. The look on their faces told her they knew something was wrong, something adult perhaps, between herself and Paul. "I have something to tell you," she said.

"Ruth, *no!*" Paul said sharply. He turned to the children. "Go to bed. School tomorrow." He took a step as if to shoo them away.

"I'm leaving you," Ruth said. "Tomorrow morning. I'm going away."

"No!" Hilary cried out at once. "Ruth, don't go away." Beside her, Bobby looked nervously at his father and then Ruth.

"It hasn't been decided," Paul said. "We're going to talk about it. Now go to bed."

"Tell them the truth," Ruth said, getting up from her chair. "It *has* been decided. I'm saying good-bye." Bobby's wide-eyed stare filled her with a bitter anger. "Yes, you'll have it just the way you want it. Just you and Hilary and your dad. No outsiders. The three of you and Mom, nice and cozy, like before *I* came along!"

"Stop it!" Paul shouted.

"Don't you understand?" Ruth shouted back. "This house is *haunted!* Jane's still here!" Whirling, she pulled the blue notebook off the shelf and tossed it wildly across the room. "There's Jane, right there in that book!" she shouted. "And here!" She kicked out with her foot, knocking the wok from its shelf so it skittered noisily onto the floor. "Jane's fucking baskets!" She reached up and knocked half a dozen to the floor. "Her *plants!*" At the

302

windowsill Ruth swept her arm across, backhanding the jade and the sansevieria so they tumbled down and smashed on the floor. *"You never needed me, never!* Because you've still got her, Lady Jane the First! You just put your wagons in a circle and kept me out. Well, okay, you win! Write it on her goddamn chalk board: Ruth zero, Jane ten. I can't compete with a ghost." Her eyes took in the line of glass jars across the countertop. "I *hate* those jars!" she shouted, and started around the stove to get at them, but Paul stepped forward and caught her, pinning her arms. "Let me go!"

"Calm down," he said. "Ruth!"

"I can't calm down!" she screamed, struggling to escape his grasp. "I'm not Miss Sweetness like she is! I get mad, I curse, I spit and scream! Let me go, Klein, leggo!" Twisting in her fury, she shook herself free and ran past the children, out of the kitchen, through the dark dining room. They heard the sound of her running footsteps on the stairs. In the silent kitchen, the slam of the guest room door resounded.

Paul covered his face with his hands. In a moment, both children were hugging him.

She lay on the narrow bed in the dark, one arm across her eyes, no more tears left to shed. From below, she heard the scrape of chairs in the kitchen as they cleaned up. Bobby came upstairs first, pausing outside the closed door but not coming in. She heard him gargling in the bathroom, the sound of his door closing. Even now, she longed to go and tuck him in, but she could not move. She heard Hilary's tread on the stairs, her light knock on the door. "Don't come in," Ruth called. At this moment, she could not bear to see them again. She was ashamed of what she'd done, sorry that they had to see her at her worst. She began thinking of which suitcase she would pack, which clothing to take in the morning.

Outside she heard a car slowing for a light on the corner.

The double lock on the front door was closed with a snap. Paul came upstairs and into the room, the hall light dim behind him. "I love you, Ruth," he said.

"I know."

He closed the door behind him, standing near the bed in the dark. "I'll take tomorrow off, babe. We'll keep the kids home and spend the whole day just talking, the four of us."

303

"No."

"Honey, please . . . we have to."

"It's too late. I can't stay here."

"We'll take a week off and go away, babe. Just you and me."

"Again?"

In the dark, she heard him sigh.

"I think I'll always love you," she said, "and I'll love them, too. Even though they wouldn't let me."

"Stay," he said. "I'll make it better for you. I'll help more. I'll get up in the morning for Bobby, I'll cook more . . ."

"And the more you do, the more they'll resent me."

She felt his hand on her arm. "What happened to us?"

"Jane," she said. "This house." She took his hand and kissed it then, not seeing his face but knowing he was smiling at the touch of her lips. "No luck," she said. "Not one goddamn piece of luck."

"You're sleeping here?" he asked. "Isn't that foolish? Come, babe."

Her low laugh was bitter. "Too late for that, too. Just go, Paul, please go."

She heard his hand turning the knob of the door. "You're not leaving yet," he said, "not without a fight from me. I'll see you in the morning. We'll talk."

"Yes," Ruth said, "we'll talk."

Night sounds.

Ruth was not spared any of them on her last night in this house. A surge of heated air moaned through the register high in the wall above her head. Ducts pinged and cracked, a floorboard creaked. From outside came the crunch of automobile tires on the frozen street. She heard the mantle clock downstairs strike two, then three. A light wind sighed through the naked branches of the Norway maple on the front lawn.

Alone in the narrow bed, she thought of her girlhood room, the half a lifetime she'd spent in a bed just like this one. Diane had the bigger room, but Ruth's had been a corner room with one more window. She remembered how the light would come into the room, the strong shadows cast on the wall, the way the swaying curtains sometimes looked ghostly before she fell asleep. How often as a young girl she had wondered with whom she'd spend her life. Yes, she would marry, she always knew that; she wanted to marry. But always there was that mystery: What would he look like, would he be handsome, rich? Would he wear a moustache like her father? Now she knew the answer to those questions, but in the way of things, she would not be spending her life with that man after all.

The sun lit the sky but not the earth. Light footsteps crunched along the snow-covered pavement. She wondered if Paul had remembered to set the clock-radio before going to sleep. Six-fifteen, her wristwatch told her. She got up and walked quietly down the hall. Paul was curled up under the quilt, lying on his side in the big bed. She looked down at his sleeping face, seeing the thick brush of eyebrow, the outline of his strong nose, the forward thrust of his rounded jaw. Sleep, my darling, she thought.

In the bathroom, she splashed water in her face, brushed her teeth, moving quietly so as not to wake Paul. She would see Bobby off to school, then Hilary, saying a proper good-bye to each of them. Let them remember her badly, she would think of them only with fondness.

Pinned beneath his tight quilt, Bobby's cupid face melted her heart. She opened his dresser, took out a shirt and underwear, the thick-soled white socks he preferred to all others. From a lower drawer she selected a pair of heavy corduroy jeans. It looked like a cold day. And the crew-neck Shetland sweater she had bought him for Christmas.

She nudged him awake and when he did not stir, leaned down to kiss his brow. That's one you won't wipe off, she thought, then took it back when he did just that. "Good morning," she said. "Rise and shine."

He came awake and looked at her, surprise showing in his eyes.

"Yes, me again," she said, smiling. "I'll see you downstairs."

His juice and vitamin pill were on the table before he came into the kitchen, along with the sports section of the newspaper and his glass of milk, with an ice cube. She had already prepared his lunch and set the brown paper bag on the counter next to the corner where he kept his pocket things.

He went to his chair and sat down, gulped his orange juice and his pill. "Are you really going?"

"Yes." She nodded. She waited for him to say more, but he

looked down at the newspaper. She brought him a bowl of Cheerios. He did not look up at her as she set it before him. "I'll miss you," she said.

"And I'll miss you," the boy said, not looking at her.

"Well," she said, "that's *something.*" A small piece of terracotta from the broken plant pot lay under the overhang of the cabinet. She told him not to crush it when he got up.

"I don't hate you," Bobby said.

"Perhaps."

"I never said you weren't nice."

"True." She waited, but he seemed to have no more to add. "I only wish, Bob-o, that you'd loved me half as well as my cat." She saw the boy's lips quiver. "Speaking of Marmaduke," she said, "you haven't put his food out in the bowl this morning. I'll do it." She went to the pantry door, then turned to look across the room at the boy. "Where *is* Marmaduke this morning?" She suddenly realized that the cat had not been asleep on the boy's bed, the first face to greet her each morning. "Bobby? He wasn't in your room?"

"Ruth," Bobby said, "don't be mad." His face had gone pale. "I didn't want you to take him."

She looked at the boy dumbly.

"When you left," he added.

A feeling of dread crept across her chest. "You thought that I . . . ? Oh, God!"

"He's your cat," the boy said.

"Oh, Bobby, how awful do you think I am?" she said. "I never would take that cat away from you, *never!* How could you think that? He's your cat now, not mine."

Bobby sobbed once, wiping at his eyes. "I'm sorry."

She came to the table and leaned against it, feeling as if she would collapse. "Where is he? What did you do?"

The boy could not speak.

"Bobby, tell me. I won't be angry. Where's Marmaduke?"

"I didn't want you—to take him away. Oh, Ruth, I'm sorry. I let him out. To hide . . . and then I'd get him later. After you . . ."

"Outside?" Her hands were trembling.

"On the porch . . . I thought . . ."

But Ruth was already running toward the front door. Marmaduke would be lost out there, in the cold, in the snow. He was only

306

a dumb inside-cat. When she opened the front door Bobby was beside her. They searched the front porch together, walking around the corner of the house to where the porch continued along the side. "Dukie!" Bobby called. There was no answer.

"Marmaduke!" Ruth shouted as they went down the steps and onto the lawn. "He's run away," she said. "He must have been so frightened."

"Dukie!" The boy looked behind the rhododendrons and the yew hedge. "Dukie boy!"

From up the street, three houses away, they heard a cold car engine starting. The driver raced it to keep it going. Ruth began to walk that way, as if drawn by the sound. Her open-toed house slipper broke through a thin crust of ice and into freezing water, but she did not notice. Bobby ran frantically across lawns, searching behind shrubs and bushes, calling, *"Dukie!"*

The car up the street pulled away from the curb. Ruth and the boy saw it at the same instant, lying broken in the street in the place where the car had been. Bobby's cry of pain was terrible to hear.

The boy ran across the street to the dead cat, falling to his knees in the dark circle of frozen blood. "Oh, Dukie," he sobbed. Ruth knelt beside him, looking against her will at the broken body, the mangled fur and brain and bone. She pulled Bobby to her, not wanting him to see any more, not wanting any more death for this little boy she loved so much. But Bobby looked and saw death plain, and knowing that, knew that the other death was real as well. He turned and leaned against Ruth; she felt him sobbing against her breast, sobbing as she sobbed too, for pain and loss and love that ends too soon, and in that moment she felt the boy's thin arms encircle her and hug tight, tight, and his broken voice crying, "Ruthie, don't go away. Please. I love you, Ruthie . . ."

23

He checked the attic first, working the house top to bottom. The June sun heated the small rooms to roasting, but Paul could not open the windows because there were no screens. He found one old plastic garment-bag hanging empty in a closet, a large tear along the side. Let the new people deal with that, he thought. They had thrown away everything else up here. In the large front room with a storage cupboard he found a batch of old wire hangers and a broken broom. He let them stay as well. Here, in this musty cupboard, he had found the boxes of Bobby's old toys, neatly packed cardboard cartons with Jane's handwriting on the top in Magic Marker.

Pack rat.

The Salvation Army had spent a whole day at the house, loading a truck almost as large as a moving van. Perhaps some other children would play with the boy's old toys; other families would use the furniture, oddments, and knickknacks of thirteen years. Let them. And let the past stay here, where it belonged.

He closed the doors to the small rooms behind him as he went, going down the steps now to the second-floor landing. Hilary's

packing had been a big problem until they decided to split her pho-
nograph record collection in two. Half went into plastic milk boxes
the girl had somehow cadged from the supermarket. These she
would take with her to Yale, come September. The rest was combined with the family's own records and was already in the new
apartment.

Only hangers remained in her closet, a long length of stereo wire
threaded through the window seat to serve the new people. The
room seemed so large now, empty of furniture, the blue carpet a
sea stretching away to the horizon. He remembered now, standing
in the empty house, the day they had moved in: Hilary a girl of
five, running from wall to wall up here and squealing with delight
at the space to play. She'd wanted all her furniture placed in one
corner of the room, so she could turn cartwheels in the rest of it.

Bobby's room was clean, except for the Rorschach stain of grape
juice on the carpet where his desk had been. Where his crib had
been in the beginning. Steady, kimosabe, he told himself: Do not
go all mushy and sentimental. It's only a room in a house.

He found a quarter on the floor of his closet and stooped to pick
it up. His closet in the co-op in Manhattan was not quite so large.
And there was no top-floor storage closet to alternate winter and
summer clothing. But he would manage. The terrace looked down
on the East River, and already Bobby was fascinated by the boats
and barges and the traffic far below on the drive. He had promised
the boy a telescope. But more important, Bobby would be able to
walk to school from there, leave later and come home earlier, and
perhaps he would find some school friends who lived nearby.

Good-bye, old bedroom. He closed the door and went downstairs. So long, stained-glass windows and fireplace and high-
ceilinged elegance. There was still that crack in the plaster of the
ceiling he'd been meaning to fix but never got around to. Well, the
new people could take care of that.

The kitchen. He stood in the empty room for several moments,
the heart of the house, Jane's headquarters in Jane's house. He'd
spent a lifetime in this room with her. A good lifetime when they
were both young and confident and knew the world was going their
way. Paul walked to the empty space where the kitchen table had
stood and looked out into the garden. He felt a chill on the back of
his neck, a prickling of the hair. Jane was still here, in everything

he saw and touched and remembered. Good-bye, Jane, he almost said aloud, good-bye.

Ruth had been right, why hadn't he seen it before it was almost too late? They needed a place to start fresh, a new home for a new family, a place where they would be free from ghosts and painful memories.

"Good-bye, Jane," he did say aloud now, tears in back of his eyes. Here I leave you, in this place I'll never forget. The three of us go on from here, to make new memories in which you will not share. But what we carry with us will be enough, for you gave each of us so much.

He walked through the foyer for the last time, checking the front closets again, although he knew they were empty. He closed the heavy iron-and-glass front door, stepping out onto the porch. The car was in the driveway; they were waiting for him.

He got in beside Hilary, winked at her, and started the engine.

"Everything copacetic?" Hilary asked.

"Finito," he said.

"When are the new people coming?" Bobby asked from the back seat.

"In two weeks, they said," he answered. "It's smart that way. They'll paint and fix up before they move in." He backed the Buick out into the street, then rolled forward to the traffic light on the corner. He looked in the rearview mirror and smiled at Ruth, who smiled back. Bobby was beside her, tucked under the curve of Ruth's arm, holding the marmalade kitten the boy had decided to call Ginger.

"Where are we going for lunch?" Hilary asked.

"Burger King?" Paul said, waiting for the reaction of the boy in the back.

"McDonald's!" Bobby said. "We always go to McDonald's. And could I not share my fries with Hilary this time?"

"This family!" Ruth exclaimed. "Do you *always* think of food?"

"Always," Paul said. When the light changed, he turned the corner, driving toward the expressway that led to Manhattan. Behind him as he looked in the mirror, he could see the tower that rose above the roofline of the house, until, two streets away, it was blocked from view.

But no one else in the car had even looked back.

310

Home delivery from Pocket Books

Here's your opportunity to have fabulous bestsellers delivered right to you. Our free catalog is filled to the brim with the newest titles plus the finest in mysteries, science fiction, westerns, cookbooks, romances, biographies, health, psychology, humor—every subject under the sun. Order this today and a world of pleasure will arrive at your door.

POCKET BOOKS, Department ORD
1230 Avenue of the Americas, New York, N.Y. 10020

Please send me a free Pocket Books catalog for home delivery

NAME _____

ADDRESS _____

CITY _____ STATE/ZIP _____

If you have friends who would like to order books at home, we'll send them a catalog too—

NAME _____

ADDRESS _____

CITY _____ STATE/ZIP _____

NAME _____

ADDRESS _____

CITY _____ STATE/ZIP _____

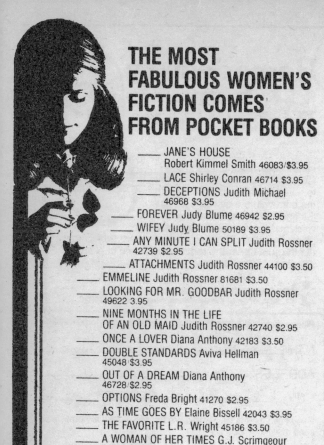
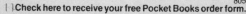

P9-APX-250

Marianela

Benito Pérez Galdós:
Marianela

El Libro de Bolsillo
Alianza Editorial
Madrid

Primera edición en «El Libro de Bolsillo»: 1983
Decimotercera reimpresión en «El Libro de Bolsillo»: 1997

© Herederos de Benito Pérez Galdós
© Alianza Editorial, S. A., Madrid, 1983, 1984, 1985, 1987, 1988, 1989,
  1990, 1991, 1992, 1993, 1994, 1995, 1996, 1997
  Calle Juan Ignacio Luca de Tena, 15; 28027 Madrid; teléf. 393 88 88
  ISBN: 84-206-9985-3
  Depósito legal: M. 15.129-1997
  Impreso en Fernández Ciudad, S. L.
  Catalina Suárez, 19. 28007 Madrid
  Printed in Spain

Se puso el sol. Tras el breve crepúsculo vino tranquila y oscura la noche, en cuyo negro seno murieron poco a poco los últimos rumores de la tierra soñolienta, y el viajero siguió adelante en su camino, apresurando su paso a medida que avanzaba el de la noche. Iba por angosta vereda, de esas que sobre el césped traza el constante pisar de hombres y brutos, y subía sin cansancio por un cerro, en cuyas vertientes se alzaban pintorescos grupos de guindos, hayas y robles. (Ya se ve que estamos en el Norte de España.)

Era un hombre de mediana edad, de complexión recia, buena talla, ancho de espaldas, resuelto de ademanes, firme de andadura, basto de facciones, de mirar osado y vivo, ligero, a pesar de su regular obesidad, y (dígase de una

7

vez, aunque sea prematuro) excelente persona
por doquiera que se le mirara. Vestía el traje
propio de los señores acomodados que viajan
en verano, con el redondo sombrerete, que debe a su fealdad el nombre de hongo; gemelos
de campo pendientes de una correa, y grueso
bastón que, entre paso y paso, le servía para
apalear las zarzas cuando extendían sus ramas
llenas de afiladas uñas para atraparle la ropa.

Detúvose, y mirando a todo el círculo del
horizonte, parecía impaciente y desasosegado.
Sin duda no tenía gran confianza en la exactitud de su itinerario, y aguardaba el paso de algún aldeano que le diese buenos informes to-
pográficos para llegar pronto y derechamente
a su destino.

«No puedo equivocarme—murmuró—. Me
dijeron que atravesara el río por la pasadera...
Así lo hice. Después, que marchara adelante,
siempre adelante. En efecto; allá, detrás de
mí, queda esa apreciable villa, a quien yo llamaría *Villafangosa* por el buen surtido de lo-
dos que hay en su calles y caminos... De modo
que por aquí, adelante, siempre adelante...
(Me gusta esta frase, si yo tuviera escudo, no
le pondría otra divisa), he de llegar a las famo-
sas minas de Socartes.»

Después de andar largo trecho, añadió:

«Me he perdido, no hay duda de que me he

perdido... Aquí tienes, Teodoro Golfín, el resultado de tu *adelante, siempre adelante*. Estos palurdos no conocen el valor de las palabras. O han querido burlarse de ti, o ellos mismos ignoran dónde están las minas de Socartes. Un gran establecimiento minero ha de anunciarse con edificios, chimeneas, ruido de arrastres, resoplido de hornos, relincho de caballos, trepidación de máquinas, y yo no veo, ni huelo, ni oigo nada... Parece que estoy en un desierto... ¡Qué soledad! Si yo creyera en brujas, pensaría que mi destino me proporcionaba esta noche el honor de ser presentado a ellas... ¡Demonio!, ¿pero no hay gente en estos lugares?... Aún falta media hora para la salida de la luna. ¡Ah, bribona, tú tienes la culpa de mi extravío!... Si al menos pudiera conocer el sitio donde me encuentro... ¡Pero qué más da!—al decir esto hizo un gesto propio del hombre esforzado que desprecia los peligros—. Golfín, tú que has dado la vuelta al mundo, ¿te acobardarás ahora?... ¡Ah! los aldeanos tenían razón: adelante, siempre adelante. La ley universal de la locomoción no puede fallar en este momento.»

Y puesta denodadamente en ejecución aquella osada ley, recorrió un kilómetro, siguiendo a capricho las veredas que le salían al paso y se cruzaban y quebraban en ángulos mil, cual si quisiesen engañarle y confundirle más.

Por grandes que fueran su resolución e intrepidez, al fin tuvo que pararse. Las veredas, que
al principio subían, luego empezaron a bajar,
enlazándose; y al fin bajaron tanto, que nuestro viajero hallóse en un talud, por el cual sólo
habría podido descender echándose a rodar.

«¡Bonita situación!—exclamó, sonriendo y
buscando en su buen humor lenitivo a la enojosa contrariedad —. ¿En dónde estás, querido
Golfín? Esto parece un abismo. ¿Ves algo allá
abajo? Nada, absolutamente nada...; pero el
césped ha desaparecido, el terreno está remo-
vido. Todo es aquí pedrusco y tierra sin vegeta-
ción, teñida por el óxido de hierro... Sin duda
estoy en las minas...; pero ni alma viviente, ni
chimeneas humeantes, ni ruido, ni un tren que
murmure a lo lejos, ni siquiera un perro que
ladre... ¿Qué haré? Hay por aquí una vereda
que vuelve a subir. ¿Seguiréla? ¿Desandaré lo
andado?... ¡Retroceder! ¡Qué absurdo! O yo
dejo de ser quien soy, o llegaré esta noche a las
minas de Socartes y abrazaré a mi querido hermano. Adelante, siempre adelante.»

Dio un paso, y hundióse en la frágil tierra
movediza.

«¿Esas tenemos, señor planeta?... ¿Conque
quiere usted tragarme?... Si ese holgazán saté-
lite quisiera alumbrar un poco, ya nos veía-
mos las caras usted y yo... Y a fe que por aquí

abajo no hemos de ir a ningún paraíso. Parece
esto el cráter de un volcán apagado... Hay
que andar suavemente por tan delicioso preci-
picio. ¿Qué es esto? ¡Ah!, una piedra. Magnífico
asiento para echar un cigarro esperando a que
salga la luna.»

El discreto Golfín se sentó tranquilamente,
como podría haberlo hecho en el banco de un
paseo; y ya se disponía a fumar, cuando sintió
una voz... Sí, indudablemente era una voz humana que lejos sonaba, un quejido patético,
mejor dicho, melancólico canto, formado de
una sola frase, cuya última cadencia se prolon-
gaba apianándose en la forma que los músicos
llaman *morendo*, y que se apagaba al fin en el
plácido silencio de la noche, sin que el oído
pudiera apreciar su vibración postrera.

«Vamos—dijo el viajero, lleno de gozo—, humanidad tenemos. Ese es el canto de una muchacha; sí, es voz de mujer, y voz preciosísima.
Me gusta la música popular de este país. Ahora
calla... Oigamos, que pronto ha de volver a em-
pezar... Ya, ya suena otra vez. ¡Qué voz tan bella, qué melodía tan conmovedora! Creeríase
que sale de las profundidades de la tierra, y
que el señor de Golfín, el hombre más serio y
menos supersticioso del mundo, va a andar en
tratos ahora con los silfos, ondinas, gnomos,
hadas y toda la chusma emparentada con la

loca de la casa...; pero si no me engaña el oído,
la voz se aleja... La graciosa cantadora se va.
¡Eh, niña, aguarda, detén el paso!»

La voz que durante breve rato había regalado
con encantadora música el oído del hombre
extraviado se iba perdiendo en la inmensidad
tenebrosa, y a los gritos de Golfín, el canto ex-
tinguióse por completo. Sin duda la misteriosa
entidad gnómica que entretenía su soledad sub-
terránea cantando tristes amores se había asus-
tado de la brusca interrupción del hombre, hu-
yendo a las hondas entrañas de la tierra, donde
moran, avaras de sus propios fulgores, las piedras preciosas.

«Esta es una situación divina—murmuró Golfín, considerando que no podía hacer mejor cosa
que dar lumbre a su cigarro—. No hay mal que
cien años dure. Aguardemos fumando. Me he
lucido con querer venir solo y a pie a las minas.
Mi equipaje habrá llegado primero, lo que prueba de un modo irrebatible las ventajas del
adelante, siempre adelante.»

Movióse entonces ligero vientecillo, y Teodoro
creyó sentir pasos lejanos en el fondo de aquel
desconocido o supuesto abismo que ante sí tenía. Puso atención, y no tardó en adquirir la
certeza de que alguien andaba por allí. Levantándose, gritó:

—¡Muchacha, hombre o quienquiera que seas!, ¿se puede ir por aquí a las minas de Socartes?

No había concluido, cuando oyóse el violento ladrar de un perro, y después una voz de hombre, que dijo:

—¡*Choto, Choto*, ven aquí!

—¡Eh!—gritó el viajero—. ¡Buen amigo, muchacho de todos los demonios, o lo que quiera que seas, sujeta pronto ese perro, que yo soy hombre de paz!

—¡*Choto, Choto!*

Vio Golfín que se le acercaba un perro negro y grande; mas el animal, después de gruñir junto a él, retrocedió, llamado por su amo. En tal punto y momento el viajero pudo distinguir una figura, un hombre que inmóvil y sin expresión, cual muñeco de piedra, estaba en pie, a distancia como de diez varas, más abajo de él, en una vereda transversal que aparecía irregularmente trazada por todo lo largo del talud. Este sendero y la humana figura detenida en él llamaron vívamente la atención de Golfín, que, dirigiendo gozosa mirada al cielo, exclamó:

—¡Gracias a Dios! Al fin sale esa loca. Ya podemos saber dónde estamos. No sospechaba yo que tan cerca de mí existiera esta senda. ¡Pero si es un camino!... ¡Hola, amiguito!, ¿puede usted decirme si estoy en Socartes?

—Sí, señor; éstas son las minas, aunque estamos un poco lejos del establecimiento.

La voz que esto decía era juvenil y agradable, y resonaba con las simpáticas inflexiones que indican una disposición a prestar servicios con buena voluntad y cortesía. Mucho gustó al doctor oírla, y más aún observar la dulce claridad que, difundiéndose por los espacios antes oscuros, hacía revivir cielo y tierra, cual si los sacara de la nada.

—*Fiat lux*—dijo, descendiendo—. Me parece que acabo de salir del caos primitivo. Ya estamos en la realidad... Bien, amiguito: doy a usted gracias por las noticias que me ha dado y las que aún ha de darme... Salí de Villamojada al ponerse el sol. Dijéronme que adelante, siempre adelante.

—¿Va usted al establecimiento?—preguntó el misterioso joven, permaneciendo inmóvil y rígido, sin mirar al doctor, que ya estaba cerca.

—Sí, señor; pero sin duda equivoqué el camino.

—Esta no es la entrada de las minas. La entrada es por la pasadera de Rabagones, donde está el camino y el ferrocarril en construcción. Por allá hubiera usted llegado en diez minutos al establecimiento. Por aquí tardaremos más, porque hay bastante distancia y muy mal camino. Estamos en la última zona de explotación, v hemos de atravesar algunas galerías y túneles, bajar escaleras, pasar trincheras, remontar taludes, descender el plano inclinado; en fin, recorrer todas las minas de Socartes desde un extremo, que es éste, hasta el otro extremo, donde están los talleres, los hornos, las máquinas, el laboratorio y las oficinas.

—Pues a fe mía que ha sido floja mi equivocación—dijo Golfín, riendo.

—Yo le guiaré a usted con mucho gusto, porque conozco estos sitios perfectamente.

Golfín, hundiendo los pies en la tierra, resbalando aquí y bailoteando más allá, tocó al fin el benéfico suelo de la vereda, y su primera acción fue examinar al bondadoso joven. Breve rato permaneció el doctor dominado por la sorpresa.

—Usted...—murmuró.

—Soy ciego, sí, señor—añadió el joven—; pero sin vista sé recorrer de un cabo a otro las minas. El palo que uso me impide tropezar, y *Choto* me acompaña, cuando no lo hace la Nela, que es mi lazarillo. Conque sígame usted y déjese llevar.

2. Guiado

—¿Ciego de nacimiento?—dijo Golfín con vivo interés, que no era sólo inspirado por la compasión.

—Sí, señor, de nacimiento—repuso el ciego con naturalidad—. No conozco el mundo más que por el pensamiento, el tacto y el oído. He podido comprender que la parte más maravillosa del Universo es esa que me está vedada. Yo sé que los ojos de los demás no son como estos míos, sino que por sí conocen las cosas; pero este don me parece tan extraordinario, que ni siquiera comprendo la posibilidad de poseerlo.

—Quién sabe...—manifestó Teodoro—. Pero ¿qué es esto que veo, amigo mío? ¿Qué sorprendente espectáculo es éste?

El viajero, que había andado algunos pasos junto a su guía, se detuvo, asombrado de la perspectiva fantástica que a sus ojos se ofrecía. Hallábase en un lugar hondo semejante al cráter de un volcán, de suelo irregular, de paredes más irregulares aún. En los bordes y en el cen-

tro de la enorme caldera, cuya magnitud era
aumentada por el engañoso claroscuro de la
noche, se elevaban figuras colosales, hombres
disformes, monstruos volcados y patas arriba,
brazos inmensos desperezándose, pies trunca-
dos, dispersas figuras semejantes a las que forma el caprichoso andar de las nubes en el cielo;
pero quietas, inmobles, endurecidas. Era su color el de las momias, color terroso tirando a
rojo; su actitud, la del movimiento febril sor-
prendido y atajado por la muerte. Parecía la
petrificación de una orgía de gigantescos demonios; sus manotadas, los burlones movimientos
de sus disformes cabezas habían quedado fijos
como las inalterables actitudes de la escultura.
El silencio que llenaba el ámbito del supuesto
cráter era un silencio que daba miedo. Creeríase que mil voces y aullidos habían quedado
también hechos piedra, y piedra eran desde
siglos de siglos.

—¿En dónde estamos, buen amigo?—dijo
Golfín—. Esto es una pesadilla.

—Esta zona de la mina se llama la Terrible
—repuso el ciego, indiferente al estupor de su
compañero de camino—. Ha estado en explotación hasta que hace dos años se agotó el mineral. Hoy los trabajos se hacen en otras zonas
que hay más arriba. Lo que a usted le maravilla
son los bloques de piedra que llaman cretácea

y de arcilla ferruginosa endurecida que han
quedado después de sacado el mineral. Dicen
que esto presenta un golpe de vista sublime,
sobre todo a la luz de la luna. Yo de nada de
eso entiendo.

—Espectáculo asombroso, sí—dijo el forastero, deteniéndose en contemplarlo—, pero que a
mí antes me causa espanto que placer, porque
lo asocio al recuerdo de mis neuralgias. ¿Sabe
usted lo que me parece? Pues que estoy viajando por el interior de un cerebro atacado de
violentísima jaqueca. Estas figuras son como
las formas perceptibles que acepta el dolor ce-
falálgico, confundiéndose con los terroríficos
bultos y sombrajos que engendra la fiebre.

—¡*Choto, Choto*, aquí!—dijo el ciego—. Caballero, mucho cuidado ahora, que vamos a entrar en una galería.

En efecto; Golfín vio que el ciego, tocando el
suelo con su palo, se dirigía hacia una puertecci-
lla estrecha cuyo marco eran tres gruesas vigas.

El perro entró primero olfateando la negra
cavidad. Siguióle el ciego con la impavidez de
quien vive en perpetuas tinieblas. Teodoro fue
detrás, no sin experimentar cierta repugnancia
instintiva hacia la importuna excursión bajo
la tierra.

—Es pasmoso—observó—que usted entre y
salga por aquí sin tropiezo.

—Me he criado en estos sitios—contestó el joven—, y los conozco como mi propia casa. Aquí se siente frío: abríguese usted si tiene con qué. No tardaremos mucho en salir.

Iba palpando con su mano derecha la pared, formada de vigas perpendiculares. Después dijo:

—Cuide usted de no tropezar en los carriles que hay en el suelo. Por aquí se arrastra el mineral de las pertenencias de arriba. ¿Tiene usted frío?

—Diga usted, buen amigo—interrogó el doctor festivamente—. ¿Está usted seguro de que no nos ha tragado la tierra? Este pasadizo es un esófago. Somos pobres bichos que hemos caído en el estómago de un gran insectívoro. ¿Y usted, joven, se pasea mucho por estas amenidades?

—Mucho paseo por aquí a todas horas, y me agrada extraordinariamente. Ya hemos entrado en la parte más seca. Esto es arena pura... Ahora vuelve la piedra... Aquí hay filtraciones de agua sulfurosa; por aquí una capa de tierra, en que se encuentran conchitas de piedras... También verá capas de pizarra: esto llaman esquistos... ¿Oye usted cómo canta el sapo? Ya estamos cerca de la boca. Allí se pone ese holgazán todas las noches. Le conozco: tiene una voz ronca y pausada.

—¿Quién, el sapo?

—Sí, señor. Ya nos acercamos al fin.

—En efecto; allá veo como un ojo que nos mira. Es la claridad de la otra boca.

Cuando salieron, el primer accidente que hirió los sentidos del doctor fue el canto melancólico que había oído antes. Oyólo también el ciego; volvióse bruscamente, y dijo sonriendo con placer y orgullo:

—¿La oye usted?

—Antes oí esa voz y me agradó sobremanera. ¿Quién es la que canta?...

En vez de contestar, el ciego se detuvo, y dando al viento la voz con toda la fuerza de sus pulmones, gritó:

—¡Nela!... ¡Nela!

Ecos sonoros, próximos los unos, lejanos otros, repitieron aquel nombre. El ciego, poniéndose las manos en la boca en forma de bocina, gritó:

—No vengas, que voy allá. ¡Espérame en la herrería..., en la herrería!

Después, volviéndose al doctor, le dijo:

—La Nela es una muchacha que me acompaña, es mi lazarillo. Al anochecer volvíamos juntos del prado grande..., hacía un poco de fresco. Como mi padre me ha prohibido que ande de noche sin abrigo, metíme en la cabaña de Remolinos, y la Nela corrió a mi casa a buscarme el gabán. Al poco rato de estar en la cabaña, acordéme de que un amigo había quedado en esperarme en casa; no tuve paciencia para aguardar a la Nela, y salí con *Choto*. Pasaba por la Terrible, cuando le encontré a usted... Pronto llegaremos a la herrería. Allí nos separaremos, porque mi padre se enoja cuando entro tarde en casa. Nela le acompañará a usted hasta las oficinas.

—Muchas gracias, amigo mío.

El túnel les había conducido a un segundo espacio más singular que el anterior. Era una profunda grieta abierta en el terreno, a semejanza de las que resultan de un cataclismo; pero no había sido abierta por las palpitaciones fogosas del planeta, sino por el laborioso azadón del minero. Parecía el interior de un gran buque náufrago, tendido sobre la playa, y a quien las olas hubieran quebrado por la mitad doblándole en un ángulo obtuso. Hasta se podían ver sus descarnados costillajes, cuyas puntas coronaban en desigual fila una de las alturas. En la concavidad panzuda distinguíanse grandes piedras, como restos de carga maltratados por las olas; y era tal la fuerza pictórica del claroscuro de la luna, que Golfín creyó ver, entre mil despojos de cosas náuticas, cadáveres medio devorados por los peces, momias, esqueletos, todo muerto, dormido, semidescompuesto y profun-

damente tranquilo, cual si por mucho tiempo
morara en la inmensa sepultura del mar.

La ilusión fue completa cuando sintió rumor
de agua, un chasquido semejante al de las olas
mansas cuando juegan en los huecos de una
peña o azotan el esqueleto de un buque náufrago.

—Por aquí hay agua—dijo a su compañero.

—Ese ruido que usted siente—replicó el ciego, deteniéndose—, y que parece... ¿Cómo lo
diré? ¿No es verdad que parece ruido de gárgaras, como el que hacemos cuando nos cura-
mos la garganta?

—Exactamente. ¿Y dónde está ese buche de
agua? ¿Es algún arroyo que pasa?

—No, señor. Aquí, a la izquierda, hay una
loma. Detrás de ella se abre una gran boca, una
sima, un abismo cuyo fin no se sabe. Se llama
la Trascava. Algunos creen que va a dar al mar
por junto a Ficóbriga. Otros dicen que por el
fondo de él corre un río que está siempre dando
vueltas y más vueltas, como una rueda, sin salir nunca fuera. Yo me figuro que será como un
molino. Algunos dicen que hay allá abajo un
resoplido de aire que sale de las entrañas de la
tierra, como cuando silbamos, el cual resoplido
de aire choca contra un raudal de agua, se ponen a reñir, se engarran, se enfurecen y produ-
cen ese hervidero que oímos de fuera.

—¿Y nadie ha bajado a esa sima?

—No se puede bajar sino de una manera.

—¿Cómo?

—Arrojándose a ella. Los que han entrado no han vuelto a salir, y es lástima, porque nos hubieran dicho qué pasaba allá dentro. La boca de esa caverna hállase a bastante distancia de nosotros; pero hace dos años, cavando los mineros en este sitio, descubrieron una hendidura en la peña, por la cual se oye el mismo hervor de agua que por la boca principal. Esta hendidura debe comunicar con las galerías de allá dentro, donde está el resoplido que sube y el chorro que baja. De día podrá usted verla perfectamente, pues basta enfilar un poco las piedras del lado izquierdo para llegar hasta ella. Hay un asiento cómodo. Algunas personas tienen miedo de acercarse; pero la Nela y yo nos sentamos allí muy a menudo a oír cómo resuena la voz del abismo. Y efectivamente, señor, parece que nos hablan al oído. La Nela dice y jura que oye palabras, que las distingue claramente. Yo, la verdad, nunca he oído palabras, pero sí un murmullo como soliloquio o meditación, que a veces parece triste, a veces alegre, tan pronto colérico como burlón.

—Pues yo no oigo sino ruido de gárgaras —dijo el doctor, riendo.

—Así parece desde aquí... Pero no nos retra-

semos, que es tarde. Prepárese usted a pasar
otra galería.

—¿Otra?

—Sí, señor. Y ésta, al llegar a la mitad, se divide en dos. Hay después un laberinto de vueltas y revueltas, porque se hicieron obras que después quedaron abandonadas, y aquello está como Dios quiere. *Choto*, adelante.

Choto se metió por un agujero como hurón que persigue al conejo, y siguiéronle el doctor y su guía, que tentaba con su palo el torcido, estrecho y lóbrego camino. Nunca el sentido del tacto había tenido más delicadeza y finura, prolongándose desde la epidermis humana hasta un pedazo de madera insensible. Avanzaron describiendo primero una curva, después ángulos y más ángulos, siempre entre las dos paredes de tablones húmedos y medio podridos.

—¿Sabe usted a lo que me parece esto?—dijo el doctor, reconociendo que los símiles agradaban a su guía—. Pues lo comparo a los pensamientos del hombre perverso. Aquí se representa la intuición del malo, cuando penetra en su conciencia para verse en toda su fealdad.

Creyó Golfín que se había expresado en lenguaje poco inteligible para el ciego; mas éste probóle lo contrario, diciendo:

—Para el que posee el reino desconocido de la luz, estas galerías deben de ser tristes; pero yo, que vivo en tinieblas, hallo aquí cierta conformidad de la tierra con mi propio ser. Yo ando por aquí como usted por la calle más ancha. Si no fuera porque unas veces es escaso el aire y otras excesiva la humedad, preferiría estos lugares subterráneos a todos los demás lugares que conozco.

—Esto es la idea de la meditación.

—Yo siento en mi cerebro un paso, un agujero lo mismo que éste por donde voy, y por él corren mis ideas desarrollándose magníficamente.

—¡Oh, cuán lamentable cosa es no haber visto nunca la bóveda azul del cielo en pleno día! —exclamó el doctor con espontaneidad suma—. Dígame, ¿este conducto donde las ideas de usted se desarrollan magníficamente, no se acaba nunca?

—Ya, ya pronto estaremos fuera. ¿Dice usted que la bóveda del cielo...? ¡Ah! Ya me figuro que será una concavidad armoniosa, a la cual parece que podremos alcanzar con las manos, sin lograrlo realmente.

Al decir esto salieron. Golfín, respirando con placer y fuerza, como el que acaba de soltar un gran peso, exclamó mirando al cielo:

—¡Gracias a Dios que os vuelvo a ver, estrellitas del firmamento! Nunca me habéis parecido más lindas que en este instante.

—Al pasar—dijo el ciego, alargando su mano,

que mostraba una piedra—he cogido este pedazo de caliza cristalizada. ¿Sostendrá usted que
estos cristalitos que mi tacto halla tan bien cor-
tados, finos y bien pegaditos los unos a los
otros, no son una cosa muy bella? Al menos
a mí me lo parece.

Diciéndolo, desmenuzaba los cristales.

—Amigo querido—dijo Golfín con emoción y
lástima— es verdaderamente triste que usted no
pueda conocer que ese pedrusco no merece la
atención del hombre mientras esté suspendido
sobre nuestras cabezas el infinito rebaño de maravillosas luces que pueblan la bóveda del cielo.

El ciego volvió su rostro hacia arriba, y dijo
con profunda tristeza:

—¿Es verdad que existís, estrellas?

—Dios es inmensamente grande y misericor-
dioso—observó Golfín, poniendo su mano sobre el hombro de su acompañante—. ¡Quién
sabe, quién sabe, amigo mío!... Se han visto,
se ven todos los días casos muy raros.

Mientras esto decía mirábale de cerca, tratando de examinar, a la escasa claridad de la
noche, las pupilas del joven. Fijo y sin mirada,
el ciego volvía sonriendo su rostro hacia donde
sonaba la voz del doctor.

—No tengo esperanza—murmuró.

Habían salido a un sitio despejado. La luna,
más clara a cada rato, iluminaba praderas ondu-

lantes y largos taludes, que parecían las escarpas de inmensas fortificaciones. A la izquierda, y a regular altura, vio el doctor un grupo de blancas casas en el mismo borde de la vertiente.

—Aquí, a la izquierda—dijo el ciego—, está mi casa. Allá arriba..., ¿sabe usted? Aquellas tres casas es lo que queda del lugar de Aldeacorba de Suso; lo demás ha sido expropiado en diversos años para beneficiar el terreno; todo aquí debajo es calamina. Nuestros padres vivían sobre miles de millones sin saberlo.

Esto decía, cuando se vino corriendo hacia ellos una muchacha, una niña, una chicuela, de ligerísimos pies y menguada de estatura.

—Nela, Nela—dijo el ciego—. ¿Me traes el abrigo?

—Aquí está—repuso la muchacha, poniéndole un capote sobre los hombros.

—¿Esta es la que cantaba?... ¿Sabes que tienes una preciosa voz?

—¡Oh!—exclamó el ciego con candoroso acento de encomio—, canta admirablemente. Ahora, Mariquilla, vas a acompañar a este caballero hasta las oficinas. Yo me quedo en casa. Ya siento la voz de mi padre que baja a buscarme. Me reñirá, de seguro... ¡Allá voy, allá voy!

—Retírese usted pronto, amigo—dijo Golfín, estrechándole la mano—. El aire es fresco y puede hacerle daño. Muchas gracias por la compañía. Espero que seremos amigos, porque estaré aquí algún tiempo... Yo soy hermano de Carlos Golfín, el ingeniero de estas minas.

—¡Ah!..., ya... Don Carlos es muy amigo de mi padre y mío; le espera a usted desde ayer.

—Llegué esta tarde a la estación de Villamojada..., dijéronme que Socartes estaba cerca y que podía venir a pie. Como me gusta ver el paisaje y hacer ejercicio, y como me dijeron que adelante, siempre adelante, eché a andar, mandando mi equipaje en un carro. Ya ve usted cuán tontamente me perdí... Pero no hay mal que por bien no venga..., le he conocido a usted, y seremos amigos, quizá muy amigos... Vaya, adiós; a casa pronto, que el fresco de septiembre no es bueno. Esta señorita Nela tendrá la bondad de acompañarme.

—De aquí a las oficinas no hay más que un cuarto de hora de camino..., poca cosa... Cuidado no tropiece usted en los raíles; cuidado al bajar el plano inclinado. Suelen dejar las vagonetas sobre la vía... y con la humedad, la tierra está como jabón... Adiós, caballero y amigo mío. Buenas noches.

Subió por una empinada escalera abierta en la tierra, y cuyos peldaños estaban reforzados con vigas. Golfín siguió adelante, guiado por la Nela. Lo que hablaron, ¿merecerá capítulo aparte? Por si acaso, se lo daremos.

—Aguarda, hija, no vayas tan aprisa—dijo
Golfín, deteniéndose—; déjame encender un
cigarro.

Estaba tan serena la noche, que no necesitó
emplear las precauciones que generalmente
adoptan contra el viento los fumadores. Encendido el cigarro, acercó la cerilla al rostro de la
Nela, diciendo con bondad:

—A ver, enséñame tu cara.

Mirábale asombrada la muchacha, y sus negros ojuelos brillaron con un punto rojizo,
como chispa, en el breve instante que duró la
luz del fósforo. Era como una niña, pues su
estatura debía contarse entre las más peque-
ñas, correspondiendo a su talle delgadísimo y
a su busto mezquinamente constituido. Era
como una jovenzuela, pues sus ojos no tenían
el mirar propio de la infancia, y su cara revelaba la madurez de un organismo que ha entrado
o debido entrar en el juicio. A pesar de esta
desconformidad, era admirablemente propor-

cionada, y su cabeza chica remataba con cierta
gallardía el miserable cuerpecillo. Alguien la de-
finía mujer mirada con vidrio de disminución;
alguno como una niña con ojos y expresión de
adolescente. No conociéndola, se dudaba si era
un asombroso progreso o un deplorable atraso.

—¿Qué edad tienes tú?—preguntóle Golfín,
sacudiendo los dedos para arrojar el fósforo,
que empezaba a quemarle.

—Dicen que tengo dieciséis años—replicó la
Nela, examinando a su vez al doctor.

—¡Dieciséis años! Atrasadilla estás, hija. Tu
cuerpo es de doce, a lo sumo.

—¡Madre de Dios! Si dicen que yo soy como
un fenómeno…—manifestó ella en tono de lástima de sí misma.

—¡Un fenómeno!—repitió Golfín, poniendo
su mano sobre los cabellos de la chica—. Podrá
ser. Vamos, guíame.

Comenzó a andar la Nela resueltamente sin
adelantarse mucho, antes bien, cuidando de ir
siempre al lado del viajero, como si apreciara
en todo su valor la honra de tan noble compañía. Iba descalza: sus pies ágiles y pequeños
denotaban familiaridad consuetudinaria con el
suelo, con las piedras, con los charcos, con los
abrojos. Vestía una falda sencilla y no muy larga, denotando en su rudimentario atavío, así
como en la libertad de sus cabellos sueltos y

cortos, rizados con nativa elegancia, cierta inde-
pendencia más propia del salvaje que del mendigo. Sus palabras, al contrario, sorprendieron
a Golfín por lo recatadas y humildes, dando
indicios de un carácter formal y reflexivo. Resonaba su voz con simpático acento de cortesía,
que no podía ser hijo de la educación; sus miradas eran fugaces y momentáneas, como no
fueran dirigidas al suelo o al cielo.

—Dime—le preguntó Golfín—, ¿vives tú en
las minas? ¿Eres hija de algún empleado de
esta posesión?

—Dicen que no tengo madre ni padre.

—¡Pobrecita! Tú trabajarás en las minas...

—No, señor. Yo no sirvo para nada—replicó
sin alzar del suelo los ojos.

—Pues a fe que tienes modestia.

Teodoro se inclinó para mirarle el rostro.
Este era delgado, muy pecoso, todo salpicado
de manchitas parduscas. Tenía pequeña la frente, picudilla y no falta de gracia la nariz, negros
y vividores los ojos; pero comúnmente brillaba
en ellos una luz de tristeza. Su cabello dorado
oscuro había perdido el hermoso color nativo
a causa de la incuria y de su continua exposi-
ción al aire, al sol y al polvo. Sus labios apenas
se veían de puro chicos, y siempre estaban sonriendo; mas aquella sonrisa era semejante a la
imperceptible de algunos muertos cuando han

dejado de vivir pensando en el cielo. La boca
de la Nela, estéticamente hablando, era desabri-
da, fea; pero quizá podía merecer elogios, aplicándole el verso de Polo de Medina: «Es tan linda su boca que no pide.» En efecto; ni hablando,
ni mirando, ni sonriendo, revelaba aquella miserable el hábito degradante de la mendicidad.

Golfín le acarició el rostro con su mano, to-
mándolo por la barba y abarcándolo casi todo
entre sus gruesos dedos.

—¡Pobrecita!—exclamó—. Dios no ha sido
generoso contigo. ¿Con quién vives?

—Con el señor Centeno, capataz de ganado
en las minas.

—Me parece que tú no habrás nacido en la
abundancia. ¿De quién eres hija?

—Dicen que mi madre vendía pimientos en
el mercado de Villamojada. Era soltera. *Me
tuvo* un día de Difuntos, y después se fue a
criar a Madrid.

—¡Vaya con la buena señora!—murmuró
Teodoro con malicia—. Quizá no tenga nadie
noticia de quién fue tu papá.

—Sí, señor—replicó la Nela, con cierto orgullo—. Mi padre fue el primero que encendió
las luces en Villamojada.

—¡Cáspita!

—Quiero decir que cuando el Ayuntamiento
puso por primera vez faroles en las calles—dijo,

como queriendo dar a su relato la gravedad de la historia—, mi padre era el encargado de encenderlos y limpiarlos. Yo estaba ya criada por una hermana de mi madre, que era también soltera, según dicen. Mi padre había reñido con ella... Dicen que vivían juntos..., todos vivían juntos..., y cuando iba a farolear me llevaba en el cesto, junto con los tubos de vidrio, las mechas, la aceitera... Un día dicen que subió a limpiar el farol que hay en el puente, puso el cesto sobre el antepecho, yo me salí fuera, y caíme al río.

—¡Y te ahogaste!

—No, señor, porque caí sobre piedras. ¡Divina Madre de Dios! Dicen que antes de eso era yo muy bonita.

—Sí, indudablemente eras muy bonita—afirmó el forastero, el alma inundada de bondad—. Y todavía lo eres... Pero dime: ¿hace mucho tiempo que vives en las minas?

—Dicen que hace tres años. Dicen que mi madre me recogió después de la caída. Mi padre cayó enfermo, y como mi madre no le quiso asistir porque era malo, él fue al Hospital, donde dicen que se murió. Entonces vino mi madre a trabajar a las minas. Dicen que un día la despidió el jefe porque había bebido mucho aguardiente...

—Y tu madre se fue... Vamos, ya me interesa esa señora. Se fue...

—Se fue a un agujero muy grande que hay allá arriba—dijo Nela, deteniéndose ante el doctor y dando a su voz el tono más patético—, y se metió dentro.

—¡Canario! ¡Vaya un fin lamentable! Supongo que no habrá vuelto a salir.

—No, señor—replicó la chiquilla con naturalidad—. Allí dentro está.

—Después de esa catástrofe, pobre criatura —dijo Golfín con cariño—, has quedado trabajando aquí. Es un trabajo muy penoso el de la minería. Estás teñida del color del mineral; estás raquítica y mal alimentada. Esta vida destruye las naturalezas más robustas.

—No, señor, yo no trabajo. Dicen que yo no sirvo ni puedo servir para nada.

—Quita allá, tonta, tú eres una alhaja.

—Que no, señor—dijo la Nela, insistiendo con energía—. Si no puedo trabajar. En cuanto cargo un peso pequeño, me caigo al suelo. Si me pongo a hacer una cosa difícil, en seguida me desmayo.

—Todo sea por Dios... Vamos, que si cayeras tú en manos de personas que te supieran manejar, ya trabajarías bien.

—No, señor—repitió la Nela con tanto énfasis, como si se elogiara—, si yo no sirvo más que de estorbo.

—¿De modo que eres una vagabunda?

—No, señor, porque acompaño a Pablo.

—¿Y quién es Pablo?

—Ese señorito ciego, a quien usted encontró en la Terrible. Yo soy su lazarillo desde hace año y medio. Le llevo a todas partes; nos vamos por los campos paseando.

—Parece buen muchacho ese Pablo.

Detúvose otra vez la Nela mirando al doctor. Con el rostro resplandeciente de entusiasmo, exclamó:

—¡Madre de Dios! Es lo mejor que hay en el mundo. ¡Pobre amito mío! Sin vista tiene él más talento que todos los que ven.

—Me gusta tu amo. ¿Es de este país?

—Sí, señor; es hijo único de don Francisco de Penáguilas, un caballero muy bueno y muy rico que vive en las casas de Aldeacorba.

—Dime: ¿y a ti por qué te llaman la Nela? ¿Qué quiere decir eso?

La muchacha alzó los hombros. Después de una pausa, repuso:

—Mi madre se llamaba la señá María Canela, pero la decían Nela. Dicen que éste es nombre de perra. Yo me llamo María.

—Mariquita.

—María Nela me llaman, y también la hija de la Canela. Unos me dicen Marianela, y otros nada más que la Nela.

—¿Y tu amo te quiere mucho?

—Sí, señor; es muy bueno. El dice que ve con mis ojos, porque como le llevo a todas partes, y le digo cómo son todas las cosas...

—Todas las cosas que no puede ver—indicó el forastero, muy gustoso de aquel coloquio.

—Sí, señor, yo le digo todo. El me pregunta cómo es una estrella, y yo se la pinto de tal modo, hablando, que para él es lo mismito que si la viera. Yo le explico cómo son las hierbas y las nubes, el cielo, el agua y los relámpagos, las veletas, las mariposas, el humo, los caracoles, el cuerpo y la cara de las personas y de los animales. Yo le digo lo que es feo y lo que es bonito, y así se va enterando de todo.

—Veo que no es flojo tu trabajo. ¡Lo feo y lo bonito! Ahí es nada... ¿Te ocupas de eso?... Dime: ¿sabes leer?

—No, señor. Si yo no sirvo para nada.

Decía esto en el tono más convincente, y con el gesto de que acompañaba su firme protesta, parecía añadir: «Es usted un majadero al suponer que yo sirvo para algo.»

—¿No verías con gusto que tu amito recibiera de Dios el don de la vista?

La muchacha no contestó nada. Después de una pausa, dijo:

—¡Divino Dios! Eso es imposible.

—Imposible no, aunque difícil.

—El ingeniero director de las minas ha dado esperanzas al padre de mi amo.

—¿Don Carlos Golfín?

—Sí, señor; don Carlos tiene un hermano médico que cura los ojos, y, según dicen, da vista a los ciegos, arregla a los tuertos y les endereza los ojos a los bizcos.

—¡Qué hombre más hábil!

—Sí, señor; y como ahora el médico anunció a su hermano que iba a venir, su hermano le escribió diciéndole que trajera las herramientas para ver si le podía dar vista a Pablo.

—¿Y ha venido ya ese buen hombre?

—No, señor; como anda siempre allá por las Américas y las Inglaterras, parece que tardará en venir. Pero Pablo se ríe de esto, y dice que no le dará ese hombre lo que la Virgen Santísima le negó desde el nacer.

—Quizá tenga razón... Pero dime: ¿estamos ya cerca?..., porque veo chimeneas que arrojan un humo más negro que el del infierno, y veo también una claridad que parece de fragua

—Sí, señor, ya llegamos. Aquéllos son los hornos de la calcinación, que arden día y noche. Aquí enfrente están las máquinas de lavado,

que no trabajan sino de día; a mano derecha
está el taller de composturas, y allá abajo, a
lo último de todo, las oficinas.

En efecto; el lugar aparecía a los ojos de
Golfín como lo describía Marianela. Esparcién-
dose el humo por falta de aire, envolvía en una
como gasa oscura y sucia todos los edificios, cuyas masas negras señalábanse confusa y fantás-
ticamente sobre el cielo iluminado por la luna.

—Más hermoso es esto para verlo una vez que
para vivir aquí—indicó Golfín, apresurando el
paso—. La nube de humo lo envuelve todo, y
las luces forman un disco borroso, como el de
la luna en noches de bochorno. ¿En dónde están las oficinas?

—Allí; ya pronto llegamos.

Después de pasar por delante de los hornos,
cuyo calor obligóle a apretar el paso, el doctor
vio un edificio tan negro y ahumado como todos los demás. Verlo y sentir los gratos sonidos
de un piano teclado con verdadero frenesí, fue
todo uno.

—Música tenemos; conozco las manos de mi
cuñada.

—Es la señorita Sofía, que toca—afirmó
María.

Claridad de alegres habitaciones lucía en los
huecos, y abierto estaba el balcón principal.
Veíase en él un ascua diminuta, era la lumbre

de un cigarro. Antes que el doctor llegase, el ascua cayó, describiendo una perpendicular y dividiéndose en menudas y saltonas chispas: era que el fumador había arrojado la colilla.

—Allí está el fumador sempiterno—gritó el doctor con acento del más vivo cariño—. ¡Carlos, Carlos!

—¡Teodoro!—contestó una voz en el balcón.

Calló el piano, como un ave cantora que se asusta del ruido. Sonaron pasos en la casa. El doctor dio una moneda de plata a su guía, y corrió hacia la puerta.

4. La familia de piedra

Menudeando el paso y saltando sobre los obstáculos que hallaba en su camino, la Nela se
dirigió a la casa que está detrás de los talleres
de maquinaria y junto a las cuadras donde co-
mían el pienso pausada y gravemente las sesen-
ta mulas del establecimiento. Era la morada
del señor Centeno de moderna construcción,
si bien nada elegante ni aun cómoda. Baja de
techo, pequeña para albergar sus tres piezas
a los esposos Centeno, a los cuatro hijos de
los esposos Centeno, al gato de los esposos
Centeno, y, por añadidura, a la Nela, la casa
figuraba en los planos de vitela de aquel gran
establecimiento ostentando orgullosa, como
otras muchas, este letrero: *Vivienda de ca-
pataces*.

En su interior, el edificio servía para probar
prácticamente un aforismo que ya conocemos,
por haberlo visto enunciado por la misma Marianela; es, a saber: que ella, Marianela, no servía más que de estorbo. En efecto; allí había
sitio para todo: para los esposos Centeno; para

las herramientas de sus hijos; para mil cachivaches de cuya utilidad no hay pruebas inconcu-
sas; para el gato; para el plato en que comía el
gato; para la guitarra de Tanasio; para los materiales que el mismo empleaba en componer
garrotes (cestas); para media docena de colle-
ras viejas de mulas; para la jaula del mirlo;
para dos peroles inútiles; para un altar en que
la Centeno ponía ofrenda de flores de trapo a
la Divinidad y unas velas seculares, coloniza-
das por las moscas; para todo absolutamente,
menos para la hija de la Canela. A menudo se
oía:

«¡Que no he de dar un paso sin tropezar con
esta condenada Nela!...»

También se oía esto:

«Vete a tu rincón... ¡Qué criatura! Ni hace ni
deja hacer a los demás.»

La casa constaba de tres piezas y un desván.
Era la primera, además de corredor y sala, alcoba de los Centenos mayores. En la segunda
dormían las dos señoritas, que eran ya mujeres, y se llamaban la Mariuca y la Pepina. Tanasio, el primogénito, se agasajaba en el desván, y Celipín, que era el más pequeño de la
familia y frisaba en los doce años, tenía su
dormitorio en la cocina, la pieza más interna,
más remota, más crepuscular, más ahumada

y más inhabitable de las tres que componían
la morada Centenil.

La Nela, durante los largos años de su residencia allí, había ocupado distintos rincones,
pasando de uno a otro conforme lo exigía la
instalación de mil objetos que no servían sino
para robar a los seres vivos el último pedazo de
suelo habitable. En cierta ocasión (no consta
la fecha con exactitud), Tanasio, que era tan
imposibilitado de piernas como de ingenio, y
se había dedicado a la construcción de cestas
de avellano, puso en la cocina, formando pila,
hasta media docena de aquellos ventrudos
ejemplares de su industria. Entonces, la hija
de la Canela volvió tristemente sus ojos en
derredor, sin hallar sitio donde albergarse;
pero la misma contrariedad sugirióle repentina
y felicísima idea, que al instante puso en ejecución. Metióse bonitamente en una cesta, y
así pasó la noche en fácil y tranquilo sueño.
Indudablemente aquello era bueno y cómodo:
cuando tenía frío, tapábase con otra cesta. Desde entonces, siempre que había *garrotes* grandes, no careció de estuche en que encerrarse.
Por eso decían en la casa: «Duerme como una
alhaja.»

Durante la comida, y entre la algazara de una
conversación animada sobre el trabajo de la
mañana, oíase una voz que bruscamente decía:

«Toma.» La Nela recogía una escudilla de manos de cualquier Centeno grande o chico, y se sentaba contra el arca a comer sosegadamente. También solía oírse al fin de la comida la voz áspera y becerril del señor Centeno diciendo a su esposa en tono de reconvención: «Mujer, que no has dado nada a la pobre Nela.» A veces acontecía que la Señana (nombre formado de señora Ana) moviera la cabeza para buscar con los ojos, por entre los cuerpos de sus hijos, algún objeto pequeño y lejano, y que al mismo tiempo dijera: «Pues qué, ¿estaba ahí? Yo pensé que también hoy se había quedado en Aldeacorba.»

Por las noches, después de cenar, rezaban el rosario. Tambaleándose como sacerdotisas de Baco, y revolviendo sus apretados puños en el hueco de los ojos, la Mariuca y la Pepina se iban a sus lechos, que eran cómodos y confortantes, paramentados con abigarradas colchas.

Poco después oíase un roncante dúo de contraltos aletargados, que duraba sin interrupción hasta el amanecer.

Tanasio subía al alto aposento, y Celipín se acurrucaba sobre haraposas mantas, no lejos de las cestas donde desaparecía la Nela.

Acomodados así los hijos, los padres permanecían un rato en la pieza principal; y mientras Centeno, sentándose junto a la mesilla y toman-

do un periódico, hacía mil muecas y visajes que
indicaban el atrevido intento de leerlo, la Señana sacaba del arca una media repleta de dinero, y después de contado y de añadir o quitar algunas piezas, lo reponía cuidadosamente
en su sitio. Sacaba después diferentes líos de
papel que contenían monedas de oro, y trase-
gaba algunas piezas de uno en otro apartadijo.
Entonces solían oírse frases sueltas como éstas:

«He tomado treinta y dos reales para el re-
fajo de la Mairuca... A Tanasio le he puesto
los seis reales que se le quitaron... Sólo nos
faltan once duros para los quinientos...»

O como éstas:

«Señores diputados que dijeron sí...» «Ayer
celebró una conferencia, etc.»

Los dedos de Señana sumaban, y el de Sinfo-
roso Centeno seguía tembloroso y vacilante los
renglones, para poder guiar su espíritu por
aquel laberinto de letras.

Las frases iban poco a poco resolviéndose en
palabras sueltas, después en monosílabos; oíase
un bostezo, otro, y al fin todo quedaba en plácido silencio, después de extinguida la luz, a
cuyo resplandor había enriquecido sus conocimientos el capataz de mulas.

Una noche, después que todo calló, dejóse
oír ruido de cestas en la cocina. Como allí ha-

bía alguna claridad, porque jamás se cerraba
la madera del ventanillo, Celipín Centeno, que
no dormía aún, vio que las dos cestas más altas, colocadas una contra otra, se separaban,
abriéndose como las conchas de un bivalvo.
Por el hueco aparecieron la naricilla y los negros ojos de Nela.

—Celipín, Celipinillo—dijo ésta, sacando también su mano—. ¿Estás dormido?

—No, despierto estoy. Nela, pareces una almeja. ¿Qué quieres?

—Toma, toma esta peseta que me dio esta
noche un caballero, hermano de don Carlos...
¿Cuánto has juntado ya?... Este sí que es regalo. Nunca te había dado más que cuartos.

—Dame acá; muchas gracias, Nela—dijo el
muchacho, incorporándose para tomar la moneda—. Cuarto a cuarto, ya me has dado al pie
de treinta y dos reales... Aquí lo tengo en el
seno, muy bien guardadito en el saco que me
diste. ¡Eres una real moza!

—Yo no quiero para nada el dinero. Guárda-
lo bien, porque si la Señana te lo descubre,
creerá que es para vicios y te pegará una paliza.

—No, no es para vicios, no es para vicios
—afirmó el chicuelo con energía, oprimiéndose
el seno con una mano, mientras sostenía su
cabeza en la otra—: es para hacerme hombre
de provecho. Nela, para hacerme hombre de

pesquis, como muchos que conozco. El domingo, si me dejan ir a Villamojada, he de comprar una cartilla para aprender a leer, ya que aquí no quieren enseñarme. ¡Córcholis! Aprenderé solo. ¡Ah!, Nela, dicen que don Carlos era hijo de uno que barría las calles en Madrid. El solo, solito él, con la ayuda de Dios, aprendió todo lo que sabe.

—Puede que pienses tú hacer lo mismo, bobo.

—¡Córcholis! Puesto que mis padres no quieren sacarme de estas condenadas minas, yo me buscaré otro camino; sí, ya verás quién es Celipín. Yo no sirvo para esto, Nela. Deja tú que tenga reunida una buena cantidad, y verás, verás cómo me planto en la villa, y allí, o tomo el tren para irme a Madrid, o un vapor que me lleve a las islas de allá lejos, o me meto a servir con tal que me dejen estudiar.

—¡Madre de Dios divino! ¡Qué calladas tenías esas picardías!—dijo la Nela, abriendo más las conchas de su estuche y echando fuera toda la cabeza.

—¿Pero tú me tienes por bobo?... ¡Ah!, Nelilla, estoy rabiando. Yo no puedo vivir así, yo me muero en las minas. ¡Córcholis! Paso las noches llorando, y me muerdo las manos, y... no te asustes, Nela, ni me creas malo por lo que voy a decirte: a ti sola te lo digo.

—¿Qué?

—Que no quiero a mi madre ni a mi padre como los debiera querer.

—Ea, pues, si haces eso, no te vuelvo a dar un real. ¡Celipín, por amor de Dios, piensa bien lo que dices!

—No lo puedo remediar. Ya ves cómo nos tienen aquí. ¡Córcholis! No somos gente, sino animales. A veces se me pone en la cabeza que somos menos que las mulas, y yo me pregunto si me diferencio en algo de un borrico... Coger una cesta llena de mineral y echarla en un vagón; empujar el vagón hasta los hornos; revolver con un palo el mineral que se está lavando. ¡Ay!...—al decir esto, los sollozos cortaban la voz del infeliz muchacho—. ¡Cor...córcholis!, el que pase muchos años en este trabajo, al fin se ha de volver malo, y sus sesos serán de calamina... No, Celipín no sirve para esto... Les digo a mis padres que me saquen de aquí y me pongan a estudiar, y responden que son pobres y que yo tengo mucha *fantesía*. Nada, nada; no somos más que bestias que ganamos un jornal... ¿Pero tú no me dices nada?

La Nela no respondió... Quizá comparaba la triste condición de su compañero con la suya propia, hallando ésta infinitamente más aflictiva.

—¿Qué quieres tú que yo te diga?—replicó al fin—. Como yo no puedo ser nunca nada,

como yo no soy persona, nada te puedo decir... Pero no pienses esas cosas malas, no
pienses eso de tus padres.

—Tú lo dices por consolarme; pero bien ves
que tengo razón..., y me parece que estás llorando.

—Yo no.

—Sí; tú estás llorando.

—Cada uno tiene sus cositas que llorar—repuso María con voz sofocada—. Pero es muy
tarde, Celipe, y es preciso dormir.

—Todavía no..., ¡córcholis!

—Sí, hijito. Duérmete y no pienses en esas
cosas malas. Buenas noches.

—Cerráronse las conchas de almeja, y todo
quedó en silencio.

Se ha declamado mucho contra el positivismo de las ciudades, plaga que entre las galas
y el esplendor de la cultura corroe los cimien-
tos morales de la sociedad; pero hay una plaga más terrible, y es el positivismo de las al-
deas, que petrifica millones de seres, matando
en ellos toda ambición noble y encerrándoles
en el círculo de una existencia mecánica, bru-
tal y tenebrosa. Hay en nuestras sociedades
enemigos muy espantosos; a saber: la especu-
lación, el agio, la metalización del hombre culto, el negocio; pero sobre estos descuella un
monstruo que a la callada destroza más que

ninguno: la codicia del aldeano. Para el aldeano codicioso no hay ley moral, ni religión, ni
nociones claras del bien; todo esto se revuelve
en su alma con supersticiones y cálculos gro-
seros, formando un todo inexplicable. Bajo el
hipócrita candor se esconde una aritmética
parda que supera en agudeza y perspicacia a
cuanto idearon los matemáticos más expertos.
Un aldeano que toma el gusto a los ochavos y
sueña con trocarlos en plata para convertir
después la plata en oro, es la bestia más inno-
ble que puede imaginarse; tiene todas las ma-
licias y sutilezas del hombre y una sequedad
de sentimientos que espanta. Su alma se va
condensando hasta no ser más que un gradua-
dor de cantidades. La ignorancia, la rusticidad,
la miseria en el vivir completan esta abomina-
ble pieza, quitándole todos los medios de disi-
mular su descarnado interior. Contando por
los dedos, es capaz de reducir a números todo
el orden moral, la conciencia y el alma toda.

La Señana y el señor Centeno, que habían hallado al fin, después de mil angustias, su *pedazo de pan* en las minas de Socartes, reunían
con el trabajo de sus cuatro hijos un jornal
que les habría parecido fortuna de príncipes en
los tiempos en que andaban de feria en feria
vendiendo pucheros. Debe decirse, tocante a
las facultades intelectuales del señor Centeno,

que su cabeza, en opinión de muchos, rivaliza-
ba en dureza con el martillo pilón montado en
los talleres; no así tocante a la de Señana,
que parecía mujer de muchísimo caletre y tras-
tienda, y gobernaba toda la casa como gober-
naría el más sabio príncipe sus Estados.

Apandaba bonitamente el jornal de su marido y de sus hijos, que era una hermosa suma,
y cada vez que había cobranza, parecíale que
entraba por las puertas de su casa el mismo
Jesús Sacramentado; tal era el gusto que la
vista de las monedas le producía.

Daba la Señana muy pocas comodidades a
sus hijos en cambio de la hacienda que con las
manos de ellos iba formando; pero como no se
quejaban de la degradante y atroz miseria en
que vivían, como no mostraban nunca pujos de
emancipación ni anhelo de otra vida mejor y
más digna de seres inteligentes, la Señana dejaba correr los días. Muchos pasaron antes que
sus hijas durmieran en camas; muchísimos antes que cubrieran sus lozanas carnes con vestidos decentes. Dábales de comer sobria y me-
tódicamente, haciéndose partidaria en esto de
los preceptos higiénicos más en boga; pero la
comida en su casa era triste, como un pienso
dado a seres humanos.

En cuanto al pasto intelectual, la Señana
creía firmemente que con la erudición de su

esposo el señor Centeno, adquirida en copiosas
lecturas, tenía bastante la familia para merecer
el dictado de sapientísima, por lo cual no trató
de alimentar el espíritu de sus hijos con las
rancias enseñanzas que se dan en la escuela. Si
los mayores asistieron a ella, el más pequeño
vióse libre de maestros, y engolfado vivía durante doce horas diarias en el embrutecedor
trabajo de las minas, con lo cual toda la familia navegaba ancha y holgadamente por el
inmenso piélago de la estupidez.

Las dos hembras, Mariuca y Pepina, no carecían de encantos, siendo los pricipales su ju-
ventud y su robusted. Una de ellas leía de corrido; la otra no, y en cuanto a conocimientos del
mundo, fácilmente se comprende que no care-
cería de algunos rudimentos quien vivía entre
risueño coro de ninfas de distintas edades y pro-
cedencias, ocupadas en un trabajo mecánico y
con boca libre. Mariuca y Pepina eran muy
apechugadas, muy derechas, fuertes y erguidas
como amazonas. Vestían falda corta, mostrando
media pantorrilla y el carnoso pie descalzo, y
sus rudas cabezas habrían lucido bien sosteniendo un arquitrabe, como las mujeres de la
Caria. El polvillo de la calamina, que las teñía
de pies a cabeza, como a los demás trabajadores de las minas, dábales aire de colosales figuras de barro crudo.

Tanasio era un hombre apático. Su falta de carácter y de ambición rayaban en el idiotismo. Encerrado en las cuadras desde su infancia, ignorante de toda travesura, de toda contrariedad, de todo placer, de toda pena, aquel joven que ya había nacido dispuesto a ser máquina, se convirtió poco a poco en la herramienta más grosera. El día en que semejante ser tuviera una idea propia, se cambiaría el orden admirable de todas las cosas, por lo cual, ninguna piedra puede pensar.

Las relaciones de esta prole con su madre, que era gobernadora de toda la familia, eran las de una docilidad absoluta por parte de los hijos, y de un dominio soberano por parte de la Señana. El único que solía mostrar indicios de rebelión era el chiquitín. En sus cortos alcances, la Señana no comprendía aquella aspiración diabólica a dejar de ser piedra. ¿Por ventura había existencia más feliz y ejemplar que la de los peñascos? No admitía, no, que fuera cambiada, ni aun por la de canto rodado. Y Señana amaba a sus hijos; ¡pero hay tantas maneras de amar! Poníales por encima de todas las cosas, siempre que se avinieran a trabajar perpetuamente en las minas, a amasar en una sola artesa todos sus jornales, a obedecerla ciegamente y a no tener aspiraciones locas ni afán de lucir galas, ni de casarse antes de tiempo ni

de aprender diabluras, ni de meterse en sabidurías, porque los pobres—decía—siempre habían de ser pobres. y como pobres portarse, sin
farolear como los ricos y gente de la ciudad,
que estaba toda comida de vicios y podrida de
pecados.

Hemos descrito el trato que tenían en casa de
Centeno los hijos, para que se comprenda el que
tendría la Nela, criatura abandonada, sola, inútil, incapaz de ganar jornal, sin pasado, sin por-
venir, sin abolengo, sin esperanza, sin persona-
lidad, sin derecho a nada más que al sustento.
Señana se lo daba, creyendo firmemente que
su generosidad rayaba en heroísmo. Repetidas
veces dijo para sí al llenar la escudilla de la
Nela: «¡Qué bien me gano mi puestecico en el
Cielo!»

Y lo creía como el Evangelio. En su cerrada
mollera no entraban ni podían entrar otras luces sobre el santo ejercicio de la caridad; no
comprendía que una palabra cariñosa, un ha-
lago, un trato delicado y amante que hicieran
olvidar al pequeño su pequeñez, al miserable
su miseria, son heroísmos de más precio que
el bodrio sobrante de una mala comida. ¿Por
ventura no se daba lo mismo al gato? Y éste,
al menos, oía las voces más tiernas. Jamás oyó
la Nela què se la llamara *michita*, *monita*, ni
que le dijeran *repreciosa*, ni otros vocablos

melifluos y conmovedores con que era obse-
quiado el gato.

Jamás se le dio a entender a la Nela que había nacido de criatura humana, como los demás habitantes de la casa. Nunca fue castigada;
pero ella entendió que este previlegio se funda-
ba en la desdeñosa lástima que inspiraba su
menguada constitución física, y de ningún modo
en el aprecio de su persona.

Nunca se le dio a entender que tenía un alma
pronta a dar ricos frutos si se la cultivaba con
esmero, ni que llevaba en sí, como los demás
mortales, ese destello del eterno saber que se
nombra inteligencia humana, y que de aquel
destello podían salir infinitas luces y lumbre
bienhechora. Nunca se le dio a entender que en
su pequeñez fenomenal llevaba en sí el germen
de todos los sentimientos nobles y delicados, y
que aquellos menudos brotes podían ser flores
hermosísimas y lozanas, sin más cultivo que
una simple mirada de vez en cuando. Nunca se
le dio a entender que tenía derecho, por el mismo rigor de la Naturaleza al criarla, a ciertas
atenciones que pueden estar exentos los robustos, los sanos, los que tienen padres y casa
propia, pero que corresponden por jurispruden-
cia cristiana al inválido, al pobre, al huérfano
y al desheredado.

Por el contrario, todo le demostraba su semejanza con un canto rodado, el cual, ni siquiera tiene forma propia, sino aquella que le dan las aguas que lo arrastran y el puntapié del hombre que lo desprecia. Todo le demostraba que su jerarquía dentro de la casa era inferior a la del gato, cuyo lomo recibía blandas caricias, y a la del mirlo, que saltaba gozoso en su jaula.

Al menos, de éstos no se dijo nunca con cruel compasión: «Pobrecita, mejor cuenta le hubiera tenido morirse.»

5. Trabajo - Paisaje - Figura

El humo de los hornos, que durante toda la noche velaban respirando con bronco resoplido, se plateó vagamente en sus espirales más remotas; apareció risueña claridad por los lejanos términos y detrás de los montes, y poco a poco fueron saliendo sucesivamente de la sombra los cerros que rodean a Socartes, los inmensos taludes de tierra rojiza, los negros edificios. La campana del establecimiento gritó con aguda voz: «Al trabajo.», y cien y cien hombres soñolientos salieron de las casas, cabañas, chozas y agujeros. Rechinaban los goznes de las puertas; de las cuadras salían pausadamente las mulas, dirigiéndose solas al abrevadero, y el establecimiento, que poco antes semejaba una mansión fúnebre alumbrada por la claridad infernal de los hornos, se animaba moviendo sus miles de brazos.

El vapor principió a zumbar en las calderas del gran automóvil, que hacía funcionar a un tiempo los aparatos de los talleres y el aparato de lavado. El agua, que tan principal papel desempeñaba en esta operación, comenzó a correr por las altas cañerías, de donde debía saltar sobre los cilindros. Risotadas de mujeres y ladridos de hombres que venían de tomar la mañana, precedieron a la faena; y al fin empezaron a girar las cribas cilíndricas con infernal chillido; el agua corría de una en otra, pulverizándose, y la tierra sucia se atormentaba con vertiginoso voltear, rodando y cayendo de rueda en rueda hasta convertirse en fino polvo achocolatado. Sonaba aquello como mil mandíbulas de dientes flojos que mascaran arena; parecía molino por el movimiento mareante; calidoscopio por los juegos de la luz, del agua y de la tierra; enorme sonajero, de innúmeros cachivaches, compuesto por el ruido. No se podía fijar la atención, sin sentir vértigo, en aquel voltear incesante de una infinita madeja de hilos de agua, ora claros y transparentes, ora teñidos de rojo por la arcilla ferruginosa. Ni cabeza humana que no estuviera hecha a tal espectáculo, podría presenciar el feroz combate de mil ruedas dentadas, que sin cesar se mordían unas a otras; de ganchos que se cruzaban royéndose, y de tornillos que, al girar, clamaban con lastimero quejido pidiendo aceite.

El lavado estaba al aire libre. Las correas de transmisión venían zumbando desde el depar-

tamento de la máquina. Otras correas se pusieron en movimiento, y entonces oyóse un estam-
pido rítmico, un horrísono compás, a la manera
de gigantescos pasos o de un violento latido
interior de la madre tierra. Era el gran martillo-
pilón del taller, que había empezado a funcionar. Su formidable golpe machacaba el hierro
como blanda pasta, y esas formas de ruedas,
ejes y carriles, que nos parecen eternas por lo
duras, empezaban a desfigurarse, torciéndose y
haciendo muecas, como rostros afligidos. El
martillo, dando porrazos uniformes, creaba formas nuevas tan duras como las geológicas, que
son obra laboriosa de los siglos. Se parecen mucho, sí, las obras de la fuerza a las de la paciencia.

Hombres negros, que parecían el carbón hu-
manado, se reunían en torno a los objetos de
fuego que salían de las fraguas, y cogiéndolos
con aquella prolongación incandescente de los
dedos a quien llaman tenazas, los trabajaban.
¡Extraña escultura la que tiene por genio el fuego y por cincel el martillo! Las ruedas y ejes de
los millares de vagonetas, las piezas estropeadas
del aparato de lavado recibían allí compostura,
y eran construidos los picos, azadas y carreti-
llas. En el fondo del taller las sierras hacían
chillar la madera, y aquel mismo hierro, edu-
cado en el trabajo por el fuego, destrozaba

las generosas fibras del árbol arrancado a la tierra.

También afuera las mulas habían sido enganchadas a los largos trenes de vagonetas. Veíaselas pasar arrastrando tierra inútil para verterla en los taludes, o mineral para conducirlo al lavadero. Cruzábanse unos con otros aquellos largos reptiles, sin chocar nunca. Entraban por la boca de las galerías, siendo entonces perfecta su semejanza con los resbaladizos habitantes de las húmedas grietas; y cuando en las oscuridad del túnel relinchaba la indócil mula, creeríase que los saurios disputaban chillando. Allá en las más remotas cañadas, centenares de hombres golpeaban con picos la tierra para arrancarle, pedazo a pedazo, su tesoro. Eran los escultores de aquellas caprichosas e ingentes figuras que permanecían en pie, atentas, con gravedad silenciosa, a la invasión del hombre en las misteriosas esferas geológicas. Los mineros derrumbaban aquí, horadaban allá, cavaban más lejos, rasguñaban en otra parte, rompían la roca cretácea, desbarataban las graciosas láminas de pizarra samnita y esquistosa, despreciaban la caliza arcillosa, apartaban la limonita y el oligisto, destrozaban la preciosa dolomía, revolviendo incesantemente hasta dar con el silicato de cinc, esa plata de Europa que, no por ser la materia de que se

hacen las cacerolas, deja de ser grandiosa fuente de bienestar y civilización. Sobre ella ha al-
zado Bélgica el estandarte de su grandeza moral y política. ¡Oh! La hoja de lata tiene también
su epopeya.

El cielo estaba despejado; el sol derramaba
libremente sus rayos, y la vasta pertenencia
de Socartes resplandecía con súbito tono rojo.
Rojas eran las peñas esculturales; rojo el precioso mineral; roja la tierra inútil acumulada
en los largos taludes, semejantes a babilónicas
murallas; rojo el suelo; rojos los carriles y los
vagones; roja toda la maquinaria; roja el agua;
rojos los hombres y mujeres que trabajaban en
toda la extensión de Socartes. El color subido
de ladrillo era uniforme, con ligeros cambian-
tes, y general en todo: en la tierra y las casas,
en el hierro y en los vestidos. Las mujeres ocupadas en lavar parecían una pléyade de equívo-
cas ninfas de barro ferruginoso crudo. Por la
cañada abajo, en dirección al río, corría un
arroyo de agua encarnada. Creeríase que era el
sudor de aquel gran trabajo de hombres y máquinas, del hierro y de los músculos.

La Nela salió de su casa. También ella, sin
trabajar en las minas, estaba teñida ligeramente de rojo, porque el polvo de la tierra calami-
nífera no perdona a nadie. Llevaba en la mano
un mendrugo de pan que le había dado la Se-

ñana para desayunarse, y, comiéndoselo, marchaba aprisa, sin distraerse con nada, formal y
meditabunda. No tardó en pasar más allá de
los edificios, y después de subir el plano inclinado, subió la escalera labrada en la tierra,
hasta llegar a las casas de la barriada de Aldeacorba. La primera que se encontraba era una
primorosa vivienda infanzona, grande, sólida,
alegre, restaurada y pintada recientemente, con
cortafuegos de piedra, aleros labrados y ancho
escudo circundado de follaje granítico. Antes
faltara en ella el escudo que la parra, cuyos sar-
mientos, cargados de hoja, parecían un bigote
que aquélla tenía en el lugar correspondiente de
su cara, siendo las dos ventanas los ojos, el escudo la nariz, y el largo balcón la boca, siempre riendo. Para que la personificación fuera
completa, salía del balcón una viga destinada a
sujetar la cuerda de tender ropa, y con tal acce-
sorio, la casa con rostro estaba fumándose un
cigarro puro. Su tejado era en figura de gorra
de cuartel, y tenía una ventana de buhardilla
que parecía una borla. La chimenea no podía
ser más que una oreja. No era preciso ser fiso-
nomista para comprender que aquella casa res-
piraba paz, bienestar y una conciencia tranquila.

Dábale acceso un corralillo circundado de ta-
pias, y al costado derecho tenía una hermosa
huerta. Cuando la Nela entró, salían las vacas,

que iban a la pradera. Después de cambiar algunas palabras con el gañán, que era un mocetón formidable..., así como de tres cuartas de alto y de diez años de edad..., dirigióse a un señor obeso, bigotudo, entrecano, encarnado, de simpático rostro y afable mirar, de aspecto entre soldadesco y campesino, el cual apareció en mangas de camisa, con tirantes, y mostrando hasta el codo los velludos brazos. Antes que la muchacha hablara, el señor de los tirantes volvióse adentro y dijo:

—Hijo mío, aquí tienes a la Nela.

Salió de la casa un joven, estatua del más excelso barro humano, suave, derecho, con la cabeza inmóvil, los ojos clavados y fijos en sus órbitas, como lentes expuestos en un muestrario. Su cara parecía de marfil, contorneada con exquisita finura; mas teniendo su tez la suavidad de la de una doncella, era varonil en gran manera, y no había en sus facciones parte alguna ni rasgo que no tuviese aquella perfección soberana con que fue expresado hace miles de años el pensamiento helénico. Aun sus ojos puramente escultóricos, porque carecían de vista, eran hermosísimos, grandes y rasgados. Desvirtuábalos su fijeza y la idea de que tras aquella fijeza estaba la noche. Falto del don que constituye el núcleo de la expresión humana, aquel rostro de Antinoo ciego poseía la fría serenidad del mármol, convertido por el genio y el cincel en estatua, y por la fuerza vital en persona. Un soplo, un rayo de luz, una sensación, bastarían para animar la hermosa piedra, que teniendo ya todas las galas de la forma, carecía tan sólo de la conciencia de su propia belleza, la cual emana de la facultad de conocer la belleza exterior.

Su edad no pasaba de los veinte años; su cuerpo, sólido y airoso, con admirables proporciones construido, era digno en todo de la sin igual cabeza que sustentaba. Jamás se vio incorrección más lastimosa de la Naturaleza que la que el tal representaba, recibiendo por una parte admirables dones, privado por otra de la facultad que más comunica al hombre con sus semejantes y con el maravilloso conjunto de lo creado. Era tal la incorrección, que aquellos prodigiosos dones quedaban como inútiles, del mismo modo que si al ser creadas todas las cosas hubiéralas dejado el Hacedor a oscuras, para que no pudieran recrearse en sus propios encantos. Para mayor desdicha, había recibido el joven portentosa luz interior, un entendimiento de primer orden. Esto y carecer de la facultad de percibir la idea visible, la forma, siendo al mismo tiempo divino como un ángel, hermoso como un hombre y ciego como un vegetal, era fuerte cosa ciertamente. No compren-

demos, ¡ay!, el secreto de estas horrendas im-
perfecciones. Si lo comprendiéramos, se abri-
rían para nosotros las puertas que ocultan pri-
mordiales misterios del orden moral y del orden
físico; comprenderíamos el inmenso misterio
de la desgracia, del mal, de la muerte, y podríamos medir la perpetua sombra que sin
cesar sigue al bien y a la vida.

Don Francisco de Penáguilas, padre del joven,
era un hombre más que bueno: era inmejora-
ble, superiormente discreto, bondadoso, afable,
honrado y magnánimo, no falto de instrucción.
Nadie le aborreció jamás; era el más respetado
de todos los propietarios ricos del país, y más
de una cuestión se arregló por la mediación,
siempre inteligente, del *señor de Aldeacorba
de Suso*. La casa en que le hemos visto fue su
cuna. Había estado de joven en América, y al
regresar a España sin fortuna, entró a servir en
la Guardia Civil. Retirado a su pueblo natal,
donde se dedicaba a la labranza y a la ganade-
ría, heredó regular hacienda, y en la época de
nuestra historia acababa de heredar otra mayor.

Su esposa, andaluza, había muerto en edad
muy temprana, dejándole un solo hijo, que a
poco de nacer demostró hallarse privado en
absoluto del más precioso de los sentidos. Esto
fue la pena más aguda que amargó los días del
buen padre. ¿Qué le importaba allegar riqueza

y ver que la fortuna favorecía sus intereses y
sonreía en su casa? ¿Para quién era esto? Para
quien no podía ver ni las gordas vacas, ni las
praderas risueñas, ni la huerta cargada de fru-
tas. Don Francisco hubiera dado sus ojos a su
hijo, quedándose él ciego el resto de sus días,
si esta especie de generosidades fuesen practi-
cables en el mundo que conocemos; pero como
no lo son, no podía don Francisco dar realidad
al noble sentimiento de su corazón sino pro-
porcionando al desgraciado joven todo cuanto
pudiera hacerle menos ingrata la oscuridad en
que vivía. Para él eran todos los cuidados y los
infinitos mimos y delicadezas cuyo secreto pertenece a las madres, y algunas veces a los padres, cuando faltan aquéllas. Jamás contraria-
ba a su hijo en nada que fuera para su consuelo
y distracción en los límites de lo honesto y moral. Divertíale con cuentos y lecturas; tratábale
con solícito esmero, atendiendo a su salud, a
sus goces legítimos, a su instrucción y a su educación cristiana; porque el señor de Penáguilas,
que era un sí es no es severo de principios,
decía: «No quiero que mi hijo sea ciego dos
veces.»

Viéndole salir, y que la Nela le acompañaba
fuera, díjoles cariñosamente:

—No os alejéis hoy mucho. No corráis...
Adiós.

3

Miróles desde la portalada hasta que dieron vuelta a la tapia de la huerta. Después entró, porque tenía que hacer varias cosas: escribir una esquela a su hermano Manuel, ordeñar una vaca, podar un árbol y ver si había puesto la gallina pintada.

Pablo y Marianela salieron al campo, precedidos de *Choto*, que iba y volvía gozoso y saltón, moviendo la cola y repartiendo por igual sus caricias entre su amo y el lazarillo de su amo.

—Nela—dijo Pablo—, hoy está el día muy hermoso. El aire que corre es suave y fresco, y el sol calienta sin quemar. ¿Adónde vamos?

—Echaremos por estos prados adelante—replicó la Nela, metiendo su mano en una de las faltriqueras de la americana del mancebo—. ¿A ver qué me has traído hoy?

—Busca, bien, y encontrarás algo—dijo Pablo, riendo.

—¡Ah, Madre de Dios! Chocolate crudo... ¡Y poco que me gusta el chocolate crudo!... Nueces..., una cosa envuelta en un papel...

—¿Adónde vamos hoy?—repitió el ciego.

—Adonde quieras, niño de mi corazón—repuso la Nela, comiéndose el dulce y arrojando el papel que lo envolvía—. Pide por esa boca, rey del mundo.

Los negros ojuelos de la Nela brillaban de
contento, y su cara de avecilla graciosa y viva-
racha multiplicaba sus medios de expresión,
moviéndose sin cesar. Mirándola, se creía ver
un relampagueo de reflejos temblorosos, como
los que produce la luz sobre la superficie del
agua agitada. Aquella débil criatura, en la cual
parecía que el alma estaba como prensada y
constreñida dentro de un cuerpo miserable, se
ensanchaba, se crecía maravillosamente al hallarse sola con su amo y amigo. Junto a él
tenía espontaneidad, agudeza, sensibilidad, gracia, donosura, fantasía. Al separarse, creeríase
que se cerraban sobre ella las negras puertas
de una prisión.

—Pues yo digo que iremos adonde tú quieras
—observó el ciego—. Me gusta obedecerte. Si
te parece bien, iremos al bosque que está más
allá de Saldeoro. Esto si te parece bien.

—Bueno, bueno, iremos al bosque—exclamó
la Nela, batiendo palmas—. Pero como no hay
prisa, nos sentaremos cuando estemos can-
sados.

—Y que no es poco agradable aquel sitio
donde está la fuente, ¿sabes, Nela?, y donde
hay unos troncos muy grandes, que parecen
puestos allí para que nos sentemos nosotros, y
donde se oyen cantar tantos, tantísimos pájaros, que es aquello la gloria.

—Pasaremos por donde está el molino, de quien tú dices que habla mascullando las palabras como un borracho. ¡Ay, qué hermoso día y qué contenta estoy!

—¿Brilla mucho el sol, Nela? Aunque me digas que sí, no lo entenderé, porque no sé lo que es brillar.

—Brilla mucho, sí, señorito mío. ¿Y a ti qué te importa eso? El sol es muy feo. No se le puede mirar a la cara.

—¿Por qué?

—Porque duele.

—¿Qué duele?

—La vista. ¿Qué sientes tú cuando estás alegre?

—¿Cuando estoy libre, contigo, solos los dos en el campo?

—Sí.

—Pues siento que me nace dentro del pecho una frescura, una suavidad dulce...

—¡Ahí te quiero ver! ¡Madre de Dios! Pues ya sabes cómo brilla el sol.

—¿Con frescura?

—No, tonto.

—Pues ¿con qué?

—Con eso.

—Con eso... ¿Y qué es eso?

—Eso—afirmó nuevamente la Nela con acento de firme convicción.

—Ya veo que esas cosas no se pueden explicar. Antes me formaba yo idea del día y de la noche. ¿Cómo? Verás: era de día, cuando hablaba la gente; era de noche, cuando la gente callaba y cantaban los gallos. Ahora no hago las mismas comparaciones. Es de día, cuando estamos juntos tú y yo; es de noche, cuando nos separamos.

—¡Ay, divina Madre de Dios!—exclamó la Nela, echándose atrás las guedejas que le caían sobre la frente—. A mí, que tengo ojos, me parece lo mismo.

—Voy a pedirle a mi padre que te deje vivir en mi casa para que no te separes de mí.

—Bien, bien—dijo María, batiendo palmas otra vez.

Y diciéndolo, se adelantó saltando algunos pasos; y recogiendo con extrema gracia sus faldas, empezó a bailar.

—¿Qué haces, Nela?

—¡Ah, niño mío, estoy bailando! Mi contento es tan grande, que me han entrado ganas de bailar.

Pero fue preciso saltar una pequeña cerca, y la Nela ofreció su mano al ciego. Después de pasar aquel obstáculo, siguieron por una calleja tapizada en sus dos rústicas paredes de lozanas hiedras y espinos. La Nela apartaba las ramas para que no picaran el rostro de su amigo, y al fin, después de bajar gran trecho, subieron una cuesta por entre frondosos castaños y nogales. Al llegar arriba, Pablo dijo a su compañera:

—Si no te parece mal, sentémonos aquí. Siento pasos de gente.

—Son los aldeanos que vuelven del mercado de Homedes. Hoy es miércoles. El camino real está delante de nosotros. Sentémonos aquí antes de entrar en el camino real.

—Es lo mejor que podemos hacer. *Choto*, ven acá.

Los tres se sentaron.

—¡Si está esto lleno de flores!...—exclamó la Nela—. ¡Madre, qué guapas!

—Cógeme un ramo. Aunque no las veo, me gusta tenerlas en mi mano. Se me figura que las oigo.

—Eso sí que es gracioso.

—Paréceme que teniéndolas en mi mano me dan a entender..., no puedo decirte cómo..., que son bonitas. Dentro de mí hay una cosa, no puedo decirte qué..., una cosa que responde a ellas. ¡Ay, Nela, se me figura que por dentro yo veo algo!

—¡Oh!, si lo entiendo...; como que todos lo tenemos dentro. El sol, las hierbas, la luna y el cielo grande y azul, lleno siempre de estrellas..., todo, todo lo tenemos dentro; quiero de-

cir que, además de las cosas divinas que hay
fuera, nosotros llevamos otras dentro. Y nada
más... Aquí tienes una flor, otra, otra, seis;
todas son distintas. ¿A que no sabes tú lo que
son las flores?

—Pues las flores—dijo el ciego, algo confundido, acercándolas a su rostro—son... unas como sonrisillas que echa la tierra... La verdad,
no sé mucho del reino vegetal.

—¡Madre divinísima, qué poca ciencia!—exclamó María, acariciando las manos de su amigo—. Las flores son las estrellas de la tierra.

—Vaya un disparate. Y las estrellas, ¿qué
son?

—Las estrellas son las miradas de los que
se han ido al cielo.

—Entonces, las flores...

—Son las miradas de los que se han muerto
y no han ido todavía al cielo—afirmó la Nela
con entera convicción—. Los muertos son en-
terrados en la tierra. Como allá abajo no pueden estar sin echar una miradilla a la tierra,
echan de sí una cosa que sube en forma y manera de flor. Cuando en un prado hay muchas
flores es porque allá..., en tiempos atrás, enterraron en él muchos difuntos.

—No, no—replicó Pablo con seriedad—. No
creas desatinos. Nuestra religión nos enseña
que el espíritu se separa de la carne y que la

vida mortal se acaba. Lo que se entierra, Nela, no es más que un despojo, un barro inservible que no puede pensar, ni sentir, ni tampoco ver.

—Eso lo dirán los libros, que, según dice la Señana, están llenos de mentiras.

—Eso lo dicen la fe y la razón, querida Nela. Tu imaginación te hace creer mil errores. Poco a poco yo los iré destruyendo, y tendrás ideas buenas sobre todas las cosas de este mundo y del otro.

—¡Ay, ay, con el doctorcillo de tres por un cuarto!... Ya..., ¿pues no has querido hacerme creer que el sol está quieto y que la tierra da vueltas a la redonda?... ¡Cómo se conoce que no los ves! ¡Madre del Señor! Que me muera en este momento si la tierra no se está más quieta que un peñón y el sol va corre que corre. Señorito mío, no se la eche de tan sabio, que yo he pasado muchas horas de noche y de día mirando al cielo, y sé cómo está gobernada toda esa máquina... La tierra está abajo, toda llena de islitas grandes y chicas. El sol sale por allá y se esconde por allí. Es el palacio de Dios.

—¡Qué tonta!

—¿Y por qué no ha de ser así? ¡Ay! Tú no has visto el cielo en un día claro, hijito. Parece que llueven bendiciones... Yo no creo que pueda haber malos; no, no los puede haber, si

vuelven la cara hacia arriba y ven aquel ojazo
que nos está mirando.

—Tu religiosidad, Nelilla, está llena de supersticiones. Yo te enseñaré ideas mejores.

—No me han enseñado nada—dijo María con
inocencia—; pero yo, cavila que cavilarás, he
ido sacando de mi cabeza muchas cosas que
me consuelan, y así, cuando me ocurre una
buena idea, digo: «Esto debe de ser así, y no
de otra manera.» Por las noches, cuando me
voy sola a mi casa, voy pensando en lo que
será de nosotros cuando nos muramos, y en
lo mucho que nos quiere a todos la Virgen
Santísima.

—Nuestra Madre amorosa.

—¡Nuestra Madre querida! Yo miro al cielo,
y la siento encima de mí como cuando nos
acercamos a una persona y sentimos el calor-
cillo de su respiración. Ella nos mira de noche y de día por medio de…, no te rías…, por
medio de todas las cosas hermosas que hay
en el mundo.

—¿Y esas cosas hermosas…?

—Son sus ojos, tonto. Bien lo comprenderías
si tuvieras los tuyos. Quien no ha visto una
nube blanca, un árbol, una flor, el agua corriendo, un niño, el rocío, un corderito, la luna paseándose tan maja por los cielos, y las estre-

llas, que son las miradas de los buenos que se han muerto...

—Mal podrán ir allá arriba si se quedan debajo de tierra echando flores.

—¡Miren el sabihondo! Abajo se están mientras se van limpiando de pecados, que después suben volando arriba. La Virgen les espera. Sí, créelo, tonto. Las estrellas, ¿qué pueden ser sino las almas de los que ya están salvos? ¿Y no sabes tú que las estrellas bajan? Pues yo, yo misma las he visto caer así, así, haciendo una raya. Sí, señor; las estrellas bajan cuando tienen que decirnos alguna cosa.

—¡Ay, Nela!—exclamó Pablo vivamente—. Tus disparates, con serlo tan grandes, me cautivan, porque revelan el candor de tu alma y la fuerza de tu fantasía. Todos esos errores responden a una disposición muy grande para conocer la verdad, a una poderosa facultad tuya, que sería primorosa si estuviera auxiliada por la razón y la educación... Es preciso que tú adquieras un don precioso de que yo estoy privado; es preciso que aprendas a leer.

—¡A leer!... ¿Y quién me ha de enseñar?

—Mi padre. Yo le rogaré a mi padre que te enseñe. Ya sabes que él no me niega nada. ¡Qué lástima tan grande que vivas así! Tu alma está llena de preciosos tesoros. Tienes bondad sin igual y fantasía seductora. De todo lo que

Dios tiene en su esencia absoluta, te dio a ti
parte muy grande. Bien lo conozco; no veo lo
de fuera, pero veo lo de dentro, y todas las
maravillas de tu alma se me han revelado desde que eres mi lazarillo... ¡Hace año y medio!
Parece que fue ayer cuando empezaron nuestros paseos... No, hace miles de años que te
conozco. ¡Porque hay una relación tan grande
entre lo que tú sientes y lo que yo siento!...
Has dicho ahora mil disparates, y yo, que conozco algo de la verdad acerca del mundo y
de la religión, me he sentido conmovido y en-
tusiasmado al oírte. Se me antoja que hablas
dentro de mí.

—¡Madre de Dios!—exclamó la Nela, cruzando las manos—. ¿Tendrá eso algo que ver con
lo que yo siento?

—¿Qué?

—Que estoy en el mundo para ser tu lazarillo, y que mis ojos no servirían para nada si
no sirvieran para guiarte y decirte cómo son
todas las hermosuras de la Tierra.

El ciego irguió su cuello repentina y vivísi-
mamente, y extendiendo sus manos hasta tocar el cuerpecillo de su amiga, exclamó con
afán:

—Dime, Nela, ¿y cómo eres tú?

La Nela no dijo nada. Había recibido una
puñalada.

Habían descansado. Siguieron adelante, hasta llegar a la entrada del bosque que hay más allá de Saldeoro. Detuviéronse entre un grupo de nogales viejos, cuyos troncos y raíces formaban en el suelo una serie de escalones, con musgosos huecos y recortes tan apropiados para sentarse, que el arte no los hiciera mejor. Desde lo alto del bosque corría un hilo de agua, saltando de piedra en piedra, hasta dar con su fatigado cuerpo en un estanquillo que servía de depósito para alimentar el chorro de que se abastecían los vecinos. Enfrente, el suelo se deprimía poco a poco, ofreciendo grandioso panorama de verdes colinas pobladas de bosques y caseríos, de praderas llanas donde pastaban con tranquilidad vagabunda centenares de reses. En el último término, dos lejanos y orgullosos cerros, que eran límite de la tierra, dejaban ver en un largo segmento el azul purísimo del mar. Era un paisaje cuya contemplación revelaba al alma sus excelsas relaciones con lo infinito.

Sentóse Pablo en el tronco de un nogal, apoyando su brazo izquierdo en el borde del estanque. Alzaba la derecha mano para coger las ramas que descendían hasta tocar su frente, con lo cual pasaba a ratos, con el mover de las hojas, un rayo de sol.

—¿Qué haces, Nela?—dijo el muchacho después de una pausa, no sintiendo ni los pasos, ni la voz, ni la respiración de su compañera—. ¿Qué haces? ¿Dónde estás?

—Aquí—replicó la Nela, tocándole el hombro—. Estaba mirando el mar.

—¡Ah! ¿Está muy lejos?

—Allá se ve por los cerros de Ficóbriga.

—Grande, grandísimo, tan grande que estaremos mirando todo un día sin acabarlo de ver; ¿no es eso?

—No se ve sino un pedazo como el que coges dentro de la boca cuando le pegas una mordida a un pan.

—Ya, ya comprendo. Todos dicen que ninguna hermosura iguala a la del mar, por causa de la sencillez que hay en él... Oye, Nela, lo que voy a decirte... ¿Pero qué haces?

La Nela, agarrando con ambas manos la rama del nogal, se suspendía y balanceaba graciosamente.

—Aquí estoy, señorito mío. Estaba pensando que por qué no nos daría Dios a nosotras las personas alas para volar como los pájaros. ¡Qué cosa más bonita que hacer... zas, y remontarnos y ponernos de un vuelo en aquel pico que está allá entre Ficóbriga y el mar!...

—Si Dios no nos ha dado alas, en cambio nos ha dado el pensamiento, que vuela más que todos los pájaros, porque llega hasta el mismo Dios... Dime tú: ¿para qué querría yo alas de pájaro, si Dios me hubiera negado el pensamiento?

—Pues a mí me gustaría tener las dos cosas. Y si tuviera alas, te cogería en mi piquito para llevarte por esos mundos y subirte a lo más alto de las nubes.

El ciego alargó su mano hasta tocar la cabeza de la Nela.

—Siéntate junto a mí. ¿No estás cansada?

—Un poquitín—replicó ella, sentándose y apoyando su cabeza con infantil confianza en el hombro de su amo.

—Respiras fuerte, Nelilla; tú estás muy cansada. Es de tanto volar... Pues lo que te iba a decir es esto: hablando del mar me hiciste recordar una cosa que mi padre me leyó anoche. Ya sabes que desde la edad en que tuve uso de razón, acostumbra mi padre leerme todas las noches distintos libros de ciencias y de historia, de artes y de entretenimiento. Esas lecturas y estos paseos se puede decir que son

mi vida toda. Diome el Señor, para compensar-
me de la ceguera, una memoria feliz, y gracias
a ella he sacado algún provecho de las lecturas, pues aunque éstas han sido sin método,
yo, al fin y al cabo, he logrado poner algún
orden en las ideas que iban entrando en mi
entendimiento. ¡Qué delicias tan grandes las
mías al entender el orden admirable del Universo, el concertado rodar de los astros, el giro
de los átomos pequeñitos, y después las leyes,
más admirables aún, que gobiernan nuestra
alma! También me ha recreado mucho la Historia, que es un cuento verdadero de todo lo
que los hombres han hecho antes de ahora, resultando, hija mía, que siempre han hecho las
mismas maldades y las mismas tonterías, aunque no han cesado de mejorarse, acercándose
todo lo posible, mas sin llegar nunca, a las
perfecciones que sólo posee Dios. Por último,
me ha leído mi padre cosas sutiles y un poco
hondas para ser penetradas de pronto, pero
que suspenden y enamoran cuando se medita
en ellas. Es lectura que a él no le agrada, por
no comprenderla, y que a mí me ha cansado
también unas veces, deleitándome otras. Pero
no hay duda que cuando se da con un autor
que sepa hablar con claridad, esas materias
son preciosas. Contienen ideas sobre las causas y los efectos, sobre el por qué de lo que

pensamos y el modo como lo pensamos, y enseñan la esencia de todas las cosas.

La Nela parecía no entender ni una palabra de lo que su amigo decía; pero atendía con toda su alma, abriendo la boca. Para apoderarse de aquellas esencias y causas de que su amo le hablaba, abría el pico como el pájaro que acecha el vuelo de la mosca que quiere cazar.

—Pues bien—añadió él—: anoche leyó mi padre unas páginas sobre la belleza. Hablaba el autor de la belleza, y decía que era el resplandor de la bondad y de la verdad, con otros muchos conceptos ingeniosos, y tan bien traídos y pensados que daba gusto oírlos.

—Ese libro—dijo la Nela, queriendo demostrar suficiencia—no será como uno que tiene padre Centeno que llaman... *Las mil y no sé cuántas noches*.

—No es eso, tontuela; habla de la belleza en absoluto...; ¿no entenderás esto de la belleza ideal?...; tampoco lo entiendes..., porque has de saber que hay una belleza que no se ve ni se toca, ni se percibe con ningún sentido.

—Como, por ejemplo, la Virgen María—interrumpió la Nela—, a quien no vemos ni tocamos, porque las imágenes no son ella misma, sino su retrato.

—Estás en lo cierto; así es. Pensando en esto,

mi padre cerró el libro, y él decía una cosa y yo otra. Hablamos de la forma, y mi padre me dijo: «Desgraciadamente, tú no puedes comprenderla.» Yo sostuve que sí; dije que no había más que una sola belleza, y que ésta había de servir para todo.

La Nela, poco atenta a cosas tan sutiles, había cogido de las manos de su amigo las flores, y combinaba sus colores risueños.

—Yo tenía una idea sobre esto—añadió el ciego con mucha energía—, una idea con la cual estoy encariñado desde hace algunos meses. Sí, lo sostengo, lo sostengo... No, no me hacen falta los ojos para esto. Yo le dije a mi padre: «Concibo un tipo de belleza encantadora, un tipo que contiene todas las bellezas posibles; ese tipo es la Nela.» Mi padre se echó a reír y me dijo que sí.

La Nela se puso como amapola, y no supo responder nada. Durante un breve instante de terror y ansiedad, creyó que el ciego la estaba *mirando.*

—Sí, tú eres la belleza más acabada que puede imaginarse—añadió Pablo con calor—. ¿Cómo podría suceder que tu bondad, tu inocencia, tu candor, tu gracia, tu imaginación, tu alma celestial y cariñosa, que ha sido capaz de alegrar mis tristes días; cómo podría suceder, cómo, que no estuviese representada en la

misma hermosura?... Nela, Nela—añadió balbu-
ciente y con afán—. ¿No es verdad que eres
muy bonita?

La Nela calló. Instintivamente se había llevado las manos a la cabeza, enredando entre sus
cabellos las florecitas medio ajadas que había
cogido antes en la pradera.

—¿No respondes?... Es verdad que eres modesta. Si no lo fueras, no serías tan repreciosa
como eres. Faltaría la lógica de las bellezas, y
eso no puede ser. ¿No respondes?...

—Yo...—murmuró la Nela con timidez, sin
dejar de la mano su tocado—, no sé...; dicen
que cuando niña era muy bonita... Ahora...

—Y ahora también.

María, en su extraordinaria confusión, pudo
hablar así:

—Ahora..., ya sabes tú que las personas dicen muchas tonterías..., se equivocan también...; a veces, el que tiene más ojos ve menos.

—¡Oh! ¡Qué bien dicho! Ven acá, dame un
abrazo.

La Nela no pudo acudir pronto, porque habiendo conseguido sostener entre sus cabellos
una como guirnalda de florecillas, sintió vivos
deseos de observar el efecto de aquel atavío en
el claro cristal del agua. Por primera vez desde
que vivía se sintió presumida. Apoyándose en
sus manos, asomóse al estanque.

—¿Qué haces, Mariquilla?

—Me estoy mirando en el agua, que es como un espejo—replicó con la mayor inocencia delatando su presunción.

—Tú no necesitas mirarte. Eres hermosa como los ángeles que rodean el trono de Dios.

El alma del ciego llenábase de entusiasmo y fervor.

—El agua se ha puesto a temblar—dijo la Nela—, y yo no me veo bien, señorito. Ella tiembla como yo. Ya está más tranquila, ya no se mueve... Me estoy mirando... ahora.

—¡Qué linda eres! Ven acá, niña mía—añadió el ciego, extendiendo sus brazos.

—¡Linda yo!—dijo ella, llena de confusión y ansiedad—. Pues esa que veo en el estanque no es tan fea como dicen. Es que hay también muchos que no saben ver.

—Sí, muchos.

—¡Si yo me vistiese como se visten otras...! —exclamó la chiquilla con orgullo.

—Te vestirás.

—¿Y ese libro dice que yo soy bonita?—preguntó ella, apelando a todos los recursos de convicción.

—Lo digo yo, que poseo una verdad inmutable—exclamó el ciego, llevado de su ardiente fantasía.

—Puede ser—observó la Nela, apartándose

de su espejo pensativa y no muy satisfecha—
que los hombres sean muy brutos y no com-
prendan las cosas como son.

—La Humanidad está sujeta a mil errores.

—Así lo creo—dijo Mariquilla, recibiendo
gran consuelo con las palabras de su amigo—.
¿Por qué han de reírse de mí?

—¡Oh, miserable condición de los hombres!
—exclamó el ciego, arrastrado al absurdo por
su delirante entendimiento—. El don de la vista
puede causar grandes extravíos..., aparta a los
hombres de la posesión de la verdad absoluta..., y la verdad absoluta dice que tú eres hermosa, hermosa sin tacha ni sombra alguna de
fealdad. Que me digan lo contrario, y les des-
mentiré... Váyanse ellos a paseo con sus formas. No..., la forma no puede ser la máscara
de Satanás puesta ante la faz de Dios. ¡Ah!,
¡menguados! ¡A cuántos desvaríos os conducen
vuestros ojos! Nela, Nela, ven acá, quiero tenerte junto a mí y abrazar tu preciosa cabeza.

María se arrojó en los brazos de su amigo.

—Chiquilla bonita—exclamó éste, estrechán-
dola de un modo delirante contra su pecho—,
¡te quiero con toda mi alma!

La Nela no dijo nada. En su corazón, lleno
de casta ternura, se desbordaban los sentimientos más hermosos. El joven, palpitante y con-

turbado, la abrazó más fuerte, diciéndole al oído:

—Te quiero más que a mi vida. Angel de Dios, quiéreme o me muero.

María se soltó de los brazos de Pablo, y éste cayó en profunda meditación. Una fuerza poderosa, irresistible, la impulsaba a mirarse en el espejo del agua. Deslizándose suavemente llegó al borde, y vio allá sobre el fondo verdoso su imagen mezquina, con los ojuelos negros, la tez pecosa, la naricilla picuda, aunque no sin gracia; el cabello escaso y la movible fisonomía de pájaro. Alargó su cuerpo para verse el busto, y lo halló deplorablemente desairado. Las flores que tenía en la cabeza se cayeron al agua, haciendo temblar la superficie, y con la superficie, la imagen. La hija de la Canela sintió como si arrancaran su corazón de raíz, y cayó hacia atrás murmurando:

—¡Madre de Dios, qué feísima soy!

—¿Qué dices, Nela? Me parece que he oído tu voz.

—No decía nada, niño mío... Estaba pensando..., sí, pensaba que ya es hora de volver a tu casa. Pronto será hora de comer.

—Sí, vamos, comerás conmigo, y esta tarde saldremos otra vez. Dame la mano; no quiero que te separes de mí.

Cuando llegaron a la casa, don Francisco de

Penáguilas estaba en el patio, acompañado de dos caballeros. Marianela reconoció al ingeniero de las minas y al individuo que se había extraviado en la Terrible la noche anterior.

—Aquí están—dijo—el señor ingeniero y su hermano, el caballero de anoche.

Miraban los tres hombres con visible interés al ciego, que se acercaba.

—Hace rato que te estamos esperando, hijo mío—indicó don Francisco, tomando al ciego de la mano y presentándole al doctor.

—Entremos—dijo el ingeniero.

—¡Benditos sean los hombres sabios y caritativos!—exclamó el padre, mirando a Teodoro—. Pasen ustedes, señores. Que sea bendito el instante en que entran en mi casa.

—Veamos este caso—murmuró Golfín.

Cuando Pablo y los dos hermanos entraron, don Francisco se volvió hacia Mariquilla, que se había quedado en medio del patio inmóvil y asombrada, y le dijo con bondad:

—Mira, Nela, más vale que te vayas. Mi hijo no puede salir esta tarde.

Y luego, como viese que no se marchaba, añadió:

—Puedes pasar a la cocina. Dorotea te dará alguna chuchería.

Al día siguiente Pablo y su guía salieron de la casa a la misma hora del anterior; mas como estaba encapotado el cielo y soplaba un airecillo. molesto que amenazaba convertirse en vendaval, decidieron que su paseo no fuera largo. Atravesando el prado comunal de Aldeacorba, siguieron el gran talud de las minas por Poniente con intención de bajar a las excavaciones.

—Nela, tengo que hablarte de una cosa que te hará saltar de alegría—dijo el ciego, cuando estuvieron lejos de la casa—. ¡Nela, yo siento en mi corazón un alborozo...! Me parece que el Universo, las Ciencias, la Historia, la Filosofía, la Naturaleza, todo eso que he aprendido, se me ha metido dentro y se está paseando por mí..., es como una procesión. Ya viste aquellos caballeros que me esperaban ayer...

—Don Carlos y su hermano, el que encontramos anoche.

—El cual es un famoso sabio que ha corrido por toda la América haciendo maravillosas

curas... Ha venido a visitar a su hermano...
Como don Carlos es tan buen amigo de mi padre, le ha rogado que me examine... ¡Qué cariñoso y qué bueno es! Primero estuvo hablando
conmigo: preguntóme varias cosas, y me contó
otras muy chuscas y divertidas. Después díjo-
me que me estuviese quieto, sentí sus dedos en
mis párpados...; al cabo de un gran rato dijo
unas palabras que no entendí: eran términos
de Medicina. Mi padre no me ha leído nunca
nada de Medicina. Acercáronme después a una
ventana. Mientras me observaba con no sé qué
instrumento, ¡había en la sala un silencio...! El
doctor dijo después a mi padre: «Se intenta-
rá.» Decían otras cosas en voz muy baja para
que no pudiera yo entenderlas, y creo que también hablaban por señas. Cuando se retiraron,
mi padre me dijo: «Niño de mi alma, no puedo
ocultarte la alegría que hay dentro de mí. Ese
hombre, ese ángel de Dios, me ha dado esperanza, muy poca; pero la esperanza parece que
se agarra más cuando más chica es. Quiero
echarla de mí diciéndome que es imposible, no,
no, casi imposible, y ella..., pegada como una
lapa.» Así me habló mi padre. Por su voz conocí que lloraba... ¿Qué haces, Nela, estás bailando?

—No, estoy aquí a tu lado.

—Como otras veces te pones a bailar desde

que te digo una cosa alegre... ¿Pero hacia dónde vamos hoy?

—El día está feo. Vámonos hacia la Trascava, que es sitio abrigado, y después bajaremos al Barco y a la Terrible.

—Bien, como tú quieras... ¡Ay, Nela, compañera mía, si fuese verdad, si Dios quisiera tener piedad de mí y me concediera el placer de verte!... Aunque sólo durara un día mi vista, aunque volviera a cegar al siguiente, ¡cuánto se lo agradecería!

La Nela no dijo nada. Después de mostrar exaltada alegría, meditaba con los ojos fijos en el suelo.

—Se ven en el mundo cosas muy extrañas —añadió Pablo—, y la misericordia de Dios tiene así... ciertos ex abruptos, lo mismo que su cólera. Vienen de improviso, después de largos tormentos y castigos, lo mismo que aparece la ira después de felicidades que se creían seguras y eternas, ¿no te parece?

—Sí, lo que tú esperas será—dijo la Nela con aplomo.

—¿Por qué lo sabes?

—Me lo dice mi corazón.

—¡Te lo dice tu corazón! ¿Y por qué no han de ser ciertos estos avisos?—manifestó Pablo con ardor—. Sí, las almas escogidas pueden en casos dados presentir un suceso. Yo lo he obser-

vado en mí, pues como el ver no me distrae
del examen de mí mismo, he notado que mi espíritu me susurraba cosas incomprensibles.
Después ha venido un acontecimiento cualquiera, y he dicho con asombro: «Yo sabía algo
de esto.»

—A mí me sucede lo mismo—repuso la Ne-
la—. Ayer me dijiste tú que me querías mucho.
Cuando fui a mi casa, iba diciendo para mí:
«Es cosa rara, pero yo sabía algo de esto.»

—Es maravilloso, chiquilla mía, cómo están
acordadas nuestras almas. Unidas por la voluntad, no les falta más que un lazo. Ese lazo lo
tendrán si yo adquiero el precioso sentido que
me falta. La idea de ver no se determina en mi
pensamiento si antes no acaricio en él la idea
de quererte más. La adquisición de este sentido
no significa para mí otra cosa que el don de
admirar de un modo nuevo lo que ya me causa
tanta admiración como amor... Pero se me figura que estás triste hoy.

—Sí que lo estoy..., y si he de decirte la verdad, no sé por qué... Estoy muy alegre y muy
triste; las dos cosas a un tiempo. ¡Hoy está tan
feo el día!... Valiera más que no hubiese día, y
que fuera noche siempre.

—No, no; déjalo como está. Noche y día, si
Dios dispone que yo sepa al fin diferenciarlos,
¡cuán feliz seré!... ¿Por qué nos detenemos?

—Estamos en un lugar peligroso. Apartémonos a un lado para tomar la vereda.

—¡Ah!, la Trascava. Este césped resbaladizo va bajando hasta perderse en la gruta. El que cae en ella no puede volver a salir. Vámonos, Nela; no me gusta este sitio.

—Tonto, de aquí a la entrada de la cueva hay mucho que andar. ¡Y qué bonita está hoy!

La Nela, deteniéndose y sujetando a su compañero por el brazo, observaba la boca de la sima, que se abría en el terreno en forma parecida a la de un embudo. Finísimo césped cubría las vertientes de aquel pequeño cráter cóncavo y profundo. En lo más hondo, una gran peña oblonga se extendía sobre el césped entre malezas, hinojos, zarzas, juncos y cantidad inmensa de pintadas florecillas. Parecía una gran lengua. Junto a ella se adivinaba, más bien que se veía, un hueco, un tragadero oculto por espesas hierbas, como las que tuvo que cortar Don Quijote cuando se descolgó dentro de la cueva de Montesinos.

La Nela no se cansaba de mirar.

—¿Por qué dices que está bonita esa horrenda Trascava?—le preguntó su amigo.

—Porque hay en ella muchas flores. La semana pasada estaban todas secas; pero han vuelto a nacer, y está aquello que da gozo verlo. ¡Madre de Dios! Hay muchos pájaros posados allí y muchísimas mariposas que están cogiendo miel en las flores... *Choto, Choto*, ven aquí, no espantes a los pobres pajaritos.

El perro, que había bajado, volvió gozoso llamado por la Nela, y la pacífica república de pajarillos volvió a tomar posesión de sus estados.

—A mí me causa horror este sitio—dijo Pablo, tomando del brazo a la muchacha—. Y ahora, ¿vamos hacia las minas? Sí, ya conozco este camino. Estoy en mi terreno. Por aquí vamos derechos al Barco... *Choto*, anda delante; no te enredes en mis piernas.

Descendían por una vereda escalonada. Pronto llegaron a la concavidad formada por la explotación minera. Dejando la verde zona vegetal, habían entrado bruscamente en la geológica, zanja enorme, cuyas paredes, labradas por el barreno y el pico, mostraban una interesante estratificación, cuyas diversas capas ofrecían en el corte los más variados tonos y los materiales más diversos. Era aquél el sitio que a Teodoro Golfín le había parecido el interior de un gran buque náufrago, comido de las olas, y su nombre vulgar justificaba esta semejanza. Pero de día se admiraban principalmente las superpuestas cortezas de la estratificación, con sus vetas sulfurosas y carbonatadas; sus sedimentos negros, sus lignitos, donde yace el negro azabache; sus capas de tierra ferruginosa, que parece amasada con sangre; sus grandes y regulares láminas de roca, quebradas en mil puntos por el arte humano, y erizadas de picos, cortaduras y desgarrones. Era aquello como una herida abierta en el tejido orgánico y vista con microscopio. El arroyo, de aguas saturadas de óxido de hierro que corría por el centro, semejaba un chorro de sangre.

—¿En dónde está nuestro asiento?—preguntó el señorito de Penáguilas—. Vamos a él. Allí no nos molestará el aire.

Desde el fondo de la gran zanja subieron un poco por escabroso sendero, abierto entre rotas piedras, tierra y matas de hinojo, y se sentaron a la sombra de enorme peña agrietada, que presentaba en su centro una larga hendidura. Más bien eran dos peñas, pegada la una a la otra, con irregulares bordes, como dos gastadas mandíbulas que se esfuerzan en morder.

—¡Qué bien se está aquí!—dijo Pablo—. A veces suele salir una corriente de aire por esa gruta; pero hoy no siento nada. Lo que siento es el gorgoteo del agua allá dentro, en las entrañas de la Trascava.

—Calladita está hoy—observó la Nela—. ¿Quieres echarte?

—Pues mira que has tenido una buena idea. Anoche no he dormido pensando en lo que mi

padre me dijo, en el médico, en mis ojos... Toda
la noche estuve sintiendo una mano que entraba
en mis ojos y abría en ellos una puerta cerrada
y mohosa.

Diciendo esto, sentóse sobre la piedra, poniendo su cabeza sobre el regazo de la Nela.

—Aquella puerta—prosiguió—, que estaba
allá, en lo más íntimo de mi sentido, abrióse,
como te he dicho, dando paso a una estancia
donde se encerraba la idea que me persigue.
¡Ay, Nela de mi corazón, chiquilla idolatrada,
si Dios quisiera darme ese don que me falta!...
Con él me creería el más feliz de los hombres,
yo, que casi lo soy, sólo con tenerte por amiga
y compañera de mi vida. Para que los dos sea-
mos uno solo me falta muy poco: no me falta
más que verte y recrearme en tu belleza, con ese
placer de la vista que no puedo comprender aún,
pero que concibo de una manera vaga. Tengo la
curiosidad del espíritu; la de los ojos me falta.
Supóngola como una nueva manera del amor
que te tengo. Yo estoy lleno de tu belleza, pero
hay algo en ella que no me pertenece todavía.

—¿No oyes?—dijo la Nela de improviso, demostrando interés por cosa muy distinta de lo
que su amigo decía.

—¿Qué?

—Aquí dentro... ¡La Trascava!...; está hablando. Y la Trascava—observó la Nela, palide-

ciendo—es un murmullo, un sí, sí, sí... A ratos
oigo la voz de mi madre, que dice clarito: «Hija
mía, ¡qué bien se está aquí!»

—Es tu imaginación. También la imaginación
habla; me olvidé de decirlo. La mía a veces se
pone tan parlanchina, que tengo que mandarla
callar. Su voz es chillona, atropellada, inaguan-
table; así como la de la conciencia es grave,
reposada, convincente, y lo que dice no tiene
refutación.

—Ahora parece que llora... Se va poquito a
poco perdiendo la voz—dijo la Nela, atenta a lo
que oía.

—De pronto salió por la gruta una ligera rá-
faga de aire.

—¿No has notado que ha echado un gran
suspiro?... Ahora se vuelve a oír la voz; habla
bajo, y me dice al oído muy bajito, muy bajito...

—¿Qué te dice?

—Nada—replicó bruscamente María, después
de una pausa—. Tú dices que son tonterías.
Tendrás razón.

—Ya te quitaré yo de la cabeza esos pensamientos absurdos—dijo el ciego, tomándole la
mano—. Hemos de vivir juntos toda la vida.
¡Oh, Dios mío! Si no he de adquirir la facultad
de que me privaste al nacer, ¿para qué me has
dado esperanzas? Infeliz de mí si no nazco de
nuevo en manos del doctor Golfín. Porque esto

será nacer otra vez. ¡Y qué nacimiento! ¡Qué
nueva vida! Chiquilla mía, juro por la idea de
Dios que tengo dentro de mí, clara, patente,
inmutable, que tú y yo no nos separaremos jamás por mi voluntad. Yo tendré ojos, Nela, tendré ojos para poder recrearme en tu celestial
hermosura, y entonces me casaré contigo. Serás
mi esposa querida..., serás la vida de mi vida,
el recreo y el orgullo de mi alma. ¿No dices
nada a esto?

La Nela oprimió contra sí la hermosa cabeza
del joven. Quiso hablar, pero su emoción no se
lo permitía.

—Y si Dios no quiere otorgarme ese don
—añadió el ciego—, tampoco te separarás de mí,
también serás mi mujer, a no ser que te repug-
ne enlazarte con un ciego. No, no, chiquilla mía,
no quiero imponerte un yugo tan penoso. Encontrarás hombres de mérito que te amarán y
que podrán hacerte feliz. Tu extraordinaria bondad, tus nobles prendas, tu belleza, han de cau-
tivar los corazones y encender el más puro
amor en cuantos te traten; asegurando un por-
venir risueño. Yo te juro que te querré mientras
viva, ciego o con vista, y que estoy dispuesto a
jurarte delante de Dios un amor grande, insa-
ciable, eterno. ¿No me dices nada?

—Sí; que te quiero mucho, muchísimo—dijo
la Nela, acercando su rostro al de su amigo—.

Pero no te afanes por verme. Quizá no sea yo
tan guapa como tú crees.

Diciendo esto, la Nela, rebuscando en su fal-
triquera, sacó un pedazo de cristal azogado,
resto inútil y borroso de un fementido espejo
que se rompiera en casa de la Señana la semana anterior. Miróse en él; mas por causa de la
pequeñez del vidrio, érale forzoso mirarse por
partes, sucesiva y gradualmente, primero un
ojo, después la nariz. Alejándolo, pudo abarcar
la mitad del conjunto. ¡Ay! ¡Cuán triste fue el
resultado de su examen! Guardó el espejillo, y
gruesas lágrimas brotaron de sus ojos.

—Nela, sobre mi frente ha caído una gota.
¿Acaso llueve?

—Sí, niño mío, parece que llueve—dijo la
Nela, sollozando.

—No, es que lloras. Pues has de saber que me
lo decía el corazón. Tú eres la misma bondad;
tu alma y la mía están unidas por un lazo misterioso y divino; no se pueden separar, ¿verdad?
Son dos partes de una misma cosa, ¿verdad?

—Verdad.

—Tus lágrimas me responden más claramente que cuanto pudieras decir. ¿No es verdad
que me querrás mucho, lo mismo si me dan
vista que si continuo privado de ella?

—Lo mismo, sí, lo mismo—afirmó la Nela,
vehemente y turbada.

—¿Y me acompañarás?...

—Siempre, siempre.

—Oye tú—dijo el ciego con amoroso arranque—: si me dan a escoger entre no ver y perderte, prefiero...

—Prefieres no ver... ¡Oh! ¡Madre de Dios divino, qué alegría tengo dentro de mí!

—·Prefiero no ver con los ojos tu hermosura, porque la veo dentro de mí, clara como la verdad que proclamo interiormente. Aquí dentro estás, y tu persona me seduce y enamora más que todas las cosas.

—Sí, sí, sí—afirmó la Nela con desvarío—; yo soy hermosa, soy muy hermosa.

—Oye tú: tengo un presentimiento..., sí, un presentimiento. Dentro de mí parece que está Dios hablándome y diciéndome que tendré ojos, que te veré, que seremos felices... ¿No sientes tú lo mismo?

—Yo... El corazón me dice que me verás...; pero me lo dice partiéndoseme.

—Veré tu hermosura, ¡qué felicidad!—exclamó el ciego, con la expresión delirante, que era su expresión más propia en ciertos momentos—. Pero si ya la veo; si la veo dentro de mí, clara como la verdad que proclamo y que me llena el alma.

—Sí, sí, sí...—repitió la Nela con desvarío,

espantados los ojos, trémulos los labios—. Yo
soy hermosa, soy muy hermosa.

—Bendita seas tú...

—¡Y tú!—añadió ella, besándole en la frente—. ¿Tienes sueño?

—Sí, principio a tener sueño. No he dormido
anoche. Estoy tan bien aquí...

—Duérmete.

Principió a cantar con arrullo, como se canta
a los niños soñolientos. Poco después Pablo
dormía. La Nela oyó de nuevo la voz de la Trascava, diciéndole: «Hija mía..., aquí, aquí.»

Teodoro Golfín no se aburría en Socartes.
El primer día después de su llegada pasó largas
horas en el laboratorio con su hermano, y en
los siguientes recorrió de un cabo a otro las
minas, examinando y admirando las distintas
cosas que allí había, que ya pasmaban por la
grandeza de las fuerzas naturales, ya por el
poder y brío del arte de los hombres. De noche,
cuando todo callaba en el industrioso Socartes,
quedando sólo en actividad los bullidores hornos, el buen doctor, que era muy entusiasta
músico, se deleitaba oyendo tocar el piano a su
cuñada Sofía, esposa de Carlos Golfín y madre
de varios chiquillos que se habían muerto.

Los dos hermanos se profesaban vivo cariño.
Nacidos en la clase más humilde, habían lucha-
do solos en edad temprana por salir de la ignorancia y de la pobreza, viéndose a punto de su-
cumbir diferentes veces; mas tanto pudo en
ellos el impulso de una voluntad heroica, que
al fin llegaron jadeantes a la ansiada orilla, de-

jando atrás las turbias olas en que se agita en constante estado de naufragio el grosero vulgo.

Teodoro, que era el mayor, fue médico antes que Carlos ingeniero. Ayudó a éste con todas sus fuerzas mientras el joven lo necesitara, y cuando le vio en camino, tomó el que anhelaba su corazón aventurero, yéndose a América. Allá trabajó, juntamente con otros afamados médicos europeos, adquiriendo bien pronto dinero y fama. Hizo un viaje a España; tornó al Nuevo Mundo; vino más tarde, para regresar al poco tiempo. En cada una de estas excursiones daba la vuelta a Europa para apropiarse los progresos de la ciencia oftálmica, que cultivaba.

Era un hombre de facciones bastas, moreno, de fisonomía tan inteligente como sensual, labios gruesos, pelo negro y erizado, mirar centelleante, naturaleza incansable, constitución fuerte, si bien algo gastada por el clima americano. Su cara, grande y redonda; su frente huesuda, su melena rebelde aunque corta, el fuego de sus ojos, sus gruesas manos, habían sido motivo para que dijeran de él: «Es un león negro.» En efecto: parecía un león, y, como el rey de los animales, no dejaba de manifestar a cada momento la estimación en que a sí mismo se tenía. Pero la vanidad de aquel hombre insigne era la más disculpable de todas las vanidades, pues consistía en sacar a relucir dos títulos de gloria, a saber: su pasión por la Cirugía y la humildad de su origen. Hablaba, por lo general, incorrectamente, por ser incapaz de construir con gracia y elegancia las oraciones. Sus frases, rápidas y entrecortadas, se acomodaban a la emisión de su pensamiento, que era una especie de emisión eléctrica. Muchas veces Sofía, al pedirle su opinión sobre cualquier cosa, decía: «A ver lo que piensa de esto la Agencia Havas.»

—Nosotros—indicaba Teodoro—, aunque descendemos de las hierbas del campo, que es el más bajo linaje que se conoce, nos hemos hecho árboles corpulentos... ¡Viva el trabajo y la iniciativa del hombre!... Yo creo que los Golfines, aunque aparentemente venimos de maragatos, tenemos sangre inglesa en nuestras venas... Hasta nuestro apellido parece que es de pura casta sajona. Yo lo descompondría de este modo: *Gold*, oro...; *to find*, hallar... Es, como si dijéramos, buscador de oro... He aquí que mientras mi hermano lo busca en las entrañas de la tierra, yo lo busco en el interior maravilloso de ese universo en abreviatura que se llama el ojo humano.

En la época de esta veraz historia venía de América por la vía de New York-Liverpool, y, según dijo, su expatriación había cesado definitivamente; pero no le creían, por haber expre-

sado lo mismo en otras ocasiones y haber hecho
lo contrario.

Su hermano Carlos era un bendito, hombre
muy pacífico, estudioso, esclavo de su deber,
apasionado por la mineralogía y la metalurgia
hasta poner a estas dos mancebas cien codos
más altas que su mujer. Por lo demás, ambos
cónyuges vivían en conformidad completa, o,
como decía Teodoro, en estado *isomórfico*,
porque cristalizaban en un mismo sistema. En
cuanto a él, siempre que se hablaba de matrimonio, decía, riendo: «El matrimonio sería para
mí una *epigénesis* o cristal *seudomórfico*, es
decir, un sistema de cristalización que no me
corresponde.»

Era Sofía una excelente señora, de regular
belleza, cada día reducida a menor expresión
por una tendencia lamentable a la obesidad. Le
habían dicho que la atmósfera del carbón de
piedra enflaquecía, y por eso fue a vivir a las
minas, con propósito de pasar en ellas todo el
año. Por lo demás, aquella atmósfera, saturada
de polvo de calamina y de humo, causábale no
poco disgusto. No tenía hijos vivos, y su principal ocupación consistía en tocar el piano y en
organizar asociaciones benéficas de señoras para socorros domiciliarios y sostenimiento de
hospitales y escuelas. En Madrid, y durante buena porción de años, su actividad había hecho

prodigios, ofreciendo ejemplos dignos de imi-
tación a todas las almas aficionadas a la caridad. Ayudada de dos o tres señoras de alto
linaje, igualmente amantes del prójimo, había
logrado celebrar más de veinte funciones dramáticas, otros tantos bailes de máscaras, seis
corridas de toros y dos de gallos, todo en be-
neficio de los pobres.

En el número de sus vehemencias, que solían
ser pasajeras, contábase una que quizá no sea
tan recomendable como aquella de socorrer a
los menesterosos, y consistía en rodearse de
perros y gatos, poniendo en estos animales un
afecto que al mismo amor se parecía. Ultima-
mente, y cuando residía en el establecimiento
de Socartes, tenía un *toy terrier* que por encargo le había traído de Inglaterra Ulises Bull,
jefe del taller de maquinaria. Era un galguito
fino y elegante, delicado y mimoso como un
niño. Se llamaba *Lili*, y había costado en Lon-
dres doscientos duros.

Los Golfines paseaban en los días buenos; en
los malos, tocaban el piano o cantaban, pues
Sofía tenía cierto chillido que podía pasar por
canto en Socartes. El ingeniero segundo tenía
voz de bajo; Teodoro también era bajo profundo; Carlos, allá se iba; de modo que armaban
una especie de coro de sacerdotes, en el cual
descollaba la voz de Sofía como sacerdotisa a

quien van a llevar al sacrificio. Todas las piezas
que se cantaban eran, o si no lo eran lo parecían, de sacerdotes sacrificadores y sacerdotisa
sacrificada.

En los días de paseo solían merendar en el
campo. Una tarde (a últimos de septiembre y
seis días después de la llegada de Teodoro a las
minas) volvían de su excursión en el orden siguiente: *Lili*, Sofía, Teodoro, Carlos. La estre-
chez del sendero no les permitía caminar de dos
en dos. *Lili* llevaba su manta o gabancito azul
con las iniciales de su ama. Sofía apoyaba en
su hombro el palo de la sombrilla, y Teodoro
llevaba en la misma postura su bastón, con el
sombrero en la punta. Gustaba mucho de pasear con la deforme cabeza al aire. Pasaban al
borde de la Trascava, cuando *Lili*, desviándose
del sendero con la elástica ligereza de sus pati-
llas como alambres, echó a correr césped abajo
por la vertiente del embudo. Primero corría,
después resbalaba. Sofía dio un grito de terror.
Su primer movimiento, dictado por un afecto
que parecía materno, fue correr detrás del animal, tan cercano al peligro; pero su esposo la
contuvo, diciendo:

—Deja que se lleve el demonio a *Lili*, mujer;
él volverá. No se puede bajar; este césped es
muy resbaladizo.

—¡*Lili*, *Lili*!...—gritaba Sofía, esperando que

sus amantes ayes detendrían al animal en su camino de perdición, trayéndole al de la virtud.

Las voces más tiernas no hicieron efecto en el revoltoso ánimo de *Lili*, que seguía bajando. A veces miraba a su ama, y con sus expresivos ojuelos negros parecía decirle: «Señora, por el amor de Dios, no sea usted tan tonta.»

Lili se detuvo en la gran peña blanquecina, agujereada, musgosa, que en la boca misma del abismo se veía, como encubriéndola. Fijáronse allí todos los ojos, y al punto observaron que se movía un objeto. Creyeron de pronto ver un animal dañino que se ocultaba detrás de la peña; pero Sofía lanzó un nuevo grito, el cual antes era de asombro que de terror.

—¡Si es la Nela!... Nela, ¿qué haces ahí?

Al oír su nombre, la muchacha se mostró toda turbada y ruborosa

—¿Qué haces ahí, loca?—repitió la dama—. Coge a *Lili* y tráemelo... ¡Válgame Dios lo que inventa esta criatura! Miren dónde ha ido a meterse. Tú tienes la culpa de que *Lili* haya bajado... ¡Qué cosas le enseñas al animalito! Por tu causa es tan mal criado y tan antojadizo.

—Esa muchacha es de la piel de Barrabás —dijo don Carlos a su hermano—. ¡Vaya dónde se ha ido a poner!

Mientras esto se decía en el borde de la Trascava, abajo la Nela había emprendido la perse-

cución de *Lili*, el cual, más travieso y calavera
en aquel día que en ningún otro de su monóto-
na existencia, huía de las manos de la chicuela.
Gritábale la dama, exhortándole a ser juicioso
y formal; pero él, poniendo en olvido las más
vulgares nociones del deber, empezó a dar brincos y a mirar con descaro a su ama, como diciéndole: «Señora, ¿quiere usted irse a paseo y
dejarme en paz?»

Al fin *Lili* dio con su elegante cuerpo en medio de las zarzas que cubrían la boca de la cueva, y allí la mantita de que iba vestido fuéle de
grandísimo estorbo. El animal, viéndose imposibilitado de salir de entre la maleza, empezó a
ladrar pidiendo socorro.

—¡Que se me pierde! ¡Que se me mata!—exclamó, gimiendo, Sofía—. ¡Nela, Nela, si me lo
sacas te doy un perro grande! ¡Sácalo..., ve con
cuidado..., agárrate bien!

La Nela se deslizó intrépidamente, poniendo
su pie sobre las zarzas y robustos hinojos que
tapaban el abismo; y sosteniéndose con una
mano en las asperezas de la peña, alargó la otra
hasta pillar el rabo de *Lili*, con lo cual le sacó
del aprieto en que estaba. Acariciando al animal, subió triunfante a los bordes del embudo.

—Tú, tú, tú tienes la culpa—díjole Sofía de
mal talante, aplicándole tres suaves coscorro-
nes—, porque si no te hubieras metido allí...

Ya sabes que va detrás de ti dondequiera que te encuentre... ¡Buena pieza!...

Y luego, besando al descarriado animal y administrándole dos nalgadas, después de cerciorarse que no había padecido avería de fundamento en su estimable persona, le arregló la mantita, que se le había puesto por montera, y lo entregó a Nela, diciéndole:

—Toma, llévalo en brazos, porque estará cansado, y estas largas caminatas pueden hacerle daño. Cuidado... Anda delante de nosotros... Cuidado, te repito... Mira que voy detrás observando lo que haces.

Púsose de nuevo en marcha la familia, precedida por la Nela. *Lili* miraba a su ama por encima del hombro de la chiquilla, y parecía decirle: «¡Ay, señora, pero qué boba es usted!»

Teodoro Golfín no había dicho nada durante el conmovedor peligro del hermoso *Lili;* pero cuando se pusieron en marcha por la gran pradera, donde los tres podían ir al lado uno de otro, sin molestarse, el doctor dijo a la mujer de su hermano:

—Estoy pensando, querida Sofía, que ese animal te inquieta demasiado. Verdad que un perro que cuesta doscientos duros no es un perro como otro cualquiera. Yo me pregunto por qué has empleado el tiempo y el dinero en hacerle un gabán a ese señorito canino, y no

se te ha ocurrido comprarle unos zapatos a la
Nela.

—¡Zapatos a la Nela!—exclamó Sofía, riendo—. Y yo pregunto: ¿para qué los quiere?...
Tardaría dos días en romperlos. Podrás reírte
de mí todo lo que quieras... Bien, yo comprendo que cuidar mucho a *Lili* es una extravagan-
cia..., pero no podrás acusarme de falta de caridad... Alto ahí..., eso sí que no te lo permito
—al decir esto, tomaba un tono muy serio con
evidente expresión de orgullo—. Y en lo de saber practicar la caridad con prudencia y tino,
tampoco creo que me eche el pie adelante persona alguna... No consiste, no, la caridad en
dar sin ton ni son cuando no existe la seguridad
de que la limosna ha de ser bien empleada.
¡Si querrás darme lecciones!... Mira, Teodoro,
que en eso sé tanto como tú en el tratado de
los ojos.

—Sí; ya sabemos, querida, que has hecho
maravillas. No me cuentes otra vez lo de las
funciones dramáticas, bailes y corridas de toros,
organizadas por tu ingenio para alivio de los
pobres, ni de los de las rifas que, poniendo en
juego grandes sumas, han servido en primer
lugar para dar de comer a unos cuantos holgazanes, quedando sólo para los enfermos un
resto de poca monta. Todo eso sólo me prueba
las singulares costumbres de una sociedad que

no sabe ser caritativa, sino bailando, toreando
y jugando a la lotería... No hablemos de eso;
ya conozco estas heroicidades y las admiro;
también eso tiene su mérito, y no poco. Pero
tú y tus amigas rara vez os acercáis a un pobre para saber de su misma boca la causa de
su miseria..., ni para observar qué clase de miseria le aqueja, pues hay algunas tan extraor-
dinarias, que no se alivian con la fácil limosna
del ochavo..., ni tampoco con el mendrugo de
pan...

—Ya tenemos a nuestro filósofo en campaña
—dijo Sofía con mal humor—. ¿Qué sabes tú
lo que yo he hecho ni lo que he dejado de
hacer?

—No te enfades, hija—replicó Golfín—; todos mis argumentos van a parar a un punto, y
es que debiste comprarle zapatos a Nela.

—Pues mira, mañana mismo los tendrá.

—No, porque esta misma noche se los com-
praré yo. No se meta usted en mis dominios,
señora.

—¡Eh..., Nela!—gritó Sofía, viendo que la
chiquilla estaba a larga distancia—. No te ale-
jes mucho; que te vea yo para saber lo que
haces.

—¡Pobre criatura!—dijo Carlos—. ¡Quién ha
de decir que eso tiene dieciséis años!

—Atrasadilla está. ¡Qué desgracia!—exclamó

Sofía—. Y yo me pregunto: ¿para qué permite
Dios que tales criaturas vivan?... Y me pregunto también: ¿qué es lo que se puede hacer
por ella? Nada, nada más que darle de comer,
vestirla... hasta cierto punto... Ya se ve..., rom-
pe todo lo que le ponen encima. Ella no puede
trabajar, porque se desmaya; ella no tiene
fuerzas para nada. Saltando de piedra en piedra, subiéndose a los árboles, jugando y enredando todo el día y cantando como los pájaros, cuanto se le pone encima conviértese
pronto en jirones...

—Pues yo he observado en la Nela—dijo Carlos—algo de inteligencia y agudeza de ingenio
bajo aquella corteza de candor y salvaje rusticidad. No, señor: la Nela no es tonta ni mucho menos. Si alguien se hubiera tomado el
trabajo de enseñarle alguna cosa, habría aprendido mejor quizá que la mayoría de los chicos. ¿Qué creen ustedes? La Nela tiene imaginación; por tenerla y carecer hasta de la enseñanza más rudimentaria, es sentimental y
supersticiosa.

—Eso es; se halla en la situación de los
pueblos primitivos—afirmó Teodoro—. Está en
la época del pastoreo.

—Ayer precisamente—añadió Carlos—pasaba
yo por la Trascava y la vi en el mismo sitio
donde la hemos hallado hoy. La llamé, hícela

salir, le pregunté qué hacía en aquel sitio, y
con la mayor sencillez del mundo me contestó que estaba hablando con su madre... Tú no
sabes que la madre de la Nela se arrojó por
esa sima.

—Es decir, que se suicidó—dijo Sofía—. Era
una mujer de mala vida y peores ideas, según
he oído contar. Nos han dicho que se embria-
gaba como un fogonero. Y yo me pregunto:
¿esos seres tan envilecidos que terminan una
vida de crímenes con el mayor de todos, que
es el suicidio, merecen la compasión del género humano? Hay cosas que horripilan; hay
personas que no debieran haber nacido, no,
señor, y Teodoro podrá decir todas las sutilezas que quiera, pero yo me pregunto...

—No, no te preguntas nada, hermana querida—dijo vivamente Teodoro—. Yo te respon-
deré que el suicida merece la más viva, la más
cordial compasión. En cuanto a vituperio, éche-
sele encima todo el que haya disponible; pero
al mismo tiempo... bueno será indagar qué
causas le llevaron a tan horrible extremo de
desesperación..., y observaría si la sociedad no
le ha dejado abierta, desamparándole en absoluto, la puerta de ese abismo horrendo que le
llama...

—¡Desamparado de la sociedad! Hay algunos
que lo están...—dijo Sofía con impertinencia—.

La sociedad no puede amparar a todos. Mira la
estadística, Teodoro; mírala y verás la cifra de
pobres... Pero si la sociedad desampara a alguien, ¿para qué sirve la religión?

—Refiérome al miserable desesperado que
reúne a todas las miserias la miseria mayor,
que es la ignorancia... El ignorante envilecido
y supersticioso sólo posee nociones vagas y ab-
surdas de la Divinidad... Lo desconocido, lejos
de detenerle, le impulsa más a cometer su crimen... Rara vez hará beneficios la idea religiosa al que vegeta en estúpida ignorancia. A
él no se acerca amigo inteligente, ni maestro,
ni sacerdote. No se le acerca sino el juez que
ha de mandarle a presidio... Es singular el rigor con que condenáis vuestra propia obra
—añadió con vehemencia, enarbolando el palo,
en cuya punta tenía su sombrero—. Estáis viendo delante de vosotros, al pie mismo de vuestras cómodas casas, a una multitud de seres
abandonados, faltos de todo lo que es necesario a la niñez, desde los padres hasta los ju-
guetes...; les estáis viendo, sí..., nunca se os
ocurre infundirles un poco de dignidad, haciéndoles saber que son seres humanos, dán-
doles las ideas de que carecen; no se os ocurre ennoblecerles, haciéndoles pasar del bestial
trabajo mecánico al trabajo de la inteligencia;
les veis viviendo en habitaciones inmundas,

mal alimentados, perfeccionándose cada día en su salvaje rusticidad, y no se os ocurre extender un poco hasta ellos las comodidades de que estáis rodeados... ¡Toda la energía la guardáis luego para declamar contra los homicidios, los robos y el suicidio, sin reparar que sostenéis escuela permanente de estos tres crímenes!

—No sé para qué están ahí los asilos de beneficencia—dijo agriamente Sofía—. Lee la estadística, Teodoro, léela, y verás el número de desdichados... Lee la estadística...

—Yo no leo la estadística, querida hermana, ni me hace falta para nada tu estadística. Buenos son los asilos; pero no, no bastan para resolver el gran problema que ofrece la orfandad. El miserable huérfano, perdido en las calles y en los campos, desamparado de todo cariño personal y acogido sólo por las Corporaciones, rara vez llena el vacío que forma en su alma la carencia de familia...; ¡oh!, vacío donde debían estar, y rara vez están, la nobleza, la dignidad y la estimación de sí mismo. Sobre este tema tengo una idea, es una idea mía; quizá os parezca un disparate.

—Dínosla.

—El problema de la orfandad y de la miseria infantil no se resolverá nunca en absoluto, como no se resolverán tampoco sus compañeros

los demás problemas sociales; pero habrá un
alivio a mal tan grande cuando las costumbres,
apoyadas por las leyes..., por las leyes, ya veis
que esto no es cosa de juego, establezcan que
todo huérfano, cualquiera que sea su origen...,
no reírse..., tenga derecho a entrar en calidad
de hijo adoptivo en la casa de un matrimonio
acomodado que carezca de hijos. Ya se arregla-
rían las cosas de modo que no hubiera padres
sin hijos, ni hijos sin **padres.**

—Con tu sistema—dijo Sofía—ya se arregla-
rían las cosas de modo que nosotros fuésemos
papás de la Nela.

—¿Por qué no?—repuso Teodoro—. Entonces
no gastaríamos doscientos duros en comprar
un perro, ni estaríamos todo el santo día haciendo mimos al señorito *Lili.*

—¿Y por qué han de estar exentos de esa graciosa ley los solteros ricos? ¿Por qué no han
de cargar ellos también con su huérfano como
cada hijo de vecino?

—No me opongo—dijo el doctor mirando al
suelo—. ¿Pero qué es esto?...; ¡sangre!...

Todos miraron al suelo, donde se veían de
trecho en trecho manchitas de sangre.

—¡Jesús!—exclamó Sofía, apretando los
ojos—. Si es la Nela. Mira cómo se ha puesto
los pies.

—Ya se ve... Como tuvo que meterse entre

las zarzas para coger a tu dichoso *Lili*. Nela,
ven acá.

La Nela, cuyo pie derecho estaba ensangren-
tado se acercó cojeando.

—Dame al pobre *Lili*—dijo Sofía, tomando el
canino de manos de la vagabunda—. No vayas
a hacerle daño. ¿Te duele mucho? ¡Pobrecita!
Eso no es nada. ¡Oh, cuánta sangre!... No puedo ver eso.

Sensible y nerviosa, Sofía se volvió de espaldas, acariciando a *Lili*.

—A ver, a ver qué es eso—dijo Teodoro, tomando a la Nela en sus brazos y sentándola en
una piedra de la cerca inmediata.

Poniéndose sus lentes, le examinó el pie.

—Es poca cosa: dos o tres rasguños... Me parece que tienes una espina dentro... ¿Te duele?
Sí, aquí está la pícara... Aguarda un momento..
Sofía, echa a correr si te molesta ver una operación quirúrgica.

Mientras Sofía daba algunos pasos para poner su precioso sistema nervioso a cubierto de
toda alteración, Teodoro Golfín sacó su estuche, del estuche unas pinzas, y en un santiamén
extrajo la espina.

—¡Bien por la mujer valiente!—dijo, observando la serenidad de la Nela—. Ahora vende-
mos el pie.

Con su pañuelo vendó el pie herido. Marianela trató de andar. Carlos le dio la mano.

—No, no, ven acá—dijo Teodoro, cogiendo a
Marianela por los brazos.

Con rápido movimiento levantóla en el aire
y la sentó sobre su hombro derecho.

—Si no estás segura, agárrate a mis cabellos,
son fuertes. Ahora lleva tú el palo con el sombrero.

—¡Qué facha!—exclamó Sofía, muerta de risa
al verlos venir—. Teodoro con la Nela al hombro, y luego el palo con el sombrero de Gessler.

—Aquí tienes, querida Sofía—dijo Teodoro—, un hombre que sirve para todo. Este es el resultado de nuestra educación, ¿verdad, Carlos? Bien sabes que no hemos sido criados con mimo; que desde nuestra más tierna infancia nos acostumbramos a la idea de que no había nadie inferior a nosotros... Los hombres que se forman solos, como nosotros nos formamos; los que, sin ayuda de nadie, ni más amparo que su voluntad y noble ambición, han logrado salir triunfantes en la *lucha por la existencia...*, sí, ¡demonio!, éstos son los únicos que saben cómo se ha de tratar a un menesteroso. No te cuento diversos hechos de mi vida, atañederos a esto del prójimo como a ti mismo, por no caer en el feo pecado de la propia alabanza, y por temor a causar envidia a tus rifas y a tus bailoteos filantrópicos. Quédese esto aquí.

—Cuéntalos, cuéntalos otra vez, Teodoro.

—No, no..., todo eso debe callarse; así lo manda la modestia. Confieso que no poseo en

alto grado esta virtud preciosa; yo no carezco
de vanidades, y entre ellas tengo la de haber
sido mendigo, de haber pedido limosna de puerta en puerta, de haber andado descalzo con mi
hermanito Carlos, y dormir con él en los huecos de las puertas, sin amparo, sin abrigo, sin
familia. Yo no sé qué extraordinario rayo de
energía y de voluntad vibró dentro de mí. Tuve
una inspiración. Comprendí que delante de
nuestros pasos se abrían dos sendas: la del
presidio, la de la gloria. Cargué en mis hombros a mi pobre hermanito, lo mismo que hoy
cargo a la Nela, y dije: «Padre nuestro que estás en los cielos, sálvanos...» Ello es que nos
salvamos. Yo aprendí a leer y enseñé a leer a
mi hermano. Yo serví a diversos amos, que me
daban de comer y me permitían ir a la escuela. Yo guardaba mis propinas; yo compré una
hucha... Yo reuní para comprar libros... Yo no
sé cómo entré en los Escolapios; pero ello es
que entré, mientras mi hermano se ganaba su
pan haciendo recados en una tienda de ultra-
marinos...

—¡Qué cosas tienes!—exclamó Sofía, muy
desazonada, porque no gustaba de oír aquel
tema—. Y yo me pregunto: ¿a qué viene el recordar tales niñerías? Además, tú las exageras
mucho.

—No exagero nada—dijo Teodoro con brío—.

Señora, oiga usted y calle... Voy a poner cáte-
dra de esto... Oíganme todos los pobres, todos
los desamparados, todos los niños perdidos...
Yo entré en los Escolapios como Dios quiso; yo
aprendí como Dios quiso... Un bendito padre
dióme buenos consejos y me ayudó con sus li-
mosnas... Sentí afición a la Medicina... ¿Cómo
estudiarla sin dejar de trabajar para comer?
¡Problema terrible!... Querido Carlos, ¿te acuerdas de cuando entramos los dos a pedir trabajo
en una barbería de la antigua calle de Cofre-
ros?... Nunca habíamos cogido una navaja en
la mano; pero era preciso ganarse el pan afei-
tando... Al principio ayudábamos..., ¿te acuerdas, Carlos?... Después empuñamos aquellos
nobles instrumentos... La flebotomía fue nuestra salvación. Yo empecé los estudios anatómi-
cos. ¡Ciencia admirable, divina! Tanto era el
trabajo escolástico, que tuve que abandonar
la barbería de aquel famoso maestro Cayeta-
no... El día en que me despedí, él lloraba... Dióme dos duros, y su mujer me obsequió con
unos pantalones viejos de su esposo... Entré
a servir de ayuda de cámara. Dios me protegía,
dándome siempre buenos amos. Mi afición al
estudio interesó a aquellos benditos señores,
que me dejaban libre todo el tiempo que podían. Yo velaba estudiando. Yo estudiaba dur-
miendo. Yo deliraba, y limpiando la ropa re-

pasaba en la memoria las piezas del esqueleto
humano... Me acuerdo que el cepillar la ropa
de mi amo me servía para estudiar la miolo-
gía... Limpiando una manga, decía: «músculo
deltoides, bíceps, cubital», y en los pantalones:
«músculos glúteos, psoas, gemelos, tibial, etc.».
En aquella casa dábanme sobras de comida, que
yo llevaba a mi hermano, habitante en casa de
unos dignos ropavejeros. ¿Te acuerdas, Carlos?

—Me acuerdo—dijo Carlos con emoción—.
Y gracias que encontré quien me diera casa
por un pequeño servicio de llevar cuentas. Luego tuve la dicha de tropezar con aquel coronel
retirado, que me enseñó las matemáticas elementales.

—Bueno; no hay guiñapo que no saquen ustedes hoy a la calle—observó Sofía.

—Mi hermano me pedía pan—añadió Teodoro—, y yo le respondía: «¿Pan has dicho?, toma
matemáticas...» Un día mi amo me dio entra-
das para el teatro de la Cruz; llevé a mi hermano y nos divertimos mucho; pero Carlos co-
gió una pulmonía... ¡Obstáculo terrible, inmenso! Esto era recibir un balazo al principio de
la acción... Pero no, ¿quién desmaya? Adelante..., a curarle se ha dicho. Un profesor de la
Facultad, que me había tomæ gran cariño, se
prestó a curarle.

—Fue milagro de Dios que me salvara en

aquel cuchitril inmundo, almacén de trapo viejo, de hierro viejo y de cuero viejo.

—Dios estaba con nosotros..., bien claro se veía... Habíase puesto de nuestra parte... ¡Oh, bien sabía yo a quién me arrimaba!—prosiguió Teodoro, con aquella elocuencia nerviosa, rápida, ardiente, que era tan suya como las melenas negras y la cabeza de león—. Para que mi hermano tuviera medicinas fue preciso que yo me quedara sin ropa. No pueden andar juntas la farmacopea y la indumentaria. Receta tras receta, el enfermo consumió mi capa, después mi levita..., mis calzones se convirtieron en píldoras... Pero mis amos no me abandonaban..., volví a tener ropa, y mi hermano salió a la calle. El médico me dijo: «Que vaya a convalecer al campo...» Yo medité... ¿Campo dijiste? Que vaya a la Escuela de Minas. Mi hermano era gran matemático. Yo le enseñé la Química; pronto se aficionó a los pedruscos, y antes de entrar en la Escuela, ya salía al campo de San Isidro a recoger guijarros. Yo seguía adelante en mi navegación por entre olas y huracanes... Cada día era más médico; un famoso operador me tomó por ayudante; dejé de ser criado... Empecé a servir a la Ciencia...; mi amo cayó enfermo; asistíle como una Hermana de la Caridad... Murió, dejándome un legado..., ¡donosa idea! Consistía en un bastón, una má-

quina para hacer cigarrillos, un cuerno de caza y cuatro mil reales en dinero. ¡Una fortuna!... Mi hermano tuvo libros, yo ropa, y cuando me vestí de gente, empecé a tener enfermos. Parece que la Humanidad perdía la salud
sólo por darme trabajo... ¡Adelante, siempre
adelante!... Pasaron años, años..., al fin vi desde lejos el puerto de refugio después de grandes tormentas... Mi hermano y yo bogábamos
sin gran trabajo..., ya no estábamos tristes...
Dios sonreía dentro de nosotros. ¡Bien por los
Golfines!... Dios les había dado la mano. Yo
empecé a estudiar los ojos, y en poco tiempo
dominé la catarata; pero yo quería más... Gané
algún dinero; pero mi hermano consumía bastante... Al fin, Carlos salió de la Escuela...
¡Vivan los hombres valientes!... Después de
dejarle colocado en Ríotinto con un buen suel-
do, me marché a América. Yo había sido una
especie de Colón, el Colón del trabajo y una
especie de Hernán Cortés; yo había descubierto en mí un nuevo mundo, y después de des-
cubrirlo, lo había conquistado.

—Alábate, pandero—dijo Sofía, riendo.

—Si hay héroes en el mundo, tú eres uno de
ellos—afirmó Carlos, demostrando gran admiración por su hermano.

—Prepárese usted ahora, señor semidiós—dijo Sofía—, a coronar todas sus hazañas ha-

ciendo un milagro, que milagro será dar la vista a un ciego de nacimiento... Mira: allí sale don Francisco a recibirnos.

Avanzando por lo alto del cerro que limita las minas del lado de Poniente, habían llegado a Aldeacorba, y la casa del señor de Penáguilas, que, echándose el chaquetón a toda prisa, salió al encuentro de sus amigos. Caía la tarde.

—Ya la están ordeñando—dijo antes de saludarles—. Supongo que todos tomarán leche. ¿Cómo va ese valor, doña Sofía?... ¿Y usted, don Teodoro?... ¡Buena carga se ha echado a cuestas! ¿Qué tiene María Canela?... ¿Una patita mala? ¿De cuándo acá gastamos esos mimos?

Entraron todos en el patio de la casa. Oíanse los graves mugidos de las vacas, que acababan de entrar en el establo, y este rumor, unido al grato aroma campesino del heno que los mozos subían al pajar, recreaba dulcemente los sentidos y el ánimo.

El médico sentó a la Nela en un banco de piedra, y ella, paralizada por el respeto, sin hacer movimiento alguno, miraba a su bienhechor con asombro.

—¿En dónde está Pablo?—preguntó el ingeniero.

—Acaba de bajar a la huerta—replicó el señor de Penáguilas, ofreciendo una rústica silla a Sofía—. Oye, Nela, ve y acompáñale.

126

—Nó, no quiero que ande todavía—objetó Teodoro, deteniéndola—. Además, tomará leche con nosotros.

—¿No quiere usted ver a mi hijo esta tarde? —preguntó el señor de Penáguilas.

—Con el examen de ayer me basta—replicó Golfín—. Puede hacerse la operación.

—¿Con éxito?

—¡Ah! ¡Con éxito...! Eso no puede decirse. Gran placer sería para mí dar la vista a quien tanto la merece. Su hijo de usted posee una inteligencia de primer orden, una fantasía superior, una bondad exquisita. Su absoluto desconocimiento del mundo visible hace resaltar más aquellas grandiosas cualidades... Se nos presentan solas, admirablemente sencillas, con todo el candor y el encanto de las creaciones de la Naturaleza, donde no ha entrado el arte de los hombres. En él todo es idealismo, un idealismo grandioso, enormemente bello. Es como un yacimiento colosal, como el mármol en las canteras... No conoce la realidad...; vive la vida interior, la vida de ilusión pura... ¡Oh! ¡Si pudiéramos darle vista!... A veces me digo: «¡Si al darle ojos le convertiremos de ángel en hombre!...» Problema, duda tenemos aquí... Pero hagámosle hombre: ése es el deber de la Ciencia: traigámosle del mundo de las ilusiones a la esfera de la realidad, y entonces sus ideas serán exactas, tendrá el don precioso de apreciar en su verdadero valor todas las cosas.

Sacaron los vasos de leche blanca, espumosa, tibia, rebosando de los bordes con hirviente oleada. Ofreció Penáguilas el primero a Sofía, y los caballeros se apoderaron de los otros dos. Golfín dio el suyo a la Nela, que, abrumada de vergüenza, se negaba a tomarlo.

—Vamos, mujer—dijo Sofía—, no seas mal criada; toma lo que te dan.

—Otro vaso para el señor don Teodoro—dijo don Francisco al criado.

Oyóse en seguida el rumorcillo de los chorros que salían de la estrujada ubre.

—Y tendrá la apreciación justa de todas las cosas—dijo don Francisco, repitiendo esta frase del doctor, la cual había hecho no poca impresión en su espíritu—. Ha dicho usted, señor don Teodoro, una cosa admirable. Y ya que de esto hablamos, quiero confiarle las inquietudes que hace días tengo. Sentaréme también.

Acomodóse don Francisco en un banco próximo. Teodoro, Carlos y Sofía se habían sentado en sillas traídas de la casa, y la Nela continuaba en el banco de piedra. La leche que acababa de tomar le había dejado un bigotillo blanco en su labio superior.

—Pues decía, señor don Teodoro, que hace días me tiene inquieto el estado de exaltación en que se halla mi hijo; yo lo atribuyo a la esperanza que le hemos dado... Pero hay más, hay más. Ya sabe usted que acostumbro leerle diversos libros. Creo que se enardece demasiado su pensamiento con mis lecturas, y que se ha desarrollado en él una cantidad de ideas superior a la capacidad del cerebro de un hombre que no ve. No sé si me explico bien.

—Perfectamente.

—Sus cavilaciones no acaban nunca. Yo me asombro de oírle y del meollo y agudeza de sus discursos. Creo que su sabiduría está llena de mil errores por la falta de método y por el desconocimiento del mundo visible.

—No puede ser de otra manera.

—Pero lo más raro es que, arrastrado por su imaginación potente, la cual es como un hércules atado con cadenas dentro de un calabozo y que forcejea por romper hierros y muros...

—Muy bien, muy bien dicho.

—Su imaginación, digo, no puede contenerse en la oscuridad de sus sentidos, viene a éste nuestro mundo de luz, y quiere suplir con sus atrevidas creaciones la falta del sentido de la vista. Pablo posee un espíritu de indagación asombroso; pero este espíritu de investigación es un valiente pájaro con las alas rotas. Hace días que está delirante, no duerme, y su afán

5

de saber raya en locura. Quiere que a todas
horas le lea libros nuevos, y a cada pausa hace
las observaciones más agudas, con una mezcla
de candor que me hace reír. Afirma y sostiene
grandes absurdos, ¡y vaya usted a contradecir-
le!... Temo mucho que se me vuelva maniático,
que se desquicie su cerebro... ¡Si viera usted
cuán triste y caviloso se pone a veces!... Y coge
un estribillo, y dale que le darás, no lo suelta
en una semana. Hace días que no sale de un
tema tan gracioso como original. Ha dado en
sostener que la Nela es bonita.

Oyéronse risas, y la Nela se quedó como
púrpura.

—¡Que la Nela es bonita!—exclamó Teodoro
Golfín cariñosamente—. Pues sí que lo es.

—Ya lo creo, y ahora más, con su bigote blanco—indicó Sofía.

—Pues sí que es guapa—repitió Teodoro, tomándole la cara—. Sofía, dame tu pañuelo...
¡Vamos, fuera ese bigote!

Teodoro devolvió a Sofía su pañuelo, después
de afeitar a la Nela. Díjole a ésta don Francisco
que fuese a acompañar al ciego, y, cojeando,
entró en la casa.

—Y cuando le contradigo—añadió el señor
de Aldeacorba—, mi hijo me contesta que el
don de la vista quizá altere en mí, ¡qué disparate más gracioso!, la verdad de las cosas.

—No le contradiga usted, y suspenda por ahora absolutamente las lecturas. Durante algunos días ha de adoptar un régimen de tranquilidad absoluta. Hay que tratar al cerebro con grandes miramientos antes de emprender una operación de esta clase.

—Si Dios quiere que mi hijo vea—dijo el señor de Penáguilas con fervor—, le tendré a usted por el más grande, por el más benéfico de los hombres. La oscuridad de sus ojos es la oscuridad de mi vida; esa sombra negra ha hecho tristes mis días, entenebreciéndome el bienestar material que poseo. Soy rico: ¿de qué me sirven mis riquezas? Nada de lo que él no pueda ver es agradable para mí. Hace un mes he recibido la noticia de una gran herencia... Ya sabe usted, señor don Carlos, que mi primo Faustino ha muerto en Matamoros. No tiene hijos; le heredamos mi hermano Manuel y yo... Esto es echar margaritas a puercos, y no lo digo por mi hermano, que tiene una hija preciosa, ya casadera; dígolo por este miserable que no puede hacer disfrutar a su hijo único las delicias honradas de la buena posición.

Siguió a estas palabras un largo silencio, sólo interrumpido por el cariñoso mugido de las vacas en el cercano establo.

—Para él—añadió el patriarca de Aldeacorba con profunda tristeza—no existe el goce del

trabajo, el primero de todos los goces. No co-
nociendo las bellezas de la Naturaleza, ¿qué
significan para él la amenidad del campo ni
las delicias de la agricultura? Yo no sé cómo
Dios ha podido privar a un ser humano de admirar una res gorda, un árbol cuajado de pe-
ras, un prado verde, y de ver apilados los frutos de la tierra, y de repartir su jornal a los
trabajadores, y de leer en el cielo el tiempo
que ha de venir. Para él no existe más vida
que una cavilación febril. Su vida solitaria ni
aun disfrutará de la familia, porque cuando yo
me muera, ¿qué familia tendrá el pobre ciego?
Ni él querrá casarse, ni habrá mujer de punto
que con él se despose, a pesar de sus riquezas;
ni yo le aconsejaré tampoco que tome estado.
Así es que cuando el señor don Teodoro me ha
dado esperanza... he visto el cielo abierto; he
visto una especie de paraíso en la tierra...; he
visto un joven y alegre matrimonio; he visto
ángeles, nietecillos alrededor de mí; he visto
mi sepultura embellecida con las flores de la
infancia, con las tiernas caricias que aun después de mi última hora subsistirán, acompa-
ñándome debajo de la tierra... Ustedes no
comprenden esto; no saben que mi hermano
Manuel, que es más bueno que el buen pan,
luego que ha tenido noticia de mis esperanzas, ha empezado a hacer cálculos y más cálcu-

los... Vean lo que dice...—sacó varias cartas, que revolvió breve rato, sin dar con la que buscaba—. En resumidas cuentas, está loco de contento, y me ha dicho: «Casaré a mi Florentina con tu Pablito, y aquí tienes colocado a interés compuesto el millón y medio de pesos del primo Faustino...» Me parece que veo a Manolo frotándose las manos y dando zancajos, como es su costumbre cuando tiene una idea feliz. Les espero a él y a su hija de un momento a otro; vienen a pasar conmigo el 4 de octubre y a ver en qué para esta tentativa de dar luz a mi hijo...

Iba avanzando mansamente la noche, y los cuatro personajes rodeábanse de una sombra apacible. La casa empezaba a humear, anunciando la grata cena de aldea. El patriarca, que parecía la expresión humana de aquella tranquilidad melancólica, volvió a tomar la palabra, diciendo:

—La felicidad de mi hermano y la mía dependen de que yo tenga un hijo que ofrecer por esposo a Florentina, que es tan guapa como la Madre de Dios, como la Virgen María Inmaculada, según la pintan cuando viene el ángel a decirle: «El Señor es contigo»... Mi ciego no servirá para el caso..., pero mi hijo Pablo, con vista, será la realidad de todos mis sueños y la bendición de Dios entrando en mi casa.

Callaron todos, hondamente impresionados
por la relación patética y sencilla del bondadoso padre. Este llevó a sus ojos la mano basta y
ruda, endurecida por el arado, y se limpió una
lágrima.

—¿Qué dices tú a eso, Teodoro?—preguntó
Carlos a su hermano.

—No digo más sino que he examinado a conciencia este caso, y que no encuentro motivos
suficientes para decir: «No tiene cura», como
han dicho los médicos famosos a quienes ha
consultado nuestro amigo. Yo no aseguro la
curación; pero no la creo imposible. El examen
catóptrico que hice ayer no me indica lesión re-
tiniana ni alteración de los nervios de la visión.
Si la retina está bien, todo se reduce a quitar
de en medio un tabique importuno... El cristalino, volviéndose opaco y a veces duro como
piedra, es el que nos hace estas picardías... Si
todos los órganos desempeñaran su papel como
les está mandado... Pero allí, en esa república
del ojo, hay muchos holgazanes que se atrofian.

—De modo que todo queda reducido a una
simple catarata congénita—dijo el patriarca
con afán.

—¡Oh!, no, señor; si fuera eso sólo, seríamos
felices. Bastaba decretar la cesantía de ese fun-
cionario que tan mal cumple su obligación...
Le mandan que dé paso a la luz, y en vez de

hacerlo, se congestiona, se altera, se endurece, se vuelve opaco como una pared. Hay algo más, señor don Francisco. El iris tiene fisura. La pupila necesita que pongamos la mano en ella. Pero de todo eso me río yo si cuando tome posesión de ese ojo, por tanto tiempo dormido, entro en él y encuentro la coroides y la retina en buen estado. Si, por el contrario, después que aparte el cristalino, entro con la luz en mi nuevo palacio recién conquistado, y me encuentro con una amaurosis total... Si fuera incompleta, habríamos ganado mucho; pero siendo general... Contra la muerte del aparato nervioso de la visión no podemos nada. Nos está prohibido meternos en las honduras de la vida...¿Qué hemos de hacer? Paciencia. Este caso ha llamado vivamente mi atención: hay síntomas de que los aposentos interiores no están mal. Su Majestad la retina se halla quzá dispuesta a recibir los rayos lumínicos que se le quieran presentar. Su Alteza el humor vítreo probablemente no tendrá novedad. Si la larguísima falta de ejercicio en sus funciones le ha producido algo de glaucoma..., una especie de tristeza..., ya trataremos de arreglarlo. Todo estará muy bien allá en la cámara regia... Pero pienso otra cosa. La fisura y la catarata permiten comúnmente que entre un poco de claridad, y nuestro ciego no percibe claridad alguna. Esto me ha hecho cavilar... Verdad es que las capas corticales están muy opacas..., los obstáculos que halla la luz son muy fuertes... Allá veremos, don Francisco. ¿Tiene usted valor?

—¿Valor? ¡Que si tengo valor!...—exclamó don Francisco con cierto énfasis.

—Se necesita no poco para afrontar el caso siguiente...

—¿Cuál?

—Que su hijo de usted sufra una operación dolorosa, y después se quede tan ciego como antes... Yo dije a usted: «La imposibilidad no está demostrada. ¿Hago la operación?»

—Y yo respondí lo que ahora repito: «Hágase la operación, y cúmplase la voluntad de Dios. Adelante.»

—¡Adelante! Ha pronunciado usted mi palabra.

Levantóse don Francisco y estrechó entre sus dos manos la de don Teodoro, tan parecida a la zarpa de un león.

—En este clima, la operación puede hacerse en los primeros días de octubre—dijo Golfín—. Mañana fijaremos el tratamiento a que debe sujetarse el paciente... Y nos vamos, que se siente fresco en estas alturas.

Penáguilas ofreció a sus amigos casa y cena; mas no quisieron éstos aceptar. Salieron todos, juntamente con la Nela, a quien don Teodoro quiso llevar consigo, y también salió don Francisco para hacerles compañía hasta el establecimiento. Convidados del silencio y belleza de la noche, fueron departiendo sobre cosas agradables: unas, relativas al rendimiento de las minas; otras, a las cosechas del país. Cuando los Golfines entraron en su casa, volvióse a la suya don Francisco, solo y triste, andando despacio, la vista fija en el suelo. Pensaba en los terribles días de ansiedad y de esperanza, de sobresalto y dudas que se aproximaban. Por el camino encontró a *Choto*, y ambos subieron lentamente la escalera de palo. La luna alumbraba bastante, y la sombra del patriarca subía delante de él, quebrándose en los peldaños y haciendo como unos dobleces que saltaban de escalón en escalón. El perro iba a su lado. No teniendo el patriarca de Aldeacorba otro ser a quien fiar los pensamientos que abrumaban su cerebro, dijo así:

—*Choto*, ¿qué sucederá?

12. El doctor Celipín

El señor Centeno, después de recrear su espíritu en las borrosas columnas del *Diario*, y la Señana, después de sopesar con embriagador deleite las monedas contenidas en el calcetín, se acostaron. Habíanse ido también los hijos a reposar sobre sus respectivos colchones. Oyóse en la sala una retahila que parecía oración o romance de ciego; oyéronse bostezos, sobre los cuales trazaba cruces el perezoso dedo... La familia de piedra dormía.

Cuando la casa fue el mismo Limbo, oyóse en la cocina rumorcillo como de alimañas que salen de sus agujeros para buscarse la vida. Las cestas se abrieron, y Celipín oyó estas palabras:

—Celipín, esta noche sí que te traigo un buen regalo; mira...

Celipín no podía distinguir nada; pero alargando la mano, tomó de la de María dos duros como dos soles, de cuya autenticidad se cercioró por el tacto, ya que por la vista difícilmente podía hacerlo, quedándose pasmado y mudo.

—Me los dio don Teodoro—añadió la Nela—
para que me comprara unos zapatos. Como yo
para nada necesito zapatos, te los doy, y así,
pronto juntarás aquello.

—¡Córcholis!, ¡que eres más buena que María Santísima!... Ya poco me falta, Nela, y en
cuanto apande media docena de reales..., ya
verán quién es Celipín.

—Mira, hijito; el que me ha dado ese dinero
andaba por las calles pidiendo limosna cuando
era niño, y después...

—¡Córcholis! ¡Quién lo había de decir!... Don
Teodoro... ¡Y ahora tiene más dinero...! Dicen
que lo que tiene no lo cargan seis mulas.

—Y dormía en las calles, y servía de criado,
y no tenía calzones...; en fin, que era más pobre
que las ratas. Su hermano don Carlos vivía en
una casa de trapo viejo.

—¡Jesús! ¡Córcholis! ¡Y qué cosas se ven por
esas tierras!... Yo también me buscaré una casa
de trapo viejo.

—Y después tuvo que ser barbero para ganarse la vida y poder estudiar.

—Miá tú..., yo tengo pensado irme derecho
a una barbería... Yo me pinto solo para rapar...
¡Pues soy yo poco listo en gracia de Dios! Desde que yo llegue a Madrid, por un lado rapando
y por otro estudiando, he de aprender en dos
meses toda la ciencia. Miá tú, ahora se me ha

ocurrido que debo tirar para médico... Sí, médico, que echando una mano a este pulso, otra mano al otro, se llena de dinero el bolsillo.

—Don Teodoro—dijo la Nela—tenía menos que tú, porque tú vas a tener cinco duros, y con cinco duros parece que todo se ha de venir a la mano. ¡Aquí de los hombres guapos! Don Teodoro y don Carlos eran como los pájaros que andan solos por el mundo. Ellos con su buen gobierno se volvieron sabios. Don Teodoro leía en los muertos y don Carlos leía en las piedras, y así los dos aprendieron el modo de hacerse personas cabales. Por eso es don Teodoro tan amigo de los pobres. Celipín, si me hubieras visto esta tarde cuando me llevaba al hombro... Después me dio un vaso de leche y me echaba unas miradas como las que se echan a las señoras.

—Todos los hombres listos somos de ese modo—observó Celipín con petulancia—. Verás tú qué fino y galán voy a ser yo cuando me ponga mi levita y mi sombrero de una tercia de alto. Y también me calzaré las manos con eso que llaman guantes, que no pienso quitarme nunca como no sea sino para tomar el pulso... Tendré un bastón con una porra dorada y me vestiré..., eso sí, en mis carnes no se pone sino paño fino... ¡Córcholis! Te vas a reír cuando me veas.

—No pienses todavía en esas cosas de remontarte mucho, que eres más pelado que un huevo —le dijo ella—. Vete poquito a poquito, hoy me aprendo esto, mañana lo otro. Yo te aconsejo que antes de meterte en eso de curar enfermos, debes aprender a escribir para que pongas una carta a tu madre pidiéndole perdón, y diciéndole que te has ido de tu casa para afinarte, hacerte como don Teodoro y ser un médico muy cabal.

—Calla, mujer... ¿Pues qué, creías que la escritura no es lo primero?... Deja tú que yo coja una pluma en la mano, y verás qué rasgueo de letras y qué perfiles finos para arriba y para abajo, como la firma de don Francisco de Penáguilas... ¡Escribir!, a mí con esas... A los cuatro días verás qué cartas pongo... Ya las oirás leer, y verás qué conceítos los míos y qué modo aquel de echar retólicas que os dejen bobos a todos. ¡Córcholis! Nela, tú no sabes que yo tengo mucho talento. Lo siento aquí dentro de mi cabeza, haciéndome *burumbum, burumbum*, como el agua de la caldera de vapor... Como que no me deja dormir, y pienso que es que todas las ciencias se me entran aquí, y andan dentro volando a tientas como los murciélagos, y diciéndome que las estudie. Todas, todas las ciencias las he de aprender, y ni una sola se me ha de quedar... Verás tú...

—Pues debe de haber muchas. Pablo, que las sabe todas, me ha dicho que son muchas, y que la vida entera de un hombre no basta para una sola.

—Ríete tú de eso... Ya me verás a mí...

—Y la más bonita de todas es la de don Carlos... Porque mira tú que eso de coger una piedra y hacer con ella latón... Otros dicen que hacen plata y también oro. Aplícate a eso, Celipillo.

—Desengáñate, no hay saber como ese de cogerle a uno la muñeca y mirarle la lengua, y decir al momento en qué hueco del cuerpo tiene aposentado el maleficio... Dicen que don Teodoro le saca un ojo a un hombre y le pone otro nuevo, con el cual ve como si fuera ojo nacido... Miá tú que eso de ver a uno que se está muriendo, y con mandarle tomar pongo el caso, media docena de mosquitos guisados un lunes con palos de mimbre cogidos por una doncella que se llame Juana, dejarle bueno y sano, es mucho aquél... Ya verás, ya verás cómo se porta don Celipín el de Socartes. Te digo que se ha de hablar de mí hasta en la Habana.

—Bien, bien—dijo la Nela con alegría—; pero mira que has de ser buen hijo, pues si tus padres no quieren enseñarte, es porque ellos no tienen talento, y pues tú lo tienes, pídele por

ellos a la Santísima Virgen, y no dejes de man-
darles algo de lo mucho que vas a ganar.

—Eso sí lo haré. Miá tú, aunque me voy de
la casa, no es que quiera mal a mis padres, y
ya verás cómo dentro de poco tiempo ves venir
un mozo de la estación cargado que se revienta
con unos grandes paquetes. Y ¿qué será? Pues
refajos para mi madre y mis hermanas y un
sombrero alto para mi padre. A ti puede que
te mande también un par de pendientes.

—Muy pronto regalas—dijo la Nela, sofocando la risa—. ¡Pendientes para mí!...

—Pero ahora se me está ocurriendo una cosa.
¿Quieres que te la diga? Pues es que tú debías
venir conmigo, y siendo dos, nos ayudaríamos
a ganar y a aprender. Tú también tienes talento, que eso del pesquis a mí no se me escapa,
y bien podías llegar a ser señora, como yo caballero. ¡Que me había de reír si te viera tocando el piano como doña Sofía!

—¡Qué bobo eres! Yo no sirvo para nada. Si
fuera contigo sería un estorbo para ti.

—Ahora dicen que van a dar vista a don Pablo, y cuando él tenga vista, nada tienes tú que
hacer en Socartes. ¿Qué te parece mi idea?...
¿No respondes?

Pasó algún tiempo sin que la Nela contesta-
ra nada. Preguntó de nuevo Celipín, sin obte-
ner respuesta.

—Duérmete, Celipín—dijo al fin la de las cestas—. Yo tengo mucho sueño.

—Como mi talento me deje dormir, a la buena de Dios.

Un minuto después se veía a sí mismo en figura semejante a la de don Teodoro Golfín, poniendo ojos nuevos en órbitas viejas, claveteando piernas rotas, y arrancando criaturas a la muerte mediante copiosas tomas de mosquitos cogidos por una doncella y guisados un lunes con palos de mimbre. Vióse cubierto de riquísimos paños, las manos aprisionadas en guantes olorosos y arrastrado en coche, del cual tiraban cisnes, que no caballos, y llamado por reyes, o solicitado de reinas, por honestas damas requerido, alabado de magnates y llevado en triunfo por los pueblos todos de la tierra.

La Nela cerró sus conchas para estar más sola. Sigámosla; penetremos en su pensamiento. Pero antes conviene hacer algo de historia.

Habiendo carecido absolutamente de instrucción en su edad primera; habiendo carecido también de las sugestiones cariñosas que enderezan el espíritu de un modo seguro al conocimiento de ciertas verdades, habíase formado Marianela en su imaginación poderosa un orden de ideas muy singular, una teogonía extravagante y un modo rarísimo de apreciar las causas y los efectos de las cosas. Exacta era la idea de Teodoro·Golfín al comparar el espíritu de la Nela con los pueblos primitivos. Como en éstos, dominaba en ella el sentimiento y la fascinación de lo maravilloso; creía en poderes sobrenaturales, distintos del único y grandioso Dios, y veía en los objetos de la Naturaleza personalidades vagas que no carecían de modos de comunicación con los hombres.

A pesar de esto, la Nela no ignoraba completamente el Evangelio. Jamás le fue bien enseñado; pero había oído hablar de él. Veía que la gente iba a una ceremonia que llamaban Misa; tenía idea de un sacrificio sublime; mas sus nociones no pasaban de aquí. Habíase acostumbrado a respetar, en virtud de un sentimentalismo contagioso, al Dios crucificado; sabía que aquello debía besarse; sabía además algunas oraciones aprendidas de rutina; sabía que todo aquello que no se posee debe pedirse a Dios, pero nada más. El horrible abandono de su inteligencia hasta el tiempo de su amistad con el señorito de Penáguilas era causa de esto. Y la amistad con aquel ser extraordinario, que desde su oscuridad explotaba con el valiente ojo de su pensamiento infatigable los problemas de la vida, había llegado tarde. En el espíritu de la Nela hallábase ya petrificado lo que podremos llamar su filosofía, hechura de ella misma, un no sé qué de paganismo y de sentimentalismo, mezclados y confundidos. Debemos añadir que María, a pesar de vivir tan fuera del elemento social en que todos vivimos, mostraba casi siempre buen sentido y sabía apreciar sesudamente las cosas de la vida, como se ha visto en los consejos que a Celipín daba. La grandísima valía de su alma explica esto.

La más notable tendencia de su espíritu era
la que le impulsaba con secreta pasión a amar
la hermosura física, dondequiera que se encon-
trase. No hay nada más natural, tratándose
de un ser criado en absoluto apartamiento de
la sociedad y de la ciencia, y en comunicación
abierta y constante, en trato familiar, digámoslo así, con la Naturaleza, poblada de bellezas
imponentes o graciosas, llena de luz y colores,
de murmullos elocuentes y de formas diversas.
Pero Marianela hubo de añadir a su admiración
el culto, y siguiendo una ley, propia también
del estado primitivo, había personificado todas
las bellezas que adoraba en una sola, ideal y
con forma humana. Esta belleza era la Virgen
María, adquisición hecha por ella en los dominios del Evangelio, que tan imperfectamente
poseía. La Virgen no habría sido para ella el
ideal más querido, si a sus perfecciones morales no reuniera todas las hermosuras, guape-
zas y donaires del orden físico, si no tuviera
una cara noblemente hechicera y seductora, un
semblante humano y divino al propio tiempo,
que a ella le parecía resumen y cifra de toda
la luz del mundo, de toda la melancolía y paz
sabrosa de la noche, de la música de los arroyos, de la gracia y elegancia de las flores, de
la frescura del rocío, de los suaves quejidos
del viento, de la inmaculada nieve de las mon-

tañas, del cariñoso mirar de las estrellas y de
la pomposa majestad de las nubes cuando gravemente discurren por la inmensidad del cielo.

La persona de Dios representábasele terrible
y ceñuda, más propia para infundir respeto que
cariño. Todo lo bueno venía de la Virgen María,
y a la Virgen debía pedirse todo lo que han
menester las criaturas. Dios reñía y ella sonreía. Dios castigaba y ella perdonaba. No es
esta última idea tan rara para que llame la
atención. Casi rige en absoluto a las clases
menesterosos y rurales de nuestro país.

También es común en éstas, cuando se jun-
ta un gran abandono a una poderosa fantasía,
la fusión que hacía la Nela entre las bellezas
de la Naturaleza y aquella figura encantadora
que resume en sí casi todos los elementos es-
téticos de la idea cristiana. Si a la soledad en
que vivía la Nela hubieran llegado menos nociones cristianas de las que llegaron; si su
apartamiento del foco de ideas hubiera sido
absoluto, su paganismo habría sido entonces
completo, adorando la luna, los bosques, el
fuego, los arroyos, el sol.

Tal era la Nela que se crio en Socartes, y así
llegó a los quince años. Desde esta fecha, su
amistad con Pablo y sus frecuentes coloquios
con quien poseía tantas y tan buenas nociones,
modificaron algo su modo de pensar; pero la

base de sus ideas no sufrió alteración. Continuaba dando a la hermosura física cierta soberanía augusta; seguía llena de supersticiones y adorando a la Santísima Virgen como un compendio de todas las bellezas naturales, encarnando en esta persona la ley moral, y rematando su sistema con extrañas ideas respecto a la muerte y la vida futura.

Encerrándose en sus conchas, Marianela habló así:

«Madre de Dios y mía, ¿por qué no me hiciste hermosa? ¿Por qué cuando mi madre me tuvo no me miraste desde arriba?... Mientras más me miro, más fea me encuentro. ¿Para qué estoy yo en el mundo?, ¿para qué sirvo?, ¿a quién puedo interesar? A uno solo, Señora y Madre mía, a uno solo que me quiere porque no me ve. ¿Qué será de mí cuando me vea y deje de quererme?...; porque, ¿cómo es posible que me quiera viendo este cuerpo chico, esta figurilla de pájaro, esta tez pecosa, esta boca sin gracia, esta nariz picuda, este pelo descolorido, esta persona mía que no sirve sino para que todo el mundo le dé con el pie? ¿Quién es la Nela? Nadie. La Nela sólo es algo para el ciego. Si sus ojos nacen ahora y los vuelve a mí y me ve, me caigo muerta... El es el único para quien la Nela no es menos que los gatos y los perros. Me quiere como quieren los novios a

sus novias, como Dios manda que se quieran
las personas... Señora Madre mía, ya que vas
a hacer el milagro de darle vista, hazme hermosa a mí o mátame, porque para nada estoy
en el mundo. Yo no soy nada ni nadie más que
para uno solo... ¿Siento yo que recobre la vista? No, eso no, eso no Yo quiero que vea.
Daré mis ojos porque él vea con los suyos;
daré mi vida toda. Yo quiero que don Teodoro
haga el milagro que dicen. ¡Benditos sean los
hombres sabios! Lo que no quiero es que mi
amo me vea, no. Antes que consentir que me
vea, ¡Madre mía!, me enterraré viva; me arro-
jaré al río... Sí, sí; que se trague la tierra mi
fealdad. Yo no debí haber nacido.»

Y luego, dando una vuelta en la cesta, pro-
seguía:

«Mi corazón es todo para él. Este cieguecito
que ha tenido el antojo de quererme mucho, es
para mí lo primero del mundo después de la
Virgen María. ¡Oh! ¡Si yo fuese grande y hermosa; si tuviera el talle, la cara y el tamaño...,
sobre todo el tamaño, de otras mujeres; si yo
pudiese llegar a ser señora y componerme!...
¡Ay!, entonces mi mayor delicia sería que sus
ojos se recrearan en mí... Si yo fuera como las
demás, siquiera como Mariuca..., ¡qué pronto
buscaría el modo de instruirme, de afinarme,
de ser una señora!... ¡Oh! ¡Madre y Reina mía,

lo único que tengo me lo vas a quitar!... ¿Para qué permitiste que le quisiera yo y que él me quisiera a mí? Esto no debió ser así.»

Y derramando lágrimas y cruzando los brazos, añadió medio vencida por el sueño:

«¡Ay! ¡Cuánto te quiero, niño de mi alma! Quiere mucho a la Nela, a la pobre Nela, que no es nada... Quiéreme mucho... Déjame darte un beso en tu preciosísima cabeza...; pero no abras los ojos, no me mires..., ciérralos, así, así.»

14. De cómo la Virgen María
    se apareció a la Nela

Los pensamientos, que huyen cuando somos vencidos por el sueño, suelen quedarse en acecho para volver a ocuparnos bruscamente cuando despertamos. Así ocurrió a Mariquilla, que habiéndose quedado dormida con los pensamientos más extraños acerca de la Virgen María, del ciego y de su propia fealdad, que ella deseaba ver trocada en pasmosa hermosura, con ellos mismos despertó cuando los gritos de la Señana la arrancaron de entre sus cestas. Desde que abrió los ojos, la Nela hizo su oración de costumbre a la Virgen María; pero aquel día la oración se compuso de la retahíla ordinaria de las oraciones y de algunas piezas de su propia invención, resultando un discurso que si se escribiera habría de ser curioso. Entre otras cosas, la Nela dijo:

«Anoche te me has aparecido en sueños, Señora, y me prometiste que hoy me consolarías. Estoy despierta, y me parece que todavía te

152

estoy mirando, y que tengo delante tu cara,
más linda que todas las cosas guapas y hermosas que hay en el mundo.»

Al decir esto, la Nela revolvía sus ojos con
desvarío en derredor de sí... Observándose a
sí misma de la manera vaga que podía hacerlo,
pensó de este modo: «A mí me pasa algo.»

—¿Qué tienes, Nela? ¿Qué te pasa, chiquilla?—le dijo la Señana, notando que la muchacha miraba con atónitos ojos a un punto fijo
del espacio—. ¿Estás viendo visiones, mar-
mota?

La Nela no respondió, porque estaba su espíritu ocupado en platicar consigo propio, di-
ciéndose:

«¿Qué es lo que yo tengo?... No puede ser
maleficio, porque lo que tengo dentro de mí
no es la figura feísima y negra del demonio
malo, sino una cosa celestial, una cara, una
sonrisa y un modo de mirar que, o yo estoy
tonta, o son de la misma Virgen María en persona. Señora y Madre mía, ¿será verdad que
hoy vas a consolarme?... ¿Y cómo me vas a
consolar? ¿Qué te he pedido anoche?»

—¡Eh..., chiquilla!—gritó la Señana con voz
desapacible, como el más destemplado sonido
que puede oírse en el mundo—. Ven a lavarte
esa cara de perro.

La Nela corrió. Había sentido en su espíritu

un sacudimiento como el que produce la repentina invasión de una gran esperanza. Miróse en
la trémula superficie del agua, y al instante sintió que su corazón se oprimía.

«Nada...—murmuró—, tan feíta como siempre. La misma figura de niña con alma y años
de mujer.»

Después de lavarse, sobrecogiéronla las mismas extrañas sensaciones de antes, al modo de
congojas placenteras. A pesar de su escasa experiencia, Marianela tuvo tino para clasificar
aquellas sensaciones en el orden de los pre-
sentimientos.

«Pablo y yo—pensó—hemos hablado de lo
que se siente cuando va a venir una cosa alegre
o triste. Pablo me ha dicho también que poco
antes de los temblores de tierra se siente una
cosa particular, y las personas sienten una cosa particular..., y los animales sienten también
una cosa particular... ¿Irá a temblar la tierra?»
Arrodillándose tentó el suelo.

«No sé..., pero algo va a pasar. Que es una
cosa buena no puedo dudarlo... La Virgen me
dijo anoche que hoy me consolaría... ¿Qué es
lo que tengo?... ¿Esa Señora celestial anda alrededor de mí? No la veo, pero la siento; está
detrás, está delante.»

Pasó por junto a las máquinas de lavado en
dirección al plano inclinado, y miraba con des-

pavoridos ojos a todas partes. No veía más que las figuras de barro crudo que se agitaban con gresca infernal en medio del áspero bullicio de las cribas cilíndricas, pulverizando el agua y humedeciendo el polvo. Más adelante, cuando se vio sola, se detuvo, y poniéndose el dedo en la frente, clavando los ojos en el suelo con la vaguedad que imprime a aquel sentido la duda, se hizo esta pregunta: «¿Pero yo estoy alegre o estoy triste?»

Miró después al cielo, admirándose de hallarlo lo mismo que todos los días (y era aquél de los más hermosos), y avivó el paso para llegar pronto a Aldeacorba de Suso. En vez de seguir la cañada de las minas para subir por la escalera de palo, apartóse de la hondonada por el regato que hay junto al plano inclinado, con objeto de subir a las praderas y marchar después derecha y por camino llano a Aldeacorba. Este camino era más bonito, y por eso lo prefería casi siempre. Había callejas pobladas de graciosas y aromáticas flores, en cuya multitud pastaban rebaños de abejas y mariposas; había grandes zarzales llenos del negro fruto que tanto apetecen los chicos; había grupos de guinderos, en cuyos troncos se columpiaban las madreselvas, y había también corpulentas encinas, grandes, anchas, redondas, oscuras, que parece se recreaban contemplando su propia sombra.

La Nela seguía andando despacio, inquieta de lo que en sí misma sentía y de la angustia deliciosa que la embargaba. Su imaginación fecunda supo al fin hallar la fórmula más propia para expresar aquella obsesión, y recordando haber oído decir *Fulano o Zutano tiene los demonios en el cuerpo*, ella dijo: «Yo tengo los ángeles en el cuerpo... Virgen María, tú estás hoy conmigo. Esto que siento son las carcajadas de tus ángeles que juegan dentro de mí. Tú no estás lejos, te veo y no te veo, como cuando vemos con los ojos cerrados.»

Cerraba los ojos y los abría de nuevo. Habiendo pasado junto a un bosque, dobló el ángulo del camino para llegar adonde se extendía un gran bardo de zarzas, las más frondosas, las más bonitas y crecidas de todo aquel país. También se veían lozanos helechos, madreselvas, parras vírgenes y otras plantas de arrimo, que se sostenían unas a otras por no haber allí grandes troncos. La Nela sintió que las ramas se agitaban a su derecha; miró... ¡Cielos divinos! Allí estaba, dentro de un marco de verdura, la Virgen María Inmaculada, con su propia cara, sus propios ojos, que al mirar reflejaban toda la hermosura del cielo. La Nela se quedó muda, petrificada, con una sensación en que se

confundían el fervor y el espanto. No pudo dar
un paso, ni gritar, ni moverse, ni respirar, ni
apartar sus ojos de aquella aparición maravillosa.

Había aparecido entre el follaje, mostrando
completamente todo su busto y cara. Era, sí,
la auténtica imagen de aquella escogida doncella de Nazareth, cuya perfección moral han
tratado de expresar por medio de la forma pictórica los artistas de dieciocho siglos, desde
San Lucas hasta los contemporáneos. La Humanidad ha visto esta sacra persona con distintos ojos, ora con los de Alberto Durero, ora
con los de Rafael Sanzio, o bien con los de
Van Dyck y Bartolomé Murillo. Aquélla que
a la Nela se apareció era según el modo Ra-
faelesco, sobresaliente entre todos si se atiende
a que en él la perfección de la belleza humana
se acerca más que ningún otro recurso artístico
a la expresión de la divinidad. El óvalo de su
cara era menos angosto que el del tipo sevilla-
no, ofreciendo la graciosa redondez del itálico.
Sus ojos, de admirables proporciones, eran la
misma serenidad unida a la gracia, a la armonía, con un mirar tan distinto de la frialdad
como del extremado relampagueo de los ojos
andaluces. Sus cejas eran delicada hechura del
más fino pincel, y trazaban un arco sutil. En
su frente no se concebían el ceño del enfado ni

las sombras de la tristeza, y sus labios, un poco
gruesos, dejaban ver, al sonreír, los más preciosos dientes que han mordido manzana del
Paraíso. Sin querer hemos ido a parar a nuestra madre Eva, cuando tan lejos está la que dio
el triunfo a la serpiente de la que aplastó su
cabeza; pero el examen de las distintas maneras de la belleza humana conduce a estos y
otros más lamentables contrasentidos. Para
concluir el imperfecto retrato de aquella estupenda visión que dejó desconcertada y como
muerta a la pobre Nela, diremos que su tez
era de ese color de rosa tostado, o más bien
moreno encendido, que forma como un rubor
delicioso en el rostro de aquellas divinas imágenes, ante las cuales se extasían lo mismo los
siglos devotos que los impíos.

Pasado el primer instante de estupor, lo que
ante todo observó Marianela, llenándose de
confusión, fue que la bella Virgen tenía una
corbata azul en su garganta, adorno que ella
no había visto jamás en las Vírgenes soñadas
ni en las pintadas. Inmediatamente notó también que los hombros y el pecho de la divina
mujer se cubrían con un vestido, en el cual
todo era semejante a los que usan las mujeres
del día. Pero lo que más turbó y desconcertó
a la pobre muchacha fue ver que la gentil ima-

gen estaba cogiendo moras de zarza... y co-
miéndoselas.

Empezaba a hacer los juicios a que daba ocasión esta extraña conducta de la Virgen, cuando oyó una voz varonil y chillona que decía:

—¡Florentina, Florentina!

—Aquí estoy, papá; aquí estoy comiendo
moras silvestres.

—¡Dale!... ¿Y qué gusto le encuentras a las
moras silvestres?... ¡Caprichosa!... ¿No te he
dicho que eso es más propio de los chicuelos
holgazanes del campo que de una señorita criada en la buena sociedad..., criada en la buena
sociedad?

La Nela vio acercarse con grave paso al que
esto decía. Era un hombre de edad madura,
mediano de cuerpo, algo rechoncho, de cara
arrebolada y que parecía echar de sí rayos de
satisfacción como el sol los echa de luz; pequeño de piernas, un poco largo de nariz, y mag-
nificado con varios objetos decorativos, entre
los cuales descollaba una gran cadena de reloj
y un fino sombrero de fieltro de alas anchas.

—Vamos, mujer—dijo cariñosamente el señor don Manuel Penáguilas, pues no era otro—,
las personas decentes no comen moras silvestres, ni dan esos brincos. ¿Ves? Te has estropea-
do el vestido..., no lo digo por el vestido, que
así como se te compró ése, se te comprará

otro...; dígolo porque la gente que te vea podrá creer que no tienes más ropa que la puesta.

La Nela, que comenzaba a ver claro, observó
los vestidos de la señorita de Penáguilas. Eran
buenos y ricos; pero su figura expresaba a maravilla la transición no muy lenta del estado de
aldeana al de señorita rica. Todo su atavío,
desde el calzado a la peineta, era de señorita
de pueblo en día del santo patrono titular. Mas
eran tales los encantos naturales de Florentina,
que ningún accidente comprendido en las con-
vencionales reglas de la elegancia podía oscu-
recerlos. No podía negarse, sin embargo, que
su encantadora persona estaba pidiendo a gritos una rústica saya, un cabello en trenzas y al
desgaire, con aderezo de amapolas, un talle en
justillo, una sarta de corales; en suma, lo que
el pudor y el instinto de presunción hubieran
ideado por sí, sin mezcla de invención cor-
tesana.

Cuando la señorita se apartaba del zarzal,
don Manuel acertó a ver a la Nela a punto que
ésta había caído completamente de su burro, y
dirigiéndose a ella, gritó:

—¡Oh!..., ¿aquí estás tú?... Mira, Florentina,
ésta es la Nela...; recordarás que te hablé de
ella. Es la que acompaña a tu primito..., a tu
primito. ¿Y qué tal te va por estos barrios?...

—Bien, señor don Manuel. ¿Y usted cómo

está?—repuso Mariquilla, sin apartar los ojos de Florentina.

—Yo tan campante, ya ves tú. Esta es mi hija. ¿Qué te parece?

Florentina corría detrás de una mariposa.

—Hija mía, ¿adónde vas?, ¿qué es eso?—dijo el padre, visiblemente contrariado—. ¿Te parece bien que corras de ese modo detrás de un insecto como los chiquillos vagabundos?... Mucha formalidad, hija mía. Las señoritas criadas entre la buena sociedad no hacen eso..., no hacen eso...

Don Manuel tenía la costumbre de repetir la última frase de sus párrafos o discursos.

—No se enfade usted, papá—repitió la joven, regresando después de su expedición infructuosa hasta ponerse al amparo de las alas del sombrero paterno—. Ya sabe usted que me gusta mucho el campo y que me vuelvo loca cuando veo árboles, flores, praderas. Como en aquella triste tierra de Campó donde vivimos hay poco de esto...

—¡Oh! No hables mal de Santa Irene de Campó, una villa ilustrada, donde se encuentran hoy muchas comodidades y una sociedad distinguida. También han llegado allá los adelantos de la civilización..., de la civilización. Andando a mi lado juiciosamente, puedes admirar la Naturaleza; yo también la admiro sin

6

hacer cabriolas como los volatineros. A las personas educadas entre una sociedad escogida
se las conoce por el modo de andar y por el
modo de contemplar los objetos. Eso de estar
diciendo a cada instante: «¡Ah!..., ¡oh!..., ¡qué
bonito!... ¡Mire usted, papá!», señalando a un
helecho, a un roble, a una piedra, a un espino,
a un chorro de agua, no es cosa de muy buen
gusto... Creerán que te has criado en algún
desierto... Conque anda a mi lado... La Nela
nos dirá por dónde volveremos a casa, porque
a la verdad, yo no sé dónde estamos.

—Tirando a la izquierda por detrás de aquella casa vieja—dijo la Nela—, se llega muy pronto... Pero aquí viene el señor don Francisco.

En efecto; apareció don Francisco, gritando:

—Que se enfría el chocolate...

—¡Qué quieres, hombre!... Mi hija estaba tan
deseosa de retozar por el campo, que no ha
querido esperar, y aquí nos tienes de mata en
mata como cabritillos..., de mata en mata como
cabritillos.

—A casa, a casa. Ven tú también, Nela, para
que tomes chocolate—dijo Penáguilas, poniendo su mano sobre la cabeza de la vagabunda—.
¿Qué te parece mi sobrina?... Vaya, que es
guapa... Florentina, después que toméis el chocolate, la Nela os llevará a pasear a Pablo y a

tı, y verás todas las hermosuras del país, las minas, el bosque, el río...

Florentina dirigió una mirada cariñosa a la infeliz criatura, que a su lado parecía hecha expresamente por la Naturaleza para hacer resaltar más la perfección y magistral belleza de algunas de sus obras. Al llegar a la casa, esperábalos la mesa con las jícaras, donde aún hervía el espeso licor guayaquileño y un montoncillo de rebanadas de pan. También estaba en expectativa la mantequilla, puesta entre hojas de castaño, sin que faltaran algunas pastas y golosinas. Los vasos de fresca y transparente agua reproducían en su convexo cristal estas bellezas gastronómicas, agrandándolas.

—Hagamos algo por la vida—dijo don Francisco, sentándose.

—Nela—indicó Pablo—, tú también tomarás chocolate.

No lo había dicho, cuando Florentina ofreció a Marianela el jicarón con todo lo demás que en la mesa había. Resistíase a aceptar el convite; mas con tanta bondad y con tan graciosa llaneza insistio la señorita de Penáguilas, que no hubo más que decir. Miraba de reojo don Manuel a su hija, cual si no se hallara completamente satisfecho de los progresos de ella en el arte de la buena educación, porque una de las partes principales de ésta consistía, según

él, en una fina apreciación de los grados de ur-
banidad con que debía obsequiarse a las diferentes personas según su posición, no dando a
ninguna ni más ni menos de lo que le corres-
pondía con arreglo al fuero social; y de este
modo quedaban todos en su lugar, y la propia
dignidad se sublimaba, conservándose en el
justo medio de la cortesía, el cual estriba en no
ensoberbecerse demasiado delante de los ricos,
ni humillarse demasiado delante de los pobres... Luego que fue tomado el chocolate, don
Francisco dijo:

—Váyase fuera toda la gente menuda. Hijo
mío, hoy es el último día que don Teodoro te
permite salir fuera de casa. Los tres pueden ir
a paseo, mientras mi hermano y yo vamos a
echar un vistazo al ganado... Pájaros, a volar.

No necesitaron que se les rogara mucho. Convidados de la hermosura del día, volaron los
jóvenes al campo.

Estaba la señorita de pueblo muy gozosa en medio de las risueñas praderas, sin la traba enojosa de las pragmáticas sociales de su señor padre, y así, en cuanto se vio a regular distancia de la casa, empezó a correr alegremente y a suspenderse de las ramas de los árboles que a su alcance veía, para balancearse ligeramente en ellas. Tocaba con las yemas de sus dedos las moras silvestres, y cuando las hallaba maduras cogía tres, una para cada boca.

—Esta para ti, primito—decía, poniéndosela en la boca—, y ésta para ti, Nela. Dejaré para mí la más chica.

Al ver cruzar los pájaros a su lado, no podía resistir movimientos semejantes a una graciosa pretensión de volar y decía: «¿Adónde irán ahora esos bribones?» De todos los robles cogía una rama, y abriendo la bellota para ver lo que había dentro, la mordía, y al sentir su amargor, arrojábala lejos. Un botánico atacado del deli-

rio de las clasificaciones no hubiera coleccio-
nado con tanto afán como ella todas las flores
bonitas que le salían al paso, dándole la bien-
venida desde el suelo con sus carillas de fiesta.
Con lo recolectado en media hora adornó todos
los ojales de la americana de su primo, los cabellos de la Nela y, por último, sus propios
cabellos.

—A la primita—dijo Pablo—le gustará ver
las minas. Nela, ¿no te parece que bajemos?

—Sí, bajemos... Por aquí, señorita.

—Pero no me hagan pasar por túneles, que
me da mucho miedo. Eso sí que no lo consien-
to—dijo Florentina, siguiéndoles—. Primo, ¿tú
y la Nela paseáis mucho por aquí? Esto es precioso. Aquí viviría yo toda mi vida... ¡Bendito
sea el hombre que te va a dar la facultad de
gozar de todas estas preciosidades!

—¡Dios lo quiera! Mucho más hermosas me
parecerán a mí, que jamás las he visto, que a
vosotras, que estáis saciadas de verlas... No
creas tú, Florentina, que yo no comprendo las
bellezas: las siento en mí de tal modo, que
casi casi suplo con mi pensamiento la falta
de la vista.

—Eso sí que es admirable... Por más que
digas—replicó Florentina—, siempre te resul-
tarán algunos buenos chascos cuando abras los
ojos.

—Podrá ser—dijo el ciego, que aquel día estaba muy lacónico.

La Nela no estaba lacónica, sino muda.

Cuando se acercaron a la concavidad de la Terrible, Florentina admiró el espectáculo sorprendente que ofrecían las rocas cretáceas, subsistentes en medio del terreno después de arrancado el mineral. Comparólo a grandes grupos de bollos, pegados unos a otros por el azúcar; después de mirarlo mucho por segunda vez, lo compará a una gran escultura de perros y gatos que se habían quedado convertidos en piedra en el momento más crítico de una encarnizada reyerta.

—Sentémonos en esta ladera—dijo—, y veremos pasar los trenes con mineral, y además veremos esto, que es muy bonito. Aquella piedra grande que está en medio tiene su gran boca, ¿no la ves, Nela?, y en la boca tiene un palillo de dientes; es una planta que ha nacido sola. Parece que se ríe mirándonos, porque también tiene ojos; y más allá hay una con joroba, y otra que fuma en pipa, y dos que se están tirando de los pelos, y una que bosteza, y otra que duerme la mona, y otra que está boca abajo sosteniendo con los pies una catedral, y otra que empieza en guitarra y acaba en cabeza de perro, con una cafetera por gorro.

—Todo eso que dices, primita—observó el ciego—, me prueba que con los ojos se ven muchos disparates, lo cual indica que ese órgano tan precioso sirve a veces para presentar las cosas desfiguradas, cambiando los objetos de su natural forma en otra postiza y fingida; pues en lo que tienes delante de ti no hay confituras, ni gatos, ni hombres, ni palillos de dientes, ni catedrales, ni borrachos, ni cafeteras, sino simplemente rocas cretáceas y masas de tierra caliza, embadurnadas con óxido de hierro. De la cosa más sencilla hacen tus ojos un berenjenal.

—Tienes razón, primo. Por eso digo yo que nuestra imaginación es la que ve y no los ojos. Sin embargo, éstos sirven para enterarnos de algunas cositas que los pobres no tienen y que nosotros podemos darles.

Diciendo esto, tocaba el vestido de la Nela.

—¿Por qué esta bendita Nela no tiene un traje mejor?—añadió la señorita de Penáguilas—. Yo tengo varios y le voy a dar uno, y además otro, que será nuevo.

Avergonzada y confusa, Marianela no alzaba los ojos.

—Es cosa que no comprendo..., ¡que algunos tengan tanto y otros tan poco!... Me enfado con papá cuando le oigo decir palabrotas contra los que quieren que se reparta por igual todo lo que hay en el mundo. ¿Cómo se llaman esos tipos, Pablo?

—Esos serán los socialistas, los comunistas —replicó el joven sonriendo.

—Pues ésa es mi gente. Soy partidaria de que haya reparto y de que los ricos den a los pobres todo lo que tengan de sobra... ¿Por qué esta pobre huérfana ha de estar descalza y yo no?... Ni aun se debe permitir que estén desamparados los malos, cuanto más los buenos... Yo sé que Nela es muy buena, me lo has dicho tú anoche, me lo ha dicho también tu padre... No tiene familia, no tiene quien mire por ella. ¿Cómo se consiente que haya tanta y tanta desgracia? A mí me quema la boca el pan cuando pienso que hay muchos que no lo prueban. ¡Pobre Mariquita, tan buena y tan abandonada!... ¡Es posible que hasta ahora no la haya querido nadie, ni nadie le haya dado un beso, ni nadie le haya hablado como se habla a las criaturas!... Se me parte el corazón de pensarlo.

Marianela estaba atónita y petrificada de asombro, lo mismo que en el primer instante de la aparición. Antes había visto a la Virgen Santísima, ahora la escuchaba.

—Mira tú, huerfanilla—añadió la Inmaculada—, y tú, Pablo, óyeme bien: yo quiero socorrer a la Nela, no como se socorre a los pobres que se encuentran en un camino, sino como se socorrería a un hermano que nos halláramos de manos a boca... ¿No dices tú que ella ha sido tu mejor compañera, tu lazarillo, tu guía en las tinieblas? ¿No dices que has visto con sus ojos y has andado con sus pasos? Pues la Nela me pertenece; yo me entiendo con ella. Yo me encargo de vestirla, de darle todo lo que una persona necesita para vivir decentemente, y le enseñaré mil cosas para que sea útil en una casa. Mi padre dice que quizá, quizá me tenga que quedar a vivir aquí para siempre. Si es así, la Nela vivirá conmigo; conmigo aprenderá a leer, a rezar, a coser, a guisar; aprenderá tantas cosas, que será como yo misma. ¿Qué pensáis? Pues sí, y entonces no será la Nela, sino una señorita. En esto no me contrariará mi padre. Además, anoche me ha dicho: «Florentina, quizá, quizá dentro de poco, no mandaré yo en ti; obedecerás a otro dueño...» Sea lo que Dios quiera, tomo a la Nela por mi amiga. ¿Me querrás mucho?... Como has estado tan desamparada, como vives lo mismo que las flores de los campos, tal vez no sepas ni siquiera agradecer, pero yo te lo he de enseñar..., ¡te he de enseñar tantas cosas!...

Marianela, que mientras oía tan nobles palabras había estado resistiendo con mucho trabajo los impulsos de llorar, no pudo al fin contenerlos, y después de hacer pucheros durante un minuto, rompió en lágrimas. El ciego, profundamente pensativo, callaba.

—Florentina—dijo al fin—, tu lenguaje no se parece al de la mayoría de las personas. Tu bondad es enorme y entusiasta como la que ha llenado de mártires la tierra y poblado de santos el cielo.

—¡Qué exageración!—e x c l a m ó Florentina, riendo.

Poco después de esto, la señorita se levantó para coger una flor que desde lejos llamara su atención.

—¿Se fue?—preguntó Pablo.

—Sí—replicó la Nela, enjugando sus lágrimas.

—¿Sabes una cosa, Nela?... Se me figura que mi prima ha de ser algo bonita. Cuando llegó anoche a las diez... sentí hacia ella grande antipatía... No puedes figurarte cuánto me repugnaba. Ahora se me antoja, sí, se me antoja que debe de ser algo bonita.

La Nela volvió a llorar.

—¡Es como los ángeles!—exclamó entre un mar de lágrimas—. Es como si acabara de bajar del cielo. En ella, cuerpo y alma son como los de la Santísima Virgen María.

—¡Oh!, no exageres—dijo Pablo con inquietud—. No puede ser tan hermosa como dices... ¿Crees que yo, sin ojos, no comprendo dónde está la hermosura y dónde no?

—No, no; no puedes comprenderlo..., ¡qué equivocado estás!

—Sí, sí...; no puede ser tan hermosa—manifestó el ciego, poniéndose pálido y revelando la mayor angustia—. Nela, amiga de mi corazón, ¿no sabes lo que mi padre me ha dicho anoche?...: que si recobro la vista me casaré con Florentina.

La Nela no respondió nada. Sus lágrimas silenciosas corrían sin cesar, resbalando por su tostado rostro y goteando sobre sus manos. Pero ni aun por su amargo llanto podían conocerse las dimensiones de su dolor. Sólo ella sabía que era infinito.

—Ya sé por qué lloras—dijo el ciego, estrechando las manos de su compañera—. Mi padre no se empeñará en imponerme lo que es contrario a mi voluntad. Para mí no hay más mujer que tú en el mundo. Cuando mis ojos vean, si ven, no habrá para ellos otra hermosura más que la tuya celestial; todo lo demás serán sombras y cosas lejanas que no fijarán mi atención. ¿Cómo es el semblante humano, Dios mío? ¿De qué modo se retrata el alma en las caras? Si la luz no sirve para enseñarnos lo real de nuestro pensamiento, ¿para qué sirve? Lo que es y lo que se siente, ¿no son una misma cosa? La forma y la idea, ¿no son como el calor y el fuego? ¿Pueden separarse? ¿Puedes dejar

tú de ser para mí el más hermoso, el más ama-
do de todos los seres de la tierra, cuando yo me
haga dueño de los dominios de la forma?

Florentina volvió. Hablaron algo más; pero
después de lo que se consigna, nada de cuanto
dijeron es digno de ser transmitido al lector.

En los siguientes días no pasó nada; mas vino uno en el cual ocurrió un hecho asombroso, capital, culminante. Teodoro Golfín, aquel artífice sublime en cuyas manos el cuchillo del cirujano era el cincel del genio, había emprendido la corrección de una delicada hechura de la Naturaleza. Intrépido y sereno, había entrado con su ciencia y su experiencia en el maravilloso recinto cuya construcción es compendio y abreviado resumen de la inmensa arquitectura del Universo. Era preciso hacer frente a los más grandes misterios de la vida, interrogarlos y explorar las causas que impedían a los ojos de un hombre el conocimiento de la realidad visible. Para esto había que trabajar con ánimo resuelto, rompiendo uno de los más delicados organismos, la córnea; apoderarse del cristalino y echarlo fuera, respetando la hialoides y tratando con la mayor consideración al humor vítreo; ensanchar con un corte las dimensiones de la pupila, y examinar por inducción o por medio

de la catóptrica el estado de la cámara poste-
rior.

Pocas palabras siguieron a esta audaz expedición por el interior de un mundo microscó-
pico, empresa no menos colosal que medir la
distancia de los astros en las infinitas magnitu-
des del espacio. Mudos y espantados presencia-
ban el caso los individuos de la familia. Cuando
se espera la resurrección de un muerto o la
creación de un mundo, no se está de otro modo.
Pero Golfín no decía nada concreto; sus palabras eran:

—Contractilidad de la pupila...; retina sensible...; algo de estado pigmentario...; nervios
llenos de vida.

Pero el fenómeno sublime, el hecho. el hecho
irrecusable, la visión, ¿dónde estaba?

—A su tiempo se sabrá—dijo don Teodoro,
empezando la delicada operación del vendaje—.
Paciencia.

Y su fisonomía de león no expresaba des-
aliento ni triunfo; no daba esperanza ni la qui-
taba. La ciencia había hecho todo lo que sabía.
Era un simulacro de creación, como otros muchos que son gloria y orgullo del siglo XIX. En
presencia de tanta audacia, la Naturaleza, que
no permite sean sorprendidos sus secretos,
continuaba muda y reservada.

El paciente fue incomunicado con absoluto

rigor. Sólo su padre le asistía. Ninguno de la familia podía verle. Iba la Nela a preguntar por el enfermo cuatro o cinco veces; pero no. pasaba de la portalada, aguardando allí hasta que salieran el señor don Manuel, su hija o cualquiera otra persona de la casa. La señorita, después de darle prolijos informes y de pintar la ansiedad en que estaba toda la familia, solía pasear un poco con ella. Un día quiso Florentina que Marianela la enseñara su casa, y bajaron a la morada de Centeno, cuyo interior causó no poco disgusto y repugnancia a la señorita, mayormente cuando vio las cestas que a la huérfana servían de cama.

—Pronto ha de venir la Nela a vivir conmigo —dijo Florentina, saliendo a toda prisa de aquella caverna—, y entonces tendrá una cama como la mía, y vestirá y comerá lo mismo que yo.

Absorta se quedó al oír estas palabras la señora de Centeno, así como la Mariuca y la Pepina, y no se les ocurrió sino que a la miserable huérfana abandonada le había salido algún padre rey o príncipe, como se cuenta en los romances.

Cuando estuvieron solas, Florentina dijo a María:

—Pídele a Dios de día y de noche que conceda a mi querido primo ese don que nosotros poseemos y de que él ha carecido. ¡En qué ansiedad tan grande vivimos! Con su vista vendrán mil felicidades y se remediarán muchos daños. Yo he hecho a la Virgen una promesa sagrada: he prometido que si da la vista a mi primo, he de recoger al pobre más pobre que encuentre, dándole todo lo necesario para que pueda olvidar completamente su pobreza, haciéndole enteramente igual a mí por las comodidades y el bienestar de la vida. Para esto no basta vestir a una persona, ni sentarla delante de una mesa donde haya sopa y carne. Es preciso ofrecerle también aquella limosna que vale más que todos los mendrugos y que todos los trapos imaginables, y es la consideración, la dignidad, el nombre. Yo daré a mi pobre estas cosas, infundiéndole el respeto y la estimación de sí mismo. Ya he escogido a mi pobre. María, mi pobre eres tú. Con todas las voces de mi alma le he dicho a la Santísima Virgen que si devuelve la vista a mi primo, haré de ti una hermana: serás en mi casa lo mismo que soy yo, serás mi hermana.

Diciendo esto, la Virgen estrechó con amor entre sus brazos la cabeza de la Nela y dióle un beso en la frente. Es absolutamente imposible describir los sentimientos de la vagabunda en aquella culminante hora de su vida. Un horror instintivo la alejaba de la casa de Aldeacorba, horror con el cual se confundía la imagen de la señorita de Penáguilas, como las figuras que se nos presentan en una pesadilla, y al propio tiempo sentía nacer en su alma admiración y simpatía muy vivas hacia aquella misma persona... A veces creía con pueril candor que era la Virgen María en esencia y presencia. De tal modo comprendía su bondad, que creía estar viendo, como el interior de un hermoso paraíso abierto, el alma de Florentina, llena de pureza, de amor, de bondades, de pensamientos discretos y consoladores. Tenía Marianela la rectitud suficiente para adoptar y asimilarse al punto la idea de que no podría aborrecer a su improvisada hermana. ¿Cómo aborrecerla, si se sentía impulsada espontáneamente a amarla con todas las energías de su corazón? La antipatía, la desconfianza, eran como un sedimento que al fin de la lucha debía quedar en el fondo para descomponerse al cabo y desaparecer, sirviendo sus elementos para alimentar la admiración y el respeto hacia la misma amiga bienhechora. Pero si la aversión desaparecía, no así el sentimiento que la había causado, el cual, no pudiendo florecer por sí ni manifestarse solo, con el exclusivismo avasallador que es condición propia de tales afectos, prodújole un aplanamiento moral que trajo consigo amarga tristeza. En casa de Cen-

teno observaron que la Nela no comía; que
permanecía en silencio y sin movimiento, como
una estatua, larguísimos ratos; que hacía mucho tiempo que no cantaba de noche ni de
día. Su incapacidad para todo había llegado a
ser absoluta, y habiéndola mandado Tanasio
por tabaco a la *Primera de Socartes,* sentóse
en el camino y allí se estuvo todo el día.

Una mañana, cuando habían pasado ocho
días después de la operación, fue a casa del
ingeniero jefe, y Sofía le dijo:

—¡Albricias, Nela! ¿No sabes las noticias que
corren? Hoy han levantado la venda a Pablo...
Dicen que ve algo, que ya tiene vista... Ulises,
el jefe del taller, acaba de decirlo... Teodoro
no ha venido aún, pero Carlos ha ido allá; muy
pronto sabremos si es verdad.

Quedóse la Nela, al oír esto, más muerta que
viva, y cruzando las manos, exclamó así:

—¡Bendita sea la Virgen Santísima, que es
quien lo ha hecho!... Ella, ella sola es quien lo
ha hecho.

—¿Te alegras?... Ya lo creo; ahora la señorita Florentina cumplirá su promesa—dijo Sofía
en tono de mofa—. Mil enhorabuenas a la señora doña Nela... Ahí tienes tú cómo, cuando
menos se piensa, se acuerda Dios de los pobres.
Esto es como una lotería..., ¡qué premio gor-
do, Nelilla!... Y puede que no seas agradeci-

da...; no, no lo serás... No he conocido a ningún pobre que tenga gratitud. Son soberbios,
y mientras más se les da más quieren... Ya es
cosa hecha que Pablo se casará con su prima.
Buena pareja; los dos son guapos chicos, y ella
no parece tonta..., y tiene una cara preciosa,
¡qué lástima de cara y de cuerpo con aquellos
vestidos tan horribles! ¡Oh!, si necesito vestir-
me, no me traigan acá a la modista de Santa
Irene de Campó.

Esto decía, cuando entró Carlos. Su rostro
resplandecía de júbilo.

—¡Triunfo completo!—gritó desde la puerta—. Después de Dios, mi hermano Teodoro.

—¿Es cierto?...

—Como la luz del día... Yo no lo creí... ¡Pero
qué triunfo, Sofía, qué triunfo! No hay para
mí gozo mayor que ser hermano de mi hermano... Es el rey de los hombres... Si es lo
que digo: después de Dios, Teodoro.

La estupenda y gratísima nueva corrió por todo Socartes. No se hablaba de otra cosa en los hornos, en los talleres, en las máquinas de lavar, en el plano inclinado, en lo profundo de las excavaciones y en lo alto de los picos, al aire libre y en las entrañas de la tierra. Añadíanse interesantes comentarios: que en Aldeacorba se creyó por un momento que don Francisco de Penáguilas había perdido la razón; que don Manuel de Penáguilas pensaba celebrar el regocijado suceso dando un banquete a cuantos trabajaban en las minas, y finalmente, que don Teodoro era digno de que todos los ciegos habidos y por haber le pusieran en las niñas de sus ojos.

No osaba la Nela poner los pies en la casa de Aldeacorba. Secreta fuerza poderosa la alejaba de ella. Anduvo vagando todo el día por los alrededores de la mina, contemplando desde lejos la casa de Penáguilas, que le parecía transformada. En su alma se juntaba, a un gozo extraordinario, una como vergüenza de sí misma; a la exaltación de un afecto noble, la inso-

portable comezón de un amor propio muy sus-
ceptible.

Halló una tregua a las congojosas batallas de
su alma en la madre soledad, que tanto había
contribuido a la formación de su carácter, y
en contemplar las hermosuras de la Naturaleza, medio fácil de comunicar su pensamiento
con la Divinidad. Las nubes del cielo y las
flores de la tierra hacían en su espíritu efecto
igual al que hacen en otros la pompa de los
altares, la elocuencia de los oradores cristia-
nos y las lecturas de sutiles conceptos místicos.
En la soledad del campo pensaba ella y decía
mentalmente mil cosas, sin sospechar que eran
oraciones. Mirando a Aldeacorba, decía:

—No volveré más allá... Ya acabó todo para
mí... Ahora, ¿de qué sirvo yo?

En su rudeza, pudo observar que el conflicto
en que estaba su alma provenía de no poder
aborrecer a nadie. Por el contrario, érale forzoso amar a todos, al amigo y al enemigo; y así
como los abrojos se trocaban en flores bajo la
mano milagrosa de una mártir cristiana, la
Nela veía que sus celos y su despecho se con-
vertían graciosamente en admiración y gratitud. Lo que no sufría metamorfosis era aquella
pasioncilla que antes llamamos vergüenza de
sí misma, y que la impulsaba a eliminar su
persona de todo lo que pudiera ocurrir ya en

Aldeacorba. Era como un aspecto singular del mismo sentimiento que en los seres educados y cultos se llamaba amor propio, por más que en ella revistiera los caracteres del desprecio de sí misma; pero la filiación de aquel sentimiento con el que tan grande parte tiene en las acciones del hombre civilizado, se reconocía en que se basaba, como éste, en la dignidad más puntillosa. Si Marianela usara ciertas voces, habría dicho:

«Mi dignidad no me permite aceptar el atroz desaire que voy a recibir. Puesto que Dios quiere que sufra esta humillación, sea; pero no he de asistir a mi destronamiento, Dios bendiga a la que por ley natural ocupará mi puesto; pero no tengo valor para sentarla yo misma en él.»

No pudiendo hablar así, su rudeza expresaba la misma idea de este otro modo:

«No vuelvo más a Aldeacorba... No consentiré que me vea... Huiré con Celipín, o me iré con mi madre. Ahora yo no sirvo para nada.»

Pero mientras esto decía, parecíale muy desconsolador renunciar al divino amparo de aquella celestial Virgen que se le había aparecido en lo más negro de su vida extendiendo su manto para abrigarla. ¡Ver realizado lo que tantas veces viera en sueños palpitando de gozo, y tener que renunciar a ello!... ¡Sentirse llamada por una voz cariñosa, que le ofrecía fraternal amor, hermosa vivienda, consideración, nombre, bienestar, y no poder acudir a este llamamiento, inundada de gozo, de esperanza, de gratitud!... Rechazar la mano celestial que la sacaba de aquella sentina de degradación y miseria para hacer de la vagabunda una persona y elevarla de la jerarquía de los animales domésticos a la de los seres respetados y queridos!...

«¡Ay!—exclamó, clavándose los dedos como garras en el pecho—. No puedo, no puedo... Por nada del mundo me presentaré en Aldeacorba. ¡Virgen de mi alma, ampárame!... ¡Madre mía, ven por mí!...»

Al anochecer marchó a su casa. Por el camino encontró a Celipín con un palito en la mano y en la punta del palo la gorra.

—Nelilla—le dijo el chico—, ¿no es verdad que así se pone el señor don Teodoro? Ahora pasaba por la charca de Hinojales y me miré en el agua. ¡Córcholis!, me quedé pasmado, porque me vi con la mesma figura de don Teodoro Golfín... Cualquier día de esta semanita nos vamos a ser médicos y hombres de provecho... Ya tengo juntado lo que quería. Verás cómo nadie se ríe del señor de Celipín.

Tres días más estuvo la Nela fugitiva, vagando por los alrededores de las minas, siguiendo

el curso del río por sus escabrosas riberas o
internándose en el sosegado apartamiento del
bosque de Saldeoro. Las noches pasábalas entre sus cestas, sin dormir. Una noche dijo tími-
damente a su compañero de vivienda:

—¿Cuándo, Celipín?

Y Celipín contestó 'con la gravedad de un
expedicionario formal:

—Mañana.

Levantáronse los dos aventureros al rayar el
día, y cada cual fue por su lado: Celipín a su
trabajo, la Nela a llevar un recado que le dio
Señana para la criada del ingeniero. Al volver
encontró dentro de la casa a la señorita Florentina, que le esperaba. Quedóse al verla María sobrecogida y temerosa, porque adivinó con
su instintiva perspicacia, o más bien con lo
que el vulgo llama corazonada, el objeto de
aquella visita.

—Nela, querida hermana—dijo la señorita
con elocuente cariño—. ¿Qué conducta es
ésa?... ¿Por qué no has aparecido por allá en
todos estos días?... Ven, Pablo desea verte...
¿No sabes que ya puede decir: «Quiero ver tal
cosa»? ¿No sabes que ya mi primo no es ciego?

—Ya lo sé—dijo la Nela, tomando la mano
que la señorita le ofrecía y cubriéndola de
besos.

—Vamos allá, vamos al momento. No hace

más que preguntar por la señorita Nela. Hoy
es preciso que estés allí cuando don Teodoro
le levante la venda... Es la cuarta vez... El día
de la primera prueba..., ¡qué día!, cuando com-
prendimos que mi primo había nacido a la luz,
casi nos morimos de gozo. La primer cara que
vio fue la mía... Vamos.

María soltó la mano de la Virgen Santísima.

—¿Te has olvidado de mi promesa sagrada
—añadió ésta—, o creías que era broma? ¡Ay!,
todo me parece poco para demostrar a la Madre de Dios el gran favor que nos ha hecho...
Yo quisiera que en estos días nadie estuviera
triste en todo lo que abarca el Universo; quisiera poder repartir mi alegría, echándola a todos lados, como echan los labradores el grano
cuando siembran; quisiera poder entrar en todas las habitaciones miserables y decir: «Ya
se acabaron vuestras penas; aquí traigo yo remedio para todos.» Esto no es posible, esto
sólo puede hacerlo Dios. Ya que mis fuerzas no
pueden igualar a mi voluntad, hagamos bien
lo poco que podemos hacer..., y se acabaron las
palabras, Nela. Ahora despídete de esta choza,
di adiós a todas las cosas que han acompañado
a tu miseria y a tu soledad. También se tiene
cariño a la miseria, hija.

Marianela no dijo adiós a nada, y como en
la casa no estaban a la sazón ninguno de sus

simpáticos habitantes, no fue preciso detener-
se por ellos. Florentina salió, llevando de la
mano a la que sus nobles sentimientos y su
cristiano fervor habían puesto a su lado en el
orden de la familia, y la Nela se dejaba llevar
sintiéndose incapaz de oponer resistencia. Pensaba que una fuerza sobrenatural le tiraba de
la mano, y que iba fatal y necesariamente con-
ducida, como las almas que los brazos de un
ángel transportan al cielo. Aquel día tomaron
el camino de Hinojales, que es el mismo donde
la vagabunda vio a Florentina por primera vez.
Al entrar en la calleja, la señorita dijo a su
amiga:

—¿Por qué no has ido a casa? Mi tío dijo que
tienes modestia y una delicadeza natural que
es lástima no haya sido cultivada. ¿Tu delicadeza te impedía venir a reclamar lo que por la
misericordia de Dios habías ganado? Eso cree
mi tío... ¡Cómo estaba aquel día el pobre señor!...; decía que ya no le importaba morirse... ¿Ves tú?, todavía tengo los ojos encarna-
dos de tanto llorar. Es que anoche mi tío, mi
padre y yo no dormimos: estuvimos formando
proyectos de familia y haciendo castillos en el
aire toda la noche... ¿Por qué callas? ¿Por qué
no dices nada?... ¿No estás tú también alegre
como yo?

La Nela miró a la señorita, oponiendo débil

resistencia a la dulce mano que la conducía.

—Sigue..., ¿qué tienes? Me miras de un modo particular, Nela.

Así era, en efecto; los ojos de la abandonada,
vagando con extravío de uno en otro objeto, tenían al fijarse en la Virgen Santísima el resplandor del espanto.

—¿Por qué tiembla tu mano?—preguntó la
señorita—. ¿Estás enferma? Te has puesto muy
pálida y das diente con diente. Si estás enferma, yo te curaré, yo misma. Desde hoy tienes
quien se interese por ti y te mime y te haga
cariños... No seré yo sola, pues Pablo te esti-
ma..., me lo ha dicho. Los dos te querremos
mucho, porque él y yo seremos como uno solo... Desea verte. Figúrate si tendrá curiosidad
quien nunca ha visto...; pero no creas..., como
tiene tanto entendimiento y una imaginación
que, según parece, le ha anticipado ciertas ideas
que no poseen comúnmente los ciegos, desde
el primer instante supo distinguir las cosas
feas de las bonitas. Un pedazo de lacre encarnado le agradó mucho, y un pedazo de carbón
le pareció horrible. Admiró la hermosura del
cielo, y se estremeció con repugnancia al ver
una rana. Todo lo que es bello le produce un
entusiasmo que parece delirio; todo lo que
es feo le causa horror y se pone a temblar como cuando tenemos mucho miedo. Yo no debí

parecerle mal, porque exclamó al verme: «¡Ay,
prima mía, qué hermosa eres! ¡Bendito sea
Dios, que me ha dado esta luz con que ahora
te siento!»

La Nela tiró suavemente de la mano de Florentina y soltóla después, cayendo al suelo
como un cuerpo que pierde súbitamente la vida. Inclinóse sobre ella la señorita, y con cariñosa voz le dijo:

—¿Qué tienes?... ¿Por qué me miras así?

Clavaba la huérfana sus ojos con terrible fijeza en el rostro de la Virgen Santísima; pero
no brillaban, no, con expresión de rencor, sino
con una como congoja suplicante, a la manera
de la postrer mirada del moribundo que pide
misericordia a la imagen de Dios, creyéndola
Dios mismo.

—Señora—murmuró la Nela—, yo no la aborrezco a usted, no..., no la aborrezco... Al contrario, la quiero mucho, la adoro...

Diciéndolo, tomó el borde del vestido de Florentina, y llevándolo a sus secos labios, lo besó
ardientemente.

—¿Y quién puede creer que me aborreces?
—dijo la de Penáguilas, llena de confusión—.
Ya sé que me quieres. Pero me das miedo...,
levántate.

—Yo la quiero a usted mucho, la adoro—repitió Marianela, besando los pies de la señorita—; pero no puedo, no puedo...

—¿Que no puedes? Levántate, por amor de Dios.

Florentina extendió sus brazos para levantarla; pero sin necesidad de ser sostenida, la Nela alzóse de un salto, y poniéndose rápidamente a bastante distancia, exclamó bañada en lágrimas:

—¡No puedo, señorita mía, no puedo!

—¿Qué?..., ¡por Dios y la Virgen!..., ¿qué te pasa?

—No puedo ir allá.

Y señaló la casa de Aldeacorba, cuyo tejado se veía a lo lejos entre árboles.

—¿Por qué?

—La Virgen Santísima lo sabe—replicó la Nela con cierta decisión—. Que la Virgen Santísima la bendiga a usted.

Haciendo una cruz con los dedos, se los besó. Juraba. Florentina dio un paso hacia ella. Comprendiendo María aquel movimiento de cariño, corrió velozmente hacia la señorita, y apoyando su cabeza en el seno de ella, murmuró entre gemidos:

—¡Por Dios..., deme usted un abrazo!

Florentina la abrazó tiernamente. Apartándose entonces con un movimiento, mejor dicho, con un salto ligero, flexible y repentino, la mujer o niña salvaje subió a un matorral cercano.

La hierba parecía que se apartaba para darle paso.

—Nela, hermana mía—gritó con angustia Florentina.

—¡Adiós, niña de mi alma!—dijo la Nela, mirándola por última vez.

Y desapareció entre el ramaje. Florentina sintió el ruido de la hierba, atendiendo a él como atiende el cazador a los pasos de la pieza que se le escapa; después todo quedó en silencio, y no se oía sino el sordo monólogo de la Naturaleza campestre en mitad del día, un rumor que parece el susurro de nuestras propias ideas al extenderse irradiando por lo que nos circunda. Florentina estaba absorta, paralizada, muda, afligidísima, como el que ve desvanecerse la más risueña ilusión de su vida. No sabía qué pensar de aquel suceso, ni su bondad inmensa, que incapacitaba frecuentemente su discernimiento, podía explicárselo.

Largo rato después hallábase en el mismo sitio, la cabeza inclinada sobre el pecho, las mejillas encendidas, los celestiales ojos mojados de llanto, cuando acertó a pasar don Teodoro Golfín, que de la casa de Aldeacorba con tranquilo paso venía. Grande fue el asombro del doctor al ver a la señorita sola y con aquel interesante aparato de pena y desconsuelo que, lejos de mermar su belleza, la acrecentaba.

—¿Qué tiene la niña?—preguntó vivamente—. ¿Qué es eso, Florentina?

—Una cosa terrible, señor don Teodoro—replicó la señorita de Penáguilas, secando sus lágrimas—. Estoy pensando, estoy considerando qué cosas tan malas hay en el mundo.

—¿Y cuáles son esas cosas malas, señorita?... Donde está usted, ¿puede haber alguna?

—Cosas perversas; pero entre todas hay una que es la más perversa de todas.

—¿Cuál?

—La ingratitud, señor Golfín.

Y mirando tras de la cerca de zarzas y helechos, dijo:

—Por allí se ha escapado.

Subió a lo más elevado del terreno para alcanzar a ver más lejos.

—No la distingo por ninguna parte.

—Ni yo—indicó, riendo el médico—. El señor don Manuel me ha dicho que se dedica usted a la caza de mariposas. Efectivamente, esas pícaras son muy ingratas al no dejarse coger por usted.

—No es eso... Contaré a usted, si va hacia Aldeacorba.

—No voy, sino que vengo, preciosa señorita; pero porque usted me cuente alguna cosa, cualquiera que sea, volveré con mucho gusto. Volvamos a Aldeacorba, ya soy todo oídos.

Vagando estuvo la Nela todo el día, y por
la noche rondó la casa de Aldeacorba, acercándose a ella todo lo que le era posible sin peligro de ser descubierta. Cuando sentía rumor
de pasos, alejábase prontamente como un la-
drón. Bajó a la hondonada de la Terrible, cuyo
pavoroso aspecto de cráter en aquella ocasión
le agradaba, y después de discurrir por el fondo contemplando los gigantes de piedra que en
su recinto se elevaban como personajes congre-
gados en un circo, trepó a uno de ellos para
descubrir las luces de Aldeacorba. Allí estaban,
brillando en el borde de la mina, sobre la oscuridad del cielo y de la tierra. Después de mi-
rarlas como si nunca en su vida hubiera visto
luces, salió de la Terrible y subió hacia la Trascava. Antes de llegar a ella sintió pasos, detúvose, y al poco rato vio que por el sendero adelante venía con resuelto andar el señor de Celipín. Traía un pequeño lío pendiente de un palo
puesto al hombro, y su marcha, como su ade-

7

mán, demostraban firme resolución de no parar hasta medir con sus piernas toda la anchura de la tierra.

—¡Celipe!..., ¿adónde vás?—le preguntó la Nela, deteniéndole.

—¡Nela!..., ¿tú por estos barrios?... Creíamos que estabas en casa de la señorita Florentina, comiendo jamones, pavos y perdices a todas horas, y bebiendo limonada con azucarillos. ¿Qué haces aquí?

—¿Y tú, adónde vas?

—¿Ahora salimos con eso? ¿Para qué me lo preguntas si lo sabes?—replicó el chico, requiriendo el palo y el lío—. Bien sabes que voy a aprender mucho y a ganar dinero... ¿No te dije que esta noche...? Pues aquí me tienes más contento que unas pascuas, aunque algo triste, cuando pienso lo que padre y madre van a llorar... Mira, Nela, la Virgen Santísima nos ha favorecido esta noche, porque padre y madre empezaron a roncar más pronto que otras veces, y yo, que ya tenía hecho el lío, me subí al ventanillo, y por el ventanillo me eché fuera... ¿Vienes tú, o no vienes?

—Yo también voy—dijo la Nela con un movimiento repentino, asiendo el brazo del intrépido viajero.

—Tomaremos el tren, y en el tren iremos hasta donde podamos—afirmó Celipín con ge-

neroso entusiasmo—. Y después pediremos limosna hasta llegar a los Madriles del Rey de
España; y una vez que estemos en los Madriles del Rey de España, tú te pondrás a servir
en una casa de marqueses y condeses, y yo en
otra, y así, mientras yo estudie tú podrás aprender muchas finuras. ¡Córcholis!, de todo lo
que yo vaya aprendiendo te iré enseñando a ti
un poquillo, un poquillo nada más, porque las
mujeres no necesitan tantas sabidurías como
nosotros los señores médicos.

Antes de que Celipín acabara de hablar, los
dos se habían puesto en camino, andando tan
aprisa cual si estuvieran viendo ya las torres
de los Madriles del Rey de España.

—Salgámonos del sendero—dijo Celipín,
dando pruebas en aquella ocasión de un gran
talento práctico—, porque si nos ven nos echa-
rán mano y nos darán un buen pie de paliza.

Pero la Nela soltó la mano de su compañero
de aventuras, y sentándose en una piedra, murmuró tristemente:

—Yo no voy.

—Nela..., ¡qué tonta eres! Tú no tienes como
yo un corazón del tamaño de esas peñas de
la Terrible—dijo Celipín con fanfarronería—.
¡Recórcholis!, ¿a qué tienes miedo? ¿Por qué
no vienes?

—Yo..., ¿para qué?

—¿No sabes que dijo don Teodoro que los que nos criamos aquí nos volvemos piedras...? Yo no quiero ser una piedra, yo no.

—Yo... ¿para qué voy?—dijo la Nela con amargo desconsuelo—. Para ti es tiempo, para mí es tarde.

La chiquilla dejó caer la cabeza sobre su pecho, y por largo rato permaneció insensible a la seductora verbosidad del futuro Hipócrates. Al ver que iba a franquear el lindero de aquella tierra donde había vivido y donde dormía su madre el eterno sueño, se sintió arrancada de su suelo natural. La hermosura del país, con cuyos accidentes se sentía unida por una especie de parentesco; la escasa felicidad que había gustado en él; la miseria misma; el recuerdo de su amito y de las gratas horas de paseo por el bosque y hacia la fuente de Saldeoro; los sentimientos de admiración o de simpatía, de amor o de gratitud que habían florecido en su alma en presencia de aquellas mismas flores, de aquellas mismas nubes, de aquellos árboles frondosos, de aquellas peñas rojas, como asociados a la belleza y desarrollo de aquellas mismas partes de la Naturaleza, eran otras tantas raíces, cuya violenta tirantez, al ser arrancadas, producíala vivísimo dolor.

—Yo no me voy—repitió.

Y Celipín hablaba, hablaba, cual si ya, su-biendo milagrosamente hasta el pináculo de su carrera, perteneciese a todas las Academias creadas y por crear.

—¿Entonces, vuelves a casa?—preguntóle al ver que su elocuencia era tan inútil como la de aquellos centros oficiales del saber.

—No.

—¿Vas a la casa de Aldeacorba?

—Tampoco.

—Entonces, ¿te vas al pueblo de la señorita Florentina?

—No, tampoco.

—Pues entonces, ¡córcholis, recórcholis! ¿adónde vas?

La Nela no contestó nada: seguía mirando con espanto al suelo, como si en él estuvieran los pedazos de la cosa más bella y más rica del mundo, que acababa de caer y romperse.

—Pues entonces, Nela—dijo Celipín, fatigado de sus largos discursos—, yo te dejo y me voy, porque pueden descubrirme... ¿Quieres que te dé una peseta, por si se te ofrece algo esta noche?

—No, Celipín, no quiero nada... Vete, tú serás hombre de provecho... Pórtate bien, y no te olvides de Socartes ni de tus padres.

El viajero sintió una cosa impropia de varón tal, formal y respetable, sintió que le venían

ganas de llorar; mas sofocando aquella emoción importuna, dijo:

—¿Cómo he de olvidar a Socartes?... ¡Pues
no faltaba más!... No me olvidaré de mis padres
ni de ti, que me has ayudado a esto... Adiós,
Nelilla... Siento pasos.

Celipín enarboló su palo con una decisión
que probaba cuán templada estaba su alma
para afrontar los peligros del mundo; pero su
intrepidez no tuvo objeto, porque era un perro
el que venía.

—Es *Choto*—dijo Nela, temblando.

—Agur—murmuró Celipín, poniéndose en
marcha.

Desapareció entre las sombras de la noche.

La geología había perdido una piedra, y la
sociedad había ganado un hombre.

Al verse acariciada por *Choto*, la Nela sintió
escalofríos. El generoso animal, después de saltar alrededor de ella, gruñendo con tanta expresión que faltaba muy poco para que sus gruñidos fuesen palabras, echó a correr con veloci-
dad suma hacia Aldeacorba. Creeríase que corría tras una pieza de caza; pero al contrario
de ciertos oradores, el buen *Choto* ladrando hablaba.

A la misma hora, Teodoro Golfín salía de la
casa de Penáguilas. Llegóse a él *Choto* y le dijo

atropelladamente no sabemos qué. Era como
una brusca interpelación pronunciada entre los
bufidos del cansancio y los ahogos del sentimiento. Golfín, que sabía muchas lenguas, era
poco fuerte en la canina, y no hizo caso. Pero
Choto dio unas cuarenta vueltas en torno de él,
soltando de su espumante boca unos al modo
de insultos, que después parecían voces cariñosas y luego amenazas. Teodoro se detuvo entonces, prestando atención al cuadrúpedo. Viendo
Choto que se había hecho entender un poco,
echó a correr en dirección contraria a la que
llevaba Golfín. Este le siguió, murmurando:
«Pues vamos allá.»

Choto regresó corriendo como para cerciorarse de que era seguido, y después se alejó de
nuevo. Como a cien metros de Aldeacorba,
Golfín creyó sentir una voz humana que dijo:

—¿Qué quieres, *Choto?*

Al punto sospechó que era la Nela quien hablaba. Detuvo el paso, prestó atención, colo-
cándose a la sombra de un roble, y no tardó
en descubrir una figura que, apartándose de la
pared de piedra, andaba despacio. La sombra
de las zarzas no permitía descubrirla bien. Des-
pacito siguióla a bastante distancia, apartándose de la senda y andando sobre el césped para
no hacer ruido. Indudablemente era ella. Cono-
cióla perfectamente cuando entró en terreno

claro, donde no oscurecían el suelo árboles ni arbustos.

La Nela avanzó después más rápidamente. Al fin corría. Golfín corrió también. Después de un rato de esta desigual marcha, la chiquilla se sentó en una piedra. A sus pies se abría el cóncavo hueco de la Trascava, sombrío y espantoso en la oscuridad de la noche. Golfín esperó, y con paso muy quedo acercóse más. *Choto* estaba frente a la Nela, echado sobre los cuartos traseros, derechas las patas delanteras, y mirándola como una esfinge. La Nela miraba hacia abajo... De pronto empezó a descender rápidamente, más bien resbalando que corriendo. Como un león se abalanzó Teodoro a la sima, gritando con voz de gigante:

—¡Nela, Nela!...

Miró y no vio nada en la negra boca. Oía, sí, los gruñidos de *Choto*, que corría por la vertiene en derredor, describiendo espirales, cual si le arrastrara un líquido tragado por la espantosa sima. Trató de bajar Teodoro, y dio algunos pasos cautelosamente. Volvió a gritar, y una voz le contestó desde abajo:

—Señor...

—Sube al momento.

No recibió contestación.

—Que subas.

Al poco rato dibujóse la figura de la vagabunda en lo más hondo que se podía ver del horrible embudo. *Choto*, después de husmear el tragadero de la Trascava, subía describiendo las mismas espirales. La Nela subía también, pero muy despacio. Detúvose, y entonces se oyó su voz, que decía débilmente:

—Señor...

—Que subas te digo... ¿Qué haces ahí?

La Nela subió otro poco.

—Sube pronto..., tengo que decirte una cosa.

—¿Una cosa?...

—Una cosa, sí; una cosa tengo que decirte.

Mariquilla acabó de subir, y Teodoro no se creyó triunfante hasta que pudo asir fuertemente su mano para llevarla consigo.

Anduvieron breve rato los dos sin decir nada. Teodoro Golfín, con ser sabio, discreto y locuaz, sentíase igualmente torpe que la Nela, ignorante de suyo y muy lacónica por costumbre. Seguíale sin hacer resistencia, y él acomodaba su paso al de la mujer-niña, como hombre que lleva un chico a la escuela. En cierto paraje del camino donde había tres enormes piedras blanquecinas y carcomidas, que parecían huesos de gigantescos animales, el doctor se sentó, y poniendo delante de sí en pie a la Nela, como quien va a pedir cuentas de travesuras graves, tomóle ambas manos y seriamente le dijo:

—¿Qué ibas a hacer allí?

—Yo..., ¿dónde?

—Allí. Bien comprendes lo que quiero decirte. Responde claramente, como se responde a un confesor o a un padre.

—Yo no tengo padre—replicó la Nela con ligero acento de rebeldía.

—Es verdad; pero figúrate que lo soy yo, y responde. ¿Qué ibas a hacer allí?

—Allí está mi madre—le fue respondido de una manera hosca.

—Tu madre ha muerto. ¿Tú no sabes que los que se han muerto están en el otro mundo?

—Está allí—afirmó la Nela con aplomo, volviendo tristemente sus ojos al punto indicado.

—Y tú pensabas ir con ella, ¿no es eso? Es decir, que pensabas quitarte la vida.

—Sí, señor; eso mismo.

—¿Y tú no sabes que tu madre cometió un gran crimen al darse la muerte, y que tú cometerías otro igual imitándola? ¿A ti no te han enseñado esto?

—No me acuerdo de si me han enseñado tal cosa. Si yo me quiero matar, ¿quién me lo puede impedir?

—¿Pero tú misma, sin auxilio de nadie, no comprendes que a Dios no puede agradar que nos quitemos la vida?... ¡Pobre criatura, abandonada a tus sentimientos naturales, sin instrucción ni religión, sin ninguna influencia afectuosa y desinteresada que te guíe! ¿Qué ideas tienes de Dios, de la otra vida, del morir?... ¿De dónde has sacado que tu madre está allí?... ¿A unos cuantos huesos sin vida llamas tu madre?... ¿Crees que ella sigue viviendo, pensando y amándote dentro de esa caverna? ¿Nadie te ha dicho que las almas, una vez que sueltan su cuerpo, jamás vuelven a él? ¿Ignoras que las sepulturas, de cualquier forma que sean, no encierran más que polvo, descomposición y miseria?... ¿Cómo te figuras tú a Dios? ¿Cómo un señor muy serio que está allá arriba con los brazos cruzados, dispuesto a tolerar que juguemos con nuestra vida y a que en lugar suyo pongamos espíritus, duendes y fantasmas, que nosotros mismos hacemos?... Tu amo, que es tan discreto, ¿no te ha dicho jamás estas cosas?

—Sí me las ha dicho; pero como ya no me las ha de decir...

—Pero como ya no te las ha de decir, ¿atentas a tu vida? Dime, tontuela; arrojándote a ese agujero, ¿qué bien pensabas tú alcanzar? ¿Pensabas estar mejor?

—Sí, señor.

—¿Cómo?

—No sintiendo nada de lo que ahora siento, sino otras cosas mejores, y juntándome con mi madre.

—Veo que eres más tonta que hecha de encargo—dijo Golfín, riendo—. Ahora vas a ser franca conmigo. ¿Tú me quieres mal?

—No, señor, no; yo no quiero mal a nadie, y menos a usted, que ha sido tan bueno conmigo y que ha dado la vista a mi amo.

—Bien, pero eso no basta; yo no sólo deseo

que me quieras bien, sino que tengas confianza
en mí y me confíes tus cosillas. A ti te pasan
cosillas muy curiosas, picarona, y todas me las
vas a decir, todas. Verás cómo no te pesa; verás
cómo soy un buen confesor.

La Nela sonrió con tristeza. Después bajó la
cabeza, y doblándose sus piernas, cayó de rodillas.

—No, tonta, así estás mal. Siéntate junto a
mí; ven acá—dijo Golfín cariñosamente, sentándola a su lado—. Se me figura que estabas
rabiando por encontrar una persona a quien
poder decirle tus secretos. ¿No es verdad? ¡Y no
hallabas ninguna! Efectivamente, estás demasiado sola en el mundo... Vamos a ver, Nela,
dime ante todo: ¿por qué?..., pon mucha atención..., ¿por qué se te metió en la cabeza quitarte la vida?

La Nela no contestó nada.

—Yo te conocí gozosa, y al parecer satisfecha de vivir, hace algunos días. ¿Por qué de la
noche a la mañana te has vuelto loca?...

—Quería ir con mi madre—repuso la Nela,
después de vacilar un instante—. No quería
vivir más. Yo no sirvo para nada. ¿De qué sirvo yo? ¿No vale más que me muera? Si Dios
no quiere que me muera, me moriré yo misma
por mi misma voluntad.

—Esa idea de que no sirves para nada es

causa de grandes desgracias para ti, ¡infeliz criatura! ¡Maldito sea el que te la inculcó, o los que te la inculcaron, porque son muchos!... Todos son igualmente responsables del abandono, de la soledad y de la ignorancia en que has vivido. ¡Que no sirves para nada! ¡Sabe Dios lo que hubieras sido tú en otras manos! Eres una personilla delicada, muy delicada, quizá de inmenso valor; pero, ¡qué demonio!, pon un arpa en manos toscas..., ¿qué harán?, romperla..., porque tu constitución débil no te permita partir piedra y arrastrar tierra como esas bestias en forma humana que se llaman Mariuca y Pepina, ¿se ha de afirmar que no sirves para nada? ¿Acaso hemos nacido para trabajar como los animales...? ¿No tendrás tú inteligencia, no tendrás tú sensibilidad, no tendrás mil dotes preciosos que nadie ha sabido cultivar? No: tú sirves para algo, aún servirás para mucho si encuentras una mano hábil que te sepa dirigir.

La Nela, profundamente impresionada con estas palabras que entendió por intuición, fijaba sus ojos en el rostro duro, expresivo e inteligente de Teodoro Golfín. Asombro y reconocimiento llenaban su alma.

—Pero en ti no hay un misterio solo—añadió el león negro—. Ahora se te ha presentado la ocasión más preciosa para salir de tu miserable abandono, y la has rechazado. Florentina, que es un ángel de Dios, ha querido hacer de ti una amiga y una hermana; no conozco un ejemplo igual de virtud y de bondad..., ¿y tú qué has hecho?..., huir de ella como una salvaje... ¿Es esto ingratitud o algún otro sentimiento que no comprendemos?

—No, no, no—replicó la Nela con aflicción—, yo no soy ingrata. Yo adoro a la señorita Florentina... Me parece que no es de carne y hueso como nosotros, y que no merezco ni siquiera mirarla...

—Pues, hija, eso podrá ser verdad; pero tu comportamiento no quiere decir sino que eres ingrata, muy ingrata.

—No, no soy ingrata—exclamó la Nela, ahogada por los sollozos—. Bien me lo temía yo..., sí, me lo temía..., yo sospechaba que me creerían ingrata, y esto es lo único que me ponía triste cuando me iba a matar... Como soy tan bruta, no supe pedir perdón a la señorita por mi fuga, ni supe explicarle nada...

—Yo te reconciliaré con la señorita..., yo; si tú no quieres verla más, me encargo de decirle y de probarle que no eres ingrata. Ahora descúbreme tu corazón y dime todo lo que sientes y la causa de tu desesperación. Por grande que sea el abandono de una criatura, por grande que sean su miseria y su soledad, no se arran-

ca la vida sino cuando tiene motivos muy poderosos para aborrecerla.

—Sí, señor, eso mismo pienso yo.

—¿Y tú la aborreces?...

Nela estuvo callada un momento. Después,
cruzando los brazos, dijo con vehemencia:

—No, señor; yo no la aborrezco, sino que la
deseo.

—¡A buena parte ibas a buscarla!

—Yo creo que después que uno se muere
tiene lo que aquí no puede conseguir... Si no,
¿por qué nos está llamando la muerte a todas
horas? Yo tengo sueños, y soñando veo felices
y contentos a todos los que se han muerto.

—¿Tú crees en lo que sueñas?

—Sí, señor. Y miro los árboles y las peñas,
que estoy acostumbrada a ver desde que nací,
y en su cara veo cosas...

—¡Hola, hola!..., ¿también los árboles y las
peñas tienen cara? ...

—Sí, señor... Para mí todas las cosas hermosas ven y hablan... Por eso cuando todas me
han dicho: «Ven con nosotras; muérete y vivi-
rás sin pena...», yo...

—¡Qué lástima de fantasía!—murmuró Golfín—. Alma enteramente pagana.

Y luego añadió en alta voz:

—Si deseas la vida, ¿por qué no aceptaste lo

que Florentina te ofrecía? Vuelvo al mismo tema.

—Porque..., porque..., porque la señorita Florentina no me ofrecía sino la muerte—dijo la Nela con energía.

—¡Qué mal juzgas su caridad! Hay seres tan infelices que prefieren la vida vagabunda y miserable a la dignidad que poseen las personas de un orden superior. Tú te has acostumbrado a la vida salvaje en contacto directo con la Naturaleza, y prefieres esta libertad grosera a los afectos más dulces de una familia. ¿Has sido tú feliz en esta vida?

—Empezaba a serlo...

—¿Y cuándo dejaste de serlo?

Después de larga pausa, la Nela contestó:

—Cuando usted vino.

—¡Yo!... ¿Qué males he traído?

—Ninguno; no ha traído sino grandes bienes.

—Yo he devuelto la vista a tu amo—dijo Golfín, observando con atención de fisiólogo el semblante de la Nela—. ¿No me agradeces esto?

—Mucho, sí, señor, mucho—replicó ella, fijando en el doctor sus ojos llenos de lágrimas.

Golfín, sin dejar de observarla ni perder el más ligero síntoma facial que pudiera servir para conocer los sentimientos de la mujer-niña, habló así:

—Tu amo me ha dicho que te quiere mucho. Cuando era ciego, lo mismo que después que tiene vista, no ha hecho más que preguntar por la Nela. Se conoce que para él todo el Universo está ocupado por una sola persona; que la luz que se le ha permitido gozar no sirve para nada si no sirve para ver a la Nela.

—¡Para ver a la Nela! ¡Pues no verá a la Nela!... ¡La Nela no se dejará ver!—exclamó ella con brío.

—¿Y por qué?

—Porque es muy fea... Se puede querer a la hija de la Canela cuando se tienen los ojos cerrados; pero cuando se abren los ojos y se ve a la señorita Florentina, no se puede querer a la pobre y enana Marianela.

—¡Quién sabe!...

—No puede ser..., no puede ser—afirmó la vagabunda con la mayor energía.

—Eso es un capricho tuyo... No puedes decir si agradas o no a tu amo mientras no lo pruebes. Yo te llevaré a la casa.

—¡No quiero, que no quiero!—gritó ella, levantándose de un salto y poniéndose frente a don Teodoro, que se quedó absorto al ver su briosa apostura y el fulgor de sus ojuelos negros, señales ambas cosas de un carácter decidido.

—Tranquilízate, ven acá—le dijo con dulzura—. Hablaremos... Verdaderamente no eres muy bonita..., pero no es propio de una joven discreta apreciar tanto la hermosura exterior. Tienes un amor propio excesivo, mujer.

Y sin hacer caso de las observaciones del doctor, la Nela, firme en su puesto como lo estaba en su tema, pronunció solemnemente esta sentencia:

—No debe haber cosas feas... Ninguna cosa fea debe vivir.

—Pues mira, hijita, si todos los feos tuviéramos la obligación de quitarnos de en medio, ¡cuán despoblado se quedaría el mundo, pobre y desgraciada tontuela! Esa idea que me has dicho no es nueva. Tuviéronla personas que viveron hace siglos, personas de fantasía como tú que vivían en la Naturaleza, y que, como tú, carecían de cierta luz que a ti te falta por tu ignorancia y abandono, y ellas porque aún esa luz no había venido al mundo... Es preciso que te cures esa manía; hazte cargo de que hay una porción de dones más estimables que el de la hermosura, dones del alma que ni son ajados por el tiempo ni están sujetos al capricho de los ojos. Búscalos en tu alma, y los hallarás. No te pasará lo que con tu hermosura, que por mucho que en el espejo la busques no es fácil que la encuentres. Busca aquellos dones preciosos, cultívalos, y cuando los veas bien grandes y florecidos, no temas; ese afán que sientes se calmará. Entonces te sobrepondrás fácilmente a la situación desairada en que hoy te ves, y elevándote tendrás una hermosura que no admirarán quizá los ojos, pero que a ti misma te servirá de recreo y orgullo.

Estas sensatas palabras, o no fueron entendidas o no fueron aceptadas por la Nela, que, sentándose otra vez junto a Golfín, le miraba atentamente. Sus ojos pequeñitos, que a los más hermosos ganaban en la elocuencia, parecían decir: «¿Pero a qué vienen todas esas sabidurías, señor pedante?»

—Aquí—continuó Golfín, gozando extremadamente con aquel asunto, y dándole, a pesar suyo, un tono de tesis psicológica—hay una cuestión principal y es...

La Nela le había adivinado, y se cubrió el rostro con las manos.

—No tiene nada de extraño; al contrario, es muy natural lo que te pasa. Tienes un temperamento sentimental, imaginativo; has llevado con tu amo la vida libre y poética de la Naturaleza, siempre juntos, en inocente intimidad. El es discreto hasta no más, y guapo como una estatua... Parece la belleza ciega hecha para recreo de los que tienen vista. Además, su bondad y la grandeza de su corazón cautivan y enamoran. No es extraño que te haya cautivado a ti, que eres una niña, casi mujer, o una

mujer que parece niña. ¿Le quieres mucho,
le quieres más que a todas las cosas de este
mundo?...

—Sí; sí, señor—repuso la chicuela sollozando.

—¿No puedes soportar la idea de que te deje
de querer?

—No; no, señor.

—El te ha dicho palabras amorosas y te ha
hecho juramentos...

—¡Oh!, sí; sí, señor. Me dijo que yo sería su
compañera por toda la vida, y yo lo creí...

—¿Por qué no ha de ser verdad?...

—Me dijo que no podría vivir sin mí, y que
aunque tuviera vista me querría siempre mucho. Yo estaba contenta, y mi fealdad, mi pequeñez y mi facha ridícula no me importaban,
porque él no podía verme, y allá en sus tinieblas me tenía por bonita. Pero después...

—Después...—murmuró Golfín, traspasado
de compasión—. Ya veo que yo tengo la culpa
de todo.

—La culpa no..., porque usted ha hecho una
buena obra. Usted es muy bueno... Es un bien
que él haya sanado de sus ojos... Yo me digo
a mí misma que es un bien..., pero después de
esto yo debo quitarme de enmedio..., porque
él verá a la señorita Florentina y la comparará
conmigo..., y la señorita Florentina es como los

ángeles, porque yo... Compararme con ella es
como si un pedazo de espejo roto se comparara
con el sol... ¿Para qué sirvo yo? ¿Para qué
nací?... ¡Dios se equivocó! Hízome una cara fea,
un cuerpecillo chico y un corazón muy grande.
¿De qué me sirve este corazón grandísimo? De
tormento, nada más. ¡Ay!, si yo no le sujetara,
él se empeñaría en aborrecer mucho; pero el
aborrecimiento no me gusta, yo no sé aborrecer,
y antes que llegar a saber lo que es eso, quiero
enterrar mi corazón para que no me atormente
más.

—Te atormenta con los celos, con el sentimiento de verte humillada. ¡Ay!, Nela, tu soledad es grande. No puede salvarte ni el saber
que no posees, ni la familia que te falta, ni el
trabajo que desconoces. Dime, la protección
de la señorita Florentina, ¿qué sentimientos ha
despertado en ti?

—¡Miedo!..., ¡vergüenza!—exclamó la Nela,
con temor, abriendo mucho sus ojuelos—. ¡Vivir con ellos, viéndoles a todas horas..., porque
se casarán; el corazón me ha dicho que se casarán; yo he soñado que se casarán!...

—Pero Florentina es muy buena, te amará
mucho...

—Yo la quiero también; pero no en Aldeacorba—dijo la chicuela con exaltación y desvarío—. Ha venido a quitarme lo que es mío...,

porque era mío, sí, señor... Florentina es como la Virgen... yo le rezaría, sí, señor, le rezaría, porque no quiero que me quite lo que es mío..., y me lo quitará, ya me lo ha quitado... ¿Adónde voy yo ahora, qué soy, ni de qué valgo? Todo lo perdí, todo, y quiero irme con mi madre.

La Nela dio algunos pasos; pero Golfín, como fiera que echa la zarpa, la detuvo fuertemente por la muñeca. Al cogerla, observó el agitado pulso de la vagabunda.

—Ven acá—le dijo—. Desde este momento, que quieras que no, te hago mi esclava. Eres mía, y no has de hacer sino lo que te mande yo. ¡Pobre criatura, formada de sensibilidad ardiente, de imaginación viva, de candidez y de superstición, eres una admirable persona nacida para todo lo bueno; pero desvirtuada por el estado salvaje en que has vivido, por el abandono y la falta de instrucción, pues careces hasta de lo más elemental! ¡En qué donosa sociedad vivimos, que hasta este punto se olvida de sus deberes y deja perder de este modo un ser preciosísimo!... Ven acá, que no has de separarte de mí; te tomo, te cazo, esa es la palabra, te cazo con trampa en medio de los bosques, florecita silvestre, y voy a ensayar en ti un sistema de educación... Veremos si sé tallar este hermoso diamante. ¡Ah, cuántas cosas ignoras!

Yo descubriré un nuevo mundo en tu alma, te
haré ver mil asombrosas maravillas que hasta
ahora no has conocido, aunque de todas ellas
has de tener tú una idea confusa, una idea vaga.
¿No sientes en tu pobre alma..., ¿cómo te lo
diré?, el brotecillo, el pimpollo de una virtud,
que es la más preciosa, la madre de todas, la
humildad; una virtud por la cual gozamos ex-
traordiariamente, ¡mira tú qué cosa tan rara!,
al vernos inferiores a los demás? Gozamos, sí,
al ver que otros están por encima de nosotros.
¿No sientes también la abnegación, por la cual
nos complacemos en sacrificarnos por los demás, y hacernos pequeñitos para que otros sean
grandes? Tú aprenderás esto; aprenderás a poner tu fealdad a los pies de la hermosura, a contemplar con serenidad y alegría los triunfos aje-
nos, a cargar de cadenas ese gran corazón tuyo,
sometiéndolo por completo, para que jamás
vuelva a sentir envidia ni despecho, para que
ame a todos por igual, poniendo por cima de
todos a los que te han hecho daño. Entonces
serás lo que debes ser, por tu natural condición
y por las cualidades que desde el nacer posees.
¡Infeliz!, has nacido en medio de una sociedad
cristiana, y ni siquiera eres cristiana; vive tu
alma en aquel estado de naturalismo poético,
sí, ésa es la palabra, y te la digo aunque no la
entiendas..., en aquel estado en que vivieron

pueblos de que apenas queda memoria. Los sentidos y las pasiones te gobiernan, y la forma es uno de tus dioses más queridos. Para ti han pasado en vano dieciocho siglos, consagrados a enaltecer el espíritu. Y esta egoísta sociedad que ha permitido tal abandono, ¿qué nombre merece? Te ha dejado crecer en la soledad de unas minas, sin enseñarte una letra sin revelarte las conquistas más preciosas de la inteligencia, las verdades más elementales que hoy gobiernan al mundo; ni siquiera te ha llevado a una de esas escuelas de primeras letras, donde no se aprende casi nada; ni siquiera te ha dado la imperfectísima instrucción religiosa de que ella se envanece. Apenas has visto una iglesia más que para presenciar ceremonias que no te han explicado; apenas sabes recitar una oración que no entiendes; no sabes nada del mundo, ni de Dios, ni del alma... Pero todo lo sabrás; tú serás otra; dejarás de ser la Nela, yo te lo prometo, para ser una señorita de mérito, una mujer de bien.

No puede afirmarse que la Nela entendiera el anterior discurso, pronunciado por Golfín con tal vehemencia y brío, que olvidó un instante la persona con quien hablaba. Pero la vagabunda sentía una fascinación singular, y las ideas de aquel hombre penetraban dulcemente en su alma, hallando fácil asiento en ella. Sin duda se efectuaba sobre la tosca muchacha el potente y fatal dominio que la inteligencia superior ejerce sobre la inferior. Triste y silenciosa, recostó su cabeza sobre el hombro de don Teodoro.

—Vamos allá—dijo éste súbitamente.

La Nela tembló toda. Golfín observó el sudor de su frente, el glacial frío de sus manos, la violencia de su pulso; pero lejos de cejar en su idea por causa de esta dolencia física, afirmóse más en ella, repitiendo:

—Vamos, vamos; aquí hace frío.

Tomó de la mano a la Nela. El dominio que sobre ella ejercía era ya tan grande, que la chicuela se levantó tras él y dieron juntos algunos pasos. Después Marianela se detuvo y cayó de rodillas.

—¡Oh!, señor—exclamó con espanto—, no me lleve usted.

Estaba pálida, descompuesta, con señales de una espantosa alteración física y moral. Golfín le tiró del brazo. El cuerpo desmayado de la vagabunda no se elevaba del suelo por su propia fuerza. Era preciso tirar de él como de un cuerpo muerto.

—Hace días—dijo Golfín—que en este mismo sitio te llevé sobre mis hombros porque no podías andar. Esta noche será lo mismo.

Y la levantó en sus brazos. La ardiente respiración de la mujer-niña le quemaba el rostro.

Iba decadente y marchita, como una planta que acaba de ser arrancada del suelo, dejando en él las raíces. Al llegar a la casa de Aldeacorba sintió que su carga se hacía menos pesada. La Nela erguía su cuello, elevaba las manos con ademán de desesperación, pero callaba.

Entró Golfín. Todo estaba en silencio. Una criada salió a recibirle, y a instancias de don Teodoro condújole sin hacer ruido a la habitación de la señorita Florentina. Hallábase ésta sola, alumbrada por una luz que ya agonizaba, de rodillas en el suelo y apoyando sus brazos en el asiento de una silla, en actitud de orar devotamente. Alarmóse al ver entrar a un hombre tan a deshora en su habitación, y a su fugaz alarma sucedió el asombro, observando la carga que Golfín sobre sus robustos hombros traía.

La sorpresa no permitió a la señorita de Penáguilas usar de la palabra, cuando don Teodoro, depositando cuidadosamente su carga sobre un sofá, le dijo:

—Aquí la traigo..., ¿qué tal, soy buen cazador de mariposas?

Retrocedamos algunos días.

Cuando don Teodoro Golfín levantó por primera vez el vendaje de Pablo de Penáguilas, éste dio un grito de espanto. Sus movimientos todos eran de retroceso. Extendía las manos como para apoyarse en un punto y retroceder mejor. El espacio iluminado era para él como un inmenso abismo, en el cual se suponía próximo a caer. El instinto de conservación obligábale a cerrar los ojos. Excitado por don Teodoro, por su padre y los demás de la casa, que sentían honda ansiedad, miró de nuevo; pero el temor no disminuía. Las imágenes entraban, digámoslo así, en su cerebro violenta y atropelladamente con una especie de brusca embestida, de tal modo que él creía chocar contra los objetos; las montañas lejanas se le figuraban hallarse al alcance de su mano, y veía los objetos y personas que le rodeaban cual si rápidamente cayeran sobre sus ojos.

Observaba Teodoro Golfín estos fenómenos con viva curiosidad, porque era aquél el segun-

lo caso de curación de ceguera congénita que
había presenciado. Los demás no se atrevían a
manifestar júbilo; de tal modo les confundía y
pasmaba la perturbada inauguración de las fun-
iones ópticas en el afortunado paciente. Pablo
xperimentaba una alegría delirante. Sus ner-
ios y su fantasía hallábanse horriblemente ex-
itados, por lo cual don Teodoro juzgó pruden-
emente obligarle al reposo. Sonriendo le dijo:

—Por ahora ha visto usted bastante. No se
pasa de la ceguera a la luz, no se entra en los
oberanos dominios del sol como quien entra
en un teatro. Es éste un nacimiento en que hay
ambién dolor.

Más tarde el joven mostró deseos tan vehe-
mentes de volver a ejercer su nueva facultad
preciosa, que don Teodoro consintió en abrirle
un resquicio del mundo visible.

—Mi interior—dijo Pablo, explicando su impresión primera—está inundado de hermosura, de una hermosura que àntes no conocía.
Qué cosas fueron las que entraron en mí lle-
nándome de terror? La idea del tamaño, que yo
no concebía sino de una manera imperfecta, se
me presentó clara y terrible, como si me arro-
aran desde las cimas más'altas a los abismos
más profundos. Todo esto es bello y grandioso,
aunque me hace estremecer. Quiero ver repeti-
las esas sensaciones sublimes. Aquella exten-

sión de hermosura que contemplé me ha dejad
anonadado; era una cosa serena y majestuosa
mente inclinada hacia mí como para recibirme
Yo veía el Universo entero corriendo hacia mí
y estaba sobrecogido y temeroso... El cielo era
un gran vacío atento, no lo expreso bien..., era
el aspecto de una cosa extraordinariamente do
tada de expresión. Todo aquel conjunto de ciel
y montañas me observaba y hacia mí corría...
pero todo era frío y severo en su gran majestad
Enséñeme una cosa delicada y cariñosa..., la
Nela, ¿en dónde está la Nela?

Al decir esto, Golfín, descubriendo nueva
mente sus ojos a la luz y auxiliándoles con an
teojos hábilmente graduados, le ponía en comu
nicación con la belleza visible.

—¡Oh, Dios mío!..., ¿esto que veo es la Nela
—dijo Pablo con entusiasta admiración.

—Es tu prima Florentina.

—¡Ah!—exclamó el joven, confuso—. Es m
prima... Yo no tenía idea de una hermosura se
mejante... ¡Bendito sea el sentido que permite
gozar de esta luz divina! Prima mía, eres como
una música deliciosa; eso que veo me parece la
expresión más clara de la armonía... ¿Y la Nela
dónde está?

—Tiempo tendrás de verla—dijo don Fran
cisco, lleno de gozo—. Sosiégate ahora.

—¡Florentina, Florentina!—repitió el ciego

on desvarío—. ¿Qué tienes en esa cara, que
arece la misma idea de Dios puesta en carnes?
Estás en medio de una cosa que debe de ser el
ol. De tu cara salen unos como rayos..., al fin
uedo tener idea de cómo son los ángeles..., y
u cuerpo, tus manos, tus cabellos vibran mos-
rándome ideas preciosas..., ¿qué es esto?

—Principia a hacerse cargo de los colores
—murmuró Golfín—. Quizá vea los objetos
odeados con los colores del iris. Aún no posee
ien la adaptación a las distancias.

—Te veo dentro de mis propios ojos—aña-
lió Pablo—. Te fundes con todo lo que pienso,
 tu persona visible es para mí como un recuer-
lo. ¿Un recuerdo de qué? Yo no he visto nada
asta ahora... ¿Habré vivido antes de esta vida?
No lo sé; pero yo tenía noticias de esos ojos tu-
os. Y tú, padre, ¿dónde estás? ¡Ah!, ya te veo.
Eres tú..., se me presenta contigo el amor que
e tengo... ¿Pues y mi tío?... Ambos os parecéis
mucho... ¿En dónde está el bendito Golfín?

—Aquí..., en la presencia de su enfermo—di-
o don Teodoro, presentándose—. Aquí estoy,
más feo que Picio... Como usted no ha visto
ún leones ni perros de Terranova, no tendrá
dea de mi belleza... Dicen que me parezco a
quellos nobles animales.

—Todos son buenas personas—dijo Pablo
on gran candor—; pero mi prima a todos les

lleva inmensa ventaja... ¿Y la Nela?, por Dios
¿no traen a la Nela?

Dijéronle que su lazarillo no aparecía por l
casa, ni podían ellos ocuparse en buscarla, l
que le causó profundísima pena. Procuraro
calmarle, y como era de temer un acceso d
fiebre, le acostaron, incitándole a dormir. A
día siguiente era grande su postración; pero d
todo triunfó su naturaleza enérgica. Pidió qu
le enseñaran un vaso de agua, y al verlo dijo
—Parece que estoy bebiendo el agua, sól
con verla.

Del mismo modo se expresó con respecto
otros objetos, los cuales hacían viva impresió
en su fantasía. Golfín, después de tratar de re
mediar la aberración de esfericidad por medi
de lentes, que fue probando uno tras otro, prin
cipió a ejercitarle en la distinción y combina
ción de los colores; pero el vigoroso entend
miento del joven propendía siempre a distingui
la fealdad de la hermosura. Distinguía estas do
ideas en absoluto, sin que influyera nada en é
ni la idea de utilidad, ni aun la de bondad. Pa
recióle encantadora una mariposa que extravia
da entró en su cuarto. Un tintero le parecía ho
rrible, a pesar de que su tío le demostró co
ingeniosos argumentos que servía para poner l
tinta de escribir..., la tinta de escribir. Entr
una estampa del Crucificado y otra de Galate

navegando sobre una concha con escolta de tritones y ninfas, prefirió esta última, lo que hizo mal efecto en Florentina, que se propuso enseñarle a poner las cosas sagradas cien codos por encima de las profanas. Observaba las caras con viva atención, y la maravillosa concordancia de los accidentes faciales con el lenguaje le pasmaba en extremo. Viendo a las criadas y a otras mujeres de Aldeacorba, manifestó desagrado, porque eran o feas o insignificantes. La hermosura de su prima convertía en adefesios a las demás mujeres. A pesar de esto, deseaba verlas a todas. Su curiosidad era una fiebre intensa que de ningún modo podía calmarse; y mientras se mostraba desconsolado por no ver a la Nela, rogaba a Florentina que no dejase de acompañarle un momento.

El tercer día le dijo Golfín:

—Ya se ha enterado usted de gran parte de las maravillas del mundo visible. Ahora es preciso que vea su propia persona.

Trajeron un espejo y Pablo se miró en él.

—Ese soy yo...—dijo con loca admiración—. Trabajo me cuesta el creerlo... ¿Y cómo estoy dentro de esta agua dura y quieta? ¡Qué cosa tan admirable es el vidrio! Parece mentira que los hombres hayan hecho esta atmósfera de piedra... Por vida mía, que no soy feo..., ¿no es verdad, prima? ¿Y tú, cuando te miras aquí, sa-

les tan guapa como eres? No puede ser. Mírate
en el cielo transparente, y allí verás tu imagen.
Creerás que ves a los ángeles cuando te veas a
ti misma.

A solas con Florentina, y cuándo ésta le pro-
digaba a prima noche las atenciones y cuidados
que exige un enfermo, Pablo le decía:

—Prima mía, mi padre me ha leído aquel
pasaje de nuestra historia, cuando un hombre
llamado Cristóbal Colón descubrió el Mundo
Nuevo, jamás visto por hombre alguno de Europa. Aquel navegante abrió los ojos del mundo conocido para que viera otro más hermoso.
No puedo figurármelo a él sino como a un Teodoro Golfín, y a la Europa como a un gran ciego
para quien la América y sus maravillas fueron
la luz. Yo también he descubierto un Nuevo
Mundo. Tú eres mi América; tú eres aquella
primera isla hermosa donde puso su pie el navegante. Faltóle ver el continente con sus inmensos bosques y ríos. A mí también me que-
dará por ver quizá lo más hermoso.

Después calló en profunda meditación, y al
cabo de ella preguntó:

—¿En dónde está la Nela?

—No sé qué la pasa a esa pobre muchacha
—dijo Florentina—. No quiere verte, sin duda.

—Es vergonzosa y muy modesta—replicó

Pablo—. Teme molestar a los de casa. Florentina, en confianza te diré que la quiero mucho.
Tú la querrás también. Deseo ardientemente
ver a esa buena compañera y amiga mía.

—Yo misma iré a buscarla mañana.

—Sí, sí..., pero no estés mucho tiempo fuera. Cuando no te veo estoy muy solo... Me he
acostumbrado a verte, y estos tres días me parecen siglos de felicidad... No me robes ni un
minuto. Decíame anoche mi padre que después
de verte a ti, no debo tener curiosidad de ver a
mujer ninguna.

—¡Qué tontería!...—dijo la señorita, rubori-
zándose—. Hay otras mucho más guapas
que yo.

—No, no; todos dicen que no—afirmó Pablo
con vehemencia, y dirigía su cara vendada hacia
la primita, como si a través de tantos obstáculos quisiera verla aún—. Antes me decían eso,
y yo no lo quería creer; pero después que tengo
conciencia del mundo visible y de la belleza
real, lo creo, sí, lo creo. Eres un tipo perfecto
de hermosura; no hay más allá, no puede haberlo... Dame tu mano.

El primo estrechó ardientemente entre sus
manos la de la señorita.

—Ahora me río yo—añadió él—de mi ridícula vanidad de ciego, de mi necio empeño de
apreciar sin vista el aspecto de las cosas... Creo

que toda la vida me durará el asombro que me produjo la realidad... ¡La realidad! El que no la posee es un idiota... Florentina, yo era un idiota.

—No primo; siempre fuiste y eres muy discreto... Pero no excites ahora tu imaginación... Pronto será hora de dormir... Don Teodoro ha mandado que no se te dé conversación a esta hora, porque te desvelas... Si no te callas me voy.

—¿Es ya de noche?

—Sí, es de noche.

—Pues sea de noche o de día, yo quiero hablar—afirmó Pablo, inquieto en su lecho, sobre el cual reposaba vestido—. Con una condición me callo, y es que no te vayas del lado mío, y de tiempo en tiempo des una palmada en la cama, para saber yo que estás ahí.

—Bueno, así lo haré, y ahí va la primer fe de vida—dijo Florentina, dando una palmada en la cama.

—Cuando te siento reír, parece que respiro un ambiente fresco y perfumado, y todos mis sentidos antiguos se ponen a reproducirme tu persona de distintos modos. El recuerdo de tu imagen subsiste en mí de tal manera, que vendado te estoy viendo lo mismo...

—¿Vuelve la charla?... Que llamo a don Teodoro—dijo la señorita jovialmente.

—No..., estáte quieta. ¡Si no puedo callar!...
Si callara, todo lo que pienso, todo lo que siento y lo que veo aquí dentro de mi cerebro me
atormentaría más... ¿Y quieres tú que duer-
ma?... ¡Dormir! Si te tengo aquí dentro Florentina, dándome vueltas en el cerebro y volvién-
dome loco... Padezco y gozo lo que no se puede
decir, porque no hay palabras para expresarlo.
Toda la noche la paso hablando contigo y con
la Nela... ¡La pobre Nela!, tengo curiosidad de
verla, una curiosidad muy grande.

—Yo misma iré a buscarla mañana... Vaya,
se acabó la conversación... Calladito... o me
marcho.

—Quédate... Hablaré conmigo mismo... Ahora voy a repetir las cosas que te dije anoche,
cuando hablábamos solos los dos..., voy a recordar lo que tú me dijiste...

—¿Yo?

—Es decir, las cosas que yo me figuraba oír
de tu boca... Silencio, señorita de Penáguilas...,
yo me entiendo solo con mi imaginación.

Al día siguiente, cuando Florentina se presentó delante de su primo, le dijo:

—Traía a Mariquilla y se me escapó. ¡Qué
ingratitud!

—¿Y no la has buscado?

—¿Dónde?... ¡Huyó de mí! Esta tarde saldré
otra vez, y la buscaré hasta que la encuentre.

—No, no salgas—dijo Pablo vivamente—. Ella aparecerá; ella vendrá sola.

—Parece loca.

—¿Sabe que tengo vista?

—Yo misma se lo he dicho. Pero sin duda ha perdido el juicio. Dice que yo soy la Santísima Virgen, y me besa el vestido.

—Es que le produces a ella el mismo efecto que a todos. La Nela es tan buena... ¡Pobre muchacha! Hay que protegerla, Florentina; protegerla, ¿no te parece?

—Es una ingrata—afirmó Florentina con tristeza.

—¡Ah!, no lo creas. La Nela no puede ser ingrata. Es muy buena...; la aprecio mucho... Es preciso que la busquen y me la traigan aquí.

—Yo iré.

—No, no; tú no—dijo prontamente Pablo, tomando la mano de su prima—. La obligación de usted, señorita sin juicio, es acompañarme. Si no viene pronto el señor Golfín a levantarme la venda y ponerme los vidrios, yo me la levantaré solo. Desde ayer no te veo, y esto no se puede sufrir; no, no se puede sufrir... ¿Ha venido don Teodoro?

—Abajo está con tu padre y el mío. Pronto subirá. Ten paciencia; pareces un chiquillo de escuela.

Pablo se incorporó con desvarío.

—¡Luz, luz!... Es una iniquidad que le tengan a uno tanto tiempo a oscuras. Así no se puede vivir...; yo me muero. Necesito mi pan de cada día, necesito la función de mis ojos... Hoy no te he visto, prima, y estoy loco por verte. Tengo una sed rabiosa de verte. ¡Viva la realidad!... Bendito sea Dios que te crió, mujer hechicera, compendio de todas las bellezas... Pero si después de criar la hermosura, no hubiera criado Dios los corazones, ¡cuán tonta sería su obra!... ¡Luz, luz!

Subió don Teodoro y le abrió las puertas de la realidad, inundando de gozo su alma. Pasó el día tranquilo, hablando de cosas diversas. Hasta la noche no volvió a fijar la atención en un punto de su vida, que parecía alejarse y disminuir y borrarse, como las naves que en un día sereno se pierden en el horizonte. Como quien recuerda un hecho muy antiguo, dijo:

—¿No ha parecido la Nela?

Díjole Florentina que no, y hablaron de otra cosa. Aquella noche sintió Pablo a deshora ruido de voces en la casa. Creyó oír la voz de Teodoro Golfín, la de Florentina y la de su padre. Después se durmió sosegadamente, siguiendo durante su sueño atormentado por las imágenes de todo lo que había visto y por los fantasmas de lo que él mismo se imaginaba. Su sueño, que principió dulce y tranquilo, fue después

agitado y angustioso, porque en el profundo
seno de su alma, como en una caverna recién
iluminada, luchaban las hermosuras y fealdades
del mundo plástico, despertando pasiones, ente-
rrando recuerdos y trastornando su alma toda.
Al día siguiente, según promesa de Golfín, le
permitirían levantarse y andar por la casa.

La habitación destinada a Florentina en Aldeacorba era la más alegre de la casa. Nadie
había vivido en ella desde la muerte de la señora de Penáguilas; pero don Francisco, creyendo
a su sobrina digna de alojarse allí, arregló la estancia con pulcritud y ciertos primores elegan-
tes que no se conocían en vida de su esposa.
Daba el balcón al Mediodía y a la huerta, por lo
cual la estancia hallábase diariamente inundada
de gratos olores y de luz y alegrada por el ar-
monioso charlar de los pájaros. En los pocos
días de su residencia allí, Florentina había dado
a la habitación el molde, digámoslo así, de su
persona. Diversas cosas y partes de aquélla
daban a entender la clase de mujer que allí vivía, así como el nido da a conocer el ave. Si hay
personas que de un palacio hacen un infierno,
hay otras que para convertir una choza en palacio no tienen más que meterse en ella.

Fue aquel día tempestuoso (y decimos aquel
día, porque no sabemos qué día era: sólo sabe-

mos que era un día). Había llovido toda la
mañana. Después aclaró el cielo, y, por último,
sobre la atmósfera húmeda y blanca apareció
majestuoso un arco iris. El inmenso arco apoyaba uno de sus pies en los cerros de Ficóbriga, junto al mar, y el otro en el bosque de Saldeoro. Soberanamente hermoso en su sencillez,
era tal que a nada puede compararse, como no
sea a la representación absoluta y esencial de
la forma. Es un arco iris como el resumen, o
mejor dicho, principio y fin de todo lo visible.

En la habitación estaba Florentina, no ensar-
tando perlas ni bordando rasos con menudos
hilos de oro, sino cortando un vestido con patrones hechos de *Imparciales* y otros periódicos. Hallábase en el suelo, en postura semejante a la que toman los chicos revoltosos cuando
están jugando, y ora sentada sobre sus pies, ora
de rodillas, no daba paz a las tijeras. A su lado
había un montón de pedazos de lana, percal,
madapolán y otras telas que aquella mañana
había hecho traer a toda prisa de Villamojada,
y corta por aquí, recorta por allá, Florentina
hacía mangas, faldas y cuerpos. No eran un
modelo de corte ni había que fiar mucho en
la regularidad de los patrones, obra también
de la señorita; pero ella, reconocimiento los defectos, pensaba que en aquel arte la buena intención salva el resultado. Su excelente padre

le había dicho aquella mañana al comenzar la obra:

—Por Dios, Florentinilla, parece que ya no hay modistas en el mundo. No sé qué me da de ver a una señorita de buena sociedad arrastrándose por esos suelos de Dios con tijeras en la mano... Eso no está bien. No me agrada que trabajes para vestirte a ti misma, ¿y me ha de agradar que trabajes para las demás? ¿Para qué sirven las modistas?..., ¿para qué sirven las modistas, eh?

—Esto lo haría cualquier modista mejor que yo—repuso Florentina, riendo—; pero entonces no lo haría yo, señor papá; y precisamente quiero hacerlo yo misma.

Después Florentina se quedó sola; no, no se quedó sola, porque en el testero principal de la alcoba, entre la cama y el ropero, había un sofá de forma antigua, y sobre el sofá dos mantas, una sobre otra. En uno de los extremos asomaba entre almohadas una cabeza reclinada con abandono. Era un semblante desencajado y anémico. Dormía. Su sueño era un letargo inquieto que a cada instante se interrumpía con violentas sacudidas y terrores. No obstante, parecía estar más sosegada cuando al mediodía volvió a entrar en la pieza el padre de Florentina, acompañado de don Teodoro Golfín.

Este se dirigió al sofá, y aproximando su cara, observó la de la Nela.

—Parece que su sueño es ahora menos agitado—dijo—. No hagamos ruido.

—¿Qué le parece a usted mi hija?—dijo don Manuel, riendo—. ¿No ve usted las tareas que se da?... Sea usted imparcial, señor don Teodoro: ¿no tengo motivos para incomodarme? Francamente, cuando no hay necesidad de tomarse una molestia, ¿por qué se ha de tomar? Muy enhorabuena que mi hija dé al prójimo todo lo que yo le señalo para que lo gaste en alfileres; pero esto, esta manía de ocuparse ella misma en bajos menesteres..., en bajos menesteres...

—Déjela usted—replicó Golfín, contemplando a la señorita de Penáguilas con cierto arrobamiento—. Cada uno, señor don Manuel, tiene su modo especial de gastar alfileres.

—No me opongo yo a que en sus caridades llegue hasta el despilfarro, hasta la bancarrota —dijo don Manuel, paseándose pomposamente por la habitación, con las manos en los bolsillos—. ¿Pero no hay otro medio mejor de hacer caridad? Ella ha querido dar gracias a Dios por la curación de mi sobrino...; muy bueno es esto, muy evangélico...; pero veamos..., pero veamos...

Detúvose ante la Nela para honrarla con sus miradas.

—¿No habría sido más razonable—añadió— que en vez de meter en nuestra casa a esta pobre muchacha hubiera organizado mi hijita una de esas solemnidades que se estilan en la corte, y en las cuales sabe mostrar sus buenos sentimientos lo más selecto de la sociedad?... ¿Por qué no se te ocurrió celebrar una rifa? Entre los amigos hubiéramos colocado todos los billetes, reuniendo una buena suma, que podrías destinar a los asilos de Beneficencia. Podías haber formado una sociedad con todo el señorío de Villamojada y su término, o con el señorío de Santa Irene de Campó, y celebrar juntas y reunir mucho dinero... ¿Qué tal? También pudiste idear una función de aficionados, o una corrida de toretes. Yo me hubiera encargado de lo tocante al ganado y lidiadores... ¡Oh! Anoche hemos estado hablando acerca de esto doña Sofía y yo... Aprende, aprende de esa señora. A ella deben los pobres qué sé yo cuántas cosas. ¿Pues y las muchas familias que viven de la administración de las rifas? ¿Pues y lo que ganan los cómicos con estas funciones? ¡Oh!, los que están en el Hospicio no son los únicos pobres. Me dijo Sofía que en los bailes de máscaras de este invierno sacaron un dineral. Verdad que una gran parte fue para la empresa del gas, para el alquiler del teatro y los empleados..., pero a los pobres les llegó su pedazo de pan... O si no, hija mía, lee la estadística..., o si no, hija mía, lee la estadística.

Florentina se reía, y no hallando mejor contestación que repetir una frase de Teodoro Golfín, dijo a su padre:

—Cada uno tiene su modo de gastar alfileres.

—Señor don Teodoro—indicó con desabrimiento don Manuel—, convenga usted en que no hay otra como mi hija.

—Sí, en efecto—manifestó el doctor con intención profunda, contemplando a la joven—; no hay otra como Florentina.

—Con todos sus defectos—dijo el padre acariciando a la señorita—, la quiero más que a mi vida. Esta pícara vale más oro que pesa... Vamos a ver, ¿qué te gusta más: Aldeacorba de Suso o Santa Irene de Campó?

—No me disgusta Aldeacorba.

—¡Ah, picarona!..., ya veo el rumbo que tomas... Bien, me parece bien... ¿Saben ustedes que a estas horas mi hermano le está echando un sermón a su hijo? Cosas de familia: de esto ha de salir algo bueno. Mire usted, don Teodoro, cómo se pone mi hija: ya tiene en su cara todas las rosas de abril. Voy a ver lo que dice mi hermano..., a ver lo que dice mi hermano.

Retiróse el buen hombre. Teodoro se acercó a la Nela para observarla de nuevo.

—¿Ha dormido anoche?—preguntó a Florentina.

—Poco. Toda la noche la oí suspirar y llorar. Esta noche tendrá una buena cama, que he mandado traer de Villamojada. La pondré en ese cuartito que está junto al mío.

—¡Pobre Nela!—exclamó el médico—. No puede usted figurarse el interés que siento por esta infeliz criatura. Alguien se reirá de esto; pero no somos de piedra. Lo que hagamos para enaltecer a este pobre ser y mejorar su condición, entiéndase hecho en pro de una parte no pequeña del género humano. Como la Nela hay muchos miles de seres en el mundo. ¿Quién los conoce? ¿Dónde están? Se pierden en los desiertos sociales..., que también hay desiertos sociales; en lo más oscuro de las poblaciones, en lo más solitario de los campos, en las minas, en los talleres. A menudo pasamos junto a ellos y no les vemos... Les damos limosna sin conocerles... No podemos fijar nuestra atención en esa miserable parte de la sociedad. Al principio creí que la Nela era un caso excepcional; pero no, he meditado, he recordado, y he visto en ella un caso de los más comunes.

Es un ejemplo del estado a que vienen los seres moralmente organizados para el bien, para
el saber, para la virtud, y que por su abandono y apartamiento no pueden desarrollar las
fuerzas de su alma. Viven ciegos del espíritu,
como Pablo de Penáguilas ha vivido ciego del
cuerpo teniendo vista.

Florentina, vivamente impresionada, parecía
comprender muy bien las observaciones de
Golfín.

—Aquí la tiene usted—añadió éste—. Posee
una fantasía preciosa, sensibilidad viva; sabe
amar con ternura y pasión; tiene su alma apti-
tud maravillosa para todo aquello que del alma
depende; pero al mismo tiempo está llena de
supersticiones groseras; sus ideas religiosas
son vagas, monstruosas, equivocadas; sus ideas
morales no tienen más guía que el sentido natural. No posee más educación que la que ella
misma se ha dado, como planta que se fecunda con sus propias hojas secas. Nada debe a
los demás. Durante su niñez no ha oído ni una
lección ni un amoroso consejo, ni una santa
homilía. Se guía por ejemplos que aplica a su
antojo. Su criterio es suyo, propiamente suyo.
Como tiene imaginación y sensibilidad, como
su alma se ha inclinado desde el principio a
adorar algo, adora a la Naturaleza lo mismo que
los pueblos primitivos. Sus ideales son natura-

listas, y si usted no me entiende bien, querida
Florentina, se lo explicaré mejor en otra ocasión. Su espíritu da a la forma, a la belleza,
una preferencia sistemática. Todo su ser, sus
afectos todos giran en derredor de esta idea.
Las preeminencias y las altas dotes del espíritu
son para ella una región confusa, una tierra
apenas descubierta, de la cual no se tiene sino
noticias vagas por algún viajero náufrago. La
gran conquista evangélica, que es una de las
más gloriosas que ha hecho nuestro espíritu,
apenas llega a sus oídos como un rumor..., es
como una sospecha semejante a la que los pueblos asiáticos tienen del saber europeo, y si
no me entiende usted bien, querida Florentina,
más adelante se lo explicaré mejor... Pero ella
está hecha para realizar en poco tiempo grandes progresos y ponerse al nivel de nosotros.
Alúmbresele un poco, y recorrerá con paso
gigantesco los siglos...; está muy atrasada, ve
poco; pero teniendo luz, andará. Esa luz no
se la ha dado nadie hasta ahora, porque Pablo
de Penáguilas, por su ignorancia de la realidad
visible, contribuía sin quererlo a aumentar sus
errores. Ese idealista exagerado y loco no es
el mejor maestro para un espíritu de esta clase. Nosotros enseñaremos la verdad a esta pobre criatura, resucitado ejemplar de otros siglos; le haremos conocer las dotes del alma;

la traeremos a nuestro siglo; daremos a su espíritu una fuerza que no tiene; sustituiremos su naturalismo y sus rudas supersticiones con una noble conciencia cristiana. Aquí tenemos un campo admirable, una naturaleza primitiva, en la cual ensayaremos la enseñanza de los siglos; haremos rodar el tiempo sobre ella con las múltiples verdades descubiertas; crearemos un nuevo ser, porque esto, querida Florentina (no lo interprete usted mal), es lo mismo que crear un nuevo ser, y si usted no lo entiende, en otra ocasión se lo explicaré mejor.

Florentina, a pesar de no ser sabihonda, algo creyó entender de lo que en su original estilo había dicho Golfín. También ella expresaría más de una observación sobre aquel tema; pero en el mismo instante despertó la Nela. Sus ojos se revolvieron temerosos observando toda la estancia; después se fijaron alternativamente en las dos personas que la contemplaban.

—¿Nos tienes miedo?—le dijo Florentina dulcemente.

—No, señora; miedo, no—balbuceó la Nela—. Usted es muy buena. El señor don Teodoro también.

—¿No estás contenta aquí? ¿Qué temes?

Golfín le tomó la mano.

—Háblanos con franqueza—le dijo—: ¿a cuál de los dos quieres más, a Florentina o a mí?

La Nela no contestó. Florentina y Golfín sonreían; pero ella guardaba una seriedad taciturna.

—Oye una cosa, tontuela—prosiguió el médico—. Ahora has de vivir con uno de nosotros. Florentina se queda aquí; yo me marcho. Decídete por uno de los dos. ¿A cuál escoges?

Marianela dirigió sus miradas de uno a otro semblante, sin dar contestación categórica. Por último, se detuvieron en el rostro de Golfín.

—Se me figura que soy yo el preferido... Es una injusticia, Nela; Florentina se enojará.

La pobre enferma sonrió entonces, y extendiendo una de sus débiles manos hacia la señorita de Penáguilas, murmuró:

—No quiero que se enoje.

Al decir esto, María se quedó lívida; alargó su cuello, sus ojos se desencajaron. Su oído prestaba atención a un rumor terrible. Había sentido pasos.

—¡Viene!—exclamó Golfín, participando del terror de su enferma.

—Es él—dijo Florentina, apartándose del sofá y corriendo hacia la puerta.

Era él. Pablo había empujado la puerta y entraba despacio, marchando en dirección recta, por la costumbre adquirida durante su larga

ceguera. Venía riendo, y sus ojos, libres de la
venda que él mismo se había levantado, miraban hacia adelante. No habiéndose familiariza-
do aún con los movimientos de rotación del
ojo, apenas percibía las imágenes laterales. Podría decirse de él, como de muchos que nunca
fueron ciegos de los ojos, que sólo veía lo que
tenía delante.

—Primita—dijo, avanzando hacia ella—. ¿Cómo no has ido a verme hoy? Yo vengo a buscarte. Tu papá me ha dicho que estás haciendo trajes para los pobres. Por eso te per-
dono.

Florentina, contrariada, no supo qué contestar. Pablo no había visto al doctor ni a la Nela.
Florentina, para alejarle del sofá, se dirigió hacia el balcón, y recogiendo algunos trozos de
tela, sentóse en ademán de ponerse a trabajar.
Bañábala la risueña luz del sol, coloreando es-
pléndidamente su costado izquierdo y dando a
su hermosa tez moreno-rosa un tono encanta-
dor. Brillaba entonces su belleza como personificación hechicera de la misma luz. Su cabello
en desorden, su vestido suelto, llevaban al último grado la elegancia natural de la gentil doncella, cuya actitud, casta y noble, superaba a las
más perfectas concepciones del arte.

—Primito—dijo, contrayendo ligeramente el
hermoso entrecejo—, don Teodoro no te ha

dado todavía permiso para quitarte hoy la venda. Eso no está bien.

—Me lo dará después—replicó el mancebo, riendo—. No puede sucederme nada. Me encuentro bien. Y si algo me sucede, no me importa. No, no me importa quedarme ciego otra vez después de haberte visto.

—¡Qué bueno estaría eso!...—dijo Florentina en tono de reprensión.

—Estaba en mi cuarto solo; mi padre había salido, después de hablarme de ti. Tú ya sabes lo que me ha dicho...

—No, no sé nada—replicó la joven, fijando sus ojos en la costura.

—Pues yo sí lo sé... Mi padre es muy razonable. Nos quiere mucho a los dos... Cuando salió, levantéme la venda y miré al campo... Vi el arco iris y me quedé asombrado, mudo de admiración y de fervor religioso... No sé por qué, aquel sublime espectáculo, para mí desconocido hasta hoy, me dio la idea más clara de la armonía del mundo... No sé por qué, al mirar la perfecta unión de sus colores, pensaba en ti... No sé por qué, viendo el arco iris, dije: «Yo he sentido antes esto en alguna parte...» Me produjo sensación igual a la que sentí al verte, Florentina de mi alma. El corazón no me cabía en el pecho: yo quería llorar..., lloré, y las lágrimas cegaron por un instante mis ojos. Te llamé, no me respondiste... Cuando mis ojos pudieron ver de nuevo, el arco iris había desaparecido... Salí para buscarte, creí que estabas en la huerta..., bajé, subí, y aquí estoy... Te encuentro tan maravillosamente hermosa, que me parece que nunca te he visto bien hasta hoy..., nunca hasta hoy, porque ya he tenido tiempo de comparar... He visto muchas mujeres..., todas son horribles junto a ti... ¡Si me cuesta trabajo creer que hayas existido durante mi ceguera...! No, no; lo que me ocurre es que naciste en el momento en que se hizo la luz dentro de mí; que te creó mi pensamiento en el instante de ser dueño del mundo visible... Me han dicho que no hay ninguna criatura que a ti se compare. Yo no lo quería creer; pero ya lo creo; lo creo como creo en la luz.

Diciendo esto puso una rodilla en tierra. Alarmada y ruborizada, Florentina dejó de prestar atención a la costura, murmurando:

—¡Primo..., por Dios!...

—¡Prima..., por Dios!—exclamó Pablo con entusiasmo candoroso—, ¿por qué eres tú tan bonita?... Mi padre es muy razonable..., nada puede oponerse a su lógica ni a su bondad... Florentina, yo creí que no podría quererte; creí posible querer a otra más que a ti... ¡Qué necedad! Gracias a Dios que hay lógica en mis afectos... Mi padre, a quien he confesado mis errores, me ha dicho que yo amaba a un monstruo... Ahora puedo decir que idolatro a un ángel. El estúpido ciego ha visto ya, y al fin presta homenaje a la verdadera hermosura... Pero yo tiemblo..., ¿no me ves temblar? Te estoy viendo, y no deseo más que poder cogerte y encerrarte dentro de mi corazón, abrazándote y apretándote contra mi peho... fuerte, muy fuerte.

Pablo, que había puesto las dos rodillas en tierra, se abrazaba a sí mismo.

—Yo no sé lo que siento—añadió con turbación, torpe la lengua, pálido el rostro—. Cada día descubro un nuevo mundo, Florentina. Descubrí el de la luz, descubro hoy otro. ¿Es posible que tú, tan hermosa, tan divina, seas para mí? ¡Prima, prima mía, esposa de mi alma!

Creyérase que iba a caer al suelo desvanecido. Florentina hizo ademán de levantarse. Pablo le tomó una mano; después, retirando él mismo la ancha manga que lo cubría, besóle el brazo con vehemente ardor, contando los besos.

—Uno, dos, tres, cuatro... ¡Yo me muero!...

—Quita, quita—dijo Florentina, poniéndose en pie, y haciendo levantar tras ella a su primo—. Señor doctor, ríñale usted.

Teodoro gritó:

—¡Pronto!... ¡Esa venda en los ojos, y a su cuarto, joven!

Confuso, volvió Pablo su rostro hacia aquel

lado. Tomando la visual recta vio al doctor junto al sofá de paja cubierto de mantas.

—¿Está usted ahí, señor Golfín?—dijo, acercándose en línea recta.

—Aquí estoy—repuso don Teodoro seriamente—. Creo que debe usted ponerse la venda y retirarse a su habitación. Yo le acompañaré.

—Me encuentro perfectamente... Sin embargo, obedeceré... Pero antes déjenme ver esto.

Observaba las mantas, y entre ellas un rostro cadavérico, de aspecto muy desagradable. En efecto; parecía que la nariz de la Nela se había hecho más picuda, sus ojos más chicos, su boca más insignificante, su tez más pecosa, sus cabellos más ralos, su frente más angosta. Con los ojos cerrados, el aliento fatigoso, entreabiertos los cárdenes labios, hallábase al parecer la infeliz en la postrera agonía, síntoma inevitable de la muerte.

—¡Ah!—dijo Pablo—, supe por mi tío que Florentina había recogido a una pobre... ¡Qué admirable bondad!... Y tú, infeliz muchacha, alégrate, has caído en manos de un ángel... ¿Estás enferma? En mi casa no te faltará nada... Mi prima es la imagen más hermosa de Dios... Esta pobrecita está muy mala, ¿no es verdad, doctor?

—Sí—dijo Golfín—, le conviene la soledad... y el silencio.

—Pues me voy.

Pablo alargó una mano hasta tocar aquella cabeza, en la cual veía la expresión más triste de la miseria y de la desgracia humanas. Entonces la Nela movió los ojos y los fijó en su amo. Creyóse Pablo mirado desde el fondo de un sepulcro; tanta era la tristeza y el dolor que en aquella mirada había. Después la Nela sàcó de entre las mantas una mano flaca, morena y áspera, y tomó la mano del señorito de Penáguilas, quien, al sentir su contacto, se estremeció de pies a cabeza, y lanzó un grito en que toda su alma gritaba.

Hubo una pausa angustiosa, una de esas pausas que preceden a las catástrofes, como para hacerlas más solemnes. Con voz temblorosa, que en todos produjo trágica emoción. la Nela dijo:

—Sí, señorito mío, yo soy la Nela.

Lentamente, y como si moviera un objeto de gran pesadumbre, llevó a sus secos labios la mano del señorito y le dio un beso..., después un segundo beso..., y al dar el tercero, sus labios resbalaron inertes sobre la piel' de la mano.

Después callaron todos. Callaban mirándola. El primero que rompió la palabra fue Pablo, que dijo:

—¡Eres tú..., eres tú!

Pasaron por su mente ideas mil; mas no pudo

expresar ninguna. Era preciso para ello que hubiera descubierto un nuevo lenguaje, así como había descubierto dos nuevos mundos: el de la luz y el del amor por la forma. No hacía más que mirar, mirar, y hacer memoria de aquel tenebroso mundo en que había vivido, allá donde quedaban perdidos entre la bruma sus pasiones, sus ideas y sus errores de ciego. Florentina se acercó derramando lágrimas para examinar el rostro de la Nela, y Golfín, que la observaba como hombre y como sabio, pronunció estas lúgubres palabras:

—¡La mató! ¡Maldita vista suya!

Y después, mirando a Pablo con severidad, le dijo:

—Retírese usted.

—Morir..., morirse así, sin causa alguna... Esto no puede ser—exclamó Florentina con angustia poniendo la mano sobre la frente de la Nela—. ¡María!... ¡Marianela!

La llamó repetidas veces, inclinada sobre ella, mirándola como se mira y como se llama, desde los bordes de un pozo, a la persona que se ha caído en él y se sumerge en las hondísimas y negras aguas.

—No responde—dijo Pablo con terror.

Golfín tentaba aquella vida próxima a extinguirse, y observó que bajo su tacto aún latía la sangre. Pablo se inclinó sobre ella, y acercando sus labios al oído de la moribunda, gritó:

—¡Nela, Nela, amiga querida!

Agitóse la mujercita, abrió los ojos, movió las manos. Parecía volver desde muy lejos. Viendo que las miradas de Pablo se clavaban en ella con observadora curiosidad, hizo un movimiento de vergüenza y terror, y quiso ocultar su pobre rostro como se oculta un crimen.

—¿Qué es lo que tiene?—dijo Florentina con ardor—. Don Teodoro, no es usted hombre si no la salva... Si no la salva, es usted un charlatán.

La insigne joven parecía colérica en fuerza de ser caritativa.

—¡Nela!—repitió Pablo, traspasado de dolor y no repuesto del asombro que le había producido la vista de su lazarillo—. Parece que me tienes miedo. ¿Qué te he hecho yo?

La enferma alargó entonces sus manos, tomó la de Florentina y la puso sobre su pecho; tomó después la de Pablo y la puso también sobre su pecho. Después las apretó allí desarrollando un poco de fuerza. Sus ojos hundidos les miraban; pero su mirada era lejana, venía de allá abajo, de algún hoyo profundo y oscuro. Hay que decir, como antes, que miraba desde el lóbrego hueco de un pozo que a cada instante era más hondo. Su respiración fue de pronto muy fatigosa. Suspiró, oprimiendo sobre su pecho con más fuerza las manos de los dos jóvenes. Don Teodoro puso en movimiento toda la casa; llamó y gritó: hizo traer medicinas, poderosos revulsivos, y trató de suspender el rápido descenso de aquella vida.

—Difícil es—decía—detener una gota de agua que resbala, que resbala, ¡ay!, por la pendiente abajo y está ya a dos pulgadas del Océano; pero lo intentaré.

Mandó retirar a todo el mundo. Sólo Florentina quedó en la estancia. ¡Ah!, los revulsivos potentes, los excitantes nerviosos, mordiendo el cuerpo desfallecido para irritar la vida, hicieron estremecer los músculos de la infeliz enferma; pero a pesar de esto, se hundía más a cada instante.

—Es una crueldad—dijo don Teodoro con desesperación, arrojando la mostaza y los excitantes—, es una crueldad lo que hacemos. Echamos perros al moribundo para que el dolor de las mordidas le haga vivir un poco más. Afuera todo eso.

—¿No hay remedio?

—El que mande Dios.

—¿Qué mal es éste?

—La muerte—vociferó con inquietud delirante, impropia de un médico.

—¿Pero qué mal le ha traído la muerte?

—La muerte.

—No me explico bien. Quiero decir que de qué...

—¡De muerte! No sé si pensar que muere de vergüenza, de celos, de despecho, de tristeza, de amor contrariado. ¡Singular patología! No, no sabemos nada..., sólo sabemos cosas triviales.

—¡Oh!, ¡qué médicos!

—No sabemos nada. Conocemos algo de la superficie.

—¿Esto qué es?

—Parece una meningitis fulminante.

—¿Y qué es eso?

—Cualquier cosa... ¡La muerte!

—¿Es posible que se muera una persona sin causa conocida, casi sin enfermedad?... Señor Golfín, ¿qué es esto?

—¿Lo sé yo acaso?

—¿No es usted médico?

—De los ojos, no de las pasiones.

—¡De las pasiones!—exclamó hablando con la moribunda—. Y a ti, pobre criatura, ¿qué pasiones te matan?

—Pregúnteselo usted a su futuro esposo.

Florentina se quedó absorta, estupefacta.

—¡Infeliz!—exclamó con ahogado sollozo—. ¿Puede el dolor del alma matar de esta manera?

—Cuando yo la recogí en la Trascava, estaba ya consumida por una fiebre espantosa.

—Pero eso no basta, ¡ay!, no basta.

—Usted dice que no basta. Dios, la Naturaleza, dicen que sí.

—Si parece que ha recibido una puñalada.

—Recuerde usted lo que han visto hace poco estos ojos que se van a cerrar para siempre; considere que la amaba un ciego, y que ese ciego ya no lo es, y la ha visto... ¡La ha visto!... ¡La ha visto!, lo cual es como un asesinato.

—¡Oh!, ¡qué horroroso misterio!

—No, misterio no—gritó don Teodoro con cierto espanto—, es el horrendo desplome de las ilusiones, es el brusco golpe de la realidad, de esa niveladora implacable que se ha interpuesto al fin entre esos dos nobles seres. ¡Yo he traído esa realidad, yo!

—¡Oh!, ¡qué misterio!—repitió Florentina, que por el estado de su ánimo no comprendía bien.

—Misterio no, no—volvió a decir don Teodoro más agitado a cada instante—; es la realidad pura, la desaparición súbita de un mundo de ilusiones. La realidad ha sido para él nueva vida; para ella ha sido dolor y asfixia, la humillación, la tristeza, el desaire, el dolor, los celos..., ¡la muerte!

—Y todo por...

—¡Todo por unos ojos que se abren a la luz..., a la realidad!... No puedo apartar esta palabra de mi mente. Parece que la tengo escrita en mi cerebro con letras de fuego.

—Todo por unos ojos... ¿Pero el dolor puede matar tan pronto?..., ¡casi sin dar tiempo a ensayar un remedio!

—No sé—replicó don Teodoro inquieto, confundido, aterrado, contemplando aquel libro humano de caracteres oscuros, en los cuales la vista científica no podía descifrar la leyenda misteriosa de la muerte y la vida.

—¡No sabe!—dijo Florentina con desesperación—. Entonces, ¿para qué es médico?

—No sé, no sé, no sé—exclamó don Teodoro, golpeándose el cráneo melenudo con su zarpa de león—. Sí, una cosa sé, y es que no sabemos más que fenómenos superficiales. Señora, yo soy un carpintero de los ojos, y nada más.

Después fijó los suyos con atención profunda en aquello que fluctuaba entre persona y cadáver, y con acento de amargura exclamó:

—¡Alma!, ¿qué pasa en ti?

Florentina se echó a llorar.

—¡El alma—murmuró, inclinando su cabeza sobre el pecho—, ya ha volado!

—No—dijo don Teodoro, tocando a la Nela—. Aún hay aquí algo; pero es tan poco... Podríamos creer que ha desaparecido ya su alma y han quedado sus suspiros.

—¡Dios mío!...—exclamó la de Penáguilas, empezando una oración.

—¡Oh!, ¡desgraciado espíritu!—dijo Golfín—. Es evidente que está muy mal alojado...

Los dos la observaron de cerca.

—Sus labios se mueven—gritó Florentina.

—Habla.

Sí, los labios de la Nela se movieron. Había articulado una, dos, tres palabras.

—¿Qué ha dicho?

—¿Qué ha dicho?

Ninguno de los dos pudo comprenderlo. Era, sin duda, el idioma con que se entienden los que viven la vida infinita. Después, sus labios no se movieron más. Estaban entreabiertos y se veía la fila de blancos dientecillos. Don Teodoro se inclinó, y besando la frente de la Nela, dijo así con firme acento:

—Mujer, has hecho bien en dejar este mundo.

Florentina se echó a llorar, murmurando con voz ahogada y temblorosa:

—Yo quería hacerla feliz, y ella no quiso serlo.

¡Cosa rara, inaudita! La Nela, que nunca había tenido cama, ni ropa, ni zapatos, ni sustento, ni consideración, ni familia, ni nada propio, ni siquiera nombre, tuvo un magnífico sepulcro, que causó no pocas envidias entre los vivos de Socartes. Esta magnificencia póstuma fue la más grande ironía que se ha visto en aquellas tierras calaminíferas. La señorita Florentina, consecuente con sus sentimientos generosos, quiso atenuar la pena de no haber podido socorrer en vida a la Nela, con la satisfacción de honrar sus pobres despojos después de la muerte. Algún positivista empedernido criticóla por esto; pero no faltó quien viera en tan desusado hecho una prueba más de la delicadeza de su alma.

Cuando la enterraron, los curiosos que fueron a verla—¡esto sí que es inaudito y raro!—la encontraron casi bonita; al menos así lo decían. Fue la única vez que recibió adulaciones. Los funerales se celebraron con pompa, y los clé-

rigos de Villamojada abrieron tamaña boca al
ver que se les daba dinero por echar responsos
a la hija de la Canela. Era estupendo, fenome-
mal, que un ser cuya importancia social había
sido casi casi semejante a la de los insectos,
fuera causa de encender muchas luces, de tender paños y de poner roncos a sochantres y sa-
cristanes. Esto, a fuerza de ser extraño, rayaba
en lo chistoso. No se habló de otra cosa en
seis meses.

La sorpresa y..., dígase de una vez, la indigna-
ción de aquellas buenas muchedumbres llegaron
a su colmo cuando vieron que por el camino
adelante venían dos carros cargados con enormes piezas de piedra blanca y fina. ¡Ah!, en el
entendimiento de la Señana se producía una
espantosa confusión de ideas, un verdadero
cataclismo intelectual, un caos, al considerar
que aquellas piedras blancas y finas eran el sepulcro de la Nela. Si ante la Señana volara un
buey o discurriera su marido, ya no le llamaría
la atención.

Fueron revueltos los libros parroquiales de
Villamojada, porque era preciso que después
de muerta tuviera un nombre la que se había
pasado sin él la vida, como lo prueba esta
misma historia, donde se la nombra de distintos modos. Hallado aquel requisito indispensa-
ble para figurar en los archivos de la muerte, la

magnífica piedra sepulcral ostentaba orgullosa,
en medió de las rústicas cruces del cementerio
de Aldeacorba, estos renglones:

R. I. P.

MARIA MANUELA TELLEZ

RECLAMOLA EL CIELO

EN 12 DE OCTUBRE DE 186...

Guirnalda de flores primorosamente tallada
en el mármol coronaba la inscripción. Algunos
meses después, cuando ya Florentina y Pablo de
Penáguilas se habían casado, y cuando (dígase
la verdad, porque la verdad es antes que todo)...
cuando nadie en Aldeacorba de Suso se acor-
daba ya de la Nela, fueron viajando por aquellos países unos extranjeros de esos que llaman
turistas, y luego que vieron el sarcófago de
mármol erigido en el cementerio por la piedad
religiosa y el afecto sublime de una ejemplar
mujer, se quedaron embobados de admiración,
y sin más averiguaciones escribieron en su car-
tera estos apuntes, que con el título de *Sketches
from Cantabria* publicó más tarde un periódico
inglés:

«Lo que más sorprende en Aldeacorba es el
espléndido sepulcro que guarda las cenizas de
una ilustre joven, célebre en aquel país por su

hermosura. *Doña Mariquita Manuela Téllez*
perteneció a una de las familias más nobles y
acaudaladas de Cantabria: la familia de Téllez
Girón y de Trastamara. De un carácter *espiri-
tual*, poético y algo caprichoso, tuvo el antojo
(take a fancy) de andar por los caminos tocando la guitarra y cantando odas de Calderón, y
se vestía de andrajos para confundirse con la
turba de mendigos, buscones, *trovadores*, tore-
ros, frailes, hidalgos, gitanos y *muleteros*, que
en las *kermesas* forman esa abigarrada plebe
española que subsiste y subsistirá siempre, in-
dependiente y pintoresca, a pesar de los *rails*
y de los periódicos que han empezado a intro-
ducirse en la Península Occidental. El *abad* de
Villamojada lloraba hablándonos de los capri-
chos, de las virtudes y de la belleza de la aristo-
crática ricahembra, la cual sabía presentarse en
los saraos, fiestas y *cañas* de Madrid con el
porte *(deportment)* más aristocrático. Es in-
calculable el número de bellos *romanceros*,
sonetos y madrigales compuestos en honor de
esta gentil doncella por todos los poetas espa-
ñoles.»

Bastaba leer esto para comprender que los
dignos *reporters* habían visto visiones. Averi-
guada la verdad, de ella resultó este libro.

Despidámonos para siempre de esta tumba,
de la cual se ha hablado en *El Times*. Volva-

mos los ojos hacia otro lado; busquemos a otro ser, rebusquémosle, porque es tan chico que apenas se ve; es un insecto imperceptible, más pequeño sobre la faz del mundo que el *philloxera* en la breve extensión de la viña. Al fin le vemos; allí está, pequeño, mezquino, atomístico. Pero tiene alientos y logrará ser grande. Oíd su historia, que no carece de interés.

Pues señor...

Pero no, este libro no le corresponde. Acoged bien el de Marianela, y a su debido tiempo se os dará el de Celipín.

Indice